ANNUAL EDITIONS

Entrepreneurship
Sixth Edition

EDITOR

Robert W. Price
Senior Research Fellow, Global Entrepreneurship Institute

Robert W. Price is a Senior Research Fellow at the Global Entrepreneurship Institute. As a researcher and writer, he enjoys world renown as an expert in the field of entrepreneurial capitalism. As a business adviser, he consults with global entrepreneurs. As an adjunct professor, he teaches classes and seminars for entrepreneurial management programs and executive MBA programs in southern California. Mr. Price received his bachelor's degree from Ohio State University and master's degree from Pepperdine University's George L. Graziadio School of Business Management in Malibu, California.

ANNUAL EDITIONS: ENTREPRENEURSHIP, SIXTH EDITION

Published by McGraw-Hill, a business unit of The McGraw-Hill Companies, Inc., 1221 Avenue of the Americas, New York, NY 10020. Copyright © 2010 by The McGraw-Hill Companies, Inc. All rights reserved. Previous edition(s) 1994–2008. No part of this publication may be reproduced or distributed in any form or by any means, or stored in a database or retrieval system, without the prior written consent of The McGraw-Hill Companies, Inc., including, but not limited to, in any network or other electronic storage or transmission, or broadcast for distance learning.

Some ancillaries, including electronic and print components, may not be available to customers outside the United States.

Annual Editions® is a registered trademark of The McGraw-Hill Companies, Inc.

Annual Editions is published by the **Contemporary Learning Series** group within the McGraw-Hill Higher Education division.

1 2 3 4 5 6 7 8 9 0 QPD/QPD 0 9

ISBN 978–0–07–352857–1
MHID 0–07–352857–9
ISSN 1520–3956

Managing Editor: *Larry Loeppke*
Senior Managing Editor: *Faye Schilling*
Developmental Editor: *David Welsh*
Editorial Coordinator: *Mary Foust*
Editorial Assistant: *Cindy Hedley*
Production Service Assistant: *Rita Hingtgen*
Permissions Coordinator: *DeAnna Dausener*
Senior Marketing Manager: *Julie Keck*
Marketing Communications Specialist: *Mary Klein*
Marketing Coordinator: *Alice Link*
Project Manager: *Joyce Watters*
Design Specialist: *Tara McDermott*
Senior Production Supervisor: *Laura Fuller*
Cover Graphics: *Kristine Jubeck*

Compositor: Laserwords Private Limited
Cover Image: © SW Productions/Getty Images/RF (inset); The McGraw-Hill Companies, Inc./John Flournoy, photographer (background)

Library in Congress Cataloging-in-Publication Data
Main entry under title: Annual Editions: State and Local Government. 14/e.
  1. Entrepreneurship—Periodicals. I. Price, Robert W., *comp.* II. Title: Entrepreneurship.
658'.05

www.mhhe.com

Editors/Academic Advisory Board

Members of the Academic Advisory Board are instrumental in the final selection of articles for each edition of ANNUAL EDITIONS. Their review of articles for content, level, and appropriateness provides critical direction to the editors and staff. We think that you will find their careful consideration well reflected in this volume.

ANNUAL EDITIONS: Entrepreneurship
6th Edition

EDITOR

Robert W. Price
Senior Research Fellow, Global Entrepreneurship Institute

ACADEMIC ADVISORY BOARD MEMBERS

Preface

Entrepreneurship is the cornerstone of the free enterprise system. In fact, research has found that nearly 500 million adults around the globe are engaged in some form of entrepreneurial activity. Entrepreneurs are, therefore, vitally important to the economic health, not only of America, but also of the rest of the world. Because of its importance, entrepreneurship should be thoroughly understood, but this is easier said than done. The field is relatively complex, and it is undergoing constant change in response to shifts in economic conditions. In addition, there is a substantial body of knowledge, concepts, and tools that entrepreneurs need to know in order to launch and grow a company successfully. All of this makes studying entrepreneurship stimulating and exciting but also challenging.

To provide a better understanding of this exciting subject matter, our latest edition of *Annual Editions: Entrepreneurship* has been revised and updated with many articles to incorporate the most current information. It is divided into five major units: *Understanding Entrepreneurship, Creating and Launching a New Business Venture, Financing a New Business Venture, Managing and Growing a New Business Venture,* and *Special Issues for the Entrepreneur.*

Looking back over the years since our first edition, I have noticed that entrepreneurship has become more popular in the United States. In 2005, more than 12 million individuals were involved in some form of entrepreneurial activity such as thinking about a new business venture or writing a business plan. On the average about 2,700 new small businesses are started every day in the United States The total number of small businesses (less than 500 employees) has soared to 26.8 million, generating 60 to 80 percent of net new jobs annually over the last decade. And small business means big business

in the United States In fact, if the 20 million sole proprietors were a nation of their own, that nation would have a larger gross domestic product than India, South Korea, or Australia.

Starting and managing a new business venture is never easy. But people can take advantage of exciting new programs at universities and colleges to learn more about entrepreneurship. According to the Kauffman Foundation, more than 5,000 entrepreneurship courses are now offered in two- and four-year institutions in the United States And today, nearly every major school has a business-planning contest for their campus entrepreneurs.

Students are motivated to study entrepreneurship for a variety of reasons. Our text is aimed at preparing you to initiate your own new business venture, work in an emerging venture, or be employed in a company that provides goods and services to entrepreneurs. *Annual Editions: Entrepreneurship* is the product of more than 30 years of entrepreneurial experience. Intended to be a practical tool that accompanies other texts, handouts, guest speakers, and in-class business planning projects, our text will provide you with a view of the complete entrepreneurial life cycle from idea to exit. Our text is designed to provide you with the most complete and current selection of readings available on entrepreneurship.

Dream It! Plan It! Do It!

Robert W. Price
Editor

Contents

UNIT 1
Understanding Entrepreneurship

The concepts in bold italics are developed in the article. For further expansion, please refer to the Topic Guide.

UNIT 2
Creating and Launching a New Business Venture

The concepts in bold italics are developed in the article. For further expansion, please refer to the Topic Guide.

UNIT 3
Financing a New Business Venture

The concepts in bold italics are developed in the article. For further expansion, please refer to the Topic Guide.

UNIT 4
Managing and Growing a New Business Venture

The concepts in bold italics are developed in the article. For further expansion, please refer to the Topic Guide.

UNIT 5
Special Issues for the Entrepreneur

The concepts in bold italics are developed in the article. For further expansion, please refer to the Topic Guide.

The concepts in bold italics are developed in the article. For further expansion, please refer to the Topic Guide.

Correlation Guide

The *Annual Editions* series provides students with convenient, inexpensive access to current, carefully selected articles from the public press. **Annual Editions: Entrepreneurship, 6/e** is an easy-to-use reader that presents articles on important topics such as *startups, success strategies, writing business plans,* and many more. For more information on *Annual Editions* and other *McGraw-Hill Contemporary Learning Series* titles, visit www.mhhe.com/cls.

This convenient guide matches the units in **Annual Editions: Entrepreneurship, 6/e** with the corresponding chapters in two of our best-selling McGraw-Hill Business textbooks by Katz/Green and Hisrich et al.

Annual Editions: Entrepreneurship, 6/e	Entrepreneurial Small Business, 3/e by Katz/Green	Entrepreneurship, 8/e by Hisrich et al.
Unit 1: Understanding Entrepreneurship	**Chapter 1:** Small Business: Its Opportunities and Rewards **Chapter 3:** Small Business Entrepreneurs: Characteristics and Competencies **Chapter 4:** Small Business Ideas: Creativity, Opportunity, and Feasibility	**Chapter 1:** Entrepreneurship and the Entrepreneurial Mind-Set **Chapter 2:** Entrepreneurial Intentions and Corporate Entrepreneurship
Unit 2: Creating and Launching a New Business Venture	**Chapter 3:** Small Business Entrepreneurs: Characteristics and Competencies **Chapter 4:** Small Business Ideas: Creativity, Opportunity, and Feasibility **Chapter 8:** Business Plans: Seeing Audiences and Your Business Clearly **Chapter 12:** Marketing Plans: Saying How You'll Get Sales	**Chapter 3:** Entrepreneurial Strategy: Generating and Exploiting New Entries **Chapter 4:** Creativity and the Business Idea **Chapter 5:** Identifying and Analyzing Domestic and International Opportunities **Chapter 6:** Intellectual Property and Other Legal Issues for the Entrepreneur **Chapter 7:** The Business Plan: Creating and Starting the Venture **Chapter 8:** The Marketing Plan **Chapter 9:** The Organizational Plan **Chapter 10:** The Financial Plan
Unit 3: Financing a New Business Venture	**Chapter 14:** Cash: Lifeblood of the Business **Chapter 15:** Small Business Finance: Using Equity, Debt, and Gifts	**Chapter 11:** Sources of Capital **Chapter 12:** Informal Risk Capital, Venture Capital, and Going Public
Unit 4: Managing and Growing a New Business Venture	**Chapter 19:** Human Resource Management: Small Business Considerations **Chapter 20:** Achieving Success in the Small Business	**Chapter 13:** Strategies for Growth and Managing the Implication of Growth **Chapter 14:** Accessing Resources for Growth from External Sources
Unit 5: Special Issues for the Entrepreneur	**Chapter 11:** Small Business Distribution and Location **Chapter 15:** Small Business Finance: Using Equity, Debt, and Gifts	**Chapter 6:** Intellectual Property and Other Legal Issues for the Entrepreneur **Chapter 15:** Succession Planning and Strategies for Harvesting and Ending the Venture

Topic Guide

This topic guide suggests how the selections in this book relate to the subjects covered in your course. You may want to use the topics listed on these pages to search the Web more easily.

On the following pages a number of websites have been gathered specifically for this book. They are arranged to reflect the units of this Annual Editions reader. You can link to these sites by going to *http://www.mhcls.com.*

All the articles that relate to each topic are listed below the bold-faced term.

Internet References

The following Internet sites have been selected to support the articles found in this reader. These sites were available at the time of publication. However, because Web sites often change their structure and content, the information listed may no longer be available. We invite you to visit http://www.mhcls.com for easy access to these sites.

Annual Editions: Entrepreneurship 6/e

General Sources

Babson College
http://www3.babson.edu/ESHIP/eship.cfm

The Arthur M. Blank Center for Entrepreneurship is the hub for entrepreneurial activity at Babson. The center's mission is to lead the global advancement of entrepreneurship education and practice through the development of academic, research, and outreach initiatives that inspire entrepreneurial thinking and cultivate entrepreneurial leadership in all organizations and society.

BusinessWeek Online
http://www.businessweek.com/smallbiz/index.html

Small Business news, advice, and resources for small businesses from the publishers of *BusinessWeek* magazine.

Data.gov
http://www.data.gov/

The purpose of Data.gov is to increase public access to high value, machine readable datasets generated by the Executive Branch of the Federal Government.

Entrepreneurship.org
http://www.entrepreneurship.org/

The Ewing Marion Kauffman Foundation and the U.S. Commerce Department's International Trade Administration (ITA) have formed a new public-private partnership focused on leveraging best practices in entrepreneurial leadership to advance economic growth around the world.

Entrepreneurship Corner
http://ecorner.stanford.edu/index.html

The Stanford Technology Ventures Program (STVP) Entrepreneurship Corner is a free online archive of entrepreneurship resources for teaching and learning. The mission of the project is to support and encourage faculty around the world who teach entrepreneurship to future scientists and engineers, as well as those in management and other disciplines.

Harvard Business Publishing (HBP)
http://harvardbusiness.org/

This organization was founded in 1994 as a not-for-profit, wholly-owned subsidiary of Harvard University. Its mission is to improve the practice of management and its impact in a changing world. HBP does this by serving as a bridge between academia and enterprises around the globe through its publications and reach into three markets: academic, enterprise, and individual managers.

Knowledge@Wharton
http://knowledge.wharton.upenn.edu/

A bi-weekly online resource that offers the latest business insights, information, and research from a variety of sources. These include analysis of current business trends, interviews with industry leaders and Wharton faculty, articles based on the most recent business research, book reviews, conference and seminar reports, and links to other websites. An in-depth, searchable database of related articles and research abstracts allows access to information through simple mouse clicks.

Network for Teaching Entrepreneurship (NFTE)
http://www.nfte.com/

This program helps young people from low-income communities build skills and unlock their entrepreneurial creativity. Since 1987, NFTE has reached more than 230,000 young people, and currently has programs in 22 states and 12 countries. NFTE has more than 1,300 active Certified Entrepreneurship Teachers, and is continually improving its innovative entrepreneurship curriculum.

Small Business Trends
http://smallbiztrends.com/

This is an award-winning, comprehensive, online publication for small business owners, entrepreneurs, and the people who interact with them. It offers a variety of features to help you stay informed about the small business market. You can track, explore, and learn from trends affecting small business through the variety of informational resources.

STAT-USA
http://www.stat-usa.gov/stat-usa.html

This essential site, a service of the U.S. Department of Commerce, contains daily economic news, frequently requested statistical releases, information on export and international trade, domestic economic news, and statistical series.

U.S. Small Business Administration (SBA)
http://www.sba.gov/index.html

The SBA was created in 1953 as an independent agency of the federal government to aid, counsel, assist, and protect the interests of small business concerns, to preserve free competitive enterprise, and to maintain and strengthen the overall economy of our nation.

Wall Street Journal Small Business and Independent Street
http://online.wsj.com/public/page/news-small-business-marketing.html

Independent Street covers the aspirations, quirks and unique challenges and opportunity of entrepreneurship.

UNIT 1: Understanding Entrepreneurship

Ayn Rand Institute
http://www.aynrand.org

A 501(c)(3) nonprofit organization introduces people to her novels, to support scholarship, and research based on her ideas, and to promote the principles of reason, rational self-interest, individual rights, and laissez-faire capitalism to the widest possible audience. The Institute is named for novelist-philosopher Ayn Rand (1905–1982), who is best known for her novels *The Fountainhead* and *Atlas Shrugged*.

Bureau of Economic Analysis
http://www.bea.gov

The BEA, an agency of the U.S. Department of Commerce, produces some of the most closely watched economic statistics that influence the decisions made by government officials,

Internet References

business people, households, and individuals. These statistics provide a comprehensive, up-to-date picture of the U.S. economy and are key ingredients in critical decisions affecting monetary policy, tax and budget projections, and business investment plans. BEA's monthly journal, *Survey of Current Business,* is available in PDF format for the years 1994 to present.

Cato Institute
http://www.cato.org

The Cato Institute seeks to broaden the parameters of public policy debate to allow consideration of the traditional American principles of limited government, individual liberty, free markets, and peace. Toward that goal, the Institute strives to achieve greater involvement of the intelligent, concerned lay public in questions of policy and the proper role of government.

Center for International Private Enterprise (CIPE)
http://www.cipe.org/index.php

The Center strengthens democracy around the globe through private enterprise and market-oriented reform. CIPE is one of the four core institutes of the National Endowment for Democracy and a non-profit affiliate of the U.S. Chamber of Commerce. For 25 years, CIPE has worked with business leaders, policymakers, and journalists to build the civic institutions vital to a democratic society.

Edward Lowe Foundation
http://edwardlowe.org/index.elf

The foundation supports entrepreneurship by focusing on second-stage entrepreneurs in the belief that they are vital to the United States economy. Develops and delivers educational programs and information that help second-stage entrepreneurs grow and thrive and produces statewide awards programs designed to help communities appreciate and support the growth of these entrepreneurs.

Entrepreneurs' Organization (EO)
http://www.eonetwork.org/Pages/default.aspx

This is a global network with more than 7,000 business owners in 38 countries. Founded in 1987 by a group of young entrepreneurs, EO is the catalyst that enables entrepreneurs to learn and grow from each other, leading to greater business success and an enriched personal life.

Ewing Marion Kauffman Foundation
http://www.kauffman.org/

This is the nation's leading not-for-profit organization dedicated to developing, supporting, and encouraging entrepreneurship education and research. The Center's nationally recognized staff works with high-growth entrepreneurs, government policymakers, entrepreneurial support organizations, and leaders in entrepreneurship education to develop and disseminate innovative, effective programs and informational resources that enhance entrepreneurial skills and abilities at all levels.

Forum for Women Entrepreneurs
http://www.fwe.org/

This is the premier entrepreneurial organization for women building and leading high-growth companies. Founded in 1993, the organization's mission is to accelerate women's opportunities to start, manage, and invest in market-leading companies by providing its members with powerful access to powerful networks. FWE offers innovative programs, access to top-tier funding sources, and a collaborative online community that accelerates women entrepreneurs' ability to launch and build world-class companies.

Global Entrepreneurship Monitor
http://www.gemconsortium.org

The research program of the Global Entrepreneurship Monitor is an annual assessment of the national level of entrepreneurial activity in 50 countries around the world.

Heritage Foundation
http://www.heritage.org

Founded in 1973, The Heritage Foundation is a research and educational institute—a think tank—whose mission it is to formulate and promote conservative public policies based on the principles of free enterprise, limited government, individual freedom, traditional American values, and a strong national defense.

U.S. Chamber of Commerce
http://www.uschamber.org

This site offers information on resources for growing businesses, and includes an online small business bookstore.

United States Association for Small Business and Entrepreneurs (USASBE)
http://www.usasbe.org

This site of USASBE, the U.S. affiliate of the International Council for Small Business, answers questions about owning a business and has search capabilities.

UNIT 2: Creating and Launching a New Business Venture

Association of University Technology Managers (AUTM)
http://www.autm.net

A nonprofit association with membership of more than 3,200 technology managers and business executives who manage intellectual property—this is one of the most active growth sectors of the U.S. economy. AUTM's members represent over 300 universities, research institutions, and teaching hospitals and a similar number of companies and government organizations.

Business Wire Press Services
http://www.businesswire.com/

This site delivers news simultaneously and in real-time directly into the newsroom editorial systems at newspapers, wire services, television and radio programs, magazines, and online news services. Journalists rely on the Business Wire file as they plan their news coverage. In addition, full-text news is placed into the news systems of leading Internet portals, financial and research databases, news and information sites, and content syndicates.

Internal Revenue Service
http://www.irs.gov/businesses/small/index.html

The Small Business and Self-Employed Community website has been designed to provide industry/profession specific information to small businesses and self employed professionals.

National Business Incubation Association (NBIA)
http://www.nbia.org

This is the website for the world's leading organization advancing business incubation and entrepreneurship. It provides thousands of professionals with the information, education, advocacy, and networking resources to bring excellence to the process of assisting early-stage companies.

Internet References

Tradepub.com
http://www.tradepub.com/

Browse through the extensive list of trade publications by industry, title, key word, or geographic eligibility to find the titles that best match your research needs. Then simply complete the application form and submit it.

U.S. Department of Labor Statistics: Industry at a Glance
http://www.bls.gov/iag/home.htm

This site consists of profiles of 12 industry supersectors. Each profile contains a variety of facts about the industry supersector, and includes links to additional statistics. The supersectors presented here are based on the North American Industry Classification System (NAICS).

U.S Patents and Trademarks Office
http://www.uspto.gov/

This is the only official website of the United States Patent and Trademark Office.

World Intellectual Property Organization (WIPO)
http://www.wipo.int/

An international organization dedicated to helping to ensure that the rights of creators and owners of intellectual property are protected worldwide and that inventors and authors are, thus, recognized and rewarded for their ingenuity. This international protection acts as a spur to human creativity, pushing forward the boundaries of science and technology and enriching the world of literature and the arts. By providing a stable environment for the marketing of intellectual property products, it also oils the wheels of international trade.

Yahoo! Industry Center
http://biz.yahoo.com/ic/index.html

Perform quick overviews of major industry sectors. Check news and search key words by industry sectors, and also perform due diligence on select leading industry performers.

YouNoodle
http://younoodle.com/

YouNoodle develops innovative ways to bring together the information, people, and technology that help startups succeed. It provides a platform for 50 of the world's top university entrepreneurship clubs and competitions, serving tens of thousands of members and thousands of startups.

UNIT 3: Financing a New Business Venture

Angel Capital Association
http://www.angelcapitalassociation.org/

This is the site of the preeminent North American association of angel investor groups. ACA's mission is to advance angel investing by supporting the development of successful angel groups, sharing best practices and industry data, building public awareness, and establishing professional standards. Currently, 60 angel groups throughout the United States and Canada are members of the organization, including 48 founding groups.

Center for Private Equity and Entrepreneurship
http://mba.tuck.dartmouth.edu/pecenter/

The Tuck Center for Private Equity and Entrepreneurship aims to advance the understanding of private equity investing—the engine behind the entrepreneurial activity that drives global innovation and productivity. The center focuses on macro and micro issues relating to private equity: capital markets, financing structures, governance, and entrepreneurship.

Center for Venture Research
http://wsbe.unh.edu/cvr

This is a multidisciplinary research unit of the Whittemore School of Business and Economics at the University of New Hampshire. The Center's principal area of expertise is in the study of early stage equity financing for high growth ventures.

National Association of Small Business Investment Companies (NASBIC)
http://www.nasbic.org

This is the site of the professional association for the Small Business Investment Company (SBIC) industry. The association's mission is to build and maintain a strong and profitable small business investment company (SBIC) industry.

National Venture Capital Association (NVCA)
http://www.nvca.org/

This is the site of the trade association that represents the venture capital industry. Its membership consists of venture capital firms and organizations who manage pools of risk equity capital designated to be invested in young, emerging companies. Currently, the NVCA represents 400+ member firms, representing the majority of venture capital invested in U.S. based companies.

Private Equity Hub
http://www.pehub.com/

An interactive forum for the private equity community, which includes venture capitalists, buyout professionals, attorneys, bankers, entrepreneurs, MBA candidates studying PE, and assorted hangers-on. Its mission is simple: to help you do your job better, by feeding your head with news and views from/about private equity industry.

Small Business Investment Companies (SBIC)
http://www.sba.gov/aboutsba/sbaprograms/inv/index.html

Congress created the Small Business Investment Company (SBIC) Program in 1958 to fill the gap between the availability of venture capital and the needs of small businesses in startup and growth situations. SBICs, licensed and regulated by the SBA, are privately owned and managed investment firms that use their own capital, plus funds borrowed at favorable rates with an SBA guarantee, to make venture capital investments in small businesses.

Venture Capital Institute
http://www.vcinstitute.org

The Venture Capital Institute began in 1974 and since then has trained more than 2,200 venture capital professionals in the principles of direct venture investing. The Venture Capital Institute is co-sponsored by NASBIC and NVCA.

UNIT 4: Managing and Growing a New Business Venture

Association for Corporate Growth (ACG)
http://www.acg.org/

This is the site of a global association for professionals involved in corporate growth, corporate development, and mergers and acquisitions for mid to large companies. Leaders in corporations, private equity, finance, and professional service firms focused on building value in their organizations belong to ACG. The group has more than 9,000 members representing Fortune 500, Fortune 1000, FTSE 100, and mid-market companies in 48 chapters in North America, Europe, and soon Asia.

Internet References

CalPERS Shareowner Forum

http://www.calpers-governance.org/

The California Public Employees' Retirement System (known as "CalPERS") has long been a leader in the corporate governance movement. This site is intended to provide an education and communication resource for those interested in the field of corporate governance and CalPERS' activities

Entrepreneur Magazine

http://www.entrepreneurmag.com

This site, self-described as "The Online Small Business Authority," addresses a number of entrepreneurship issues, from finding a location for your business to raising money.

Foundation for Enterprise Development/Beyster Institute

http://www.fed.org

A non-profit organization dedicated to advancing the use of entrepreneurial employee ownership nationally and internationally, in both the public and private sectors, as a way to build high-performing enterprises and improve corporate performance.

Inc.com

http://www.inc.com/

The website for *Inc.* magazine, delivers advice, tools, and services to help business owners and CEOs start, run, and grow their businesses more successfully. You'll find information and advice covering virtually every business and management task, including marketing, sales, finding capital, managing people, and much, much more.

Moot Corp.

http://www.mootcorp.org/

The original intercollegiate new-venture competition offering the largest guaranteed prize of any student contest in the world. It's "The Super Bowl of World Business-Plan Competition."

National Federation of Independent Business (NFIB)

http://www.nfib.org/

With over 600,000 members, this is the largest advocacy organization representing small and independent businesses in Washington, DC and all 50 state capitals.

Service Corps of Retired Executives (SCORE)

http://www.score.org/

A nonprofit association and resource partner with the U.S. Small Business Administration, SCORE is dedicated to entrepreneurship and the formation, growth, and success of small businesses nationwide. Since 1964, SCORE has helped nearly 4.5 million entrepreneurs.

UNIT 5: Special Issues for the Entrepreneur

Ashoka

http://www.ashoka.org/

The mission of Ashoka is to shape a citizen sector that is entrepreneurial, productive, and globally integrated, and to develop the profession of social entrepreneurship around the world. Ashoka identifies and invests in leading social entrepreneurs—extraordinary individuals with unprecedented ideas for change in their communities—supporting them, their ideas, and institutions through all phases of their careers.

Bill & Melinda Gates Foundation

http://www.gatesfoundation.org/Pages/home.aspx

Guided by the belief that every life has equal value, the Bill & Melinda Gates Foundation works to reduce inequities and improve lives around the world. In developing countries, it focuses on improving health, reducing extreme poverty, and increasing access to technology in public libraries. In the United States, the foundation seeks to ensure that all people have access to a great education and to technology in public libraries.

Center for Advancing Social Entrepreneurship (CASE)

http://www.caseatduke.org/

Based at Duke University's Fuqua School of Business, CASE's current programs and activities fall into three broad areas: knowledge development and dissemination; MBA involvement in the social sector; and increasing awareness of the field.

Center for Social Innovation

http://www.gsb.stanford.edu/csi/

The Center, at Stanford Graduate School of Business, builds and strengthens the capacity of individuals and organizations to develop innovative solutions to social problems for a more just, sustainable, and healthy world.

Grameen Foundation

http://www.grameen-info.org/

This foundation provides credit to the poorest of the poor in rural Bangladesh without any collateral. The bank sees credit as an empowering agent, an enabling element in the development of socioeconomic conditions of the poor who have been kept outside the banking orbit on the simple ground that they are poor and hence not bankable.

Milken Institute

http://www.milkeninstitute.org

The Institute's Capital Access Index (CAI) ranks countries by the ability of their entrepreneurs to gain access to capital. Each year, the Institute hosts the Global Conference, which attracts more than 1,500 leading businesspeople and policymakers from around the globe.

Global Entrepreneurship Week

http://www.unleashingideas.org/

This event connects young people everywhere through local, national, and global activities designed to help them explore their potential as self-starters and innovators. Students, educators, entrepreneurs, business leaders, employees, non-profit leaders, government officials, and many others will participate in a range of activities, from online to face-to-face, and from large-scale competitions and events to intimate networking gatherings.

VolunteerMatch.org

http://www.volunteermatch.org/

The organization offers a variety of online services to support a community of nonprofit, volunteer, and business leaders committed to civic engagement. This website welcomes millions of visitors a year and has become a popular Internet recruiting tool for more than 40,000 nonprofit organizations.

UNIT 1

Understanding Entrepreneurship

Unit Selections

1. **Wanted: Entrepreneurs (Just Don't Ask for a Job Description),** Ronald A. Wirtz
2. **An Idea Whose Time Has Come,** *The Economist*
3. **Creative Disruption,** Douglas Clement
4. **The World Discovers the Laffer Curve,** Stephen Moore
5. **Building Entrepreneurial Economies,** Carl J. Schramm
6. **The Role of Small and Large Businesses in Economic Development,** Kelly Edmiston
7. **Success Rules!,** Thomas Melville
8. **The Greatest Entrepreneurs of All Time,** John Tozzi
9. **The Secrets of Serial Success,** Gwendolyn Bounds, Kelly K. Spors, and Raymund Flandez

Key Points to Consider

- What is entrepreneurship?

- What exactly do entrepreneurs do?

- Why is studying entrepreneurship important?

- What is your definition of a typical entrepreneur?

- What impact does entrepreneurship have on the economy?

- What is the typical path of a new business venture?

- Who starts a business and becomes an entrepreneur?

- What are the different types of entrepreneurs?

- Who are some of the most successful entrepreneurs? Why?

- What characteristics will separate the winners from the losers?

Student Website
www.mhcls.com

Internet References

Ayn Rand Institute
http://www.aynrand.org

Bureau of Economic Analysis
http://www.bea.gov

Cato Institute
http://www.cato.org

Center for International Private Enterprise(CIPE)
http://www.cipe.org/index.php

Edward Lowe Foundation
http://edwardlowe.org/index.elf

Entrepreneurs' Organization (EO)
http://www.eonetwork.org/Pages/default.aspx

Ewing Marion Kauffman Foundation
http://www.kauffman.org/

Forum for Women Entrepreneurs
http://www.fwe.org/

Global Entrepreneurship Monitor
http://www.gemconsortium.org

Heritage Foundation
http://www.heritage.org

U.S. Chamber of Commerce
http://www.uschamber.org

United States Association for Small Business and Entrepreneurs (USASBE)
http://www.usasbe.org

Facing the global economic crisis, the role of the entrepreneur has become increasingly important in restoring the competitive position of the United States in the global marketplace. Entrepreneurs in the United States have created an economic sector that is worth trillions. More than 635,000 small businesses are created each year—joining the some 26.8 million that already exist. The total number of small businesses generated 60 to 80 percent of net new jobs annually over the last decade.

Entrepreneurial capitalism is key to the success of entrepreneurship. Entrepreneurial capitalism is defined as private capital, investing in private startups, with potential for a viable harvest. The concept of entrepreneurship has been in our modern society for thousands of years and in the history of economic study the word has been overused, and in some cases underused. So, what do entrepreneurs do? What makes an entrepreneur successful? What is governments' role in supporting entrepreneurial capitalism? Most will agree that the answers are not simple.

Starting with practically nothing, an entrepreneur is one who organizes a new venture, manages it, and assumes the associated risk. In theory, entrepreneurship includes several subdisciplines that include small business or lifestyle entrepreneurs, high-growth potential entrepreneurs, professional or serial entrepreneurs, corporate entrepreneurs, and social entrepreneurs. An entrepreneur's principal objectives are profit and growth, and they will employ formal strategic management practices to achieve them.

Entrepreneurship begins with an idea and opportunity analysis. Its meaning can be found in the exciting process of putting together a unique team of creative individuals in pursuit of a limited opportunity before anyone else does. But being an entrepreneur also means taking on risks. No such "venture team" led by an entrepreneur can control all the necessary "critical capital resources," such as employees, equipment, raw materials, and startup money, because pursuing such opportunity requires a bridging of the resource gap. Prudent decision making requires that the entrepreneur act in a manner that is consistent with risk reduction and growth.

The exciting lure of entrepreneurship draws a lot of people who really aren't prepared for it into trying to be entrepreneurs. In fact, this is one reason why so many new startups fail, and, obviously, not all startups are profitable. The average annual net income for the millions of sole proprietorships in the United States is less than $50,000 for the first year. And about 25 percent of these ventures do not make a penny of profit during a typical year.

Faced with these odds, entrepreneurs exhibit many of the qualities of the early pioneers because they are prepared to take enormous risks. They innovate in areas where most say that it cannot be done. They work incredibly long hours over extended periods of time, and even suffer personal problems, all for the excitement of developing a product or building an enterprise. Their passion brings a concentrated

© BananaStock Ltd.

focus to their projects. Most have an ability to sell themselves and their ideas, but few understand that they can't do it all by themselves.

Entrepreneurs essentially start with nothing more than an idea and a blueprint or roadmap. Along the "entrepreneurial life cycle" they create "venture teams" that have the ability and resources to develop ideas to the point at which the startup can sustain itself and internally generate a positive cash flow. Typically, they are starting from scratch; they have no offices, no salespeople, no computers, no suppliers, and no customers. Their job at hand is to quickly gain a "critical mass" by putting all the ideas and resources together and yet somehow make a profit as quickly as possible. Professional or "serial" entrepreneurs are masters of this entrepreneurial life cycle. They know how to overcome hurdles and they know how to bounce back from roadblocks and failures.

An entrepreneur is someone who perceives a new idea and creates an organization to harvest the opportunity; the activity involved in that pursuit is called the entrepreneurial life cycle. The entrepreneurial life cycle is very much a series of fits, starts, and brainstorms. What makes an entrepreneur successful is the ability to navigate through uncharted waters and, when faced with a tough challenge, continue on. The economist Joseph Schumpeter said, "As the inventor produces ideas, the entrepreneur gets things done."

The education of potential entrepreneurs is a difficult task, one that is complicated due to the absence of any clear career patterns. Also, there is really no such thing as a "true entrepreneurial profile" from which to learn. Entrepreneurs come from a variety of educational backgrounds. It doesn't necessarily take an MBA graduate to start and harvest a business successfully. Entrepreneurs have a special way of thinking, reasoning, and obsessing with harvesting an opportunity. In a holistic approach, they create teams that are leadership balanced, injecting imagination, motivation, commitment, passion, teamwork, and vision. A definition of tomorrow's entrepreneur may be as follows: one who is involved in the process of finding, leading, and coaching a close-knit group of talented people committed to pursuing an idea, as well as providing, marshaling, and allocating the resources needed to take advantage of a limited opportunity.

Some say that entrepreneurship is like driving fast on an icy road. To survive the journey, it requires unique industry insight through domain expertise, anticipation, and "traction" with sales. More importantly, it is a matter of finding the right balance between the individual and the opportunity. Entrepreneurs are rewarded with the freedom to do what they want, the ability to selectively control and reduce risks; they are rewarded with the potential to generate unlimited amounts of income. To accomplish this requires a good, solid plan and a far-reaching vision.

Wanted: Entrepreneurs (Just Don't Ask for a Job Description)

If entrepreneurship is so important, why don't we know more about it?

RONALD A. WIRTZ

All the world loves an entrepreneur. They are the business equivalent of the date you bring home to your mother, or the people you consider role models for your kids, because they are seen as honest, bright, hard-working and successful. Most of us want to be one ourselves. Indeed, most countries and their policymakers are busy trying to find, encourage and grow more entrepreneurs.

But despite their prized status, not to mention their ubiquitous presence in many economies, entrepreneurs are like Heffalumps, the exotic creatures hunted by Winnie-the-Pooh and his friends. Everyone "knows" what Heffalumps and entrepreneurs are. But ask for details, and you get a wide range of physical, behavioral and environmental descriptions.

Wesleyan University economist Peter Kilby first made the Heffalump analogy close to 40 years ago. Since then, research on entrepreneurship has multiplied considerably, especially in the past decade. Still, the Heffalump syndrome continues to plague the study of the topic. "Although entrepreneurship has become a buzzword in the public debate," notes a 2008 article in the journal *Foundations and Trends in Entrepreneurship,* "a coherent definition of entrepreneurship has not yet emerged."[1]

Such irony is not lost on those who have spent careers trying to build a better mousetrap for measuring entrepreneurship. "It's a wonderful word for raising money, but terrible for conducting research. It's too vague of a word. . . . There are so many different ideas of entrepreneurship," says Paul Reynolds, professor of management at Florida International University and principal investigator in three major efforts to gather data on entrepreneurs.

Some might pooh-pooh (so to speak) the semantic worries of researchers pursuing this elusive economic phenomenon and the person who brings it to life. But countries ignore the matter at their own peril, because entrepreneurship is increasingly seen as the wellspring of healthy, growing economies, and failure to understand the dynamics of the person and the process makes it unlikely that economies will get optimum levels of either.

> **Some might pooh-pooh (so to speak) the semantic worries of researchers pursuing this elusive economic phenomenon and the person who brings it to life. But countries ignore the matter at their own peril, because entrepreneurship is increasingly seen as the wellspring of healthy, growing economies.**

Much has been accomplished in the research community in the past 10 years or so. As a result, certain traits and other descriptive matters regarding entrepreneurs are better understood. But large gaps remain, in part because researchers have generally avoided stating what they really mean by "entrepreneurship" or generating a convenient definition of their own. As a result, some of the most important insights regarding entrepreneurship's role in state and national economies, and its behavior in different economic environments, remain beyond our grasp.

A Working Definition

So let's start from the beginning—that comfortable spot where we talk about entrepreneurs with nodding agreement.

An entrepreneur is a person who conceives, develops and operates a new business venture, assuming both the risk and reward for his or her effort. Entrepreneurs are often celebrated for their vision, derring-do and conviction to do it their way. Those who succeed make society better off for the jobs created and new goods or services delivered that make life more productive, comfortable or convenient. Success typically leads to financial gain for the entrepreneur, and sometimes extreme personal wealth. Such traits make entrepreneurship the seed and roots of the American Dream.

Still Hunting Heffalumps

- Entrepreneurship is the new buzzword, and policymakers in many nations and states are trying to develop more entrepreneurs because of their positive effect on jobs and productivity.
- But while the term is familiar, there is little agreement about what entrepreneurship is, what it does and how it happens. Recent research has improved understanding of some descriptive features of the entrepreneur, but we still don't know much about the entrepreneurial process itself—conception, development and entry into economic life. As a result, some of the most important insights regarding entrepreneurship—and any ability to encourage more of it—remain beyond our grasp.

And there are a lot of dreamers out there. In the United States, about 12 million people are undertaking some entrepreneurial endeavor, according to the U.S. Panel Study on Entrepreneurial Dynamics. It also estimates that "perhaps up to one-half of all adults are engaged in self-employment or the creation of a new business at some point during their work career."[2] Worldwide, the Global Entrepreneurship Monitor estimates, a half-*billion* people are trying to create a new business every year.

Cultures differ in their regard for entrepreneurs. The pedestal is high in the United States. Robert Litan is vice president of research and policy at the Kauffman Foundation, based in Kansas City, Mo., and believed to be the largest foundation with a focus on entrepreneurship. Litan says entrepreneur-ship has been noticeably on the rise, something he attributes to certain conspicuous successes of the 1980s, when garage-born, pioneering firms like Microsoft and Apple came into prominence. That momentum was further boosted in the 1990s when the Internet opened untold opportunities for new business ideas.

Cultures differ in their regard for entrepreneurs. The pedestal is high in the United States. . . . Entrepreneurship has been noticeably on the rise, [attributed] to certain conspicuous successes of the 1980s, when garage-born, pioneering firms like Microsoft and Apple came into prominence. That momentum was further boosted in the 1990s when the Internet opened untold opportunities for new business ideas.

"America has seen a regeneration of its economy largely on the growth of entrepreneurs, and it has become part of the culture," Litan says.

Not all cultures hold entrepreneurship in such high esteem. The German, French and Japanese economies, for instance, have historically placed high value on the security and stability of large, mature firms. But in Europe, too, the profile of entrepreneurship is rising. In a 2008 report, the Paris-based Organisation for Economic Co-operation and Development says that in recent years "entrepreneurship has become a buzzword that's entered the mainstream. Politicians continuously cite its importance and the need to create more entrepreneurial societies, and newspapers and television programmes frequently create themes around successful entrepreneurs."[3] The OECD itself has a center devoted to the promotion of entrepreneurship.

Research has shown that economic growth is strongly associated with the creation of new firms because they generate jobs and improve productivity through adaptation and change. New firms tend to push out old ones, and this churn is believed to rejuvenate economies—a critical matter in a hyper-competitive global economy.

But we don't know much about the entrepreneurial process itself—the conception, development and entry into economic life. We know about this stuff anecdotally, but we don't know it systematically. Many perceive entrepreneurship to be similar to biological gestation, where all firms develop in similar, predictable stages. Reynolds says such a model "is really inappropriate" because surveying to date has shown "that there is no one thing people do first or last." There are general patterns, he says, but enough variety to frustrate any paint-by-numbers model.

Government statistics offices have only recently started paying the topic much formal attention. The topic of entrepreneurship "has been around for hundreds of years," says Tim Davis, head of the new OECD Statistics Directorate program tracking entrepreneur-ship performance. "But it is true that only in the last 10 years or so that government and serious statistical offices have said there's something there to measure."

A bird's-eye view shows a lot of research on this topic of late. For example, the Entrepreneurship Research & Policy Network (part of the Social Science Research Network) was started in March 2006 and already consists of more than 4,300 papers. Babson College's most recent annual compendium of entrepreneurship research includes close to 200 papers in 26 categories. Universities are adding faculty and entire programs to study and teach entrepreneurship. In 1996, the Kauffman Foundation and the University of Maryland started what would later become the Global Consortium of Entrepreneurial Centers. Today, the network includes more than 200 universities.

Such activity and attention has improved our understanding of entrepreneurship, particularly here in the United States. For example, we have a much better idea of the socio-demographic characteristics of entrepreneurs: Men are more likely than women to start their own business; immigrants have higher entrepreneurial rates than native-born; people in their 30s and 40s have the highest rates by age. Reams of descriptive details about entrepreneurs exist on topics ranging from financing to household and educational background to human resource management and psychological makeup. Says Reynolds, "The increase in knowledge of basic features of entrepreneurship has grown dramatically in the last 15 years."

You Think You're So Smart

But that's less progress than you might think. It seems that the more we study and the more we learn about entrepreneurship, the more vast and complex the subject becomes. We see how little a dent has been made. Most important, existing research does not address the dynamism of the entrepreneurial process that society is ultimately most interested in encouraging; it describes the sorcerer's features without revealing how the magic occurs.

In a 2006 essay, New York University economist William Baumol writes that while the entrepreneur is often mentioned and his or her role emphasized, "the discussion of the subject is most frequently very brief, and consists generally of a listing of the tasks of the entrepreneur—organizing of the firm, risk bearing, etc., with little that aspires to the status of sophisticated theory." Baumol says this gap in the literature "is not neglect of a peripheral matter, but a gaping hole in our understanding of the economic mechanism."[4]

Getting at the enchantment of entrepreneurship might seem an impossible task. But doing so is fundamental if the hope is to somehow understand and channel that magic for society's benefit. And this brings us back to Pooh's hunting party and the elusive Heffalump. One of the few things the research community seems to agree on is that there is no agreement on what entrepreneurship is or does. Says Litan, from Kauffman, "That's a very contentious issue."

Worse yet, researchers haven't really bothered to stop and argue it through. They each hunt their own particular Heffalump, which may or may not resemble others'. As a result, the challenge of studying and understanding entrepreneurship "is made all the more demanding because of the considerable confusion that exists in the way that people use the term entrepreneurship," says a January OECD report. "Indeed, even the OECD itself has contributed to the confusion since virtually every study that has focused on entrepreneurship has presented a different definition of the term."[5]

The problem can be traced in part to society's casual agreement on what an entrepreneur is and does. The term itself is attributed to Irish economist Richard Cantillon, whose 1732 essay on commerce, written in French, devoted attention to those who *undertake* economic activities that involve both risk and potential gain. In English translation, that person is an "undertaker," but in French, he or she is the far more elegant "entrepreneur," from the same root as "enterprise."

Austrian economist Joseph Schumpeter, who made popular the phrase "creative destruction," is widely viewed as the father of modern entrepreneur theory for his extensive work on capitalism, business cycles and the role of innovation. But save for his emphasis on innovation, Schumpeter never went much beyond fairly general notions of the entrepreneur.

Trying to Define

But aside from creating a general identification and exultation of the entrepreneur, analysis of the entrepreneurial process has remained primitive. The lack of something as basic as a definition of entrepreneurship—much less a sophisticated model of

it—effectively crumbles research efforts into mini camps of decentralized thought, many of them inapplicable to each other because each uses a subtly different definition, whether about the entrepreneur or his or her endeavor.

Don't believe it? Here's a quick test: When does entrepreneurship start? With the idea? When the first dollar is spent developing the idea? When a tax identification number is issued? Or maybe when the first dollar of revenue is earned, or the first employee hired? And when does a firm discontinue being an entrepreneurial activity? How do we know? And what does it transition into, exactly? All of these are discrete stages of the entrepreneurial process, but research to date assigns no particular empirical significance to any of them.

There are many other distinctions to haggle over. For example, we all know that entrepreneurship sometimes comes out of necessity—after the loss of a job or the inability to find a job, for example. Other times, entrepreneurship springs from the recognition of a market opportunity. Purists believe that entrepreneurship—at least the kind with the most economic potential—comes from capitalizing on a new idea or product, not from bootstrap undertakings.

> **We all know that entrepreneurship sometimes comes out of necessity—after the loss of a job or the inability to find a job, for example. Other times, entrepreneurship springs from the recognition of a market opportunity. Purists believe that entrepreneurship—at least the kind with the most economic potential—comes from capitalizing on a new idea or product, not from bootstrap undertakings.**

To go a step further, many believe that genuine entrepreneurship transcends the recognition of a market opportunity and must involve innovation as well; to Schumpeter, innovation was fundamental. Litan subscribes to the innovation theory, because the underlying social goal of entrepreneurship is growth.

"It's too easy to equate entrepreneurship with small businesses," he says. "Most small business is what we call replicative"—businesses that take existing services or products and bring them to new markets, or tweak existing services and products for a new niche. "We're not dismissing those that do it. But innovative entrepreneurship provides substantially more benefits" to owners and society, Litan argues. "They are the engines of growth."

Maybe so, but our ability to measure innovative entrepreneurship is almost nil; U.S. data systems can't even distinguish between endeavors undertaken out of necessity and by market opportunity. Not everyone buys into the innovation-only model. Some argue that it undervalues the added competition brought by replicative businesses, which keeps a lid on prices.

Indeed, the definition of innovation itself is another argument waiting to happen. For example, is Starbucks considered innovative? Its signature product—coffee—certainly isn't new, or even particularly different from anything that came before it. The firm's corporate franchising model isn't particularly new or different either. But with stores worldwide, tens of thousands of employees and a market cap in the billions, the company undoubtedly qualifies as innovative in some capacity and as entrepreneurial at some point in its development.

And that's fundamentally the problem: We don't know—or agree on—when a firm has started, what qualifies it as entrepreneurial or when it stops being entrepreneurial. Though research is trying to fill in the gap, too often study populations are subjectively defined in terms of their entrepreneurial characteristics and qualifications. While such studies certainly offer some utility, a shifting study population undermines any attempt to build coherent theory or models.

The Big Dig

Getting at these complex empirical research matters is both a problem and an opportunity for the research community. Indeed, you might say the research community is confronted with its own entrepreneurial test.

Litan estimates that there are more than 50 journals dedicated to the topic of entrepreneurship; many of these journals occupy narrow intellectual niches and have few readers. Litan wants to see the topic tackled by mainstream academic journals. "Unless [entrepreneurship research] is mainstream, it will be marginalized," he says. But economists "can't work without the data."

By anyone's standard, however, gathering good data is a slow process. Part of the problem is institutional inertia. Governments have long been data warehouses, cranking out and storing vast troves of information on businesses. Today, little of that data-gathering is dedicated to entrepreneurship, or even small business, because it hasn't been part of the research agenda in the past.

That orientation is not accidental, or even necessarily ill-conceived. In 2007, the National Research Council (NRC) published a lengthy report on the nation's ability to track business dynamics—the formal name given to birth and death cycles of business. It points out that, historically speaking, government's "predominant focus" in data-gathering was to measure output and jobs, with a focus on large firms because they account for most of the economy's output and employment (and one of the reasons the somewhat ironically named Small Business Administration defines its core audience as any firm with fewer than 500 workers). As a result, the report states, "the U.S. business data system is inadequate for understanding many of the mechanisms leading to greater productivity and innovation or the dynamics of firm and job creation."[6]

Some matters that seem both simple and necessary for understanding today's economy, and entrepreneurs' role in it, are left to guesswork. For example, business data are disaggregated along numerous dimensions—employment, geography, industry sector—but virtually no published data exist on the age of firms. As a result, it's often assumed that small businesses are young and that large businesses are old, even though we know that's not the case.

The NRC report notes that available data have improved: Government agencies like the Census Bureau, Bureau of Labor Statistics and Internal Revenue Service have long had administrative records with data on key developments in the life of a firm, such as receipt of an employer identification number or when positive cash flow or profits are achieved. Agencies, as well as independent researchers, have been digging into these databases to construct better longitudinal data sets for young and small businesses. The Census Bureau, for example, is expected to release new data this year on firm births and deaths, and employment changes attached to each, going back to the late 1970s. Currently, such data go back only to the 1990s.

Yet despite recent progress, according to the NRC report, "substantial data gaps remain." That's because shifting the government's data collection system to new objectives is not a quick or easy matter. "It changes paradigms and they are not comfortable with it. They know what they've got [regarding existing data collection] and they want to keep it," says Reynolds.

Brick by Data Brick

Without assertive buy-in from government statistics offices, the creation of good data sets will evolve slowly. But the needle is moving.

The Kauffman Foundation has been pushing hard for better data sets, funding academic pursuits and pushing the envelope with its own research. For example, the Kauffman Index of Entrepreneurial Activity resulted from mutual interests with economist Robert Fairlie, of the University of California Santa Cruz, and is one of the few nationwide measures of entrepreneurship at the state level.

In March, the foundation released the Kauffman Firm Survey, a panel survey that tracks about 4,900 businesses founded in 2004. The survey's origin, according to the report, stems from the disconnect that "entrepreneurial activity is an important part of a capitalist economy, [yet] only a small amount of data are available about U.S. businesses in their first years of operation."

In March, the foundation released the Kauffman Firm Survey, a panel survey that tracks about 4,900 businesses founded in 2004. The survey's origin, according to the report, stems from the disconnect that "entrepreneurial activity is an important part of a capitalist economy, [yet] only a small amount of data are available about U.S. businesses in their first years of operation."

Kauffman also supported two of the earliest—and to date, still most significant—efforts to build longitudinal data sets on entrepreneurs. The godfather of such efforts—going "way back" to 1998—is the U.S. Panel Study on Entrepreneurial Dynamics, a project that evolved out of earlier survey work by Reynolds who was later joined by Richard Curtin at the University of

Michigan. PSED was ground-breaking because it captured early stages of entrepreneurship (what Reynolds and Curtin refer to as the "nascent" stage) before an endeavor was picked up on official government registries. It's the period we all know exists, but previously had only anecdotes to work from to identify.

> To date, over 60 countries have participated at least once, and GEM [Global Entrepreneurship Monitor] has more than 200 researchers worldwide participating in the project. It touts itself as "the largest single study of entrepreneurial activity in the world."

PSED provided the first readings of this developmental stage by screening 62,000 households to find 830 active nascent entrepreneurs, which it defined as anyone admitting to startup activity in the past 12 months, who also had the expectation of owning all or part of the new firm, and having no positive cash flow covering all expenses and employees for six of last 12 months.

Study participants were initially interviewed for 60 minutes and then three additional times over a four-year period. They were asked almost 500 questions, providing a level of detail about entrepreneurs and the firm development process that is unmatched. That's both a problem and an opportunity, according to Reynolds.

"It's very hard to get nascents on the phone because they are very busy people. They've got full-time jobs and families and kids and everything else," says Reynolds. But "once we get them on the phone, we can't get them off, because it's a very sophisticated interview. It's like low-level consulting. [The nascent entrepreneurs] stop the interview to take notes." A new and enhanced project—dubbed PSED II—started the process over again in 2005 with a new batch of about 1,200 nascent entrepreneurs.

The original PSED also sparked the first effort at comparing entrepreneurial activity among countries, ultimately developing into a separate project called the Global Entrepreneurship Monitor. GEM had to overcome enormous hurdles—shoestring budgets, translation of the survey into dozens of languages, lack of sophisticated survey firms in some countries—but has managed to conduct 2,000 interviews per year per country (with a few exceptions), starting with 10 countries in the first year (1999) and expecting to increase to 42 countries this year. To date, over 60 countries have participated at least once, and GEM has more than 200 researchers worldwide participating in the project. It touts itself as "the largest single study of entrepreneurial activity in the world."

Among many findings from these ongoing surveys, GEM has found an inverse relationship between entrepreneurship and gross domestic product—in other words, poor countries tend to have very high rates of entrepreneurship, much of it based on necessity.

As coordinating principal investigator of the GEM project in its early years, Reynolds acknowledges that GEM is "not a perfect data set." But he points out that it "is the only harmonized comparison of business creation across this wide range of countries in existence." And with a half-billion nascent or operating entrepreneurs worldwide, "this [is] on the scale of a lot of other major social phenomena," Reynolds says. "It's that scale of activity that you begin to realize that entrepreneurial activity is really this phenomenal activity that we didn't really understand before."

And the rising profile of entrepreneurship is motivating more countries to take a closer look at the phenomenon. In most OECD countries, entrepreneurship is becoming a policy priority, says Davis, of the OECD's Statistics Directorate. That might not seem surprising, he admits, but even recently "there was very limited involvement of official national statistics offices in anything that was called entrepreneurship. In fact, you could go to all of the national statistic offices, and never see the word 'entrepreneurship.'"

In the fall of 2006, the OECD and Eurostat kicked off an "entrepreneurial performance" program to track employer firms and their growth over time among a voluntary group of 15 member countries, with the hope that all OECD countries would join eventually. The effort is not plowing new ground in terms of surveying and other data-gathering. Rather, the project has established fundamental definitions and a framework of performance indicators. National statistics offices are being asked to mine existing databases because these repositories have the highest quality data and attention to detail, factors that facilitate credibility and comparability of the data, which is the whole point.

"We want to make entrepreneurship data boring. We want to make it mainstream. We want to make it part of the statistical program of the member countries, and develop a common language," Davis says.

It Was Bigger than I Dreamed

In April, the OECD released its first set of findings on entrepreneurial performance indicators, like employment growth. But knowing performance "is only the first step," says Davis. Over time, the project will cobble together many data that will eventually allow researchers to investigate the many determinants of successful entrepreneurship. "That's the next step, and a harder step."

Kauffman's Litan talks about "new frontiers" of research that help identify the red and green lights that entrepreneurs encounter. For example, talk to any entrepreneur about obstacles, and "you'll very quickly have a legal discussion," whether it be about government regulations, intellectual property or other matters of law, he says.

PSED I and II also offer the first attempt to aggregate the time and money put into startups, the latter of which they estimate at between $40 billion and $50 billion annually. What it shows is "how much (investment) never leads to a business. This is the social cost of this Darwinian process," says Reynolds. He adds that future research might help reduce those dead-weight costs to society. Only about one-third of serious nascent entrepreneurs end up with an operating business, says Reynolds. "If we could get that to 50 percent, that would be a hell of a payoff. It wouldn't take much for a lower social cost."

This is why the Heffalump hunt matters. Only a better understanding of entrepreneurship in its living environment will give policymakers a chance at encouraging its propagation, or ensuring a better survival rate. The January 2008 OECD report says the absence of clear definitions and performance indicators for entrepreneurship has left policymakers "somewhat rudderless when it comes to developing policies" to facilitate entrepreneurship, particularly in the sense of international best practices.[7] Many countries, for example, actively seek high-growth firms to fuel job and wealth creation. But in the absence of empirical data, policymakers play a game of how-about-this.

And in the end, the goal of coming up with a single definition of entrepreneurship might be terribly nearsighted. Likely more useful would be a model that identifies the many moving parts, traits and stages of entrepreneurship.

"The challenge of the future," Reynolds says, is getting all of the research "into a more conceptualized scheme" that starts at idea generation and moves through the various stages of becoming a business (or not) and finally through the maturation period or termination. "It's a fun challenge when you realize how complicated it is."

But he also points out that we're not chasing this Heffalump for the fun of it. As market economies spread worldwide, entrepreneurship and innovation are widely believed to be the comparative advantage for national economies; a better understanding of both likely holds an important key to future growth.

As market economies spread worldwide, entrepreneurship and innovation are widely believed to be the comparative advantage for national economies; a better understanding of both likely holds an important key to future growth.

The nice part is that once researchers have decoded the DNA of entrepreneurship, and recognize the environment in which it thrives, a perfect title awaits the tell-all book that will unmask this phenomenon:

What color is your Heffalump?

Notes

1. Iversen, Jens, Rasmus Jørgensen and Nikolaj Malchow-Møller, "Defining and Measuring Entrepreneurship," *Foundations and Trends in Entrepreneurship* 4 (1), 2008.

2. Reynolds, Paul D., and Richard T. Curtin, "Business Creation in the United States: Panel Study of Entrepreneurial Dynamics II, Initial Assessment," *Foundations and Trends in Entrepreneurship* 4 (3): 155–307, 2008.

3. Ahmad, Nadim, and Anders N. Hoffmann, "A Framework for Addressing and Measuring Entrepreneurship," OECD Statistics Working Paper, January 2008.

4. Baumol, William J., "Entrepreneurship and Small Business: Toward a Program of Research," *Entrepreneurship Research: Past Perspectives and Future Prospects,* 2006. The volume consists of essays from Baumol and other winners of the international research award given by the Swedish Foundation for Small Business Research and the Swedish National Board for Industrial and Technical Development (dubbed the FSF-NUTEK Award). The essays were published in the 10th anniversary edition of the journal *Foundations and Trends in Entrepreneurship,* 2006.

5. Ahmad, Nadim, and Richard G. Seymour, "Defining Entrepreneurial Activity: Definitions Supporting Frameworks for Data Collection," OECD Statistics Working Paper, January 2008.

6. National Research Council of the National Academies, *Understanding Business Dynamics: An Integrated Data System for America's Future,* 2007.

7. Ahmad, Nadim, and Anders N. Hoffmann, "A Framework for Addressing and Measuring Entrepreneurship," OECD Statistics Working Paper, January 2008.

An Idea Whose Time Has Come

Entrepreneurialism Has Become Cool

Victor Hugo once remarked: "You can resist an invading army; you cannot resist an idea whose time has come." Today entrepreneurship is such an idea.

The triumph of entrepreneurship is driven by profound technological change. A trio of inventions—the personal computer, the mobile phone and the internet—is democratising entrepreneurship at a cracking pace. Today even cash-strapped innovators can reach markets that were once the prerogative of giant organisations.

The internet provides a cheap platform for entrepreneurs to build interactive businesses. Meg Whitman grew rich by developing an online marketplace, eBay, where people could buy and sell without ever meeting. An army of pyjama-clad bloggers has repeatedly outsmarted long-established newspapers on breaking stories. Automated news-collecting services such as RealClear-Politics and Memeorandum, using tiny amounts of capital, have established themselves as indispensable tools for news junkies.

The development of "cloud computing" is giving small outfits yet more opportunity to enjoy the advantages of big organisations with none of the sunk costs. People running small businesses, whether they are in their own offices or in a hotel half-way round the world, can use personal computers or laptops to gain access to sophisticated business services.

The mobile phone has been almost as revolutionary. About 3.3 billion people, or half the world's population, already have access to one. The technology has allowed entrepreneurs to break into what used to be one of the world's most regulated markets, telecoms. And many developing countries have been able to leapfrog rich ones by going straight to mobile phones, cutting out landlines.

This has resulted in a cascade of entrepreneurship. Iqbal Quadir, a Bangladeshi who emigrated to America to become an investment banker and then a business academic, had a dream of bringing mobile phones to his homeland. He struck up a relationship with Muhammad Yunus, the founder of Grameen Bank, which provides microfinance, to turn the dream into reality. If the bank was willing to lend women money to buy cows, why not mobile phones? Bangladesh now has 270,000 phone ladies who borrow money to buy specially designed mobile-phone kits equipped with long-lasting batteries, and sell time on their phones to local villagers. Grameen has become Bangladesh's largest telecoms provider, with annual revenues of around $1 billion; and the entrepreneurial phone ladies have plugged their villages into the wider economy.

The Best and the Worst

Ease of Doing Business Rankings

Top Ten

2009	2008	Business Region
1	1	Singapore
2	2	New Zealand
3	3	United States
4	4	Hong Kong
5	5	Denmark
6	6	Britain
7	7	Ireland
8	8	Canada
9	10	Australia
10	9	Norway

Bottom Ten

2009	2008	Business Region
172	171	Niger
173	173	Eritrea
174	175	Venezuela
175	176	Chad
176	177	São Tomé and Principe
177	174	Burundi
178	178	Congo-Brazzaville
179	179	Guinea-Bissau
180	180	Central African Republic
181	181	Congo

Source: World Bank *Doing Business* database

Thanks to the combination of touch-screen technology and ever faster wireless networks, the mobile phone is becoming the platform of choice for techno-entrepreneurs. Since July last year Apple has allowed third parties to post some 20,000

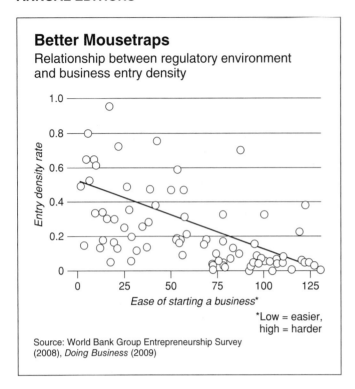

Better Mousetraps
Relationship between regulatory environment and business entry density

Entry density rate

Ease of starting a business*

*Low = easier,
high = harder

Source: World Bank Group Entrepreneurship Survey
(2008), *Doing Business* (2009)

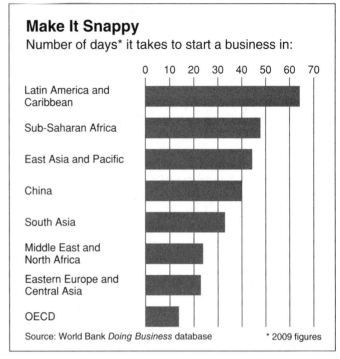

Make It Snappy
Number of days* it takes to start a business in:

Latin America and Caribbean
Sub-Saharan Africa
East Asia and Pacific
China
South Asia
Middle East and North Africa
Eastern Europe and Central Asia
OECD

Source: World Bank *Doing Business* database   * 2009 figures

programs or applications on its "app store", allowing phones to do anything from identifying the singer of a song on the radio to imitating the sound of flatulence. So far around 500m "apps" have been downloaded for about a dollar a time.

These developments have been reinforced by broad cultural changes that have brought entrepreneurialism into the mainstream. An activity that was once regarded as peripheral, perhaps even reprehensible, has become cool, celebrated by politicians and embraced by the rising generation.

Britain's Oxford University used to nurture one of the longest traditions of anti-entrepreneurial prejudice in the world. The dons valued "gentlemanly" subjects such as classics or philosophy over anything that smacked of "utility". ("He gets degrees in making jam/at Liverpool and Birmingham," went one popular ditty.) The students dreamed of careers in the civil service or the law rather than business, still less entrepreneurship. "How I hate that man," was the writer C.S. Lewis's tart comment on Lord Nuffield, his city's greatest entrepreneur and his university's most generous benefactor.

Today Oxford has a thriving business school, the Saïd School, with a centre for entrepreneurship and innovation and a growing business park that tries to mix the university's scientists with entrepreneurs. Oxford Entrepreneurs is one of the university's most popular societies, with 3,600 student members and a record of creating about six start-ups a year.

No Longer Niche

The story of Oxford's conversion to entrepreneurship is being repeated the world over as a growing number of respectable economists discover the new creed. For most of the post-war period entrepreneurs were all but banished from economics. Practitioners concentrated on the traditional factors of production—land, labour and capital—and on the price mechanism. Schumpeter was almost alone in arguing that the most vital competitive weapon was not lower prices but new ideas.

Today entrepreneurship is very much part of economics. Economists have realised that, in a knowledge-based economy, entrepreneurs play a central role in creating new companies, commercialising new ideas and, just as importantly, engaging in sustained experiments in what works and what does not. William Baumol has put entrepreneurs at the centre of his theory of growth. Paul Romer, of Stanford University, argues that "economic growth occurs whenever people take resources and rearrange them in ways that are more valuable . . . [It] springs from better recipes, not just more cooking." Edmund Phelps, a Nobel prize-winner, argues that attitudes toward entrepreneurship have a big impact on economic growth.

Another reason for entrepreneurship becoming mainstream is that the social contract between big companies and their employees has been broken. Under managed capitalism, big companies offered long-term security in return for unflinching loyalty. But from the 1980s onwards, first in America and then in other advanced economies, big companies began slimming their workforces. This made a huge difference to people's experience at the workplace. In the 1960s workers had an average of four different employers by the time they reached 65. Today they have had eight by the time they are 30. People's attitudes toward security and risk also changed. If a job in a big organisation can so easily disappear, it seems less attractive. Better to create your own.

Yet another reason for the mainstreaming of entrepreneurship is that so many institutions have given it their support. In 1998 HBS made entrepreneurship one of the foundation stones of business education, partly in response to demand from students. The school's Arthur Rock Centre for Entrepreneurship now employs over 30 professors. Between 1999 and 2003 the number of endowed chairs in entrepreneurship in America grew from 237 to 406 and in the rest of the world from 271 to 536.

The media have also played a part. "Dragons' Den", a television programme featuring entrepreneurs pitching their ideas to businesspeople in order to attract venture capital, is shown in 12 countries. "The Apprentice", a programme that had Donald Trump looking for a protégé, has produced numerous spin-offs. Even China's state-owned Central Television has a show about entrepreneurs pitching ideas to try to win $1.3m in seed money.

A Welcome Mat for Business

The world's governments are now competing to see who can create the most pro-business environment. In 2003 the World Bank began to publish an annual report called *Doing Business,* rating countries for their business-friendliness by measuring things like business regulations, property rights and access to credit. It demonstrated with a wealth of data that economic prosperity is closely correlated with a pro-business environment. This might sound obvious. But *Doing Business* did two things that were not quite so obvious: it put precise numbers on things that people had known about only vaguely, and it allowed citizens and investors to compare their country with 180 others.

This "naming and shaming" caused countries to compete fiercely to improve their position in the World Bank's rankings. Since 2004 various countries have brought in more than 1,000 reforms. Three of the top reformers in 2007–08 were African—Senegal, Burkina Faso and Botswana. Saudi Arabia too has made a lot of progress. *Doing Business* is also encouraging countries to learn from each other.

Most rich countries are working all the time to make it easier to start new businesses. In Canada, for example, it is now possible to start a business with just one procedure. But the list of top reformers includes all sorts of unexpected places, and the range of reforms that have been undertaken is impressive. India has concentrated on technology, for example, introducing electronic registration for businesses; China has put a great deal of effort into improving access to credit. Robert Litan, of the Kauffman Foundation, suggests that the World Bank may have done more good by compiling *Doing Business* than by lending much of the money that it has.

Creative Disruption

Economic theory has been unable to explain the bond between competition and innovation. Until now.

DOUGLAS CLEMENT

Over the past decade, a steady flow of research has shown a strong real-world relationship between competitive markets, technological innovation and higher productivity. This work argues powerfully that if nations wish to grow economically, they should eliminate obstacles to competition—whether from trade barriers, patents or other forms of anticompetitive practice.

But the theoretical case for this relationship is far weaker than the empirical evidence. Indeed, standard theory is ambiguous as to whether a competitive or monopolistic environment is more likely to be innovative and productive. Some schools of thought suggest that monopolies have less incentive to innovate; others argue that competition is less favorable to the spread of innovation.

In a recent Minneapolis Fed staff report, three economists suggest that standard theory—of both schools—has been built on a flawed assumption; when that assumption is corrected, they argue, theory aligns with data in finding that competition is more conducive than monopoly to innovation and productivity.

The flawed assumption? That adopting a new innovation is a smooth, problem-free process. The correction: Technological innovation is subject to "switchover disruptions," those troublesome glitches or outright disasters that accompany virtually every change in procedure or process. Think of when you switched your cell phone company. Expand that to a corporate-wide adoption of a new process, and the potential for disruption becomes obvious. When this disruption is taken into account, standard theory is brought into line with real-world experience: Monopolies are *less* likely to innovate.

"If firms face switchover disruptions, then they may temporarily lose some unit sales upon adoption," write Thomas Holmes, David Levine and James Schmitz in "Monopoly and the Incentive to Innovate When Adoption Involves Switchover Disruptions," a Minneapolis Fed staff report and National Bureau of Economic Research working paper. (See "Publications and Papers" online at minneapolisfed.org.)"Greater market power will mean higher prices on those lost units of output, and hence a reduced incentive to innovate."

The concept is fairly straightforward. Change isn't easy, and because monopolists make higher profits than competitors, their opportunity cost of change is higher as well. As Levine put it in an e-mail, "Monopolists tend to be more conservative in innovating because they have more to lose."

The Austrian School

Straightforward? Perhaps. But some of the field's brightest minds have viewed this quite differently. Austrian economist Joseph Schumpeter, a prominent Harvard scholar, was the first theoretician to devote substantial attention to innovation. He considered it a crucial step in the process of what he termed "creative destruction," in which new firms incessantly overtake the old as capitalist economies evolve.

Monopolies didn't really worry Schumpeter. Indeed, he thought most economists held competition on too high a pedestal. "Perfect competition is not only impossible but inferior, and has no title to being set up as a model of ideal efficiency," he wrote in his 1942 classic, *Capitalism, Socialism and Democracy.* "Most of the facts and arguments . . . tend to dim the halo that once surrounded perfect competition as much as they suggest a more favorable view of its alternative."

According to Schumpeter, monopolies and innovation are closely related. . . . They can take advantage of increasing returns prevalent in R&D, they have greater capacity to take on the inherent risk, . . . and "a monopolist does not have competitors ready to imitate his innovation."

According to Schumpeter, monopolies and innovation are closely related. As French economist Jean Tirole points out in *The Theory of Industrial Organization,* Schumpeter

Disruptive Innovation

- Economic theorists have been of two minds on the relationship between monopoly power and innovation. Kenneth Arrow argued that competitors have more incentive to innovate than monopolists. Others suggested that monopolists are more likely to encourage innovation.
- A recent Minneapolis Fed staff report argues that both models implicitly assume that adoption of innovation is trouble-free. When "switchover disruptions" are incorporated into either model, theory shows that competitive environments are more favorable to innovation.
- The crux of the argument: Because monopolists make higher profits than competitors, they have higher opportunity costs. Disruptive switchovers therefore pose a greater disincentive to innovation for monopolists.

argued "that monopolies are natural breeding grounds for R&D and that if one wants to induce firms to undertake R&D one must accept the creation of monopolies as a necessary evil." Schumpeter was vague about whether monopolies per se or simply big firms are more conducive to R&D than small competitive firms, but he did suggest several reasons large establishments are "better-qualified or more eager to undertake R&D than smaller firms," according to Tirole: They can take advantage of increasing returns prevalent in R&D, they have greater capacity to take on the inherent risk, their large production facilities ease implementation of innovations and "a monopolist does not have competitors ready to imitate his innovation."

Arrow's Point

Schumpeter's theories were controversial on several fronts, and even as economists came to accept his ideas about the importance of entrepreneurs and innovation, many would continue to argue that monopolies squelched rather than nurtured innovation. Stanford's Kenneth Arrow was the first to offer a rigorous mathematical treatment of the issue, and his seminal 1962 article, "Economic Welfare and the Allocation of Resources for Invention," drew a conclusion directly at odds with Schumpeter. "The incentive to invent," wrote Arrow, "is less under monopolistic than under competitive conditions."

Arrow set down simple equations for unit costs of production before and after an invention, and the corresponding prices, quantities, inventor royalties and monopolist profits. He assumed a downward-sloping demand curve, so that a higher product price would result in a lower quantity demanded by consumers (price elasticity). And he assumed that only the monopolist could adopt a cost-saving innovation; that is, the

incumbent firm wouldn't have to worry about a potential rival buying this new technology and entering the market. (Of course, for some innovations, rivalry isn't an issue. A monopolist might simply consider adopting a new supply system, not a new physical invention.)

In this situation, Arrow showed, a monopolist would have a lower incentive to adopt innovation because monopolies maximize profit by raising price and reducing quantity supplied compared with competitive markets. A monopolist would therefore have relatively few units of output over which to spread the fixed cost of the new technology.

Arrow's argument, later termed "the replacement effect," was convincing. A firm in a competitive market would have high output levels, and so the cost of an innovation could be spread thinly, but a monopolist, with lower output, would be less inclined to incur that additional cost. That isn't to say a monopolist would never innovate, simply that its motivation would always be lower than that of a firm in a competitive environment. "The preinvention monopoly power acts as a strong disincentive to further innovation," Arrow concluded.

> **Arrow's argument, later termed "the replacement effect," was convincing. A firm in a competitive market would have high output levels, and so the cost of an innovation could be spread thinly, but a monopolist, with lower output, would be less inclined to incur that additional cost.**

(Another way to look at it: A firm with a weak monopoly position because of low tariff protection against foreign competition is going to produce more output than a firm enjoying higher tariff protection; the latter will have less incentive to innovate because—again—it has less output to "justify" the fixed cost.)

On the Other Hand

In 1982, University of California, Berkeley, economist Richard Gilbert and David Newbery of Cambridge University presented a counterargument. Arrow, they wrote, had "assumed that entry was blockaded" by the monopolist—that is, for the sake of argument he presupposed that only the incumbent firm could choose whether or not to adopt an innovation.

But in reality, innovations are often available to both incumbents and rivals in any particular market. Inventors create, and firms can vie for that creation. Both Microsoft and Yahoo, for instance, could have owned YouTube, but Google bought it. And if a potential rival might adopt an innovation that would put an incumbent monopolist at a competitive disadvantage, that implies a very different incentive structure than Arrow imagined.

The Gilbert-Newbery model, then, says that a monopolist must choose between adopting an innovation and allowing a rival to adopt it. The monopoly firm must calculate not only the value of the innovation to its own operation, but the repercussions of allowing a rival to have it. In this situation, the economists showed, monopolists often have a strong incentive to innovate, if only to preempt their rivals.

> **The Gilbert-Newbery model says that a monopolist must choose between adopting an innovation and allowing a rival to adopt it. The monopoly firm must calculate not only the value of the innovation to its own operation, but the repercussions of allowing a rival to have it.**

"Under certain conditions," Gilbert and Newbery wrote, "a firm with monopoly power has an incentive to maintain its monopoly power by patenting new technologies before potential competitors. . . . The monopolist will preempt if the cost is less than the profits gained by preventing entry."

Monopolists, they pointed out, might never implement the new technology, but in the long run this "patent shelving" isn't necessarily harmful. "Preemption need not have adverse consequences for economic welfare. Preemption requires investment in product development with only a probability of successful entry deterrence. Society gains from the development of new technology at a pace at least as rapid as would occur with more competition."

The Gilbert-Newbery analysis—sometimes called the "efficiency effect"—led economists to a more favorable view of monopoly and innovation, closer to that envisioned by Schumpeter. And indeed, they reference the Austrian. "Since entry at some date is inevitable, to the extent that preemption does occur it is a phase in the Schumpeterian process of creative destruction."

Disruption

So, we're back where we started: Theory on the relationship between monopoly and innovation remains unclear. Schumpeter believed that innovation required a significant measure of monopoly. Arrow demonstrated the reverse—that monopolists are less likely to innovate. Gilbert-Newbery showed the opposite could be true.

For empirical economists, this messy theoretical debate has produced more smoke than fire, but over the past decade, their research has nonetheless found—in a wide variety of contexts— that more competition tends to result in increased innovation and higher productivity. Still, without solid theory to explain the data, economists feel ill at ease.

Finding the link in theory that exists in fact required a flash of inspiration—a disruptive innovation, if you will—for

Minneapolis Fed visiting scholar Tom Holmes of the University of Minnesota, David Levine of Washington University, and Minneapolis Fed senior economist Jim Schmitz. Interviewed together at the Minneapolis Fed, Holmes and Schmitz recalled that the genesis of their collaboration with Levine on this project was the mutual need to bring theory into line with reality.

"It's been like a folk idea, the notion that monopoly is less efficient," observes Holmes, "but when we sit down and write our models, we haven't been able to get it to go that way. Yes, there's an empirical link between competition and productivity, but the theory has been tough. Why wouldn't a monopolist be just as efficient as a competitor? Why would they leave money on the table? Just to try to understand that has been a bit of a trick."

"I like to think it went back to my iron ore paper," says Schmitz, referring to a seminar he gave in the fall of 2002 at the University of California, Los Angeles, where Levine taught for many years. Schmitz's research found that iron ore producers in countries faced with tough international competition exhibited increased productivity, while those facing little competition showed no increase in productivity.

"David saw my presentation at UCLA," says Schmitz, "and later he would send e-mails about what might be going on to explain why, when competition came, we saw productivity gains in the iron mines."

"This is pretty hard to understand," observes Holmes who has collaborated frequently with Schmitz, but never before with Levine. "And David wanted to understand it. He's a brilliant theorist—really one of the top theorists, bar none, in the entire world—and he's trying to figure out, why is that? Why is that?"

"The question of why monopolies are so stagnant has puzzled me for a very long time," says Levine, via e-mail. "Jim's iron ore research was instrumental in that he had a very clear micro-level examination of how this happens in practice."

Initially, Schmitz and Levine corresponded about the problem; then Holmes joined the discussions during Levine's visits to the Minneapolis Fed. (Levine was a consultant at the Bank in 2004–05; his work on intellectual property was the focus of a September 2002 *Region* article, available at minneapolisfed.org under "Publications and Papers.")

Jim and I talked about the whys quite a bit, recalls Levine. "Tom has also been interested in these issues for a long time; he's collaborated with Jim, and I've known him and admired his work for an equally long time. I think at some point when I was visiting at the Bank the three of us started talking more about it, and the paper grew out of those ideas."

The Innovation

Like many powerful concepts, the idea behind their paper is quite simple: Innovation is disruptive, and disruption is more costly to a monopolist than to a competitive firm. Schumpeter, Arrow, and Gilbert and Newbery all had implicitly assumed that adoption of innovation is a seamless, trouble-free process. And that assumption hardly jibes with the world as we know it.

> Like many powerful concepts, the idea behind their paper is quite simple: Innovation is disruptive, and disruption is more costly to a monopolist than to a competitive firm. Schumpeter, Arrow, and Gilbert and Newbery all had implicitly assumed that adoption of innovation is a seamless, trouble-free process.

Consider Boeing. Standard practice for the airplane manufacturer had long been for all outside suppliers to ship parts to company facilities in Everett, Wash., and do virtually all assembly on site. To produce its highly anticipated 787 Dreamliners, however, the company initiated a new production plan under which suppliers would preassemble large sections of the plane and Boeing would perform only the final stages of assembly. Major gains in efficiency were anticipated.

But suppliers were unable to stay on schedule, and eventually Boeing reversed itself, calling on suppliers to ship unassembled work to Everett. That plan also went awry. "Boeing has ended up with a pile of parts and wires, and lots of questions about how they all fit together," reported the *New York Times* in January this year, "not unlike a frustrating Christmas morning at home." Airlines had ordered 817 of the planes, worth more than $100 billion, and delivery had been scheduled for late 2008. With the switchover disruption, Boeing says it hopes to start making deliveries in 2009.

Regardless of when the planes actually arrive, Boeing is— for a significant period of time—losing money. "The sales are being pushed to the future," notes Schmitz. "Boeing could have sold these planes earlier if they'd stuck to the old technology. But because they innovated, sales are delayed, and that's a substantial loss."

Newspaper headlines and daily life provide an ongoing series of plans that don't work out when institutions change their standard operating procedure, when corporations innovate and the innovations fail. New Coke, anyone?

The economists cite switchover disruptions in General Motors car manufacturing robotics, Denver airport's baggage-handling system, Japanese steel makers shifting from open-hearth to basic-oxygen furnaces, work rule changes, and new workplace compensation schemes. "And, of course," they write, "introducing new information technology systems often leads to significant disruptions."

The Model

Since disruption is an empirical reality when innovations are adopted, models hoping to illuminate the process should account for disruption. So in their paper, Holmes, Levine and Schmitz take the standard models used by economists to understand innovation and monopoly—Arrow and Gilbert-Newbery—and introduce disruption.

They begin with the Arrow model. The standard setup assumes elastic demand, and Arrow's classic result of monopolies having less incentive to innovate hinges on this assumption. But when Holmes, Levine and Schmitz introduce switchover disruption into the Arrow model, they find that Arrow's elasticity assumption is no longer necessary.

"If demand is perfectly inelastic, the Arrow effect goes away. No difference between competition and monopoly," observes Holmes. "Put that elastic demand in, and of course you get [the Arrow effect]. But we found that even if you strip out the thing that Arrow's model focused on, putting in switchover disruption gets back the inverse relationship between monopoly and incentive to innovate."

The Arrow model is the easier case; the economists' paper deals at greater length with Gilbert-Newbery. But to give the Gilbert-Newbery argument (the efficiency effect) its full power, the economists strip out Arrow's replacement effect by assuming inelastic demand: Quantity demanded isn't affected by changing prices, so monopolists won't necessarily have fewer units over which to spread the cost of innovation.

> Since disruption is an empirical reality when innovations are adopted, models hoping to illuminate the process should account for disruption. So in their paper, Holmes, Levine and Schmitz take the standard models used by economists to understand innovation and monopoly— Arrow and Gilbert-Newbery—and introduce disruption.

They set up their mathematical model so that an incumbent and a rival firm can bid for an innovation. Their object is to determine—first without switchover disruption and then with—how willingness to pay for innovation varies with degree of monopoly power. Without switchover disruption, their model replicates the Gilbert-Newbery result. "Innovation is worth more to the incumbent than a new entrant and so the incumbent will preemptively patent before a rival," they write. "The incumbent will take into account that if it does not preemptively innovate and the entrant adopts instead, the incumbent will lose its monopoly rent. In contrast, the rivals have no rent to forgo if they don't innovate."

Then, for five pages of mathematical propositions and proofs (plus a short appendix devoted to proving a lemma), the paper examines the Gilbert-Newbery model, *with* switchover disruption. The authors derive the incumbent's return (or profit) if it acquires and adopts the innovation, the incumbent's return if it acquires but idles the innovation, the incumbent's return if it doesn't acquire (so the rival gets it) and the rival's return if it acquires and adopts. And then they determine willingness to pay for innovation in the face of switchover disruption.

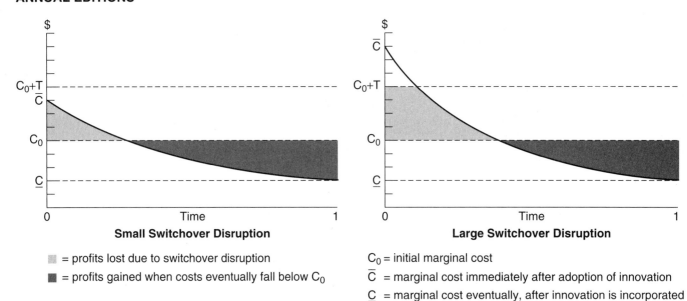

Figure 1 Large switchover costs discourage innovation by monopolists.

In the end, they find that large disruptions overturn Gilbert-Newbery. That is, that "with 'enough' switchover disruption, increases in market power now lead to decreases in industry innovation." If disruptions are minor—if the road bumps toward more efficient production are small—then Gilbert and Newbery's finding still holds. But if change is difficult and costly—truly disruptive—monopolies have a large incentive not to change. After all, they'll be sacrificing monopoly rents for as long as disruption ensues.

In two simple graphs (Figure 1), they represent the finding symbolically.

The first graph in Figure 1 shows the small-disruption scenario. A firm changing its production technology initially incurs higher marginal costs than it did with the old technology, but as time goes on, the kinks are smoothed, and the cost savings of the innovation kick in. A firm contemplating this scenario weighs the size of the initial area—when costs were higher—against the size of the later area— when savings occur.

The second graph in Figure 1 shows the large-disruption story. Adopting the new technology is so difficult that marginal costs of production soar well above not only the original marginal cost but also the original marginal cost plus the monopolist's market power, represented by T (representing a trade tariff, perhaps, or transportation costs). A firm facing this kind of disruption weighs the relative sizes of the two areas—before and after costs drop below the original marginal cost—and finds the initial losses so daunting that it will be unlikely to innovate.

"To the extent you think switchover costs are important, it's not ambiguous," notes Holmes. "If you set the problem up like Arrow did or if you set the problem up like Gilbert and Newbery did, once you throw in switchover costs, it goes only one way. And the economics are pretty clean, right? It's just that it's costly to give up monopoly rents. Adoption involves some sort of sacrifice."

The Elusive Link

This then may be the link between theory and reality, the elusive explanation for higher productivity that appears to be unleashed when competition undermines monopoly power. Providing that link is crucial to understanding how the structure of an economy can affect its prospects for growth, and for all three economists, this is incentive for further research.

This may be the link between theory and reality, the elusive explanation for higher productivity that appears to be unleashed when competition undermines monopoly power. Providing that link is crucial to understanding how the structure of an economy can affect its prospects for growth, and for all three economists, this is incentive for further research.

"It's a powerful idea and brings to mind other possible examples," notes Schmitz. "Like CEOs. Do you replace a CEO or not? You can have switchover disruptions." As an empiricist, Schmitz is envisioning future applications. "It makes me think about data and where to look. I've done this work on iron ore and cement, and it seems this is a more general idea. It opens up new avenues for empirical work."

The new avenues will mesh with previous collaborations. "There's the tariff paper we wrote a while back," says Holmes, referring to a 1995 *Quarterly Review* article with a model in which competition via trade reduced resistance to new technology. "And then our railroad paper [a 2001 *QR*] and then a

Journal of Monetary Economics paper [in April 2001]. This is a different angle on all that."

And as Levine points out, all of this research is not simply academic deliberation. Clarifying the relationship between industry structure and productivity has strong policy implications. "Empirically, it is well understood that monopoly is inimical to innovation," he says. "Understanding why is key to public policies that lead to greater innovation. For example: Should we engage in antitrust? Or remove impediments to foreign competition? Will this lead to greater rates of technological progress?"

"This," concludes Holmes, "is just one piece of a long-running research program looking at the connection between productivity and competition."

Stay tuned.

The World Discovers the Laffer Curve

Stephen Moore

For 15 years, the *Index of Economic Freedom* has provided an indispensable road map for countries that want to achieve prosperity. The rules aren't complicated. As the *Index* has revealed, lasting prosperity is a result of a persistent commitment to low tax rates, a stable currency, limited government, strong private property rights, openness to global trade and financial flows, and sensible regulation. Together, these factors empower the individual and induce dynamic entrepreneurial activity.

Over the 15-year course of the *Index,* politicians have evidently been listening. Tax rates have been ratcheted down substantially. Inflation, despite recent setbacks, has been tamed in many parts of the world. Government spending is still growing, but not as fast as in the 1970s and 1980s, and in many countries, private-sector growth is outpacing the public sector. In other words, economic freedom is on the march, spreading more opportunities and higher standards of living around the world.[1]

In this chapter, I focus on the extraordinary tax-cutting revolution that started in the early 1980s, gathered momentum in the 1990s, and is now the most important economic policy trend on the planet. The movement was captured in a May 2007 story on Bloomberg News, which reported: "A tax-cut bidding war is spreading across Europe as leaders of the continent's biggest economies give up criticizing smaller neighbors for cutting business tax rates and decide to join them instead."[2]

The Wall Street Journal reports the same phenomenon. "Many countries have slashed their corporate rates," a July 1, 2008, story proclaimed.[3] Scott Hodge, president of the nonpartisan Tax Foundation, adds that "[t]ax rates are being cut so quickly around the world that it's hard to keep a good tally of all the latest developments."[4]

This essay investigates how much tax rates have fallen, where they have fallen, and what the consequences have been.

The Low-Tax Revolution

Let's start the story in Sofia, Bulgaria. In early 2008, I met the instigator of the world's lowest flat tax, Svetla Kostadinova, director of the Institute for Market Economics in Sofia. Ms. Kostadinova persuaded a socialist government in Bulgaria to adopt a flat tax. She and her free-market think tank colleagues managed to persuade the politicians that the flat tax would increase revenues to the government—money that could be used for social programs.

Ms. Kostadinova told me that "the situation was getting desperate in Bulgaria. We were losing our population and our best workers. They were leaving for Western Europe to find jobs, and the number one form of foreign capital came from remittances." That changed when the corporate tax was cut to 10 percent in 2007 and the personal income tax to 10 percent in January of 2008. "We told the politicians that it would be symbolically important for Bulgaria to have the lowest flat tax," she noted. Today, a nation that 10 years ago had a double-digit unemployment rate now has a 6 percent jobless rate. And instead of people leaving Bulgaria to find jobs overseas, she laughed, "now it is the reverse. Western Europeans come to Bulgaria for jobs. We're gaining population now."[5]

I asked her: Don't the socialists say that the rich should pay more? "Of course, many do, and they want to raise the rates, but most understand that the flat tax gives us more jobs and more revenues."[6] In an interview in Washington later that year, Richard Rahn, the former chief economist for the U.S. Chamber of Commerce and now a senior fellow at the Cato Institute and chairman of the Institute for Global Economic Growth, agreed and added: "These countries understand that the flat tax is the key to enhancing their prosperity—even the former Communists know this."

Mart Laar, the former Prime Minister of Estonia, was the first politician to bring the flat tax to Eastern Europe. Mr. Laar told me when I met him in 2007 that when he first pushed the flat tax, the major opponents were not the Estonian citizens, "who love the flat tax," but the economists and other wise men of government "both inside and outside of this tiny country. Almost all of the smartest minds told me 'We cannot have a flat tax. It is untested. It will not work. It will cause budget deficits,'" he recalls about their litany of objections.

But remembering the virtues of the flat tax in Milton Friedman's classic book, *Free to Choose,* Mr. Laar insisted that the plan would work. So, in 1994, he heroically and wisely ignored the economic pundits and snapped in place one of the world's first flat taxes at 23 percent. Since then, Estonia has had one of the most rapid growth spurts of any nation in the world, and the country's adoption of the flat tax has been widely heralded as a cornerstone of its prosperity.

The U.S. has never had a flat tax, but the global tax-cutting spree, in fact, began in the U.S. when Ronald Reagan enacted two tax cuts—one in 1981 and another in 1986—that reduced the highest marginal personal income tax rate to 28 percent from

Country	1980	2007	Change (Percentage Points)
United Kingdom	83%	40%	−43
Portugal	84	42	−42
Norway	75	40	−35
United States	**73**	**39**	**−34**
Sweden	87	56	−31
Italy	72	43	−29
Mexico	55	28	−27
Belgium	76	50	−26
New Zealand	62	39	−23
Spain	66	43	−23
Canada	64	44	−20
Germany	65	45	−20
Netherlands	72	52	−20
Ireland	60	42	−18
Finland	68	51	−17
Australia	62	49	−13
Austria	62	50	−12
France	60	48	−12
Denmark	66	59	−7
Switzerland	38	34	−4
Average	68	45	−23

Figure 1 Top personal income tax rates are falling.

Source: Organisation for Economic Co-operation and Development, OECD Tax Database, Table 1.4, at http://www.oecd.org/document/60/0,3343,en_2649_34533_1942460_1_1_1_1,00.html; World Tax Database, at http://www.bus.umich.edu/optr/optr/introduction.htm.

70 percent. Reagan also tamed the double-digit inflation that had crippled the U.S. economy in the late 1970s. Those policies proved to be a gravitational pull on foreign investment capital of more than $5 trillion from 1982 to 2007. This tax advantage for the U.S. forced other nations to cut rates themselves or face a loss of competitiveness.

Over the past 20 years, and especially in the past five years, global personal and corporate tax rates have fallen at a faster pace than at any time in the past 100 years. (See Figures 1 and 2.) The average personal income tax rate among industrialized countries in 1980 was 68 percent. That rate fell to 50 percent in 1995 and today stands at 45 percent. This means that average personal income tax rates at the top of the income scale have fallen by over one-third. On the corporate income tax side, the tax-cutting momentum is even more pronounced. The average tax rate in industrialized nations has fallen by half, to 25 percent from 48 percent since the start of the Reagan era.

In the late 1980s, there was one nation in the world with a true flat tax: Hong Kong. Now there are 24 such jurisdictions, and most of these are in Eastern Europe. (See Table 1.) These nations, formerly behind the Iron Curtain of Communism, endured suffocating economic controls and declining living standards for half a century. Now they are capitalists par excellence and avid flat-tax partisans. The average flat tax rate is 20 percent, which has made the tax rates of Old Europe (40 percent to 60 percent) look as high as the Swiss Alps.

For many decades after it adopted a flat tax rate of 15 percent in 1947, Hong Kong enjoyed the benefits of a competitively low tax rate with no tax on dividends or capital gains or money earned outside of the island. Hong Kong has also embraced

Table 1 Flat-Tax Jurisdictions and Their Rates

Iceland	35.7%	Mauritius	15%
Lithuania	27%	Montenegro	15%
Jamaica	25%	Ukraine	15%
Latvia	25%	Russia	13%
Estonia	21%	Georgia	12%
Guernsey	20%	Albania	10%
Jersey	20%	Bulgaria	10%
Slovakia	19%	Kazakhstan	10%
Romania	16%	Kyrgyzstan	10%
Czech Republic	15%	Macedonia	10%
Hong Kong	15%	Mongolia	10%
Iraq	15%	Prednestrovie	10%

Source: Daniel J.Mitchell, "The Global Flat Tax Revolution: Lessons for Policy Makers," The Center for Freedom and Prosperity, *Prosperitas,* Vol. VIII, Issue I (February 2008), at http://www.freedomandprosperity.org/papers/flattax/flattax.shtml.

free trade, which explains why it has evolved into a capitalist paradise brimming with entrepreneurial spirit. The tax code is about 180 pages, compared to tens of thousands of pages for the U.S. tax code. The result has been that Hong Kong, over several decades, evolved into one of the richest places on Earth despite its tiny land mass and no natural resources. The only mystery is why it took nearly half a century for the rest of the world to start copying the Hong Kong flat-tax model.

Country	1980	2007	Change (Percentage Points)	
Ireland	45.0%	12.5%	−32.5	
Austria	55.0	25.0	−30.0	
Netherlands	48.0	25.5	−22.5	
United Kingdom	52.0	30.0	−22.0	
Portugal	47.2	26.5	−20.7	
Germany	56.0	38.9	−17.1	
Finland	43.0	26.0	−17.0	
Australia	46.0	30.0	−16.0	
France	50.0	34.4	−15.6	
Denmark	40.0	25.0	−15.0	
Belgium	48.0	34.0	−14.0	
Mexico	42.0	28.0	−14.0	
New Zealand	45.0	33.0	−12.0	
Sweden	40.0	28.0	−12.0	
Luxembourg	40.0	30.4	−9.6	
Italy	40.0	33.0	−7.0	
United States	**46.0**	**39.3**	**−6.7**	
Canada	37.8	33.5	−4.3	
Japan	42.0	39.5	−2.5	
Norway	29.8	28.0	−1.8	
Spain	33.0	32.5	−0.5	
Average	43.5	30.3	−13.2	

Figure 2 Corporate tax rates are falling.

Source: Organisation for Economic Co-operation and Development, OECD Tax Database, Table II.I, at http://www
.oecd.org/document/60/0,3343,en_2649_34533_1942460_1_1_1_1,00.html#table_III; World Tax Database, at
http://www.bus.umich.edu/optr/optr/introduction.htm.

Tax reductions are also an underappreciated part of the story of China's economic surge. In 1978, the late Chinese leader Deng Xiaping unleashed a series of free market–based economic reforms, including the legalization of privately owned farms (which caused a near doubling of food output above what the communist state-owned farms produced), the establishment of coastal economic enterprise zones, new opportunities for foreign investment and the privatization of state-owned enterprises.

But as Alvin Rabushka of the Hoover Institution points out, "The application of supply-side tax policies was the main component."[7] It helped to generate the double-digit rates of economic growth on the mainland that have become the stuff of economic legend. China is staying on the supply-side course. Effective January 2008, the Chinese corporate tax rate became 25 percent, down from 33 percent.

Europe Discovers the Supply Side

Even the fat welfare-state nations of Western Europe, whose tax rates climbed to hopelessly uncompetitive levels in the 1970s and 1980s, have been getting into the supply-side tax-cutting act.

The economic growth rate of European Union nations between 2002 and 2006 was about half the pace of U.S. economic growth. In the 1990s, European unemployment rates were consistently about 50 percent higher than the U.S. jobless rate. Euroland was no workers' paradise.

The Europeans are now slowly shedding many of the excesses of cradle-to-grave socialism and their confiscatory tax rates. In 2007, Germany under Chancellor Angela Merkel chopped the corporate income tax rate by about nine percentage points.[8] Now, amazingly, Germany, which started this century with an effective corporate income tax rate of over 50 percent, has sliced and diced the corporate rate down to slightly less than 30 percent.[9] Ms. Merkel sounds a lot like Jack Kemp or Ronald Reagan when she says that the purpose of the tax cuts is to boost "Germany's attractiveness as a location for international investment."[10]

Spain has also driven its taxation lower. Under José María Aznar, the former conservative Prime Minister, as well as under the leadership of José Luis Rodríguez Zapatero, the current socialist Prime Minister, measures to reform Spain's taxation have been implemented. Spain's top personal income tax rate has been reduced to 43 percent from 56 percent while its corporate tax rate has been cut to 30 percent from 35 percent.[11] Prime Minister Zapatero may have taken a staunchly anti-American stand on the war in Iraq, but he was able to recognize a bad tax when he saw one, and Spain's wealth tax was abolished in 2008.

The surest sign of all that there is a new economic paradigm taking hold in Europe is that just two years ago, Sweden, the socialist workers' paradise, completely eliminated its estate tax because the political leaders realized that the tax was economically counterproductive. In promising to "abolish the wealth tax," Swedish Prime Minister Fredrik Reinfelt said, "We hope to give a boost to the desire to invest in Sweden and to create a condition for new, expansive companies to create more jobs."[12] So now Sweden and, more recently, Russia have no estate tax, while the land of the free, America, taxes death at 45 percent. In late 2008, Sweden also announced a plan to reduce its corporate tax rate by another percentage point to 24 percent, which is 11 points lower than the U.S. statutory rate.

Nor is Asia being left behind in this competition. South Korea cut its income tax to 40 percent by the late 1990s from 87 percent in 1978. Its tax revenues soared from $2 billion in 1980 to $24 billion by 1996 to nearly $50 billion in 2007. Vietnam announced in 2008 that it intends to reduce the corporate rate to 25 percent from 28 percent while removing other government barriers to growth.

The motivation for this tax-slashing on every continent is the free flow of investment. In this age of information and technology, borders don't matter much any more. The world has become one massive shopping market for capital. Nations are in a contest to climb past each other in a race up the economic growth ladder. Singapore, for example, recently approved a corporate tax cut to keep pace with its low-tax rival Hong Kong. Northern Ireland is making a bid to lower its corporate tax rate to 12.5 percent in an effort to catch up to the economic gazelle of Europe: Ireland. When I recently met with the Prime Minister of Scotland, Alex Salmond, he related the same story. "Supply-side economics works. We've seen that in Ireland." Then he added: "Their low tax rates are attracting all the capital of Europe, and if we want to compete, our rates need to fall to near theirs."

I call this global phenomenon Reaganomics 2.0. The supply-side economics model, which the Gipper installed with such great controversy 28 years ago, is now the economic operating system around the globe. Foreigners have witnessed with envy the American prosperity boom of the past quarter-century. Where American politicians have decried "tax cuts for the rich," the rest of the world has taken note of the impressive and sustained rates of growth. Now it is possible that capital will begin to flow back as many of these economies start to treat investors and capital more kindly at home.

Revisiting the Irish Miracle

Ireland does not qualify as a flat-tax country because it only has a low flat-rate corporate tax. Regrettably, it still has steeply graduated personal rates. Yet the Irish economic miracle may be the greatest supply-side economics success story of recent times (other than the Reagan revolution). Ireland turned to the idea only when the nation was on its knees and all other inferior alternatives had been tried.

Just over a century and a half ago, Ireland had a population of some 8 million, but by 1980, that number had dwindled to 4 million, with far more Irish living in America than in Ireland. From the 1960s to the 1980s, Ireland became a giant welfare state burdened with high taxation, generous benefits for not working, and an industrial base in demise. The movie *The Commitments* depicted a rock-and-roll band with several of the struggling band members collecting free welfare benefits from the government. "It beats working," was the famous response of one band member when asked why he stood in long lines for monthly benefits. Indeed, it did, and Ireland's GDP stagnated.

In the 1990s, things began to change. Welfare was reformed; government services and enterprises became more efficient through privatizations; and, most important, the corporate income tax rate was cut to 12.5 percent—not just the lowest in Euroland, but one-third the average rate on the continent. In the succeeding 10 years, the population grew for the first time in decades, rising to 5.7 million; GDP rose at twice the rate of Europe's; and more than 1,000 international companies, such as Intel, Bristol–Myers Squibb, Microsoft, Dell, and Motorola, moved in. By 2000, Ireland's growth rate hit 8.7 percent a year and, perhaps most astonishing of all, with the lowest corporate tax rate in all of Europe, it achieved the biggest budget *surplus* as a share of GDP.

The winners in this economic transformation have been rank-and-file workers. The average hourly manufacturing wage soared by 126 percent from 1985 to 2004 at a time when many industrial nations were experiencing stagnant wage growth. The country's real GDP per person has climbed up to $30,736 from $9,957,[13] and the Irish on a per capita basis are now more than three times as rich as they were in 1980.

In 1991, Germany had a per capita income that was twice that of Ireland. By 2004, Ireland's per capita purchasing power exceeded Germany's.[14] In less than a decade and a half, Ireland climbed from last to first in Europe. That's economic development at warp speed. The Irish brain drain, which started during the potato famine of 1845 and continued almost unabated for the next 150 years, has finally reversed course. Now brains are coming back to Ireland where more job opportunities have been created. The unemployment rate has fallen to 4.5 percent from over 17 percent in 1985. (See Figure 3.)

Cutting Corporate Taxes

As the Irish success story illustrates, one of the taxes that has a large impact on a nation's ability to compete in global markets is the corporate tax, which is coming down rapidly just about everywhere—except the U.S. In 2006 and 2007, 12 nations cut their corporate rates, including Germany, Spain, and the Netherlands. In 2008, nine of the 30 most developed nations and 20 countries worldwide—from Israel to Germany to Turkey—cut corporate tax rates. For the first time ever, the U.S. statutory rate is now a full 50 percent higher than the average of our international competitors. (See Figure 4.)

The *Index of Economic Freedom* has shown that commitment to lower taxation is a key component of a country's effort to create a virtuous cycle of entrepreneurship, growth, and lasting prosperity for its citizens. A 2008 study by the Organisation for Economic Co-operation and Development, "Tax and Economic Growth," examines why some countries are becoming more prosperous than others and concludes that "corporate taxes are found to be most harmful for growth, followed by personal income taxes, and then consumption taxes."[15] The study finds, not surprisingly, that investment rates fall when corporate tax rates rise and that the most profitable and most rapidly expanding companies tend to be the most sensitive to corporate tax rates.

High corporate tax rates are also self-defeating because they don't produce much if any revenue. The average European

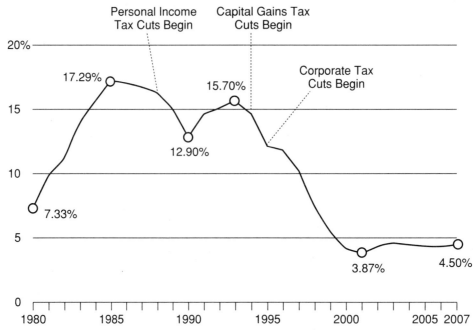

Figure 3 Ireland's Unemployment Rate Plummets Joblessness in Ireland decreased from 17% to less than 4% in the span of 16 years, primarily due to tax cuts.

Source: International Monetary Fund 2008 World Economic Outlook, April 2008, at http://www.imf.org/external/ pubs/ft/weo/2008/01/weodata/index.aspx; Central Statistics of Ireland, Labor Market, Principal Statistics, at http:// www.cso.ie/statistics/sasunemprates.htm.

nation's tax rates on corporate income are 10 percentage points *lower* than those in the U.S., but those countries on average raise almost twice the share of GDP in corporate taxes. Ireland, with its bargain-basement 12.5 percent rate, captures a higher share of its GDP in corporate taxes than the U.S. captures with a tax rate that is *three times higher* than Ireland's.

Policymakers in the two highest corporate tax nations, the U.S. and Japan, may want to take a look at a 2006 study by two scholars, Kevin Hassett and Aparna Mathur, at the American Enterprise Institute (AEI).[16] They find that the burden of the corporate income tax rate is borne in large part by workers in the form of lower wages. In a study of 72 nations, they found that manufacturing wages were negatively associated with high corporate tax rates.

The Laffer Curve effect suggests that nations will increase their economic output and competitive stature in the global race for capital by cutting business tax rates even further. Alan Reynolds, an economist at the Cato Institute (and formerly of the Hudson Institute), has confirmed this relationship: Countries that cut tax rates sharply outperform those that don't. He labels the tax rate reduction countries "supply-side economies" and the countries that raised tax rates in the 1990s "demand-side economies." The "supply-side economy nations—whose tax rates fell to an average of 34 percent from 61 percent—experienced economic growth rates three times higher than the demand-side countries." (See Table 2, work Mr. Reynolds did while an economist at the Hudson Institute.) "Hong Kong, Singapore, and most other economies that have adopted supply-side tax strategies, have seen their private consumption, and investment, good measures of living standards, increase three times the pace of the demand-side economies,"[17] he wrote in a later paper.

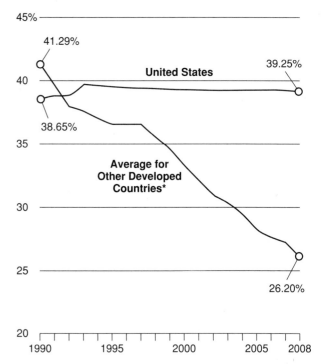

* Combined central and subcentral government corporate tax rate.

Figure 4 Comparing Corporate Tax Rates On average, other developed nations have decreased their corporate tax rates, while the U.S.'s rate has remained relatively flat.

Source: Organisation for Economic Co-operation and Development, Taxation of Corporate and Capital Income, Table II.I, at *http://www.oecd .org/dataoecd/26/56/3317459.xls*.

Table 2 Comparing Supply-Side and Demand-Side Economies

Top Marginal Tax Rate

	Supply-Side Economies	Demand-Side Economies
1979	61%	63%
1989	43%	46%
1995	34%	49%

Average Growth in GDP

	Supply-Side Economies	Demand-Side Economies
1985–1994	5.10%	1.40%

Source: Hudson Institute.

Why Rates Matter

Very high tax rates can distort economic behavior and reduce the incentive to work and earn. Consider celebrities. Rock stars and highly paid actors regularly engage in tax-minimization strategies, much to the consternation of their home countries, as a January 2007 story in *The Economist* explained:

> Sometimes it takes a rock star. By moving to Switzerland to flee punitive French taxes, Johnny Hallyday, France's 63-year-old rock idol, has set off a new debate. Many other high-earning French celebrities have become tax exiles, prompting periodic moral outrage. But this departure is politically embarrassing: Mr Hallyday's friend, Nicolas Sarkozy, is set to be the centre-right's presidential candidate. "If he reforms the wealth and inheritance law," Mr. Hallyday told *Paris-Match,* "well, then I will come back to France."[18]

Hallyday said that 70 percent of his earnings goes to the state and that he had "a particular gripe about the annual wealth tax, or ISF, which is applied to almost all assets, whether revenue-generating or not." According to *The Economist*'s account, "Even Thierry Breton, the finance minister, once called the wealth tax 'economically dangerous.'"[19]

Ségolène Royal, then the Socialist presidential candidate, "said top earners should 'set an example' and pay their taxes without a fuss."[20] But they do put up a fuss, because rock stars are like everyone else: They don't want to pay confiscatory taxes. The academic evidence confirms these anecdotes. One 2004 study by Nobel prize–winning economist Edward Prescott for the National Bureau of Economic Research (NBER) found that people work more when tax rates are lowered:

> Americans now work 50 percent more than do Germans, French and Italians. This was not the case in the early 1970s. . . . [T]his marginal tax rate accounts for the predominance of the differences at points in time and the large change in relative labor supply over time.[21]

Another NBER study found that among rich nations, a lowering of tax rates in the 1990s led to an increase in hours worked and an increase in the number of people in the labor force. It also found that the "shadow economy"—i.e. underground activity—rises "by 3.8 percent of GDP for every 12.8 percentage point increase in the tax rate."[22]

Finally, in a 2007 study financed by the National Science Foundation, Christina Romer and David Romer examined tax policy changes in the United States from 1947 through today. Their study found that "tax increases are highly contractionary. The effects are strongly significant, highly robust, and much larger than those obtained [in earlier studies]. The large effect stems in considerable part from a powerful negative effect on investment."[23]

Conclusion

Fifteen years ago, when the first edition of the *Index of Economic Freedom* was published, the supply-side idea of the Laffer Curve—that high tax rates reduce growth and can even reduce revenues—was still highly controversial and disregarded among the political class and even trained economists. Today, however, more nations around the globe are embracing the idea.

The sentiment among the tax-chopping nations is that lower tax rates are a critical component of the process of capitalizing on the globalization of financial markets. Hundreds of billions of dollars of investment capital are traded every day across international boundaries, and investors are attentive to each jurisdiction's tax rates.

But there is still one place on the globe where the idea that lower tax rates generate more entrepreneurial activities and economic growth is being disparaged: the United States. James Surowiecki, a *New Yorker* financial page columnist, argued in 2007 that supply-side tax prescriptions for the economy are the equivalent of "saying that the best way to treat sick people is to bleed them to let out the evil spirits."[24]

Today much of the talk in Washington is of higher income taxes, capital gains taxes, dividend taxes, payroll taxes, energy taxes, and hedge fund taxes. The threat of this tax assault on wealth and capital is taking a toll on investor confidence in the U.S. economy. Michael Darda, a top Wall Street economic analyst for MKM Partners, hypothesizes that this is "one reason the U.S. dollar has fallen relative to the currencies of other nations."

What this suggests is that if the U.S. refuses to cut its tax rates—or, even worse, if it follows the "tax-hike on the rich" course that has become so popular among many politicians in Washington—America's economic freedom, competitiveness and prosperity will be in great peril.

References

1. Evidence of this comes from a Millennium Project assessment of how nations are working to alleviate poverty. Entitled *The State of the Future,* the report concludes that, beginning in 1985 and projected through 2015, 600 million people—twice as many as live in the United States—will have escaped dire poverty across the globe. Most of the progress comes from the two most populous nations, China and India, which are following

free-market supply-side economic policies to the great economic benefit of their citizens. See Jerome C. Glenn and Theodore J. Gordon, *2007 State of the Future,* Millennium Project, 2007. The Millennium Project functions under the auspices of the World Federation of UN Associations, an "independent, non-governmental organization with Category One Consultative Status at the Economic and Social Council (ECOSOC) and consultative or liaison links with many other UN organizations and agencies," and "is a global participatory futures research think tank of futurists, scholars, business planners, and policy makers who work for international organizations, governments, corporations, NGOs, and universities." See Millennium Project Web site, at http://www.millennium-project.org.

2. Simon Kennedy, "Tax-Cut War Widens in Europe as U.K., France, Germany Jump In," Bloomberg.Com, May 29, 2008, at http://www. bloomberg.com/apps/news?pid=20601085&sid=aev_LMGsw3aw&refer=europe.

3. "Corporate Tax Cut Windfall," *The Wall Street Journal,* July 1, 2008, p. A16.

4. Interview, July 2008.

5. Interview, August 2008.

6. *Ibid.*

7. Alvin Rabushka, "The Great Tax Cut of China," *Hoover Digest* 1998, No. 1, Hoover Institution, at http://www.hoover.org/publications/digest/3523046.html.

8. Invest in Germany, "Company Taxation," at http://www .invest-in-germany.com/homepage/business-guide-to-germany/the-tax-system/company-taxation.

9. *Ibid.* Germany's standard federal corporate tax rate is 15 percent.

10. Kennedy, "Tax-Cut War Widens in Europe as U.K., France, Germany Jump In."

11. Economist Intelligence Unit, "Spain," *Country Briefing,* September 30, 2008, at http://www.economist.com/countries/Spain/profile.cfm?folder=Profile-FactSheet; Economist Intelligence Unit, *Country Commerce,* 1997 and 2000, available with subscription.

12. "Björn Borg, Come Home," *The Wall Street Journal,* April 11, 2007.

13. Figures are in real GDP per capita (in constant 2000 U.S. dollars). See World Bank, *World Development Indicators Online,* available with subscription at http://www.worldbank .org/data.

14. Eurostat, "GDP per Capita in 2004: GDP per Capita Varied by One to Five Across the EU25 Member States," news release 75/2005, June 3, 2005, at http://epp.eurostat.ec.europa.eu/pls/portal/docs/PAGE/PGP_PRD_CAT_PREREL/PGE_CAT_PREREL_YEAR_2005/PGE_CAT_PREREL_YEAR_2005_MONTH_06/2-03062005-EN-BP.PDF.

15. Åsa Johansson, Christopher Heady, Jens Arnold, Bert Brys, and Laura Vartia, "Tax and Economic Growth," Organisation for Economic Co-operation and Development, Economics Department *Working Paper* No. 620, July 2008, at http://www .olis.oecd.org/olis/2008doc.nsf/LinkTo/NT00003502/$FILE/JT03248896.PDF.

16. Aparna Mathur and Kevin A. Hassett, "Taxes and Wages," American Enterprise Institute *Papers and Studies,* March 6, 2006, at http://www.aei.org/publications/pubID.24063/pub_detail.asp.

17. Alan Reynolds, "A Depressing Situation," *The Washington Times,* May 4, 2003, at http://www.cato.org/pub_display.php?pub_id=5674.

18. "Tax 'n' Wealth and Rock 'n' Roll," *The Economist,* January 4, 2007.

19. *Ibid.*

20. *Ibid.*

21. Edward Prescott, "Why Do Americans Work So Much More Than Europeans?" National Bureau of Economic Research *Working Paper* No. 10316, February 2004.

22. Steven J. Davis and Magnus Henrekson, "Tax Effects on Work Activity, Industry Mix, and Shadow Economy Size: Evidence from Rich-Country Comparisons," National Bureau of Economic Research *Working Paper* No. 10509, May 2004.

23. Christina Romer and David Romer, "The Macroeconomic Effects of Tax Changes: Estimates Based on a New Measure of Fiscal Shocks," University of California, Berkeley, November 2006, at http://www.economics.ucr.edu/seminars/fall06/ets/Romer11-27-06.pdf.

24. James Surowiecki, "Tax Evasion: The Great Lie of Supply-Side Economics," *The New Yorker,* October 29, 2007, at http://www .newyorker.com/online/2007/10/29/071029on_onlineonly_surowiecki.

Building Entrepreneurial Economies

Carl J. Schramm

Poor Imitation

The United States, using its own direct-aid programs and its influence over development agencies, has encouraged other nations to adopt the features and institutions of post–Cold War American capitalism. But this approach—the so-called Washington consensus—has often yielded disappointing results. Many economies in Latin America, eastern Europe, and elsewhere are stagnant or backsliding, and most of the world's poorest economies show few signs of new life. Going forward, the American economic model should not be abandoned, as some development economists advocate, but it must be improved. The current template is incomplete. In particular, it fails to reproduce a vital element of the U.S. economy: support for entrepreneurship.

The ability to support entrepreneurship is a vital element of the U.S. economy.

Not only does the United States have a high rate of new business starts, it breeds a constant flow of new high-impact firms—the kind that create value and stimulate growth by bringing new ideas to market, be they new technologies, new business methods, or simply new and better ways of performing routine tasks. These firms do not appear automatically, as a natural by-product of having free-market institutions. Nor are they the result of any single factor. Rather, the United States has evolved a multifaceted "system" for nurturing high-impact entrepreneurship—a system that, with the right development policies, might be cultivated in many other countries as well.

With the right policies, the U.S. system of entrepreneurship could be cultivated in other countries too.

Such an approach has been missing so far. The Washington consensus focuses on macroeconomic issues such as finance and trade, along with general institution building. Nations are urged to create good banking systems, reasonable interest and exchange rates, and stable tax structures. They are expected to privatize, deregulate, and invest in infrastructure and basic education. Entrepreneurship, meanwhile, is considered only as an afterthought and in piecemeal fashion. Some policymakers, for instance, have suggested that venture capital firms should be added to the list of financial institutions that developing countries ought to have. But venture capital will do no good without ventures to support. Microenterprises are not sufficient either. Existing programs to support small businesses, such as those promoted by the U.S. Agency for International Development and nongovernmental organizations, offer livelihoods to many people. But these ventures tend to involve cottage industries that add little to the economy in terms of productivity or growth. Even microentrepreneurs with great potential cannot succeed without national mechanisms to feed and sustain them. Nor can a developing nation prosper in the long term only by attracting outsourced work, which has a disturbing tendency to migrate to still lower-cost locales. Real opportunities arise only when a nation is the initiator: a breeder of new firms, based on new ideas that add unique value.

Start-Ups' Starring Role

The system that generates and supports entrepreneurship in the United States is surprisingly unappreciated. Perhaps this is because when modern economic thought first took shape in the early and middle decades of the twentieth century, the West already had a mature industrial economy. With a universe of large corporations and modern equity markets already in place, economists were preoccupied with impersonal market forces, business cycles, capital markets, and government stimuli via fiscal and monetary policy. Microeconomic thinking also focused on big-firm behavior, rather than on the start-up process.

Few people realize how many Americans today still make their living in entrepreneurial settings. More than 500,000 "employer firms" (businesses with employees) are started in the United States every year.

The latest Global Entrepreneurship Monitor (GEM) survey, funded by the Ewing Marion Kauffman Foundation, found that in 2003, approximately 11 of every 100 working adults in the United States were engaged in entrepreneurial activity, either starting a business or playing a lead role in one less than three and a half years old. That rate is higher than any in Europe and roughly twice that of Germany or the United Kingdom. And although most Americans work in large or mid-sized firms, research for the U.S. Census Bureau and others has found that most net new jobs are created either by start-up activity or by firms in a rapid-expansion phase. Among other benefits, this relieves the nation's mature companies from being hobbled by guaranteed-employment practices. Instead of maintaining jobs artificially, they can trim staff as needed to stay competitive, with the entrepreneurial base cushioning the blow by providing a steady supply of new jobs.

The United States is also unusual in that many of its big, strategically important corporations were created very recently. Dell and Cisco Systems, for example, were started in 1985 and 1984, respectively. New firms have been national leaders in creating wealth and raising living standards: Charles Schwab has pioneered low-cost securities trading, enabling more people to participate in equity markets, while large retailers such as Wal-Mart have reinvented business models, reducing the cost of consumer goods.

Overall, new firms play two essential roles in the U.S. economy. First, they are engines of innovation. Although large, established firms innovate, they tend to do so only in certain ways, wary of straying too far from their existing fines of business. Compare the birth of two industries: nuclear power and software. Innovation in the first was driven mainly by big companies such as Westinghouse Electric that were already in the power-generation business. By contrast, there was no software industry in the early days of computing. Computer programs were either custom written or sold along with the machinery; writing and selling them separately, for widespread use, was not seen as a viable business strategy. People such as John Swanson, an engineer who left Westinghouse in 1969 to become an entrepreneur, turned this conventional wisdom on its head. Realizing that the kind of design work he was doing could be greatly enhanced by writing a general-purpose computer simulation program, he started a company now called Ansys. Its software has been used to help design goods ranging from automobiles to shoes. Thanks to the efforts of thousands of similar entrepreneurs, the software industry has done what nuclear power was once expected to do: benefited every sector of the economy and spurred tremendous growth.

The second essential role that new firms play in the U.S. economy is smoothing the exigencies of the business cycle. Time and again, the breeding of new companies, new jobs, and new industries has helped pull the economy out of a slump and fuel a rebound—as occurred after the recession in the early 1990s. Japan, in contrast, has many innovative large firms but the lowest per-capita rate of entrepreneurial activity of 37 countries studied by GEM—a possible explanation for its prolonged stagnation.

Entrepreneurship is thus what enables American-style capitalism to be generative and self-renewing. The problem confronting policymakers is to model the entrepreneurial dimension of the U.S. economy in a way that is comprehensive enough to capture all the important dynamics and is also transferable to other economies. Such a model is proposed here.

The Four-Sector Model

The American entrepreneurial system involves four sectors of the economy: high-impact entrepreneurs, large mature firms, the government, and universities.

The first sector is inhabited by new firms. The people who start them need not be scientists or inventors of new products themselves. Henry Ford did not invent the automobile and Michael Dell did not invent any computer technology. Both built their firms largely around production and marketing ideas, freely borrowing from existing concepts.[1]

New companies require more than just ideas, however: money, skilled people, and other resources are also needed. In the United States, entrepreneurs often obtain these things from large, mature firms—the second sector. Business mythology portrays new firms as adversaries of established ones, with the nimble newcomers trying to outwit lumbering dinosaurs who are in turn trying to flatten the upstarts. Something like that may occur at times, but a powerful symbiotic relationship is more common.

There are several ways in which new and established businesses work together. First, and most obvious, established firms often become customers of the new firms. U.S. corporations have learned to use new companies as reliable sources of innovation, buying from them, for example, specialized software and business services or components that can be embedded in their own products. Second, large U.S. firms today effectively "outsource" much of their research and development to start-ups. Rather than take on all of the effort and risk of developing an idea internally, they help a new firm do so, via strategic investments or working partnerships. There are many twists on this strategy. Intel, for example, tries to build markets for its chips by investing in companies that develop new systems and products that will use the chips; it has invested in more than a thousand such start-ups. Third, once a new company has developed a good product, a larger outfit often simply buys the start-up, thus acquiring a complete package of proven technology and expertise. This practice is now common in the pharmaceutical and health care product industries. Finally, mature firms support start-up firms by providing human capital. Bright young people often develop their skills and learn about a particular industry by working at a big corporation, and then leave to start or join a new one.

The third important contributor to entrepreneurship is the government, which, in the United States, uses some of its tax revenues to foster new businesses. One way it does this is by funding large programs that traffic in innovation, such as defense and space exploration. The Department of Defense is always in the market for new systems and technologies, not only for weaponry, but also for communications, intelligence, logistics, and support. Government agencies also invest directly in new firms through channels such as the Small Business Innovation Research Program and the Central Intelligence Agency's In-Q-Tel venture fund. More indirectly, the U.S. government promotes entrepreneurship by funding research in fields of knowledge from information technology to medicine and the physical and human sciences. Total federal spending on research and development equals about one percent of the U.S. GDP. Although some of this funding goes to the government's own laboratories (such as Argonne and Sandia) or to private firms and industry consortia, much of it flows into the fourth sector of the U.S. entrepreneurial system, the nation's universities.

U.S. universities generate a constant flow of ideas for new businesses. Since the 1960s, the number of faculty members and students doing university research has expanded greatly, due to investment from both the federal and the state governments. An invention or discovery moves out of a university into the entrepreneurial sector when investors and businesspeople help to form a company that commercializes the idea. Typically, universities own a share in any patent developed on their premises and will then license these rights in exchange for an equity share of the new company. (The Bayh-Dole Act of 1980, which allowed this process to be followed even for discoveries and inventions derived from federally funded research, greatly accelerated the transfer of technology from universities to the U.S. economy.)

The resulting economic growth has been tremendous. It has been estimated that the companies spun out from just one university, the Massachusetts Institute of Technology (MIT), would constitute a nation with the twenty-fourth largest GDP in the world. Returns to the universities also have been significant. Earnings from just one spinoff company, Lycos, enabled Carnegie Mellon University to construct a new building and create three endowed faculty chairs. Research professors often take leaves to help start a new company, typically holding a title such as "chief technology officer" while an experienced businessperson manages the firm.

Practical Steps

The Four-Sector Model of the U.S. economy provides a useful framework for guiding policies to promote entrepreneurship in the developing world.

With respect to the first sector, developing nations must establish certain underlying conditions that allow the entrepreneurial process to flourish: favorable business policies and regulations, and access to investment and human capital. U.S. laws make it easy to start, fund, grow, and sell a company. An American citizen can incorporate a new business under state law and obtain all the federal identity needed from the Internal Revenue Service in an afternoon. U.S. tax laws encourage private investment in new firms, and bankruptcy laws provide an orderly end to a failed business, reducing the risk for creditors and allowing entrepreneurs to start anew.

In many developing countries, by contrast, starting a business is fraught with expensive and time-consuming red tape. The Peruvian economist Hernando DeSoto notes that entrepreneurs and property holders in such countries will often adapt by setting up a complete parallel economy outside the law, with its own complex rules and written contracts. An oft-cited drawback of this approach is that the government does not get tax revenue. But perhaps the greater cost is that the entrepreneurs involved are seriously constrained by the resources and horizons of their underground world, finding themselves unable to attract major investments, recruit skilled managers and technicians from outside, or legally protect, convert, and transfer their assets. The "official" economy, meanwhile, remains the province of a select few: privileged insiders, existing firms, and state-related enterprises.

Another important factor in the first sector is sources of capital for new firms. Development experts tend to focus on replicating the U.S. venture capital system. The system is a powerful one, but many entrepreneurs do not even want venture capital, since they would have to give up a great deal of ownership and control in exchange for the investment. Most of the firms on *Inc.* magazine's list of the 500 fastest-growing small companies in the United States have not used venture capital. And despite the common misconception, venture capitalists do not usually provide start-up money. In 1996, according to the National Venture Capital Association (NVCA), 77 percent of venture-capital-funded companies were at least three years old when they received their first round of investment. That changed during the Internet start-up frenzy, but normal patterns have returned since then. In the first quarter of 2004 (again, according to NVCA figures), only 17 percent of venture-capital dollars in the United States were invested in "early stage" companies, with the rest going to "expansion stage" and "later stage" firms.

Entrepreneurs in the United States get early-stage capital from a variety of sources. Many take second mortgages on their homes, as the founders of Cisco Systems did. Many make liberal use of credit cards for short-term operating funds. Virtually all solicit investments or personal loans from family and friends. Some find wealthy individuals called "angels"—frequently successful entrepreneurs themselves—who provide advice and contacts along with money. And once they are started, many entrepreneurs "bootstrap" their firms, reinvesting revenues or obtaining bank credit.

In countries where personal wealth is not as widespread as it is in the United States, emulating this diversity of financial resources will not be easy. But the process might be started by persuading wealthier individuals to invest in new ventures (perhaps through tax incentives), or encouraging banks and pension funds to commit a portion of assets to such ventures. Moreover, countries' labor policies should not tie economic security to long-term employment. Americans have many close-at-hand ways to obtain support for starting a company; and at the same time they have little incentive to stay with a big firm for job security.

The Washington consensus approach to development—which stresses privatization of state-owned companies and the freeing up of local business environments to help existing firms—already has a positive impact in the second sector, that of large firms. But more needs to be done to induce a real symbiosis between established firms and entrepreneurs. First off, developing countries must ensure that there is a level playing field between old and new firms. The United States tries achieve this in a variety of ways, such as by protecting intellectual property and discouraging monopolies and unfair trade practices. Developing nations must resist pressures from existing businesses to preserve markets and prevent innovation. And the "treaty" between large and small firms must be built on an understanding that large firms benefit from entrepreneurial activity. The most promising entrepreneurs should be helped to find big corporations as partners—which, in today's global economy, can include corporations based in the United States or elsewhere. Developing countries' own large firms and government agencies also could be given incentives to "farm out" and support employees who have good ideas for starting spinoff companies.

In the third sector—the government—nations should do as much as possible to invest in infrastructure that supports entrepreneurship. South Korea offers a good example with its efforts to promote end user connectivity to the Internet. An estimated 60 to 70 percent of the country already has high-speed broadband access. One rationale for this investment has been to make government more efficient and responsive by moving citizens' interactions online. But the policy is also helping to build a countrywide platform for entrepreneurship: every South Korean will soon be linked to massive online flows of knowledge and to online markets.

Another infrastructure investment that can help entrepreneurs is subsidizing laboratories and testing facilities for shared use, which young technology firms often need but cannot afford on their own. Shared facilities also encourage entrepreneurs to cluster geographically, as they do in the United States—gathering in certain cities or around research universities—thereby gaining a dense network of peers for partnering and mentoring.

In the fourth sector, the Washington consensus rightly calls for countries to invest in education, but it emphasizes primary education. Higher education should be made a priority, too. Consider India: in 1951, shortly after gaining independence, it launched the Indian Institute of Technology (IIT), modeling it on world-class universities such as MIT. This may be one of the best decisions a newly liberated nation ever made. The IIT now has seven campuses across India. Its alumni make up part of India's formidable and growing professional class (the group from which many high-impact entrepreneurs emerge), and it has fueled interest in primary education by giving young Indians and their parents a great university toward which to aim. A similar approach has also benefited older industrial nations with stalled economies. In recent decades, the government of Ireland has invested heavily in higher education, which has helped produce a period of rapid growth, accompanied by a dramatic increase in high-tech business start-ups, that has been dubbed the "Irish miracle." Universities not only train skilled people; they also attract them. In the United States, for example, about one-fourth of the new businesses in Silicon Valley since 1980 have been started by immigrants, many of whom were first drawn to the region to study or teach at its universities.

High-impact entrepreneurship will thrive most in countries that pay proper attention to all four sectors of the entrepreneurial system. China is an example of a developing nation that currently does this. While adopting policies that actively encourage entrepreneurship, Beijing is pushing to have more of its college-age population enrolled in higher education, for example. And it is developing high-skill, high-tech business in tandem with low-wage contract manufacturing, steel making, and other basic industries. China seems to understand that the commodities it currently manufactures can be obtained from less developed countries—and that many of the world's highly sought-after goods will come from laboratories, skilled people, and entrepreneurs. As a result, it may well arrive at its post-industrial stage very quickly.

The Culture Chimera

Critics may object that the four-sector approach does not give enough weight to cultural factors. It is often argued, for instance, that whereas "individualistic" cultures such as that of the United States are conducive to entrepreneurship, more "collectivist" cultures are not. Yet the example of China, with its communist cultural legacy, suggests that this objection is weak. The cultural argument also looks flimsy in light of U.S. history. American culture in the 1950s was by no means favorable to entrepreneurship. Bright young men of that era were expected to join an established firm and climb the ladder while their wives stayed home taking care of the children. William Whyte's book *The Organization Man* warned that the United States was becoming a "nation of bureaucrats," with a "conspiracy of the mediocre" threatening to stifle innovation. Yet by the 1980s, a potent new generation of entrepreneurs had emerged, and people such as Steve Jobs and Bill Gates quickly became national icons.

Developing countries and development agencies, then, should not worry too much about cultural intangibles. They should try to emulate the practical features of the U.S. entrepreneurial system, as expressed in the four-sector model, with the knowledge that culture can change as incentives and conditions change. Encouraging entrepreneurship may do developing countries more good, in terms of long-term growth and gains in productivity, than policies aimed at accelerating near-term growth. And as individuals step into the market, assume risk, and work to turn their aspirations into businesses, they will insist on political and economic liberalization—the very goals prioritized by the Washington consensus. Ironically, entrepreneurs, who are by nature agents of change, may prove to be among the most important forces for global stability.

Note

1. Ford's moving assembly fine was famously said to have been inspired by a meatpacking plant. To this model he added a vigorous dealer network, making the automobile a mass-market good. Dell lowered the cost of PCs by building them to order rather than carrying inventory and by selling directly so as to eliminate the dealer—two ideas that have been used in other industries.

CARL J. SCHRAMM is President and Chief Executive Officer of the Ewing Marion Kauffman Foundation.

From *Foreign Affairs*, Vol. 83, No. 4, July/August 2004, pp. 104–107, 109–115. Copyright © 2004 by Council on Foreign Relations. Reprinted by permission.

The Role of Small and Large Businesses in Economic Development

KELLY EDMISTON

Increasingly, economic development experts are abandoning traditional approaches to economic development that rely on recruiting large enterprises with tax breaks, financial incentives, and other inducements. Instead, they are relying on building businesses from the ground up and supporting the growth of existing enterprises. This approach has two complementary features. The first is to develop and support entrepreneurs and small businesses. The second is to expand and improve infrastructure and to develop or recruit a highly skilled and educated workforce. Both efforts depend in large part on improving the quality of life in the community and creating an attractive business climate.

The reason for the shift in approaches is clear. Experience suggests that economic development strategies aimed at attracting large firms are unlikely to be successful—or successful only at great cost. Smokestack chasing can be especially costly if it generates competition for firms among jurisdictions. Further, because of the purported job creation role and innovative prowess of entrepreneurs and small businesses, creating an environment conducive to many small businesses may produce more jobs than trying to lure one or two large enterprises. The hope is not only that new businesses will create jobs in the local community, but, through innovation, some new businesses may grow into rapid-growth "gazelle" firms, which may spawn perhaps hundreds of jobs and become industry leaders of tomorrow.

This article evaluates this shift in economic development strategies. The first section describes traditional economic development strategies. The second section explores the role that small businesses play in creating jobs. The third section compares job quality between small firms and larger firms. The fourth section examines how important small businesses are in the development of new products and new markets.

The overarching question is whether promoting entrepreneurship and small businesses makes sense as an economic development strategy. This article concludes that it probably does but with some caveats. Small businesses are potent job creators, but so are large businesses. The attribution of the bulk of net job creation to small businesses arises largely from relatively large job losses at large firms, not to especially robust job creation by small firms. More importantly, data show that, on average, large businesses offer better jobs than small

businesses, in terms of both compensation and stability. Further, there is little convincing evidence to suggest that small businesses have an edge over larger businesses in innovation. More research is needed to properly evaluate the case for a small business strategy, and, indeed, to determine whether or not public engagement in economic development itself is a cost-effective and worthwhile pursuit.

I. Issues with Traditional Economic Development Policies

On the surface, one might think that a large firm would spur local economic growth by yielding significant gains in employment and personal income. The direct effect—the jobs and income generated directly by the firm—would certainly suggest this to be the case. In reality, however, it is often the effects on other firms in the area—the *indirect* effects—that carry the greatest weight in the net economic impact. Experience suggests that because of these typically large indirect effects and the costs of incentives and competition, economic development strategies aimed at attracting large firms are unlikely to be successful or are likely to succeed only at great cost.

A recent study of new-firm locations and expansions in Georgia suggests that, on net, the location of a new large (300+ employees) firm often retards the growth of the existing enterprises or discourages the establishment of enterprises that would otherwise have located there (Edmiston). Specifically, the location of a new plant with 1,000 workers, on average, adds a net of only 285 workers over a five-year period. That is, the average firm would add 1,000 workers in its own plant but would also drive away 715 other jobs that would have been generated (or retained) if the new large firm had chosen not to locate there. Another recent study suggests that the net employment impact of large-firm locations may actually be closer to zero (Fox and Murray).

Much has been made of the indirect effects, or spillovers, of new large firms. The positive spillovers include links with suppliers, increased consumer spending, the transfer of knowledge from one firm to another, and the sharing of pools of workers. But negative spillovers are important as well. They include

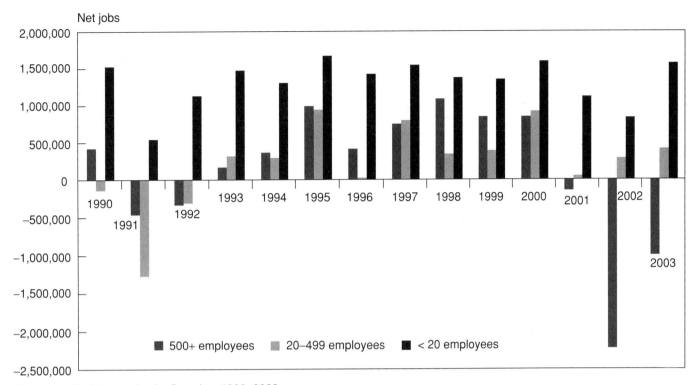

Figure 1 Net job creation by firm size, 1990–2003.

Source: U.S. Census Bureau Statistics of U.S. Business.

constraints on the supply of labor and other inputs, upward pressure on wages and rents, congestion of infrastructure, and (if fiscal incentives are provided to the locating firm) budget pressures from increased spending without commensurate increases in public revenues. Even perceptions of these negative effects can drive away firms, whether or not they actually materialize. The evidence suggests that the negative effects dominate with many large-firm locations (Edmiston; Fox and Murray).

Expansions of existing firms, however, tend to have multiplicative positive employment impacts. On average, a plant expansion adding 1,000 employees is expected to generate a net employment impact of 2,000. This result supports the notion that internal business generation and growth has potentially better prospects as a strategy than firm recruitment.

The costs per job of incentive packages are generally measured in terms of gross new jobs at the new firm. The dollars of incentives are divided by the number of jobs. During the recruitment stage, these costs are often substantially underestimated. For example, the cost per job created for an enterprise creating 1,000 new jobs and offering $20 million in incentives is $20,000. But if the net job impact is only 285, the true cost per job created soars to $70,175.

In many cases, states or local communities could arguably receive greater returns by investing the same resources in creating a more conducive business environment for existing firms—both large and small. Thus, recruiting large firms is often costly, in both direct expenditures and the lost opportunities for other forms of economic development.

Recruitment of large firms is also costly because it may engender a competitive economic development landscape.

For example, decisions by local governments to use tax abatements to lure firms are highly dependent on the decisions of their neighbors (Edmiston and Turnbull). The likelihood that a county uses tax abatements to lure firms increases 41 percentage points if its neighbors use them. In other words, a county that has a 20 percent probability of using tax abatements when none of its neighbors use them would have a 61 percent probability when all of its neighbors use them. The presence of a border with a neighboring state may also encourage the use of tax abatements.

This type of competition can be very costly. Recruiting a firm will generate costs for infrastructure, such as roads, sewers, and public services. If a community gets into a bidding war with another community, fewer resources will be available for absorbing these costs, and neither community gains an advantage by aggressive recruiting. If, for example, one community offers tax incentives to win the new firm, it will face increased costs but no property taxes to offset them. The recruitment of firms can therefore be a losing proposition for all involved.

Perhaps most important, from the perspective of society at large, aggressive courting of large firms can distort rational behavior, causing a waste of economic resources. For example, one region may offer a lower cost option for a newly locating enterprise because of a larger supply of labor, cheaper costs of transport to market, or other natural advantages. If another region is able to capture the firm away from its optimal location by offering lucrative financial incentives, resources will be expended needlessly. For example, shipping the final product over longer distances will be more expensive. While welfare in the winning region may improve (but not necessarily), welfare

Table 1   Job Creation and Destruction by Firm Size Class, 1990–2001

Employment Size Class	Share of Total Employment (2003)	Share of Gross Job Creation (1990–2003)	Share of Gross Job Destruction (1990–2003)	Share of Net New Jobs Created (1990–2003)
>20	18.4	29.3	23.9	79.5
20–499	32.3	30.7	32.6	13.2
500 +	49.3	39.9	43.5	7.3

Source: U.S. Census Bureas, Statistics of U.S. Businesses.

for the larger community encompassing the region will suffer: Fewer resources would be available for production than would be the case if the firm chose its economically optimal location.

II. Small Businesses and Job Creation

An alternative to recruiting large firms with tax incentives and other inducements is to focus on the small business sector. Perhaps the greatest generator of interest in entrepreneurship and small business is the widely held belief that small businesses in the United States create most new jobs. The evidence suggests that small businesses indeed create a substantial majority of net new jobs in an average year. But the widely reported figures on net job growth obscure the important dynamics of job creation and destruction. Nevertheless, small businesses remain a significant source of new jobs in the United States.

Net Job Creation

Data published by the U.S. Census Bureau clearly show that the bulk of net new jobs are generated by firms with less than 20 employees (Figure 1). *Net* new jobs are the total of new jobs created by firm startups and expansions (gross job creation) minus the total number of jobs destroyed by firm closures and contractions (gross job destruction). From 1990 to 2003, small firms (less than 20 employees) accounted for 79.5 percent of the net new jobs, despite employing less than 18.4 percent of all jobs in 2003.[1] Midsize firms (20 to 499 employees) accounted for 13.2 percent of the net new jobs, while large firms (500 or more employees) accounted for 7.3 percent.[2]

At first glance, the net new job figures are difficult to reconcile with the fact that, over the same period, small firms' share of total employment actually fell. In 1990, small firms employed 20.2 percent of all workers, while large firms employed 46.3 percent. In 2003, the numbers for small firms dropped to 18.4 percent but climbed to 49.3 percent for large firms.

The explanation lies in the migration of firms across size classes from year to year. In any given year, some small firms will grow beyond 20 workers and join a larger size class. Such migration trims the share of firms in the smallest class size, in the same way that small business failures trim the class size.[3] Likewise, some large firms will contract, falling below the 500-employee level and dropping into a smaller size class. Also, new small businesses are born, increasing the share of jobs in the small-firm class. The data, thus, suggest that the effects of migration of small firms into larger size classes and small business failures outweigh the effects of the migration of large firms into smaller size classes and small business startups. Migration also makes it difficult to attribute job growth to firm size.[4]

Gross Job flows

While striking, the net job growth figures presented above can also be somewhat deceiving. Gross job flows are considerably larger than net job flows. Roughly 23 million net new jobs were created from 1990 to 2003, but these figures represent the difference between 239 million gross new jobs created and 216 million gross jobs lost. Clearly, net employment figures mask a great deal of volatility in the labor market.

The relatively high share of net new jobs created by small businesses stems mainly from relatively large gross job losses among larger firms—not from massive job creation by small firms. From 1990 to 2003, small firms created almost 80 percent of *net* new jobs but less than 30 percent of *gross* jobs (Table 1).[5] Small firms also accounted for about 24 percent of gross job losses. Large firms created almost 40 percent of gross new jobs but suffered 43.5 percent of gross job losses.

Most gross and net new jobs at small businesses stem from existing business expansions rather than from new business startups. Small business startups created about 36 percent of gross new jobs from 1990 to 2004, an average of roughly 1.8 million jobs per year. At the same time, the death of small firms was responsible for an average loss of more than 1.6 million gross jobs each year. Thus, the net job growth from small business startups in the 1990s and early 2000s (new jobs created minus job losses) was relatively small, representing less than 13 percent of total net job growth among the smallest firms.

Self-Employment

In the United States, 75 percent of business establishments represent the self-employed and, therefore, have no payroll at all. Some of the self-employed have other jobs as well, but for many, self-employment is their primary source of income. Clearly, many entrepreneurs start their businesses as self-employed people. They acquire new employees as their businesses expand.

Mainly because these establishments generate only about 3 percent of total receipts (sales) annually, data for the sector are generally less available than for the employer sector. But the Census Bureau annually collects limited information from business tax returns filed with the Internal Revenue Service. In

2004, more than 19.5 million individuals were self-employed or operated businesses with no payroll. This number is roughly 12 percent of the working population and about 26 percent higher than in 1997. The number also corresponds to a compound annual growth rate of about 3.4 percent over the period. By contrast, total private employment over the same period increased 0.8 percent annually.[6]

III. Job Quality at Small Businesses

Knowing that small businesses create a significant share of new jobs, it is natural to ask how these jobs compare to those at larger firms. Simply put, large firms offer better jobs and higher wages than small firms. Benefits appear to be better at large firms as well, for everything from health insurance and retirement to paid holidays and vacations. Finally, job turnover, initiated by both employers and employees, is lower at large firms. The lower rates of employee-initiated turnover suggest that job satisfaction and mobility are relatively greater at larger firms. Lower rates of employer-initiated separations suggest that jobs at larger firms are more stable.

Earnings

Large firms pay higher wages than small firms. In 2005, the average hourly wage in establishments with less than 100 workers was $15.69 and increased consistently with establishment size. Wages increased to $27.05 (a 72 percent premium) for establishments with 2,500 or more workers (Figure 2). Smaller businesses are also much more likely to employ low-wage workers. In 2004, establishments with less than 100 workers paid nearly a fourth of their workers less than $8 per hour. Establishments with 2,500 or more workers paid only 3 percent of their workers less than $8 per hour (Bureau of Labor Statistics 2004). Again, the percentage of workers earning low wages declines consistently as establishment size increases. The gap does not appear to be narrowing, as research finds wage growth at large firms equals or exceeds that at small firms (Hu).[7]

There are several explanations for the general wage discrepancies across workers or classes of workers. Workers doing the same job might be willing to accept a lower wage for increased job stability, better fringe benefits, or other positive job attributes. In fact, research has found that many workers accept lower wages in exchange for health benefits (Olson). But this is not a plausible explanation for the size-wage effect because large firms tend to offer more stable employment and better benefits than small firms.

Large firms often have undesirable working conditions, such as weaker autonomy, stricter rules and regulations, less flexible scheduling, and a more impersonal working environment. But, to the extent that empirical evidence can capture these differences, working conditions cannot explain the firm size-wage effect (Brown and Medoff).

Demographics may offer a plausible explanation: Women and minorities typically earn less than their white male counterparts. But evidence shows that, with the exception of Hispanics,

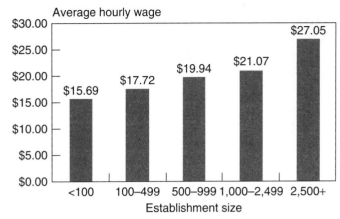

Figure 2 Average Hourly Wage, by Establishment Size, 2005.
Source: Bureau of Labor Statistics, U.S. Department of Labor (2007). *National Compensation Survey: Occupational Wages in the United States, June 2005.*

women and minorities are generally more likely to work for larger firms. Blacks make up about 10 percent of smaller firms (less than 500), compared to 13 percent of larger firms (Headd).[8] Similarly, women make up 45 percent of smaller firms but 48 percent of larger firms. This pattern holds for higher paying jobs as well. Professional women are disproportionately employed by large establishments (Mitra). The same is true for minorities in science and engineering fields (National Science Foundation). Only Hispanics show a contrary trend, making up 12 percent of smaller firms but only 9 percent of larger firms.

Another potential explanation for the size-wage effect is the difference in average firm size across industries. If the industries that pay better wages generally have larger firms, part of the size-wage effect would arise from industry makeup. In reality, however, the size-wage effect persists across industries (Table 2). There are a few minor exceptions (shaded in the table), but, for the most part, the exceptions are industries that offer relatively low pay overall.

Analysts have explored many other possibilities. But even after controlling for variables such as "collar color," union status, plausibility of a union threat, and industry makeup, researchers have been unable to explain away the persistent firm size-wage effect (Brown and Medoff). The relationship persists even for piece-rate workers and for workers moving across different-sized employers. In 1989, Brown and Medoff finally concluded: "Our bottom line is that the size-wage differential appears to be both sizable and omnipresent; our analysis leaves us uncomfortably unable to explain it, or at least the part of it that is not explained by observable indicators of labor quality."

Other theories to explain the size-wage effect have surfaced since the Brown and Medoff study, some of which have empirical support. Among these are theories suggesting that larger employers may make greater use of high-quality workers. This might occur, for example, because larger firms are more capital-intensive and require higher skilled employees to operate the plant and equipment. Empirical data seem to bear this out, as 25.5 percent of workers at larger firms in 1998 had a bachelor's degree or higher, compared to 20.3 percent at smaller firms (Headd). Further, some argue that workers at large firms have

Table 2 Salary Data by Industry and Firm Size

Industry	Ann. Salary Small Firms ($) [2]	Ann. Salary Medium Firms ($) [3]	Ann. Salary Large Firms ($) [4]	Ratio (%) [4]/[2]
Forestry, Fishing, Hunting, and Agriculture Support	26,324	NA	NA	NA
Mining	41,234	51,712	63,046	152.9
Utilities	30,644	NA	NA	NA
Construction	32,456	42,087	50,690	156.2
Manufacturing	30,933	37,563	47,835	154.6
Wholesale Trade	39,845	44,882	58,058	145.7
Retail Trade	**20,058**	**27,998**	**19,486**	**97.1**
Transportation and Warehousing	27,772	32,307	39,101	140.8
Information	40,728	52,292	60,308	148.1
Finance and Insurance	45,001	59,279	69,971	155.5
Real Estate and Rental and Leasing	29,794	35,352	39,194	131.6
Professional, Scientific, and Technical Services	43,135	58,776	62,227	144.3
Management of Companies and Enterprises	58,360	57,612	81,530	139.7
Administrative and Support, Waste Management and Remediation Services	**26,968**	**25,553**	**27,180**	**100.8**
Educational Services	19,966	25,406	30,348	152.0
Health Care and Social Assistance	**37,624**	**30,868**	**37,153**	**98.7**
Arts, Entertainment, and Recreation	**28,580**	**25,716**	**24,079**	**84.3**
Accommodation and Food Services	11,138	12,219	15,745	141.4
Other Services (except Public Administration)	19,905	23,177	28,406	142.7
Unclassified	13,164	NA	NA	NA
ALL FIRMS	29,213	33,639	41,373	141.6

Note. NA indicates that data were not available.

Source: Author's calculations using data from *Statistics of U.S. Businesses,* U.S. Census Bureau.

a greater incentive to gain additional education and new skills because of greater opportunities for upward mobility (Zabojnik and Bernhardt). Others suggest that because employee monitoring is more costly at larger firms, these firms pay higher wages to deter shirking on the job—but this explanation is not supported by the data (Oi and Idson). Another possibility is simply that the larger scale of larger firms in some industries means lower costs (Pull; Idson and Oi). Or perhaps less stable employees, who are likely to have lower wages, are attracted to small firms (Evans and Leighton; Mayo and Murray).

Many explanations for the size-wage effect have been explored with little success. Lacking a satisfying explanation, however, workers still tend to earn higher wages at large firms.

Fringe Benefits

Small business owners and their employees are much less likely to have employer-based health insurance policies or health insurance policies of any kind. Survey data from the Census Bureau reveals that in 2002 about 31 percent of workers at small businesses (25 or less employees) had employer-based health insurance policies in their own name, compared to 69 percent at large businesses (1,000 or more employees) (Mills and Bhandari).[9] Of the nearly 44 million uninsured people in the United States in 2002, fully 60 percent were in families who owned or worked at small businesses.[10] Among the self-employed, about 32 percent are uninsured, compared to 18 percent of all workers.[11]

Perhaps the best source of information on fringe benefits by employer size is the National Compensation Survey conducted by the Bureau of Labor Statistics (2006). Workers at large firms are much more likely to receive retirement benefits; life insurance; and health, dental, and vision insurance (Table 3). Eligibility for both short-term and long-term disability benefits are about twice as likely at large firms than at small firms. Aggravating the discrepancy in disability benefits is the fact that very small employers generally are not required to provide employees with workers' compensation insurance.[12] The average number of paid holidays is almost 13 percent higher at large firms, and paid vacation days are roughly 20 percent to 40 percent greater at large firms, depending on length of service. The difference

Table 3 Fringe Benefits Availability by Firm Size, March 2006

Fringe Benefit	100+ Employees	1–99 Employees
Retirement benefits (%)		
Any type	78	44
Defined benefit	35	9
Defined contribution	70	41
Health care (%)		
Medical care	84	59
Dental care	64	31
Vision care	40	20
Outpatient prescription drug coverage	80	56
Insurance (%)		
Life Insurance	69	36
Short-term disability benefits	53	27
Long-term disability benefits	43	19
Paid vacation days (#)		
After 1 year of service	10.1	7.8
After 5 years of service	15.0	12.3
After 25 years of service	22.3	16.3
Paid holidays (#)	9	8
Nonproduction bonus (% eligible)	49	44

Source: U.S. Department of Labor, Bureau of Labor Statistics, *National Compensation Survey: Employee Benefits in Private Industry in the United States, March 2006.*

in paid vacation days tends to increase in both absolute and relative terms with length of service. Eligibility for nonproduction bonuses (that is, bonuses not based on sales or output) is comparable at large and small firms, but benefits generally appear to be much more generous at larger firms.

Job Stability

Perhaps the best measure of job satisfaction is the propensity of employees to separate from their employers. Likewise, the likelihood of being dismissed from a job is an important factor in determining the quality of jobs. Turnover in general, that is, both employer-and employee-initiated separations, is therefore indicative of lower quality jobs—due to job instability in the former case and (relative) job dissatisfaction in the latter.

Tabulations show a consistent downward trend in annual rates of permanent job separations as firm size increases (Anderson and Meyer). Permanent separation rates were close to 22 percent for firms with less than 100 employees, 13 percent for firms with 500-1,999 employees, and only 8 percent for firms with 2,000 or more employees. Temporary separations, which are about 28 percent of all turnover, occurred at roughly equal rates at small and large firms. The authors back up their tabulations with more sophisticated statistical analyses that show a significant negative relationship between job dissolution

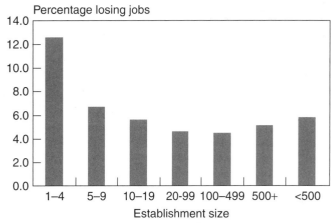

Figure 3 Job losses from business failures, 2002–2003.

Source: *Statistics of U.S. Businesses*, U.S. Census Bureau.

and firm size (Groothuis). While these separations include both employer- and employee-initiated separations, other research shows a significant negative relationship between firm size and probability of layoff (Winter-Ember; Campbell). Similarly, quit rates decline with firm size (Brown and Medoff).

A natural reason for lower quit rates at large firms is the higher average wage and better fringe benefits at large firms, which would be expected to reduce employee decisions to separate. This is especially true for pensions, which reward long tenure specifically. As shown in Table 3, retirement benefits are available to 78 percent of large-firm workers but only 44 percent of small-firm workers. The presence of labor unions, which are much more common at large firms, may indirectly reduce turnover through the higher wages generally paid to unionized workers, but unions may also directly reduce turnover by giving dissatisfied workers a "voice" in their employment situation, offering an alternative to leaving (Anderson and Meyer). Further, larger firms offer more on-the-job training and more advancement opportunities, which makes it easier for them to maintain long employment relationships with their workers (Idson). Finally, some argue that the size-layoff relationship may be a spurious relationship resulting from the tendency of smaller businesses to attract less stable and capable workers, which also would work to explain part of the size-wage relationship (Winter-Ember).

A critical factor in greater labor turnover at smaller businesses is that the failure rate of small businesses is somewhat greater than that of larger businesses, which leads to higher rates of employer-initiated separations (Dunne and others; Idson). Failure rates of establishments drop markedly as firm size increases to 100 employees, but then turn upward again such that firms with 500 or more employees have larger failure rates than firms with 20–99 employees. Nevertheless, the failure rates for the smallest firms (one to four employees) generally are about one and one-half times higher than those of the largest firms. More important for this analysis is the loss of jobs from business failures. As seen in Figure 3, approximately 12.6 percent of all workers in the smallest firms (one to four employees) lost their jobs from business failures in 2002–03, compared to 5.1 percent at the largest firms (500 or more employees).

IV. Small Business and Innovation

Joseph Schumpeter, the renowned analyst and advocate of capitalism, asserted that the hallmark of capitalism is innovation: "The sweeping out of old products, old enterprises, and old organizational forms by new ones." He referred to this process as "creative destruction." In capitalism, therefore, the only survivors are those who constantly innovate and develop new products and processes to replace the old ones.

Small businesses are largely thought to be more innovative than larger firms for three reasons: a lack of entrenched bureaucracy, more competitive markets, and stronger incentives (such as personal rewards). Small businesses are indeed crucial innovators in today's economy and are the technological leaders of many industries. But the conventional wisdom—that small businesses are the cornerstone of innovative activity and that large firms are too big and bureaucratic to make significant innovations—is false. Both small and large firms make significant innovations, and both types of firms are critical to the success of today's economy.

Schumpeter asserted that larger firms are better positioned to make innovations, especially if operating in a concentrated market (such as a monopoly or a market in which only a few firms dominate). Several concepts underlie his reasoning (Vossen; Symeonidis).

Research and development (R&D) expenditures involve very large fixed (sunk) costs. R&D costs can be recovered only with a large sales volume, so that the costs can be spread over a large number of items. Further, larger firms generally have better access to external financing, and monopolistic firms, which tend to be larger, have better access to internal financing because of their generally higher profitability. Larger firms also have a greater capacity to undertake several R&D projects at once and, hence, dilute the risk of any one project in a diversified portfolio.

There are several other advantages to innovation at large firms beyond financing and managing R&D. Large firms tend to have established reputations and name recognition, which make it easier to enter new markets and/or established marketing channels. Thus, larger firms are often better able to take advantage of innovations through production and sale. In addition, having a large number of colleagues, which is more likely at a large firm, facilitates a division of labor and the solution of problems (for example, by seeking the assistance of colleagues) and increases the likelihood that "serendipitous discoveries [are] recognized as important" (Vossen). Finally, many of the largest firms operate in industries in which only a few firms operate or dominate the market. For the most part, these firms do not compete with one another on the basis of price, but rather on the basis of quality and product differentiation. Given this market structure, large firms may, therefore, have greater incentive to innovate.

While large-firm strengths are mostly material in nature, small-firm strengths are mostly behavioral (Vossen). Perhaps the most critical strength is the lack of an entrenched bureaucracy that often characterizes larger firms. An entrenched bureaucracy can lead to long chains of command and subsequent communication inefficiency, inflexibility, and loss of managerial coordination. Further, small firms, to the extent that they operate in more competitive environments, may have a greater incentive to innovate so as to stay ahead of rivals. Finally, because ownership and management are more likely to be intertwined at smaller firms, the personal rewards of potential innovators are higher. As a related factor, smaller firms may be better able to structure contracts to reward performance (Zenger).

Given the relative strengths of large and small firms, whether small businesses are more innovative is an empirical question. Numerous studies have presented results on the relationship between firm size and R&D or innovative activity using a myriad of measures (Symeonidis). Unfortunately, the results are mixed.

The large majority of small firms (especially those with less than 100 employees) do not engage in formal R&D, and the degree to which they engage in informal R&D is difficult to gauge (Symeonidis). Total R&D increases with firm size, but studies have offered differing views on the intensity of R&D. Intensity is generally measured across firm size classes as R&D expenditure per employee or relative to sales. The preponderance of the evidence suggests two tendencies. First, R&D intensity increases with firm size in some industries and decreases in others, as do R&D outcomes, such as patents (Scherer; Acs and Audretsch; Pavitt and others). Thus, a general statement about the relationship between R&D and firm size probably is not sensible. Second, to the extent that a generalization can be made, the relationship is likely a moderate U-shape, meaning that both smaller firms (above a threshold size) and very large firms engage in R&D more intensively than medium-sized firms (Gellam Research Associates; Bound and others; Pavitt and others).

More clear is that smaller businesses are more efficient at innovation, which means they produce more innovations for a given amount of R&D than do larger firms (Vossen). Thus, they often create more innovation value per given amount of R&D. Part of this may be due simply to underestimation of R&D expenditure at smaller firms, but others suggest that small firms are more effective in taking advantage of knowledge spillovers from other firms (Acs and others).

Perhaps the industry with the greatest history of innovations by lone entrepreneurs and small businesses is the computer industry.[13] The consensus first personal computer, the MITS' Altair (1975), and the first personal computer as we know them today, the Apple II, were developed and marketed by what were, at the time, very small businesses.[14] The first software written specifically for the personal computer (BASIC) was developed and marketed by Paul Allen and Bill Gates as part of a small business, Traf-O-Data, which would later evolve into Microsoft (1975).

The PC era arguably would have been substantially delayed if not for entrepreneurs starting small businesses. The large computer companies seemed to have little initial interest in personal computers. Hewlett-Packard, for example, rejected as nonviable the first Apple computer when it was developed by employee Steve Wozniak in 1976. It was the rapid sales of the Apple II that spawned development of IBM's PC, which was not introduced until 1981. Xerox rejected a proposal in 1971 to design a "portable" computer and rejected multiple proposals in 1976 to market its personal computer, Alto, which was designed in the early 1970s for research use.

Clearly, many of the great innovations in this industry were made by lone entrepreneurs and small businesses. Nevertheless, the innovations were made possible by years of R&D by large firms like AT&T and IBM and their precursory innovations (like the transistor). Many of the enhancements in personal computing since then have come from large firms as well, including the hard drive (IBM PC/XT), although enhancements in personal computing, software, and their marketing continue to be made by both small and large firms.

The message seems to be that both small firms and large firms make significant innovations that keep the economy moving and growing, although small firms may be more efficient at innovation. Small firms are the great innovators in some industries, while large firms are the great innovators in others. Moreover, small and large businesses interact in innovative activity. The computer industry was largely developed by large firms (AT&T and IBM), small firms advanced computing through the development of personal computers (MITS and Apple), large firms brought the innovation to the public at large through mass marketing (the IBM PC), and both small and large firms continue to improve computing today with additional innovations and enhancements.

Often entrepreneurs leave large enterprises to start small firms, either because innovation was hampered in their existing enterprise or because the entrepreneurs wanted to ensure the rewards for themselves. And many small firms grow rapidly to become the largest of the large firms. Further, innovative small businesses often benefit enormously from the basic R&D of large firms.

V. Conclusion

This analysis evaluated the economic development role of small businesses vis-à-vis large businesses. It suggests that small businesses may not be quite the fountainhead of job creation they are purported to be, especially when it comes to high-paying jobs that are stable and offer good benefits. Big-firm jobs are typically better jobs. Moreover, while small businesses are important innovators in today's economy, so are large businesses. There is no clear evidence that small businesses are more effective innovators. Further, the innovations of both small businesses and large businesses are inextricably linked. Still, small firms create the majority of net new jobs and are critical innovators, and efforts to encourage the formation and growth of small enterprises are probably sensible in most cases.

While large firms offer better jobs on average and contribute significantly to job creation and innovation, research and experience suggest that attempts to recruit large enterprises to a specific community are unlikely to be successful (because of competition from competing communities). And they are not likely to be cost-effective even if they are successful. More generally, an economic development strategy that focuses on a particular business or industry is very risky because sorting prospective winners and losers is difficult at best.

Where do these facts leave economic development strategy? As noted earlier, net employment impacts from firm expansions tend to be much greater than those associated with new-firm locations. This suggests that concentrating on organic growth, or the growth of existing or "home-grown" businesses, is likely to be a much more successful strategy than the recruitment of new firms. Given the role of small businesses in employment growth, supporting entrepreneurs and budding businesses is also likely to be an effective strategy. The hope is that some of these small businesses can grow to become the large firms of tomorrow and offer the kinds of benefits that typically come with employment in a large firm.

The key to a successful strategy is to get the policies right. Evidence increasingly suggests that the right approach is usually to focus on developing an attractive and supportive environment that might enable any business, whether small or large, to flourish, and to allow the market to sort out which businesses succeed. Many communities have had success in creating this environment. They have developed and fostered a high-quality workforce through great schools, community colleges, and universities. They have provided life-long learning opportunities; built and maintained high-quality public infrastructure; created a business climate with reasonable levels of taxation and regulation; and, through good government and quality amenities, have created the kinds of communities where highly educated and skilled people want to live and work.

Notes

1. The latest date for which data were available is 2003. All Figures in this article use data through the latest year in which they were available.

2. These numbers are somewhat obscured by large job losses in 2002 and 2003, especially at large firms. Through 2001, small firms created 69.1 percent of net new jobs, compared to 10.1 percent for midsized firms and 21.2 percent for large firms.

3. For this reason, it would be misleading to measure net employment changes as total employment in a size class at the end of the year less total employment in the size class at the beginning of the year. The numbers presented in this section were generated by the U.S. Census Bureau from longitudinal data from individual firms.

4. The job figures presented in Figure 1 classify firms into size classes based on their size at the beginning of the period, which favors a finding of higher growth among small firms, rather than at the end of the period (Appendix).

5. Some research suggests that the size-job creation nexus operates in reverse for manufacturing plants: Small firms create most gross jobs and suffer the most gross job losses, but larger firms contribute the most to net job creation (Davis and others).

6. According to the Bureau of Labor Statistics, total private nonfarm employment increased from 104.6 million in 1997 to 110.7 million in 2004. Private employment grew at a much faster 2.2 percent annual rate in the prerecession period from 1997 to 2000. Recessions often find individuals moving out of traditional employment and into self-employment, which explains some of the discrepancy in growth rates.

7. The firm size-wage effect persists across other countries as well. Similar results have been found, for example, in Canada (Morisette), Germany (Schmidt and Zimmerman), Austria (Winter-Ember), the United Kingdom (Belfield and Wei), and Switzerland (Winter-Ember and Zweimüller), among others.

8. Kraybill and others show that the large-firm wage premium is higher for blacks than for whites.

9. Some workers may have been covered by another family member's employer-based policy.

10. U.S. Census Bureau, Current Population Survey, 2003 Annual Social and Economic Supplement.

11. Some research suggests, however, that health-care utilization rates for the self-employed generally are the same as those for wage earners, despite their much lower rate of health insurance coverage (Perry and Rosen). This suggests that self-employed people may have been finding other means for financing their medical care other than health insurance.

12. See National Academy of Social Insurance, 2003. The maximum number of workers who can be employed without coverage varies from state to state but generally is in the range of three to five workers. Texas does not mandate workers' compensation coverage.

13. The source for much of the historical information in this section is "Chronology of Personal Computers." Accessed March 23, 2007, at http://www.islandnet.com/~kpolsson/comphist/index.htm.

14. The Altair was preceded by the Scelbi and the Mark-8, both in 1974.

References

Acs, Z.J., and D.B. Audretsch. 1987. "Innovation, Market Structure and Firm Size," *Review of Economics and Statistics,* vol. 69, no. 4, pp. 567–75.

Acs, Z.J., D.B. Audretsch, and M.B. Feldman. 1994. "R&D Spillovers and Recipient Firm Size," *Review of Economics and Statistics,* vol. 76, no. 2, pp. 336–39.

Anderson, P.M., and B.D. Meyer. 1994. "The Extent and Consequences of Job Turnover," *Brookings Papers on Economic Activity: Microeconomics,* pp. 177–248.

Belfield, C.R., and X. Wei. 2004. "Employer Size-Wage Effects: Evidence from Matched Employer-Employee Survey Data in the UK," *Applied Economics,* vol. 36, no. 3, pp. 185–93.

Bound, J., C. Cummins, Z. Griliches, B.H. Hall, and A. Jaffe. 1984. "Who Does R&D and Who Patents?" in Z. Griliches, ed., *R&D, Patents, and Productivity.* Chicago: University of Chicago Press.

Brown, C., and J. Medoff. 1989. "The Employer Size-Wage Effect," *Journal of Political Economy,* vol. 97, no. 5, pp. 1027–59.

Bureau of Labor Statistics, U.S. Department of Labor. 2006. "National Compensation Survey: Employee Benefits in Private Industry in the United States, March 2006," August.

_____. 2004. "Low Pay and Establishment Size," *Monthly Labor Review: The Editor's Desk,* February 3.

Campbell, C.M. 1994. "The Determinants of Dismissals: Tests of the Shirking Model with Individual Data," *Economics Letters,* vol. 46, no.1, pp. 89–95.

Davis, S.J., J. Haltiwanger, and S. Schuh. 1996. "Small Business and Job Creation: Dissecting the Myth and Reassessing the Facts," *Small Business Economics,* vol. 8, no. 4, pp. 297–315.

Dunne, T., M.J. Roberts, and L. Samuelson. 1989. "The Growth and Failure of U.S. Manufacturing Plants," *Quarterly Journal of Economics,* vol. 104, no. 3, pp. 671–98.

Edmiston, K.D. 2004. "The Net Effects of Large Plant Locations and Expansions on County Employment," *Journal of Regional Science,* vol. 44, no. 2, pp. 289–319.

Edmiston, K.D., and G.K. Turnbull. 2007. "Local Competition for Economic Development," *Journal of Urban Economics,* forthcoming.

Evans, D.S., and L.S. Leighton. 1989. "Why Do Smaller Firms Pay Less?" *Journal of Human Resources,* vol. 24, no. 2, pp. 299–318.

Fox, W.F., and M.N. Murray. 2004. "Do Economic Effects Justify the Use of Fiscal Incentives?" *Southern Economic Journal,* vol. 71, no. 1, pp. 78–92.

Gellam Research Associates. 1976. *Indicators of International Trends in Technological Innovation,* Jenkintown, Penn.

Groothuis, P.A. 1994. "Turnover: The Implications of Establishment Size and Unionization," *Quarterly Journal of Business and Economics,* vol. 33, no. 2, pp. 41–53.

Headd, B. 2000. "The Characteristics of Small-Business Employees," *Monthly Labor Review,* vol. 123, no. 4, pp. 13–18.

Hu, L. 2003. "The Hiring Decisions and Compensation Structures of Large Firms," *Industrial and Labor Relations Review,* vol. 56, no. 4, pp. 663–81.

Idson, T.L. 1996. "Employer Size and Labor Turnover," *Research in Labor Economics,* vol. 15, pp. 273–304.

Idson, T.L., and W.Y. Oi. 1999. "Workers Are More Productive in Large Firms," *American Economic Review,* vol. 89, no. 2, pp. 104–08.

Kraybill, D.S., M.J. Yoder, and K.T. McNamara. 1991. "Employer Size, Human Capital, and Rural Wages: Implications for Southern Rural Development," *Southern Journal of Agricultural Economics,* vol. 23, no. 2, pp. 85–94.

Mayo, J.W., and M.N. Murray. 1991. "Firm Size, Employment Risk, and Wages: Further Insights on a Persistent Puzzle," *Applied Economics,* vol. 23, no. 8, pp. 1351–60.

Mills, R.J., and S. Bhandari. 2003. "Health Insurance Coverage in the United States: 2002," U.S. Census Bureau, *Current Population Reports,* September.

Mitra, A. 2003. "Establishment Size, Employment, and the Gender Wage Gap," *Journal of Socio-Economics,* vol. 32, no. 3, pp. 317–30.

Morisette, R. 1993. "Canadian Jobs and Firm Size: Do Smaller Firms Pay Less?" *Canadian Journal of Economics,* vol. 26, no. 1, pp. 159–74.

National Academy of Social Insurance. 2003. *Workers' Compensation: Benefits, Coverage, and Costs, 2001,* Washington, July.

National Science Foundation, Division of Science Resources Studies. 1999. *Will Small Business Become the Nation's Leading Employer of Graduates with Bachelor's Degrees in Science and Engineering?* NSF 99–322, Project Officers: John Tsapogas and Lawrence M. Rausch; Mary Collins, Westat, Arlington, Va.

Oi, W.Y., and T.L. Idson. 1999. "Firm Size and Wages," in O. Ashenfelter and D. Card, eds., *Handbook of Labor Economics.* Amsterdam: North-Holland, 3rd ed.

Okolie, C. 2004. "Why Size Class Methodology Matters in Analyses of Net and Gross Job Flows, *Monthly Labor Review,* vol. 127, no. 7, pp. 3–12.

Olson, C.A. 2002. "Do Workers Accept Lower Wages in Exchange for Health Benefits?" *Journal of Labor Economics,* vol. 20, no. 2, part 2, pp. S91–S114.

Pavitt, K., M. Robson, and J. Townsend. 1987. "The Size Distribution of Innovating Firms in the UK: 1945–1983," *Journal of Industrial Economics,* vol. 35, no. 3, pp. 297–316.

Perry, C.W., and H.S. Rosen. 2001. "Insurance and the Utilization of Medical Services Among the Self-Employed," *National Bureau of Economic Research* Working Paper No. 8490.

Pull, K. 2003. "Firm Size, Wages, and Production Technology," *Small Business Economics,* vol. 21, no. 3, pp. 285–88.

Schmidt, C.M., and K.F. Zimmerman. 1991. "Work Characteristics, Firm Size, and Wages," *Review of Economics and Statistics,* vol. 73, no. 4, pp. 705–10.

Scherer, F.M. 1984. *Innovation and Growth: Schumpeterian Perspectives.* Cambridge, Mass.: MIT Press.

Schumpeter, J.A. 1942. *Capitalism, Socialism, and Democracy.* New York: Harper & Row.

Symeonidis, G. 1996. "Innovation, Firm Size, and Market Structure: Schumpeterian Hypotheses and Some New Themes," *OECD Economic Studies,* vol. 27, pp. 35–70.

Vossen, R.W. 1998. "Combining Small and Large Firm Advantages in Innovation: Theory and Examples," *SOM Research Report 98B21,* Research School Systems Organisation and Management, Universiteitsbibliotheek Groningen.

Winter-Ember, R. 2001. "Firm Size, Earnings, and Displacement Risk," *Economic Inquiry,* vol. 39, no. 3, pp. 474–86.

Winter-Ember, R., and J. Zweimüller. 1999. "Firm Size-Wage Differentials in Switzerland: Evidence from Job Changes," *American Economic Review,* vol. 89, no. 2, pp. 89–93.

Zabojnik, J., and D. Bernhardt. 2001. "Corporate Tournaments, Human Capital Acquisition, and the Firm Size-Wage Relation," *Review of Economic Studies,* vol. 68, no. 3, pp. 693–716.

Zenger, T.R. 1994. "Explaining Organizational Diseconomies of Scale in R&D: Agency Problems and the Allocation of Engineering Talent, Ideas, and Effort by Firm Size," *Management Science,* vol. 40, no. 6, pp. 708–29.

KELLY EDMISTON is a senior economist in Community Affairs at the Federal Reserve Bank of Kansas City. This article is on the bank's website at www.KansasCityFed.org.

Appendix
Firm Migration, Classification, and Growth

The migration of firms into and out of size categories also makes attributing job growth to size categories difficult (Okolie). The job figures presented in Figure 1 classify firms into size classes based on their size at the beginning of the period, which favors a finding of higher growth among small firms, rather than at the end of the period. Table A1 decomposes job growth from the second quarter of 2000 into job classes using beginning size of firm, mean size of firm over the period, and end size of firm. If the beginning size of the firm is used to classify firms, small firms with less than 20 employees are responsible for 53.2 percent of net job growth in the quarter, whereas if end-of-period size is used, small firms are responsible for only

Table A1 Share of Net Job Growth by Firm Size, Second Quarter 2000, by Size Classification Scheme

Employees	Beginning Size	Mean Size	End Size
>20	53.2	34.5	16.2
20–499	34.7	45.3	55.7
500 +	12.1	20.2	28.1

Source: Okolie.

16.2 percent of net job creation in the quarter. Again, this pattern is consistent with significant movement of small firms into larger class sizes.

Success Rules!

Succeed with these five rules from five entrepreneurs who have made it.

THOMAS MELVILLE

J oe Mancuso, a burly sexagenarian with a white beard and an easy laugh, knows about success. He has founded seven businesses, along with the Center for Entrepreneurial Management and the Chief Executive Officers Club, written 24 business books, and is a much sought-out corporate motivational speaker. Mancuso, who is often called "the entrepreneur's entrepreneur," has spent a life-time being successful and being around the successful.

"Entrepreneurs and CEOs accomplish more because they are always thinking," says Mancuso. "Success is not only about financial success, it is about a life-style—people doing what they want to do. It's a classic cliché, but people that make a lot of money are not always happy."

But are there definitive rules that someone could follow to success?

Ask the businessman's Buddha, Mancuso, who relishes his role as mentor, and he will give you his 20 commandments (see some of them in the sidebar included in this article).

Twenty is a lot to remember. SUCCESS went looking for five rules essential to startup success and found them in five entrepreneurs who have made it. Some are serial entrepreneurs who have succeeded several times over, and some have nurtured one business for years, but all have one thing in common—they are winners.

"Don't cling to ownership. Give employees stock options."

—Steven Cash Nickerson, CEO, Mucho.com

1 Always Start with the Exit in Mind

Steven Cash Nickerson's mother may have been clairvoyant. She worked as a vacuum salesman at J.C. Penney in Philadelphia, while carrying Nickerson to term. After giving birth she wanted to name her son Cash, after James Cash Penny, but her husband talked her out of it. Instead Cash became Steven's middle name, literally and figuratively. Now a 41-year-old serial entrepreneur

who has founded 11 and sold eight companies, Nickerson has proved his mother's psychic abilities correct.

"Everybody calls me Cash now," says Nickerson, who sold his last startup company, Workforce Strategies, for $8.4 million.

Currently Nickerson, based in Lafayette, Calif., is busy launching his latest venture, Mucho.com, an Internet portal designed to provide small business owners a single source for all business needs. But it was starting and running Workforce Strategies where Nickerson learned some valuable lessons.

He was a partner in a large law firm in Chicago in the 1990s, earning a nice paycheck and feeling quite secure when he decided to jump ship and start his own business. Workforce Strategies ended up bringing in $25 million in revenue before he sold it in 1997.

"My plan from the start was to sell it," he says. "Always start with the exit in mind, otherwise you work for 40 years and become a penny stacker."

Nickerson also advises owners to share equity. "Don't cling to ownership. Give employees stock options." Nickerson sets aside 10 percent of the stock for employees at the beginning.

"Another big rule is not to lie to yourself when things are not going well," he says. "Always be assessing—what are your stars and your dogs? It's like keeping score when you were a kid. If things are not working, do not be afraid to cut loose. And always, hire slowly, but fire quickly. Swallow your pride, admit you made a mistake in hiring someone, and move on."

2 Communicate with Employees and be Flexible

Last year Jeff Lawrence learned about truth from about 50 students at UCLA, and it has helped him run his business. He gave a two-hour lecture to a class on engineering ethics, and afterward the students wrote a one-page report on what they heard.

"Fifty people had heard 50 different things," Lawrence says. "I read their reports and everyone had their own interpretations. You can have a set of facts and then everyone has his own point of view about it. Truth is relative."

Lawrence, who started Trillium Digital Systems, a $20 million-plus internet-working communications software company

Highlights from Joe Mancuso's 20 Commandments

Joe Mancuso, founder of the Chief Executive Officers Club, created 20 commandments for CEOs. "I chose 20 rather than 10 in remembrance of my favorite scene in a Mel Brooks movie, *The History of the World, Part I.* As Moses came down from Mount Sinai with three inscribed stone tablets, he bellowed out to the masses: 'I have spoken directly to God, and he has given me these 15 commandments.' As he spoke, he slipped and one of the three tablets in his hand fell and shattered. Thank God!"

In honor of the shattered tablet, here are five of Mancuso's 20.

Beg for forgiveness rather than ask permission. When you discover you are in a hole, maybe it's time to stop digging. Ready. Fire. Aim.

Abdicate vs. Delegate. You can get anything you want if you help enough other people get what they want.

Avoid the "sandbox syndrome." A company's weakest vice president often shares the CEO's area of expertise. Pity the vice president for marketing who reports to a CEO who came up through the ranks in marketing. Whether by accident or design, it seems that vice presidents in a CEO's discipline are seldom as effective as those in other areas. It's the sandbox syndrome as the CEOs with certain skills just can't help meddling in their old favorite sand-box.

Use your company's mission statement as a touchstone. The mission statement of an organization is the most tangible measure of a CEO's effectiveness.

Make sure that all objectives are clear and attainable. Both the entrepreneurial and the professional CEO agree that every person in a well-run organization can say: "I know what I'm supposed to accomplish and by when. My boss has agreed to my objectives and has allocated to me the resources I need to attain them. If conditions change, I can shift my effort and still attain my objectives."

Six Rules of How Not to Fail

Seek out quality, supportive relationships. Entrepreneurs go through more ups and downs than a roller coaster. Without the supportive relationships of a spouse, significant other, business coach, family, mentors, or friends it can be a lonely and confidence-shattering journey.

Pick a strategy for every step of the way. Entrepreneurs spend most of their time focusing on the projected growth of their company. They don't spend enough time thinking about how far they are willing to go, in terms of time and money, on their startup. Success may always be right around the corner, but knowing when to pull the plug can save you many sleepless nights.

Volunteer in your community. Building a successful company will depend heavily upon the quality and diversity of your relationships. I have found no better way to build personal relationships that ultimately lead to valuable business relationships than through my volunteer efforts in the community.

Maintain your health and well-being. Entrepreneurs tend to invest far too much of their time and energy into their business and forget about their own well-being.

Diversify your interests. Pursue your hobbies and interests as passionately as you pursue the growth of your startup. It will help your brain to relax and rest. You will also find that you will be a far more interesting person to others as well as to yourself.

Maintain a life vision. Too often, entrepreneurs have their entire future invested in their startup. By maintaining a vision for all areas of their life they will keep their mind focused on today and the future, not worried about what worked or didn't work in the past.

—Nicholas Hall

in Los Angeles, knows about facing truths. In 1988 he was laid off from Doelz Networks and decided to start his own company.

"You should be as fair as possible with employees and customers. And encourage creativity from employees. Creativity sets you apart from other businesses in the same industry."

—Mary Ella Gabler, CEO, Peacock Alley

"My father was self-employed most of his life, so I always thought about it," says the soft-spoken Lawrence. "Getting laid off was the catalyst. Then it came down to assessing what I could do. I had knowledge in telecommunications software development. And I figured if it didn't work out I still had the skills to go back and work for someone else."

Lawrence's initial $1,000 investment with partner Larisa Chistyakov has spawned a 250-employee company that takes up most of the Trillium Building in west L.A., is projected to have $30 million in revenues for 2000, and has a long list of Fortune 500 clients. And last year he raised $14 million in venture capital from Intel and Rader, Reinfrank & Co.

"I think we have been successful because we have good people, smart people, nice people," says Lawrence. "To be successful you have to listen to people and be willing to change. You need to communicate with your people so they know what is going on. Encourage their input."

3 Hire Smart People

He talks in an authentic you-know-what-I'm-talking-about New York accent straight out of the city that never sleeps' mean streets. Glenn Schlossberg was raised on the ultra-competitive

Making a Success of Failure

Nicholas Hall has had more comebacks than George Foreman. After his first three startups went under, the 30-year-old entrepreneur kept climbing back in the ring for more punishment. Hall's latest creation, startupfailures.com, has been a cult hit as people get sick of hearing about overnight dot-com millionaires.

The website, www.startupfailures.com, Hall says, is a service for the many who don't make it and need some support. "The reality is that most startups are going to go through some tough time or fail. Entrepreneurs who fail have an emotional need, and I thought I could provide some support for these people," says Hall, who as president of the Silicon Valley Association of Software Entrepreneurs has witnessed a few startups crash and burn. Not to mention his own failures (for what he's learned see Six Rules of How Not To Fail).

First, as a young man in Cincinnati, he started a financial services company. "I tried to build it myself. I was headstrong, but I realized you can't do it alone," he says. Next he took a bath in the beverage industry when his coffee/hard-cider shop plan was scuttled. "By the time we went out to raise capital, that coffee shop market got hammered. So it was bad timing." Hall then had an idea for an Internet community site and decided to move to the San Francisco Bay area to drum up some interest. But he couldn't raise enough money to keep going. "I should have gone out and found some partners and potential customers instead of spending all my time trying to raise money."

With the support of his wife, Jennifer, Hall keeps bouncing back. He recently completed *The Future Scrapbook: Having the Design of Your Life,* a book that helps people plan out their futures. He's taking music lessons and is trying out for a musical.

"I've had some success," he says. "I'm not focusing on what did not work or how I screwed up. I have a network of supportive people to lean on. I wasn't born with a silver spoon in my mouth, nor did I receive a big inheritance. I'm just trying to make it like a lot of people."

streets of New York City's garment district. And at age 36, he has made it there and proved he can make it anywhere.

In 1989, Schlossberg, who at the time worked in the family business in the clothing industry, broke out on his own at age 25 and started Jump Apparel, which manufactures social-occasion dresses. By 1999, the company was making $70 million in revenue and Schlossberg had spun off one separate company, Onyx Nite, and co-founded two other affiliated apparel companies—Helen Blake and Danielle Casey.

"I found a financial backer, borrowed from my family and used my life savings to start," Schlossberg says. "I put my blood on the table next to theirs."

Schlossberg, who arrives at work in a chauffeured Bentley from his Manhattan apartment every morning at 6:30, believes that hiring the best people and providing top-notch service to his clients have led to his success. "You need to hire smart people.

I have more than 200 employees, and they are my championship team. It's all about the people."

It is not about being scared to fail. "Never show fear," he says. "*Show no fear* are the words to live by. I have a big sign on the front of my desk that says 'It can be done.' You have to have the guts to take the shots. You miss 100 percent of the shots you do not take."

4 Stick to a Realistic Business Plan

Jeff Parker has been to battle on the two great stages of the 20th century—in war and on Wall Street—and has survived and thrived. In the mid-1960s he worked in the Pentagon while in the Army, and through the 1970s he did his tour at Fidelity, becoming an extremely successful bond salesman.

Throughout the next 20 years he became an entrepreneur and founded six companies including his latest, CCBN.com, an Internet portal that organizes and delivers easy-to-use investment-related information for the corporate marketplace. It had $9 million in revenues in 1999 and is projected to bring in $25 million next year. Street-Events, a leading service of CCBN.com, allows users to track significant company events such as earnings release dates and investor conferences.

"When I left my high-paying job at Fidelity to start my own business, people said 'Is he nuts?'" Parker says. "But I had an innate desire to do something better, which is what makes someone an entrepreneur. But I was also at a time in my life where it wasn't that risky. I was a well-known bond salesman. I don't think entrepreneurs are great risk takers; they should have a fall-back position."

Parker, who describes himself as so organized he is anal, knew he could provide a service that on one else had, but needed. "As a bond-selling professional, it was a service I wish I had." His first business, started in 1980, was one of the first to provide organized, detailed, and easy-to-use information about the bond market. It clicked—and has been a springboard for the rest of Parker's successes.

"A successful business is about execution," he says. "You need laser focus and then do everything you can possibly do to stay on your business plan. But you need to be realistic about your business plan. I see ridiculous numbers from these young entrepreneurs sometimes, where they expect to go from zero in the first year to $42 million in revenue the next year."

Then, after the plan is set, you must create revenue. "All my businesses have had a heavy sales and marketing side," Parker says. "If you sit around and count expenses you will go out of business. You have to go out and sell it. Remember that cash is king."

5 Never Give Up

In the late 1980s Mary Ella Gabler made one of the toughest decisions in her professional life. Should she give up, get out, and try something else, or should she sink her life savings into her dream and hope for the best? Gabler, who in 1964 was one of the first women to work on Wall Street and had seen her share of successes and failures, made the decision to stick it out.

"All of Texas had a big downturn in the economy in the late '80s, and I was right in it," says Gabler, who started the fine-linen company Peacock Alley 27 years ago in Dallas. "It was a great lesson in not giving up. I came very close to quitting." When the bank foreclosed on her note, Gabler, a single mother of two small children at the time, believed in herself and her business and decided to use her savings to retire the debt and keep the business afloat.

Now, she has retail stores in Dallas, New York City, and Los Angeles, 31 instore boutiques across the country, 105 employees, $20 million in annual sales, and celebrity clients such as Kathie Lee Gifford, John Travolta, and Jimmy Buffet. Even Pope John Paul II sleeps on Peacock Alley's solo white sheets.

"I don't give up," Gabler says. "If one plan does not work I always try to find a plan B. I have a desire to achieve and have confidence in my decisions. I figured I was better than the competition, and I would persevere. It takes a toll on you and you do have setbacks, but you keep going forward."

Gabler grew up in an entrepreneurial family. Her father and his three brothers owned and ran a furniture store in Chambersburg, Pa. "Seeing their success was inspirational to me," she says. "It was a wonderful combination of family and business ethics."

Gabler also recommends spending money on professional strategic planing. "That is absolutely critical for a growing company. It is something you cannot afford *not* to do."

The Greatest Entrepreneurs of All Time

To compile our top 30, we sought the selections of professors and authors, whose criteria included mass commerce and distribution of wealth.

JOHN TOZZI

Who are the greatest entrepreneurs of all time? We could spend a lifetime compiling a list without ever agreeing on who deserves a mention. From the pirates of Silicon Valley to the captains of industry, there are far too many figures to choose from to give anyone the final say.

In other words, we acknowledge our list's inherent subjectivity. To compile it, we picked the brains of professors, authors, and *BusinessWeek* staffers. Our criteria for entrepreneurs to be considered among the greatest was simple. If they had the vision to create new markets or tap into underserved markets, changing the way people lived in the process, then they were candidates on a list we whittled down to 30 players.

More than Just Wealth

Some founders won recognition not just for their companies' success, but for what they did with the wealth they accumulated. For Jeff Cornwall, director of the Center for Entrepreneurship at Belmont University, entrepreneurs-turned-philanthropists like Andrew Carnegie and Bill Gates made the top of his list.

"Look at entrepreneurs who had a profound impact that goes beyond just raw business success, as we often define it on Wall Street," says Cornwall, whose book on the subject, *The Good Entrepreneur* (Regal), will be published next year. "The great ones to me are the ones that understood they were building more than just that wealth."

Many of the pioneers we chose also created businesses that in turn encouraged others to start their own enterprises. Microloans from Muhammad Yunus' Grameen Bank have helped thousands of poor Bangladeshi women lift themselves from destitution (see BusinessWeek.com, 10/13/06, "What the Nobel Means for Microcredit"). And how many businesses has Pierre Omidyar's eBay (EBAY) made possible? "He wants to encourage free enterprise around the world," Cornwall said. (See BusinessWeek.com, 6/21/07, "Axe the SBA.")

Popular Transformation

Todd Buchholz, author of *New Ideas from Dead CEOs* (Collins, 2007), says the founders on his list distinguished themselves by a belief in "the democratization of commerce."

"The 20th century, socially and economically, was about more people participating in a large way," says Buchholz. Ray Kroc, for example, made many of his McDonald's (MCD) franchisees rich before him. Sam Walton created the world's largest retailer in Wal-Mart Stores (WMT) by giving customers the world's lowest prices. "A theme that goes through many of the stories that I chose is kind of betting on the masses." (See BusinessWeek.com, 6/6/07, "Book Views: Todd Buchholz").

Above all, the entrepreneurs we chose transformed their times. Admiral Zheng He created a vast trade empire for China during the Ming Dynasty. Henry Ford brought the car to the mass market.

And Gates, Steve Jobs, and Andy Grove ushered in the information age. "All three of them played key roles in putting computers on everybody's desks and now in everybody's pockets," says Richard Tedlow, a Harvard Business School professor and Grove biographer. "That's why you have one on your desk right this minute."

So, who are the 30 greatest entrepreneurs of all time? Click through *BusinessWeek*'s slide show to find out.

Join a debate about whether SBA loans should continue.

JOHN TOZZI is an intern for BusinessWeek.com.

The Secrets of Serial Success

How some entrepreneurs manage to score big again and again and . . .

GWENDOLYN BOUNDS, KELLY K. SPORS, AND RAYMUND FLANDEZ

Five years ago, Tom Scott and Tom First realized they would never have to work again. Friends from college, the pair had launched a juice brand called Nantucket Nectars from the back of their island boat and catapulted themselves—the self-dubbed "juice guys"—into the stuff of entrepreneurial legend as their beverage took off nationwide.

Factoring isn't for everybody. But for companies that need cash quickly—or don't want to hassle with banks—it's one way to go. Plus, new online services offer small businesses an affordable opportunity to advertise on television.

They sold a majority of their company to Ocean Spray Cranberries Inc., and when Cadbury Schweppes PLC later bought the entire business for an estimated $100 million in March of 2002, both men were set for retirement—and they were only in their mid-30s.

But there was no retiring in their futures. Today Messrs. Scott and First are both deep into new ventures that, for now at least, appear headed for success. Mr. Scott leads Plum TV, a New York-based company that operates local television channels in historic, affluent markets such as Aspen, Nantucket and Martha's Vineyard, and has had notable investors including Starwood Capital Group CEO Barry Sternlicht, singer Jimmy Buffett and former Viacom CEO Tom Freston.

Mr. First is in the midst of a new start-up: O Beverages LLC, in Cambridge, Mass., which markets a line of naturally flavored waters already sold in nearly 20 states through Safeway, Balducci's and Bristol Farms, among other stores. In between Nantucket Nectars and their current ventures, the two men started a beverage-distribution-software company that was sold to a publicly traded technology company.

"I'm a crazy competitive person, so there's no way I'm stopping," Mr. First says. "I like being in the trenches."

Call them serial-preneurs. While some entrepreneurs struggle their whole lives to bring one idea or product to market, there's another breed: those who do it once, twice or three times more, disproving the notion of beginner's luck. In some cases, the brands and people are household names, such as Steve Jobs with Apple, Pixar and NeXT. But the ranks also are populated with lesser-known entrepreneurs who fly under the radar, hitting one start-up home run after the other.

"I really believe that some people are kind of entrepreneurial adrenaline freaks," says Wayne Stewart, a management professor at Clemson University in Clemson, S.C. "They really get their kicks by starting businesses."

In 2000, Mr. Stewart published a study with two other researchers looking for common traits among serial entrepreneurs—which he defined as those who had owned and operated three or more businesses. Of the 664 entrepreneurs studied, only 12% fit the bill. But those who did scored higher in all three categories examined: They had a higher propensity for risk, innovation and achievement. They were less scared of failure. And they were more able to recover when they did fail.

Beyond that, many serial-preneurs bring tactical advantages from their first venture to apply the second and third time around. For instance, they recruit top talent from their original companies to subsequent ventures. They double-dip financially, getting money—and connections—from people who backed their earlier brainstorms. Several lean heavily on a trusted partner for financial, professional and emotional support in whatever endeavor they undertake.

More than anything, however, the greatest, and more crucial, challenge among repeat entrepreneurs is figuring out how to rekindle for future ventures the innocence, love and hunger that fueled their first enterprise. Despite hitting it big early with Nantucket Nectars, Messrs. First and Scott both struggled after the sale to find a business that inspired them as much as being the juice guys.

"A lot of the drive early on was the drive to not have to leave Nantucket, or write the résumé, or go do anything else. We were hustlers," says Mr. First. Adds Mr. Scott: "What happened was that while approaching the things we love—boats, water, weather—we stumbled on juice. I've learned from this that it doesn't matter what I'm good at. It matters what I like."

What's the Motivation?

So why do some entrepreneurs who strike gold once continue to start over? A general contractor might launch a business because he has certain skills, and then stick with it until retirement. Or a banker will work her way up the corporate ladder, happy with the security of a paycheck and benefits, and retire once she has saved enough. By contrast, serial entrepreneurs' main job is the act of creation—and thus they keep creating new businesses, often after they no longer need the paycheck.

"Most people can't understand why someone who made $10 million would do it again," says Seth Godin, who founded Yoyodyne, an interactive direct-marketing company bought by Yahoo in late 1998. He's now running a new online venture called Squidoo, a free tool that lets users build Web pages about any topic within a searchable community. "That's because most people don't like working, and they think it's irrational to keep working," he says. "But most entrepreneurs don't care about money; it's a tool."

For instance, Scott Jones was a multimillionaire by age 30, having co-founded the company Boston Technology, maker of a voice-mail system now used by many telephone companies world-wide. He retired, and learned how to fly planes and perform aerobatics, but was quickly bored. So he went back to work and has since co-founded Gracenote Inc., an Internet-accessible music database used by iTunes, as well as a robotic-lawn-mower company and a search engine that uses human guides in real time. Those years not creating, he says, were "the most unhappy years of my life."

Moreover, serial entrepreneurs harbor an unusual appetite for risk—something they can inherit from their parents. Dan Bricklin, 56, has started four companies in his lifetime; his first Software Arts, was sold to Lotus Development Corp. in the mid-1980s. Mr. Bricklin's father was a small-business owner who ran a printing business, as did his grandfather.

Mr. Bricklin, who now runs Software Garden Inc. in Newton Highlands, Mass., says he feeds on the thrill of starting something new and untested. "It's like that sense of walking across a stream on the rocks—sort of knowing where you're going, but sort of not." As for risk? "If you've actually seen the ups and downs of a business, and your family isn't terrified, that makes it a lot easier to do yourself."

Likewise, Tim Miller caught the entrepreneurial bug at age 18 when he received about $500,000 after his father sold a company. Mr. Miller stashed that money away, planning to invest in his own company one day. Fifteen years later, he dipped into the fund to start a software firm called Avitek Inc. based on an idea his then-employer didn't want to explore. Mr. Miller recalls how family members fretted about the danger of going it alone, with his brother specifically questioning his judgment after he hired his fourth employee: How could he possibly put other people's livelihoods on the line?

"But it never truly occurred to me that I would potentially need to let any of them go at any point," Mr. Miller says, adding that he believes successful entrepreneurs "see opportunities where other see risk." He sold Avitek in 1999 for about $13.5 million, without layoffs, and is now running a venture called Rally Software Development Corp., based in Boulder, Colo.

The Value of Teamwork

Mr. Miller didn't succeed alone; he had a partner, Ryan Martens, who now works with him at Rally Software. Their compatibility is an asset whose value Mr. Miller finds hard to quantify. While Mr. Martens as the chief technology officer is deeply invested in software development, Mr. Miller is the business guy. "I think great leaders build teams," Mr. Miller says, "and those teams have some glue and they tend to stick together."

Whether by design or not, on second and third ventures, serials often surround themselves with familiar faces. Partly it's about familiarity and trust. Messrs. Scott and First both tapped ex-Nantucket Nectar employees for their newest ventures. They typically talk to each other several times a week, and Mr. Scott is an investor in O Beverages. "We've never doubted the other's total respect and having the other person's good interest at heart," Mr. First says.

Repeat relationships are also about expediency. Elizabeth Cogswell Baskin has run four companies, including two advertising agencies and a book-packaging operation. Now 46, she's the CEO of Tribe Inc., a $3 million Atlanta advertising agency that works with brands including Porsche, Home Depot and UPS, and peppered throughout Tribe's ranks are faces from her previous companies. "I think it is a huge shortcut to hire someone you already have a relationship with," Ms. Baskin says.

At age 77, Jack Goeken lays claim to having helped start a string of well-known enterprises: MCI, InFlight Phone, Airfone and several others. Now, he's deeply involved in a new start-up, Polybrite International Inc., a Naperville, Ill., company that produces a screw-in LED light bulb that will fit in normal lamps. His daughter Sandra, 49, has worked with him on every venture since MCI, and says one of her father's greatest strengths is "herding tigers"—that is, finding entrepreneurial, and sometimes difficult to manage, individuals who can make a project happen, but then making sure they don't stick around too long.

"A team can come in and do a great start-up and make history, but the team that does that isn't the team to run it for 10 years," Ms. Goeken says. The key, she says, is to let those people know they'll be taken care of after a sale, so they don't hold a company's progress back worrying about a job. Bringing them on in the next venture is one inducement. Plus, she says, "they are a known entity and you take the risk out of the equation."

There are drawbacks to repeat employees. Mr. Godin, for one, believes the strategy can inhibit a fresh start. "One good thing is 'beginner's mind'—people looking at something for the first time often have a fresh insight," he says. Plus, new businesses have different needs. At his first start-up, Yoyodyne, he says his team worked 21 hours a day in "emergency mode"—a pattern he didn't want to repeat. "If I put the whole team together again, I don't know if we could have worked in anything but emergency mode."

More Money, Please

By contrast, hitting up the same investors, Mr. Godin believes, is almost always smart—particularly if you made them money the first go-around. "They are doing everything on trust," he says.

David Neeleman, the founder of JetBlue Airways Corp., says treating investors fairly and staying close to them between ventures is critical—as is giving them an opportunity to invest in subsequent ventures. In fact, he says, all of JetBlue's investors, except George Soros, had been investors in his first airline, Morris

Air. "I just went back to the investors of Morris Air and said, 'Do you want to do it again?' " He raised $90 million for JetBlue from his old investors and $40 million from Mr. Soros. Mr. Neeleman stepped down as JetBlue's CEO earlier this year after a series of high-profile flight cancellations, though he remains chairman.

What's more, serial entrepreneurs find many of the contacts, and information, they pick up with early ventures can pay off down the road. They court vendors, customers, trade groups, chambers of commerce—even if they don't need them right away. While working in earlier ventures for her father, Ms. Goeken often spent weekends in foreign countries instead of going home, inviting business contacts to dinner. For many years, she mailed 1,400 Christmas cards all over the world, learned about different religions and picked the brains of partners' low-level employees about their country's customs.

"It may not be that important to you right now, but they might have something to teach you," she says. "I'd invest more than just getting the deal done. And time and time again, I went back to the same people in new ventures."

A Question of Desire

One of the hardest tasks serial entrepreneurs face is recapturing the drive and direction that fueled their first venture, without letting the first success overshadow or dictate what they do next. Sometimes, it's as simple as learning to let go. Says Ms. Goeken: "Walking out of Airfone was the saddest day of my life. When I finally pulled myself together, I never looked back. I don't miss a single company now."

Other times, it isn't so clear-cut. After Nantucket Nectars was sold, the founders started a beverage-distribution-software company because it seemed a natural evolution from being the juice guys. Trouble was, both men hated software, and left before the company was sold.

"I felt like I was turning into a sheep," says Mr. Scott. "I started wondering what I'd do about the rest of my life and was insecure, afraid and slightly depressed." Finally he pushed himself to understand what got him to Nantucket Nectars, and arrived at a rather amorphous answer: passion.

"We were passionate about ice, and pumping out sewage systems on boats; juice was just one of 50 things that we liked," Mr. Scott says. With Plum TV, he loves the civic nature of local TV—even though it's about as far from juice as you can get. "I think the best entrepreneurs are like artists and painters," Mr. Scott says. "It's about creating. It's not about business."

Likewise, his partner, Mr. First, also fumbled at different enterprises, including starting a grocery store, until his wife said to him, "You're bored stiff, aren't you?" That set off a period of his own soul-searching—eventually, leading him full circle. What he loved most, it turned out, was what he had already done: building a consumer-products company. So in early 2005, he launched O, and the first bottles hit the Boston market that spring.

Mr. First concedes that he sometimes feels the burden of re-entering a field he once dominated. Consumers don't pick up O and want to drink it just because Nantucket Nectars was a big hit; he doesn't have the "Tom and Tom" story—he doesn't even have the other Tom.

"I constantly think about how I was the cool guy at Nantucket Nectars, a juice guy," Mr. First says. "I'm risking going back into the same industry and being a loser."

Still, Mr. First says, he's slowly learning to use the previous success to grease wheels where he can: Grocery chains, for instance, believe if he can do it once, he can do it again. The same is true with investors. "It gives me credibility," he says, "and the fight is too tough to leave a weapon in the bag."

Ms. Bounds, *The Wall Street Journal's* small-business news editor in New York, served as contributing editor of this report. **Mr. Flandez** is a staff reporter in the *Journal's* New York bureau and **Ms. Spors** is a staff reporter for the *Journal* in South Brunswick, N.J.

UNIT 2

Creating and Launching a New Business Venture

Unit Selections

Key Points to Consider

- What economic forces are shaping entrepreneurship? Why?

- What is the most exciting aspect of entrepreneurship? What is the most worrisome?

- How can entrepreneurs measure the dimensions of the "window of opportunity"?

- How can entrepreneurs be more successful in planning their startup?

- Which resources are most difficult for entrepreneurs to obtain?

- What marketing research should entrepreneurs use to analyze new opportunities?

- What information should a good business plan contain?

- Why do investors need to see a well-prepared business plan before they invest?

- In what other ways can writing a business plan benefit an entrepreneur?

- Why do some business plans fail?

Student Website

www.mhcls.com

Internet References

Association of University Technology Managers (AUTM)
http://www.autm.net

Business Wire Press Services
http://www.businesswire.com/

Internal Revenue Service
http://www.irs.gov/businesses/small/index.html

National Business Incubation Association (NBIA)
http://www.nbia.org

Tradepub.com
http://www.tradepub.com/

U.S. Department of Labor Statistics: Industry at a Glance
http://www.bls.gov/iag/home.htm

U.S Patents and Trademarks Office
http://www.uspto.gov/

World Intellectual Property Organization (WIPO)
http://www.wipo.int/

Yahoo! Industry Center
http://biz.yahoo.com/ic/index.html

YouNoodle
http://younoodle.com/

Entrepreneurs see opportunity where others see risks. They generate lots of ideas as they pursue business opportunities. But for professional or "serial" entrepreneurs with eyes on limited resources, and knowing how difficult it is to raise venture capital, launching a new business means more than just "scratching the cerebral itch." Very seldom do they act on impulse. Experts say that an entrepreneur can never be too prepared—screening out unpromising ventures requires a methodology based on experience, judgment, and internal reflection, but not always upon mounds of new data. With a little insight and diligent preparation, people who yearn for their own business can feel confident of forthcoming success or, at the very least, can decide rationally that they should not start one.

The key to creating and starting the new business venture successfully is to look at the window of market opportunity, create and fit the new business strategy, and then measure the appropriate risk, considering whether or not the opportunity fits personal goals and needs. Assessing viability requires analyzing a venture's ability to not only profitably win customers, employees, and resources, but also to secure financing. This unit discusses legal issues entrepreneurs face and creating the business and marketing plans. Subsequent units cover financing issues and managing rapid growth.

The opportunity should be based on a distinct "competitive advantage" that creates a "barrier to entry," preventing others from following. A competitive advantage may be based on an invention, unique "intellectual property" like software code, or the entrepreneur may be a "domain expert" having unique insight about solving a particular problem in a sector of a large industry. In fact, 60 percent of the *Inc.* 500 CEOs say that the idea for their company came from working in the same industry. No venture will have the resources or ability to compete against all competitors and should not attempt to do so. Instead, an entrepreneur should target a few key competitors and act to ensure success against them. The opportunity should be a niche with potential for plenty of growth and high gross margins in order to make sure that the startup has enough capital to achieve long-term viability.

What form should the new business venture take? One of the key issues that an entrepreneur must resolve very early in the entrepreneurial process is what legal form of organization the venture should adopt. Creating the legal entity that best supports the opportunity is almost always a challenge. Each of the forms differs from the others along several dimensions. It is very important that the entrepreneur carefully evaluate the pros and cons of the various legal forms when organizing the new venture. This requires the entrepreneur to determine the priority of each of the factors mentioned in this unit. Variations, and their advantages and disadvantages, are numerous. Finally, these decisions about the legal entity must be made prior to the submission of a business plan and the request for venture capital, loans, lines of credit, and joint ventures.

Successful entrepreneurs don't take risks blindly. They carefully craft strategies that work. But still, reports indicate that 90% of the small businesses don't have a business plan or business strategy. Some claim that they lack the time and money

© Royalty-Free/Corbis

to research business opportunities. Others indicate that they don't understand the value of strategic planning and consider it a waste of time. But all are in a race with time because by the time an opportunity is investigated fully, they know that it may no longer exist. If done wisely though, strategic planning can help entrepreneurs reach a higher level of success in their ventures.

Few areas of entrepreneurship attract as much attention as the business plan. Professional entrepreneurs, advisers, and consultants, as well as educators know that writing a business plan is part art and part science. The business plan is probably the single most important document to any entrepreneur at the startup stage because it is the preferred mode of communication between entrepreneurs and potential investors and becomes a selling document that conveys its excitement and promise to any potential investor or stakeholder.

Preparing a business plan that needs to both guide the growth of the new venture and to attract interest from outside stakeholders requires a great amount of skill, time, and analysis. A well-prepared business plan is used internally to help the venture team decide what choices are to be made about startup costs and to help figure out how the venture will be managed. Most importantly, the plan should help the team to identify the resources required to pursue the opportunity, explain how the team will bootstrap itself to gather the resources required, and, finally, propose methodologies for controlling and allocating such critical capital resources. A business plan can also be used externally for raising financing. The plan should be able to convince and communicate to investors that the new venture has identified an opportunity and that the venture team has the entrepreneurial talent to exploit that opportunity and the management skills for achieving positive cash flow targets on time.

Finally, the selection of stakeholders and organizational structure for any business venture requires some major decisions that will affect long-term effectiveness and profitability. When it comes to successful entrepreneurs and entrepreneurial teams, most investors will agree that they prefer a grade A entrepreneur with a grade B business idea to a grade B entrepreneur with a grade A idea. In other words, they prefer to bet on the jockey and not the horse. Since no one individual can possess all the attributes that venture capitalists and academics say are important for success, it is generally a strong entrepreneurial management team, not a lone entrepreneur, that investors will back. Regardless of how great the opportunity may seem to be, it will not become a successful venture unless it is developed by a venture team with strong entrepreneurial and management skills.

Startups in a Downturn

Entrepreneurs who helped build their startups into tech stalwarts—companies like Cisco, Oracle, and Google—share lessons on how to thrive during tough times.

SPENCER E. ANTE

December 1987 was no time to be raising money for a startup. Computer engineer Len Bosack was trying to attract funding for a young enterprise called Cisco Systems (CSCO). But the stock market had just crashed and the Dow Jones industrial average had plummeted 40% since October. Gun-shy venture capitalists either didn't get the new-fangled technology or deemed it too risky.

Making matters worse, Bosack was running low on the savings he had used to bootstrap the business, and competition was gaining steam. It wasn't until this 75th meeting that he found a receptive audience. The willing financier was Donald Valentine of Sequoia Capital, a venture capital firm in Silicon Valley. On Dec. 14, two months after Black Monday, Sequoia invested $2.5 million in Cisco. "Valentine's reasoning was pretty simple," recalls Bosack, now CEO of telecom gear-maker XKL. "It doesn't matter what they are. They are selling stuff in a bad market. With a little bit of capital and more experienced help they should be able to do better."

Better is just what Cisco did. By the time of its initial share sale three years later, in February 1990—during a recession—the maker of telecom networking equipment was worth $224 million. Within a decade, Cisco Systems had become one of the world's most valuable companies.

Greatness Can Emerge from a Slump

Today, some of America's sharpest financiers and entrepreneurs say Cisco's story holds a profound lesson easily forgotten amid financial turmoil: Great companies can be built during tough times. "For us, Cisco is always the company we think of when we think about bad times," says Michael Moritz, a general partner with Sequoia Capital who was a young associate when the firm made its investment.

Cisco is just one example. In the history of technology, many other great companies either were founded during downturns or forged business models during bad times. In 1939, at the tail end of the Great Depression, two engineers started Hewlett-Packard (HPQ) in a garage in northern California. During the recession of 1957, Digital Equipment, the first computer company to challenge IBM (IBM), set up shop in a Civil War-era wool mill, sparking a high-tech boom in Massachusetts. "It makes sense to do research and development counter-cyclically," says Tom Nicholas, associate professor in the Entrepreneurial Management Group of Harvard Business School. "Recessions can be really useful strategic opportunities."

Entrepreneurs, financiers, and historians point to several reasons for this phenomenon. For starters, everything is cheaper during a downturn, including the cost of labor, materials, and office space. There's less competition, both from incumbents that are trying to put out their own fires and from startups that find it harder to raise money. And the tough times force entrepreneurs to work on their business models earlier, so they end up reaching profitability more quickly than when money comes cheap. "The companies are tougher because they were tested during a tougher time," says Carl Schramm, president of the Kauffman Foundation, an organization that promotes entrepreneurship.

In fact, Silicon Valley itself was largely created during the nasty recession of the mid-1970s. During that decade, entrepreneurs and financiers built companies that pioneered three entirely new industries: video games through Atari, personal computers with Apple (AAPL), and biotechnology thanks to Genentech (DNA).

Find Your Passion

Talk to the entrepreneurs who built great companies during bad times, and they'll tell you there are a number of lessons that help explain their success. Atop the list: Founders of the most successful companies are motivated less by the lure of riches than the dream to solve an important problem and benefit the world. As a young, self-taught computer engineer, Mitch Kapor saw an opportunity in the early 1980s, another recessionary period, to create software tools for personal computers that would help businesses be more productive. So in 1982 he founded his own software company called Lotus.

The startup was an immediate hit because it was the first software program to demonstrate the value of a personal computer to the business world. During an October 1982 conference, Kapor showed off his initial product, Lotus 1-2-3, the first software tool to integrate spreadsheets and graphing programs. After taking $900,000 in orders during the conference, he had to tear up all of his sales forecasts. "It was one of the biggest shocks of my life," he recalls. "It turned out there was an enormous latent demand for what we did."

Kapor also noticed that market leaders such as Microsoft (MSFT) had taken their eyes off the ball. In 1981, IBM had introduced its first PC with a 16-bit microprocessor. Microsoft, contracted to provide the operating system for IBM, was also building a spreadsheet, but it was based on code built for machines with slower, 8-bit processors. Kapor realized Microsoft had left him an opening. He set about creating spreadsheet software tailored to the new chips. In 1983, its first full year of business, Lotus sold an astonishing $53 million in software. "If a product meets an unmet need, it doesn't matter if the economy is bad," Kapor says.

Cater to Your Market

Another key lesson is to pick markets strategically, says Umang Gupta, who joined database maker Oracle (ORCL) in 1980 as employee No. 17 and wrote its first business plan. Ultimately, the company wanted to build a database program that would work with multiple types of computers, from minicomputers to PCs to mainframes, those hulking machines that crunched massive amounts of data. But Oracle couldn't do it all at once. It started out creating a database that worked on minicomputers such as Digital Equipment's PDP-11. Then Oracle methodically went upstream, pursuing mainframes next, rather than going for mainframes and PCs at the same time. "We concentrated our bets," says Gupta, now CEO of Internet measurement firm Keynote (KEYN). "We built a culture of an extremely focused, aggressive company."

For some companies, it may be tempting to slough off belt-tightening customers loath to place new orders amid a slump. Bad move, financiers say. The best companies go the extra mile during a cold spell, engendering goodwill that pays off when the economy bounces back and companies have more money to spend.

At Cisco, Bosack launched a customer advocacy group, one of whose jobs was to help customers design their computer networks before they spent even one penny with the company. Employees would spend weeks holed up in the basements of customer offices fixing the glitches that popped up. "We were

happy to help," Bosack says. "We didn't expect a big order . . . People sell products today and abandon their customers. It's bad business."

Embrace Frugality

Almost all great companies built during bad times also learn how to run extremely efficiently. Workers wear multiple hats, buy used furniture, and look for any way to cut costs. Tales of frugality are legendary in the tech industry. At the headquarters of Digital Equipment, the company's founders didn't even go to a garage sale. They appropriated desks that had been left by the previous tenants, and they didn't install doors, even in bathrooms, because they cost too much.

But while companies need to watch their bottom line, downturns also present an excellent opportunity to hire high-quality labor on the cheap. A lot of good talent gets laid off during downturns, and workers are more open to joining new companies since there are fewer jobs to be had in big corporations.

After the dot-com bust early this decade, Google (GOOG) took huge advantage of the surfeit of talent. At the end of 2001, Google had 281 full-time employees. By the end of 2004, the number had swelled to more than 3,000. Those employees, many of whom Google poached from big rivals such as IBM and Microsoft, allowed Google to handle and generate explosive growth. In 2001, Google earned $7 million on $86 million in sales; by the end of 2004, Google reaped $399 million in profit from $3.2 billion in sales. "When I joined Google we were the only place hiring," says Sheryl Sandberg, a former executive at Google who is now the chief operating officer of Facebook.

There's Room for Optimism

Today, when venture capitalist Moritz surveys the economy, he admits times are sobering. It was his venture capital firm that spooked the entire tech industry with a presentation, leaked on the Web, that was titled "RIP: Good Times" and detailed for startups the gloomy state of the economy. As he and others have noted, selling anything in this economy is more of a challenge. And it's harder than ever to raise money because the IPO market is dead and mergers have dried up.

Moritz nevertheless sees a lot of opportunity, and says great companies will emerge from this downturn, just as they have in the past. "Things get overblown in the Valley," he says. "As the obituaries are currently being penned, those are overstated, too. Good ideas and brilliant people will find us very willing to step out into the cold with them. It's as easy for me to be excited today by the unknown 23-year-olds as I was in the past."

ANTE is an associate editor for *BusinessWeek*.

So, You Want to Be an Entrepreneur?

First, answer these questions to see if you have what it takes.

KELLY K. SPORS

Thinking about starting a business? Make sure you're cut out for it first.

In this bleak economy, lots of people are contemplating striking out on their own—whether they're frustrated job seekers or people who are already employed but getting antsy about their company's prospects.

For some people, entrepreneurship is the best option around, a way to build wealth and do something you love without answering to somebody else. But it's also a huge financial gamble—and some people, unfortunately, will discover too late that it's not the right fit for them.

Building a successful business can take years filled with setbacks, long hours and little reward. Certain personalities thrive on the challenge and embrace the sacrifices. But it can be a hard switch for someone who has spent years sitting in a cubicle with a steady paycheck.

So, how can you figure out whether you're suited for self-employment? We spoke with entrepreneurship researchers, academics and psychologists to come up with a list of questions you should ask yourself before making a big leap. Entrepreneurs, of course, come from all sorts of backgrounds, with all sorts of personalities. But our experts agreed that certain attributes improve the odds people will be successful and happy about their decision.

Keep in mind that any self-analysis is only as useful as the truthfulness of the answers—and most people aren't exactly the best judges of their own character. So, you might enlist a friend's help.

Here, then, are 10 questions to ask to see whether you're up for the challenge of entrepreneurship.

1. Are You Willing and Able to Bear Great Financial Risk?

Roughly half of all start-ups close within five years, so you must be realistic about the financial risks that come with owning a business—and realize that you could very well lose a sizable chunk of your net worth.

Consider how much you'll have to ante up and how losing it would affect your other financial goals, such as having a sound retirement or paying your kids' college tuition. Weigh the importance of starting a business against the sacrifices you might face.

Entrepreneurs should be sure that "if they lose this capital, it either won't destroy their financial situation, or they can accept the concept of bankruptcy," says Scott Shane, an entrepreneurship professor at Case Western Reserve University in Cleveland. "Some people thrive on the financial risk; others are devastated by the thought of losing even $10,000."

And don't assume you'll be able to lower your risk substantially by finding investors. Less than 10% of start-up financing comes from venture capitalists, angel investors and loans from friends and family combined, Prof. Shane says. And that's true even in *good* economic times. Banks, meanwhile, often won't lend to start-up founders without a proven track record. When they do, they generally require the founders to guarantee the loan or credit line with their personal savings or home—an incredibly risky proposition. (To learn how to mitigate risk by keeping your old job while starting a new venture, see "A Toe in the Water".)

2. Are You Willing to Sacrifice your Lifestyle for Potentially Many Years?

If you're used to steady paychecks, four weeks' paid vacation and employer-sponsored health benefits, you might be in for an unpleasant surprise.

Creating a successful start-up often entails putting in workweeks of 60 hours or more and funneling any revenue you can spare back into the business. Entrepreneurs frequently won't pay themselves a livable salary in the early years and will forgo real vacations until their business is financially sound. That can often take eight years or longer, says William Bygrave, a professor emeritus of entrepreneurship at Babson College in Wellesley, Mass.

Even if you can steal away, it's hard to find somebody who can fill in for you. Many entrepreneurs must tow along their cellphone and laptop, so they can be available to answer questions from clients or employees.

Jennifer Walzer learned those lessons the hard way. In 2002, after being laid off from a $100,000 consulting job when the company closed, she started Backup My Info! Inc., which sells online data-backup services to businesses.

For the first year, the New York-based company brought in just $29,000 in gross revenue. Ms. Walzer didn't pay herself a salary until the third year, and even then it was a slim $30,000. She could have taken more out, but she wanted to shovel as much money into the business as possible to keep it financially sound.

Having no income for two years meant that Ms. Walzer had to be extremely frugal; she virtually never ate out or went on vacations or clothes-shopping trips. Twenty-nine years old at the time, she says, "I got very jealous of my girlfriends who got home at 5 o'clock every night and could go out gallivanting and pretty much do whatever they pleased." She'd occasionally meet friends for coffee instead of drinks, since coffee was less expensive.

Now that her business generates about $2 million in annual revenue, the tables have turned. Ms. Walzer says she earns more from the business than she did as a consultant, and "I have friends who are struggling to keep their jobs because they have bosses."

3. Is Your Significant Other on Board?

Don't ignore the toll running a business will take on your loved ones. Failed ventures frequently break up marriages, and even successful ones can cause lots of stress, because entrepreneurs devote so much time and money to the business.

"I'm always surprised at the number of husbands who start a business and don't tell their wives," says Bo Fishback, vice president of entrepreneurship at the Ewing Marion Kauffman Foundation.

You can avoid the heartache by talking at length with your spouse and family about how the business will affect home life, including the time commitment, changes in daily schedules and chores, financial risks and sacrifices. They must also understand the huge financial gamble they're making with you.

4. Do You Like all Aspects of Running a Business?

You better. In the early stages of a business, founders are often expected to handle everything from billing customers to hiring employees to writing marketing materials. Some new entrepreneurs become annoyed that they're spending the majority of their time on administration when they'd rather be focused on the part of the job they enjoy, says Donna Ettenson, vice president of the Association of Small Business Development Centers in Burke, Va.

"All of a sudden, they have to think about all these things they never had to think about before," she says.

Jeromy Stallings, the 33-year-old founder of Ninthlink Inc., a San Diego interactive-marketing firm with 15 employees, always felt he had plenty of passion for entrepreneurship and self-motivation. But when starting his agency in 2003 and hiring his first couple of employees, he realized he wasn't prepared for the day-to-day challenges of managing other people.

Mr. Stallings had assumed his passion would rub off on employees and they would do their jobs as enthusiastically as he did. But some clients started calling him directly, complaining that his employees weren't returning phone calls or that projects were behind schedule.

"My clients were saying, 'We love your passion, we love your skill, we're just having a really hard time with your management style,'" he says.

So, Mr. Stallings turned to peers, mentors and guidebooks for help. He realized he needed to work more closely with employees and create a more structured project-management system. "I didn't really have a plan in place for how they spend their time," he says.

5. Are You Comfortable Making Decisions on the Fly with no Playbook?

With a new business, you're calling all the shots—and there are a lot of decisions to be made without any guidance. You might not be used to that if you've spent years working in corporate America, says Bill Wagner, author of *The Entrepreneur Next Door,* a book that lays out the characteristics of successful entrepreneurs.

"For most entrepreneurial ventures, there's no structure," he says. "You're going into a business, and nobody has told you how to be successful."

Mr. Wagner has surveyed more than 10,000 entrepreneurs to find out what traits distinguish successful start-up founders from less-successful ones. Among other things, most entrepreneurs he interviewed said they liked making decisions. He doesn't rule out the idea that less-decisive people could become better at the leadership role. It's just that they will have to work a lot harder at it.

6. What's Your Track Record of Executing Your Ideas?

One of the biggest differences between successful entrepreneurs and everyone else is their ability to implement their ideas, says Prof. Bygrave of Babson College. You might have a wonderful concept, but that doesn't mean you possess that special mix of drive, persuasiveness, leadership skills and keen intuition to actually turn the idea into a lucrative business.

So, examine your past objectively to see whether you have assumed leadership roles or initiated solo projects—anything that might suggest you're good at executing ideas. "Were you senior class president? Did you play varsity sports?" Prof. Bygrave suggests asking.

You might even find clues back in your childhood, he adds: "A lot of successful entrepreneurs were starting businesses when they were still kids."

7. How Persuasive and Well-Spoken are You?

Nearly every step of the way, entrepreneurship relies on selling. You'll have to sell your idea to lenders or investors. You must sell your mission and vision to your employees. And you'll ultimately have to sell your product or service to your customers. You'll need strong communication and interpersonal skills so you can get people to believe in your vision as much as you do.

If you don't think you're very convincing or have difficulty communicating your ideas, you might want to reconsider starting your own company—or think about getting some help.

In 2007, Brad Price left a $135,000-a-year job as an associate at a Baltimore law firm to purchase a PuroClean Emergency Restoration Services franchise, which cleans up property damage such as mold and flooded basements. A former Naval officer, Mr. Price felt he was very self-motivated and a good leader. But he was less comfortable cold-calling and striking deals—something he'd never had to do in previous jobs.

"There's a big difference in waiting for the phone to ring and getting an assignment and having to make the phone ring," says the 33-year-old Mr. Price.

Mr. Price says he now has his wife handle the marketing and networking. "My wife is very good at that, 'Hey, next time a call comes in, how about you give it to us?' " he says.

8. Do You have a Concept You're Passionate about?

Every morning you want to jump out of bed eager to get to work. If you're not that exuberant about how you'll be spending your time—or the business concept itself—running a business is going to be a rough ride.

Ms. Ettenson of the Association of Small Business Development Centers has coached many prospective entrepreneurs about their chosen business. She always asks why they're doing it. If they suggest it's mostly for the prospect of making a lot of money or because they're tired of working for someone else, she steers them toward something more in line with their interests or avoiding self-employment altogether.

"If you hate doing paperwork, the last thing you want to do is become a bookkeeper," Ms. Ettenson says. "If you'd rather be outside taking people into the wilderness, then that's the type of business you should be in."

But it's also usually wise to find a business in an industry you are very familiar with; it will be much harder to succeed if you know little about the field. Mr. Fishback at Kauffman says he has steered a doctor and other professionals away from starting restaurants because they often don't grasp how difficult and risky restaurant ownership is. And they'd be competing against restaurateurs with years of experience.

9. Are You a Self-Starter?

Entrepreneurs face lots of discouragement. Potential buyers don't return calls, business sours or you face repeated rejection. It takes willpower and an almost unwavering optimism to overcome these constant obstacles.

John Gartner, an assistant clinical-psychiatry professor at Johns Hopkins University and author of the book *The Hypomaniac Edge,* theorizes that many well-known entrepreneurs have a temperament called hypomania. They're highly creative, energetic, impatient and very persistent—traits that help them persevere even when others lose faith.

"One of the things about having this kind of confidence is they're kind of risk-blind because they don't think they could fail," Prof. Gartner says. And, he adds, "if they fail, they're not down for that long, and after a while they're energized by a whole new idea."

You don't have to be as driven as, say, Steve Jobs to succeed. But somebody who gets deterred easily, or too upset when things go wrong, won't last.

10. Do You have a Business Partner?

If you don't have all the traits you need to run the show, it's not necessarily a hopeless endeavor. Finding a business partner who compensates for your shortcomings—and has equal enthusiasm for the business concept—can help mitigate the risks and even boost the odds of success.

David Gage, co-founder of BMC Associates, an Arlington, Va., business-mediation practice, points to a Marquette University study of 2,000 businesses. The researchers found that partner-run businesses are far more likely to become high-growth ventures than those started by solo entrepreneurs.

The key, Mr. Gage says, is finding a partner who prefers handling different aspects of the business, so you're complementing each other—and not constantly at each other's throats.

Someone who likes to take risks and be in the spotlight, for instance, might choose a cautious partner who prefers to work in the back room. "If they're willing to work with that person, and not just look at them as a wet blanket, then it can be great," Mr. Gage says.

But taking on a partner isn't a light decision. Many partnerships split due to conflicts over everything from attitudes about money to miscommunication and contrasting work ethics. Mr. Gage recommends that potential partners spend several days hashing out the specifics of the business and how the arrangement will work to see if they're compatible.

Ms. Spors is a staff reporter of *The Wall Street Journal* in Minneapolis. E-mail: kelly.spors@wsj.com

The B!g Idea

Entrepreneurs reveal their eureka moments—and how they turned a burst of inspiration into a business.

JOAN RAYMOND

Walt Disney was at a local carnival with his grandkids when he was inspired to create Disneyland. A cold winter day of skating in Farmington, Me., got Chester Greenwood thinking up earmuffs. And Bill Bowerman saw in his morning waffles the design for the Nike (**NKE**) Waffle running shoe.

Eureka moments—those sudden bursts of inspiration—can happen anywhere. But for most of us, they come when we step out of our routine and go someplace different, someplace special. Children seem to know instinctively the importance of having a special place to sort out their thinking. When I was a child, mine was the woods behind our house, which at various times hosted a castle, a fort, a spaceship—in reality, a couple of pieces of plywood and some two-by-fours nailed together. As a teenager I spent summers leading Boy Scouts on canoe trips. At one of the camping areas was a set of granite rocks where I would sit and think about the world as I watched the sun set. Many years later, sitting beside a lake or ocean at sunset still calms my mind, setting up an opportunity for new connections. For many adults, it's often visiting new places that opens the mind to new ideas.

Most of us spend our days working in dim offices, so it's no surprise that many entrepreneurs find insight outdoors. Disney believed so much in the power of sunlight to kick-start creativity that he designed his animation studios to leverage natural light.

Recent research backs him up: A study of more than 21,000 students found that children in classrooms with the most daylight learned 20% to 26% faster than those whose classrooms got the least light. Even math and reading scores on standardized tests increased significantly.

No matter where you are, the key to inspiration is to relax. A rested mind makes fresh connections that are obvious in retrospect but hard to see during our overworked, overstressed lives. Millions of people have enjoyed the fresh smell of pine or briny ocean air. But Mark Peltier, one of the entrepreneurs featured on the pages that follow, turned that appreciation into a business that takes the scents of the outdoors indoors. Millions of adults have attended awkward networking events, but Tom Jaffee thought about those uncomfortable moments in an innovative way and built a new kind of events management business.

You can't force eureka moments, but you can increase their odds of happening by preparing your mind. Cram your cranium with your problems, challenges, ideas, and insights. Then relax and let your mind work. But don't forget to listen. Be conscious of your thoughts, so that when inspiration does strike, you can grab the idea and run with it.

The last step is the hardest. Ideas are everywhere. What's rare is the courage and conviction to act on them. In the end, creativity means the audacity to believe in yourself and your ideas.

How to Build a Bulletproof Startup

Got a great idea? There's never been a better time to turn it into a great company. Here's a 16-step guide to help you do it right.

MICHAEL V. COPELAND AND OM MALIK

It's the spring of 2006, and the sweet scent of entrepreneurship is in the air. Growing numbers of Americans are pursuing their startup dreams. According to the National Venture Capital Association, seed-level VC funding nearly doubled in 2005. This year, based on current trends, it could double again. In Delaware, the country's incorporation capital, new business formation was up 19 percent last year, the highest one-year growth rate on record.

In other words, there's never been a better time to start your own company. New technologies are creating new business opportunities on the Internet, on mobile phones, in consumer products, and in information services. At the same time, many of these technologies have radically reduced the costs associated with launching a new venture. In the late 1990s, a typical VC-funded startup needed roughly $10 million to amass the infrastructure and staff required to carry the company from its first business plan to its first product launch. Today that cost has been reduced to just $4 million—and in many cases way, way less. The barriers to entry have never been lower.

While birthing a company is easier, succeeding is as difficult as ever. The general rule in the investment community is that only about a third of all startups ever turn a profit. Another third limp along at a break-even level, and the rest end in failure. Top among the reasons young companies fail are problems such as incorrect market focus and misguided executive leadership. With that in mind, we wanted you to have all the benefit of hard-earned experience without having to actually endure the pain of making your own mistakes. We spoke to dozens of experts—seasoned entrepreneurs, early-stage investors, venture capitalists, and first-time CEOs—to understand what they've learned about the art of getting a new company off the ground. Then we set out to create a set of blueprints describing just how to do it.

There are no guarantees in the world of entrepreneurship. But there is a right way to go about it, and we've mapped the process out for you here. As for the rest—well, that's entirely up to you. You can thank us later.

PHASE ONE
Establish a Company ($$$ Required: $15K to $25K)

Your role as a spectator who merely watches as other adventurous souls launch their own startups is about to end. The decisions you make at this early stage of the game will do much to shape the long-term destiny of your venture. Most of all, don't procrastinate. If you don't act on your burst of business insight, someone else surely will.

Tools You'll Need

Whiteboard: Treat it like an incubator for your best thinking. Write. Revise. Erase. Repeat.

Mobile Phone: The one you have is fine, but make sure you've signed up for 1,000 prepaid minutes.

New Credit Card: American Express's Platinum Business offers zero percent interest for six months.

Accounting Software: Nothing fancy for now. QuickBooks Simple Start does the trick for $50.

YOU ARE
HERE

| 1 | 2 | 3 | 4 | 5 | 1 | 2 | 3 | 1 | 2 | 3 | 4 | 1 | 2 | 3 | 4 |

ESTABLISH   PROTOTYPE   BETA   LAUNCH

Step 1

Stress-Test Your Big Idea (Objective: Debug and Perfect Your Business Brainstorm.)

You have a brilliant idea. It's shrewd. It's timely. You think about it so much it keeps you up at night. It might even make you rich. There's just one thing left to do: Make sure it really has legs. The only way to do that is by bouncing your idea off as many people as possible. Friends and family probably can't provide the critical insight you need. Track down at least a dozen people with expertise in the market you intend to enter. You want candor and honesty, not diplomacy. Understanding why your idea is flawed is as useful as knowing that it's pure genius. Many will likely express support, but the real question is this: Would they pay money for your proposed product? Use each conversation to sharpen how you explain what your company will sell—if you can't describe the product clearly and concisely, how can you possibly sell it? Finally, before saying good-bye, always get the name of another person with whom you can discuss your idea.

Words of Wisdom

"People pooh-poohed our idea for more than a year. We took that to mean either we weren't explaining it well or we were dead wrong. Yet the more we studied the problem, the more clear it became that we weren't wrong. What you forget—because you've been living and breathing this idea for so long—is that others may not see what's obvious to you. You need to connect the dots for them. We did that by finding a metaphor that explained what our company would do."

—Gibu Thomas, CEO and
co-founder of personal media
synchronization startup Sharpcast

Step 2

Build Your Founding Team (Objective: Join Forces with Other Execs to Navigate the Challenges Ahead.)

Starting a company isn't just a full-time job; in many cases, it's three full-time jobs. The ideal founding team is a triumvirate that includes an ace technologist, a big strategic thinker, and a dealmaker who focuses on sales and marketing. Although everyone must have relevant industry experience, a good Rolodex, and the willingness to wear many hats, trust and good judgment are the most essential ingredients. Expectations should be clearly laid out, and the founders' financial interests should be mutually aligned. "You need to feel confident that your co-founder will fight for a deal as hard as you would," says Dan Gould, co-founder of online news aggregator Newroo. It's tempting to partner with good friends, but that's not necessarily a pathway to success. In fact, it's dangerous—under the stress of running a business, your friendship will surely be tested and quite possibly destroyed.

Tip
Five Qualities to Look for in a Co-Founder

1. Loyalty to the business idea.
2. Honesty, including the ability to acknowledge errors and mistakes.
3. Versatility to focus on more than one aspect of the company.
4. Connections and the ability to attract talent to the team.
5. Flexibility in the face of changing circumstances.

(continued)

HOW TO BUILD A BULLETPROOF STARTUP

YOU ARE HERE

1 | 2 | 3 | 4 | 5 || 1 | 2 | 3 || 1 | 2 | 3 | 4 || 1 | 2 | 3 | 4

ESTABLISH PROTOTYPE BETA LAUNCH

PHASE ONE *(continued)*

Step 3

Draft a Business Plan (Objective: Map Out the Market and Explain How You Fit in It.)

A business plan is neither a core asset nor a sacred text. It's just a tool to help focus your ideas and a conceptual summary to share with potential investors, advisers, and employees. The business plan sells your vision for the company: why it's viable, why it's better than anything else out there, and why your team has what it takes to make it happen. It should also detail key factors that relate to the company—target markets, goals, product attributes, revenue projections, competitive differentiators, and founders' resumes. Visit the Small Business Administration's website (www.sba.gov) or Bplans.com for an overview of the structure and components of a typical business plan, as well as links to dozens of sample plans. But the most important thing is a well-honed executive summary that's no more than three pages long. Grab the reader's attention by starting with a simple two-sentence description of your company and what it will do. (Rest assured, you'll use those two sentences often.) And no matter what, don't fall in love with your business plan— it'll change many times in the months ahead.

Things to Avoid
Four Common Business Plan Mistakes

1. **Asking potential investors to sign a nondisclosure agreement.** It's a rookie move. Besides, they won't sign anyway.
2. **Spending too much time describing the market.** Instead, provide lots of detail on your strategy to dominate it.
3. **Making wildly optimistic projections and assumptions.** Nothing will get the door slammed in your face faster. Save the hockey sticks for the NHL.
4. **Exaggerating your experience.** They'll eventually learn the truth, and when they do, your credibility will be compromised. Permanently.

Step 4

Play the Name Game (Objective: Give Your Startup a Handle That Works.)

What's in a name? Plenty. It will make a first impression, carry brand equity, and provide a foundation for every marketing effort you'll ever launch. Naming gurus like David Placek of Lexicon Branding argue that startups should look for names that are either simple and easy to understand (like Salesforce.com) or quirky and memorable (like Google). Some names combine the two: Narendra Rocherolle settled on 30Boxes, an easy-to-remember name for his calendaring startup that also alludes to a monthly datebook. But creativity is only part of the naming challenge; there are legal concerns as well. Before you become attached to any name, check the U.S. government's trademark website (www.uspto.gov) to make sure no company serving an overlapping market has staked out a similar moniker. You don't need a lawyer to file a trademark of your own, but the $500 to $700 you'll spend for a professional trademark search—from a company like Thomson CompuMark—is a smart investment before you sign papers that make your name official.

Tip
Become Master of Your Domain

About 30 million new dotcom domain names are registered each month. Which means that coming up with a name for your company and matching it to an available Internet domain is very difficult. Check Instantdomainsearch.com to see what's available. If your preferred domain is in use, you have three choices:

1. **Adapt.** In the Google age, it's not quite as important to get a URL that exactly matches your company name. Come up with a relevant adaptation, like acmewidget .com, instead of just acme.com. The Nameboy.com website generates lists of available permutations.
2. **Buy from a Broker.** Some names are owned by squatters who sell online real estate through brokerage services run by popular domain-name registrars. Prices range from $10 to the tens of thousands. Discounters like GoDaddy.com and 1and1.com offer brokerage services, as do Networks Solutions and Register.com.
3. **Make an Offer.** If your desired name is already in use by an individual, politely inquire about buying it. Tony Conrad, co-founder of search company Sphere, spent months tracking down the owner of Sphere.com, which he then bought in exchange for cash and equity. "The equity was the important part, because it allowed [the former owner] to stay connected to the name," Conrad says. If cash is your only currency, don't over-pay: $25,000 should be your absolute top end.

| 1 | 2 | 3 | 4 | 5 | 1 | 2 | 3 | 1 | 2 | 3 | 4 | 1 | 2 | 3 | 4 |

ESTABLISH · PROTOTYPE · BETA · LAUNCH

Step 5

Incorporate Thyself (Objective: Adopt the Corporate form That's Best for Your Growth Plans.)

Your startup may consist of just a few warm bodies crammed into a living room, but you still need to establish it as a legal entity. A formal corporate structure solidifies the standing of the founders and provides potential investors with the assurances they need to participate in the company's financial evolution. Incorporation also provides tax benefits and all-important liability protection. Hire an experienced lawyer who specializes in setting up startups—many will even defer payment until the first round of financing. If your lawyer likes your business plan, he or she may also become a crucial source for later introductions.

The Fine Print

What's Right for You Inc.

There are three main types of incorporation. Here's how to figure out which is most appropriate.

S Corporation: Fine if you don't plan to raise money from outside angels or VCs. Only one class of stock is allowed. Taxed at a lower rate than larger corporations, but enjoys the same liability benefits.

Limited Liability Company: Functions like an S-corp, but with no outside shareholders. A good choice for professional services firms that don't need to solicit investment. Can be converted to a C-corp later.

C Corporation: Preferred by most medium-size to large companies. Allows for multiple classes of stock (a common requirement for angel and VC investors). Taxation rates for C-corps are higher than for S-corps.

PHASE TWO
Prototype the Product ($$$ Required: $100K to $500K)

A prototype is where the rubber starts to hit the road: It's the first physical embodiment of your business idea, and a tool you'll use to attract the resources you need to grow. Don't confuse a prototype with the final product—a distracting and potentially fatal mistake. Pretty looks aren't important. A good prototype is just a working demonstration that showcases what your product will do. Show your finished prototype to a dozen or so potential customers and investors who can validate your idea, define key features, and guide your product development.

Tools You'll Need

Spec-Document Software: Omni Outliner and Microsoft Visio simplify writing product definitions.

Development Server: Lease one for $300 a month from a Web hosting company like ServerBeach.

Collaboration Tools: Basecamp is a cheap Web-based application for sharing files and documents.

Voip Calling Service: Skype is a free application that lets you make long-distance calls from your PC.

Step 1

Stake out Intellectual Property (Objective: Avoid Infringing on Others' Patents and Secure Some of Your Own.)

Patents and patent law are a major headache for tech and Web-based startups, so you'll want legal guidance. Gordon Davidson, a partner with Fenwick & West in Mountain View, Calif., warns that the most important thing is to avoid falling afoul of a "blocking patent"—one that defies any engineering work-arounds. Just ask Research in Motion, maker of the BlackBerry, how onerous that can be.

(continued)

PHASE TWO (continued)

As you start to share your ideas with outsiders, you also want to protect your intellectual property. For that, consider filing for a provisional patent; it doesn't require the formal claims of a full patent but allows you to lay claim to an idea as "patent pending." Submitting a provisional patent application costs about $200 if you do it yourself, while a full patent application costs $12,000 to $15,000, including legal fees.

The Fine Print

Patent Law 101

The U.S. Patent and Trademark Office will grant a patent to any new and useful process, machine, manufacture, composition of matter, or new and useful improvement thereof. Confused? Just remember there are two main types of patents:

Technology Patents describe and protect how a particular device, mechanism, or software program works—the classic "better mousetrap."

Business Process Patents describe and protect a mechanism for making money and how it interacts with underlying technologies. Amazon.com holds such a patent for its one-click shopping feature.

Step 2

Create an Advisory Board (Objective: Formalize the Network of People Who Can Help You Most.)

Your advisory board is a group of 6 to 12 people who will provide expertise in the industry you hope to tackle, useful connections, potential funding, or (ideally) all three. At this early stage, it makes sense to load the board with people who can provide technical insight about your product, but you'll also want a few startup veterans who can answer questions about running a young company. In exchange for equity in the company—typically 0.1 to 1 percent—you should expect at least four hours a month of their time. Avoid big group meetings; they're inefficient. Instead, bring in specific advisers for task-oriented discussions as needed.

Words of Wisdom

"We wouldn't be here today without the advisers we picked specifically for their expertise in our technology. They led me to my co-founder and CTO and were able to help on technical issues. It doesn't work to bring on general, name-brand technology people as advisers. They end up frustrated that they don't have much to contribute, and though you think they'll impress potential investors, they don't."

—**Munjal Shah,** CEO and co-founder of photo search startup Riya

Step 3

Build Your Prototype (Objective: Take Your Product out For Its First Test-Drive.)

Prototyping is an iterative process. Start simple, with a basic mock-up, artist's rendering, or Photoshop screen shots. Show these to a few potential customers and use their feedback to define the specifications of your working prototype. Hire independent contractors if you need specialized expertise to build or code the thing, but it's best to stay local. You'll be gathering input on a daily basis and making revisions almost as often, so you'll want your contractors nearby—in town, if not under your roof. Keep them close, but be paranoid. Your attorney should draw up confidentiality agreements and noncompete clauses; make all contractors sign them.

Tip

Finding Contract Talent

Design: Scour local schools. The American Institute of Graphic Arts (www.aiga.org) and Creative Hotlist (www.creativehotlist.com) list designers looking for work.

Hardware: If you need help with the electronic, mechanical, or physical configuration of your prototype, try the directory at Coroflot (www.coroflot.com) to find freelance professionals.

Software: You can post jobs to Craigslist, Dice.com, Monster.com, and SimplyHired.com. Marketplaces like Elance, IPswap, and RentACoder match talent with projects.

YOU ARE HERE

| 1 | 2 | 3 | 4 | 5 | 1 | 2 | 3 | **1** | 2 | 3 | 4 | 1 | 2 | 3 | 4 |

ESTABLISH   PROTOTYPE   BETA   LAUNCH

Parts List

Prototyping Essentials

Design And Photo Editing: GIMP is an excellent and free alternative to expensive programs like Adobe Photoshop.

Product Design: QCad is an open-source, 2-D computer-aided design package that sells site licenses for $260.

Collaboration Software: Subversion is an open-source tool for tracking changes in files or code.

Searching for Angels

What to look for in early-stage Investors

The right time to raise the first round of money varies from startup to startup. Some companies—mostly software or Web-based ventures—need little cash to get off the ground. But if you're building a physical product, you'll be looking for funding earlier in the game. That's where angel investors come in: Unlike venture capitalists, who usually wait until a company has a working product, they specialize in early-stage startups.

The main thing to understand is that not all money is the same. Friends and family are a natural place to start, but keep their investments modest to avoid throwing your relationships off balance. Never take investments from anyone who is not a so-called accredited investor—an individual with a net worth of at least $1 million. Remember, it's not just money you want; you also want brainpower, connections, and experience. "You always want at least one heavy hitter in an angel round," says veteran Silicon Valley angel Jeff Clavier. Instead of treating their investment as a loan, some angels may expect a stake in your company, so set aside 10 to 15 percent of your equity to allocate among early-stage investors. Get used to giving away ownership: In a venture-funded startup, the original founders may ultimately retain as little as 5 to 10 percent of the original equity.

PHASE THREE
Develop the Beta Product ($$$ Required: $500K to $1M)

If a prototype is the first manifestation of your big idea, the beta transforms it into a product you might actually sell. The focus here is on usability and design. Your task is to create something so simple, so powerful, and so effective that people beg to become beta testers. As you amass comments and feedback, look for opportunities to simplify production and keep your cost structure lean—that's much harder to do after the product is released.

Tools You'll Need

Enterprise-Level E-Mail: Providers like the Message Center offer hosted exchange service for about $10 a month per user.

Phone Service: A hosted system from M5 Networks costs about $50 a month per extension for unlimited calling.

T-1 Broadband: $500 per month buys you heavy-duty service from a provider such as AT&T, Covad, or Verizon Business.

Feedback Collection: SurveyMonkey is a handy tool for setting up online questionnaires and compiling user comments. Prices start at $20 per month.

Step 1

Start Staffing Up (Objective: Build the Core Team That Will Carry You into the Future.)

You're ready to make some permanent (or semipermanent) hires. For most startups, the bulk of your hiring here will be technical—people who can get your product to beta. Although it's shrewd to source talent globally, your core product-development team should be local. Enthusiasm is a precious commodity; look for people who are excited about your planned product. Hire the best you can afford, but as a general rule, Silicon Valley startups assume a burn-rate cost of $11,000 per person per month.

Tip

Where to Find Workers

Contracting: Part-timers can help get a company started, but director-level staff should be permanent hires. Always visit new overseas contractors to launch the relationship. Nasscom.org provides listings of India's top outsourcing shops. Russoft.org does the same for Eastern Europe.

(continued

HOW TO BUILD A BULLETPROOF STARTUP

YOU ARE HERE

| 1 | 2 | 3 | 4 | 5 | 1 | 2 | 3 | 1 | 2 | 3 | 4 | 1 | 2 | 3 | 4 |

ESTABLISH   PROTOTYPE   BETA   LAUNCH

PHASE THREE *(continued)*

Recruiting: Job boards can be useful, but old-fashioned networking often yields better results. When you interview, go with your gut: If the potential hire doesn't feel right, it probably isn't.

Poaching: Snatching workers away from rivals is ideal for adding sales staff or senior-level talent. You'll need to offer better compensation than they have now, but the most effective lure is the opportunity for them to put their stamp on an all-new venture.

Tip
Better Living across Time Zones
Contract talent is a global commodity, but location matters if you want to avoid middle-of-the-night teleconferences. On the East Coast, that means hiring in Eastern Europe, where the end of their work-day corresponds to the middle of yours. West Coast companies should opt for China and India, where your day ends as theirs is getting started.

Step 2

Assemble Your Back Office (Objective: Let Pros Handle the Admin So You Can Focus on the Rest.)

Accounting, payroll, and benefits administration aren't glamorous, but they're important parts of maximizing limited resources and keeping staff motivated. Early on, many startups tap one of the founders to keep the books using software like QuickBooks. That's fine when you have fewer than a dozen employees, but as you grow, a part-time bookkeeper or administrative assistant can help. Call in professionals for the heavy lifting, in the form of outsourced payroll and benefits administration services. Staffing is the opposite: In a small company, each personality impacts the team, so avoid using outside recruiters and headhunters.

Parts List
Who's Who in Administrative Outsourcing
Paycycle automates payroll processing and tax reporting. Best for smaller companies.

Paychex works with small to midsize firms to manage payroll and tax compliance.

Ceridian provides services ranging from payroll to benefits administration.

Trinet provides health-plan and benefits services to larger firms. May be too expensive for early-stage companies.

Step 3

Launch Your Beta Test (Objective: Solicit the Comments You Need to Perfect the Product.)

Beta testing used to be a drawn-out ordeal, but for software, Web services, and online media companies, "agile development" has redefined the rules by emphasizing the release of fully functional products, asking end users for input, and addressing suggestions quickly to iron out bugs or add features. The lessons of agile development apply to other kinds of startups as well. Physical objects are obviously harder to alter, but the important thing is to solicit large amounts of user feedback (often by e-mail), respond to each comment, and incorporate changes quickly. Keep in mind that the factors that distinguish a successful product from a dud aren't always obvious. Guidance comes from highly granular research that measures the effectiveness of individual attributes and features.

Words of Wisdom
"Test everything with real people—it's unbelievable how helpful this is. Go find civilians, real people who use [products like yours] because they have to and not because they love to. Find them in Starbucks or at the library or in a college computer lab. Give them $20 for 20 minutes, and you'll be paid back a hundred times over."
—"Entrepreneurial proverb" from Marc Hedlund, entrepreneur-in-residence at O'Reilly Media. (For more of Hedlund's proverbs, visit radar.oreilly.com/archives/2006/03/entrepreneurial_proverbs.html.)

YOU ARE
HERE

| 1 | 2 | 3 | 4 | 5 | 1 | 2 | 3 | 1 | 2 | 3 | 4 | 1 | 2 | 3 | 4 |

ESTABLISH   PROTOTYPE   BETA   LAUNCH

Step 4

Revisit the Business Plan (Objective: Translate All That You've Learned into a More Realistic Blueprint.)

The product your company was created to sell may not be the thing you later unveil in the marketplace. "You're going to change your business three times by the time you're ready to launch," says angel investor Jeff Clavier. "Get used to it." You may be focused on the wrong market, or even the wrong product. Listen carefully, keep an open mind, and revise your projections and analysis accordingly. The assumption these days is that software and Web companies should break even after $20 million in investment; a hardware or consumer product company should do so with $30 million.

Case Study

Flickr's New Image

Ludicorp, the original parent company of online photo site Flickr, began as a startup developing a massively multiplayer game called the Game Neverending. As part of the initial software development, the company developed a tool that allowed people to share photos and chat about them. As more and more of the internal team and their friends began to use the tool, it became clear that providing technology to share photos in a unique way was the real opportunity—a shift that led to the creation of the Flickr website and an all-new business model. The Game Neverending was never launched, but Flickr was acquired by Yahoo in 2005 for an estimated $30 million.

What a VC Wants to See in You

How to Woo Those Fussy Venture Capitalists

Most venture capitalists will tell you that they invest in people, not business plans. They like experienced entrepreneurs they've worked with before. With luck, you've got one of those people on your team, preferably as CEO. But if you're not a veteran and can't find one, don't fret. A common misstep is to pitch the wrong partner at a VC firm—that will get your business plan nixed immediately. Find the partner whose expertise aligns with your business and send that person your well-honed executive summary. (Save the full-blown plan for later.) If you get a meeting, highlight your experience and what differentiates your startup from others, but keep your ego in check. In such a close-knit business relationship, VCs much prefer to work with people they get along with easily.

In an early-stage round, VCs will want 40 percent of the company in return for their investment. VC term sheets are notoriously demanding, but the place where entrepreneurs can suffer most is in the liquidation preferences. In essence, liquidation preferences determine how money gets divvied up if your company is sold. Your VCs are entitled to protect their downside, of course, but not to the exclusion of common stockholders—management and employees—who also want their equity to be worth something. Proceed with caution.

PHASE FOUR
Launch the Product ($$$ Required: $1M to $3M)

The testing is done, the product has been refined, and it's almost ready for release. Now you need to find paying customers, which means it's time to reassess your staffing needs. A rule of thumb is that a company should have about 20 employees at the time of launch, with roughly 60 percent of its headcount devoted to product development and engineering and the rest focusing on management, sales, and marketing. Ideally, this is just the first of many launches to come. Try to nurture the momentum your team will need to think beyond the excitement of the initial release.

Tools You'll Need

In-House Networking: Make it your own. You'll need networked storage, commodity servers, and a place to put it all.

E-Mail/Collaboration Software: Zimbra is more affordable than Microsoft Exchange.

A PBX Phone System: Asterisk PBX is a free telephone exchange that can be installed on any cheap server.

Business Process Software: NetSuite and Salesforce.com offer monthly subscriptions for customer-relationship management tools.

(continued)

YOU ARE
HERE

HOW TO BUILD A
BULLETPROOF
STARTUP

| 1 | 2 | 3 | 4 | 5 | 1 | 2 | 3 | 1 | 2 | 3 | 4 | 1 | 2 | 3 | 4 |

ESTABLISH　　PROTOTYPE　　BETA　　LAUNCH

PHASE FOUR *(continued)*

Step 1

Build a New Board of Directors (Objective: Expand Your Network and Create the Perfect Brain Trust.)

You have new investors, a broader network of contacts, and a slew of enthusiastic backers. Put the best of them together to create a formal board of directors. Your board will likely include at least one representative from your funders. Angel investors may not demand a seat on the board, but most VCs insist on it. The rest of your board should consist of people who understand your business, have practical operating experience, and can leverage their relationships to open doors with potential customers. Cultivate a range of expertise on your board, spanning finance, technology, marketing, management, and merchandising. The excitement of being involved in a red-hot startup is usually the main incentive for prospective board members. Equity is secondary, but here's a general guideline: Board members should receive the same equity package as your director-level employees.

Words of Wisdom

"The people on my board are people I would love to hire but could never afford. They sit on our board because they're excited about our company and want to have a real impact."

—**Brad Oberwager,** *CEO and founder of startup juice and produce company Sundia, who just landed outgoing Sunkist CEO Jeff Gargiulo to serve on the board of his year-old company*

Step 2

Develop the Sales and Marketing Plan (Objective: Establish a Team to Implement a Targeted Strategy.)

As you get ready to come to market, your staffing priorities will shift from the technical team that built the product to the marketing and sales team that will sell it. Your VP for sales and marketing should need only one or two salespeople to start pounding on customers' doors. It's great if they can close a few early deals, but the initial emphasis should be to assess how potential customers respond to your sales pitch. Once they find the pitch that works, institutionalize it throughout your company. Marketing efforts should have a specific goal that supports your company's strategic objectives. Make sure all your sales and marketing initiatives are precisely targeted to achieve them.

Case Study

Focus! Focus! Focus!

When Krugle launched at the Demo conference in February, it became one of the great successes of the semiannual startup dog-and-pony show—not so much for what happened at the show, but for what happened afterward. Krugle is a search company that helps programmers find open-source software code. Most startups at Demo don't have a marketing strategy for the event, beyond just showing up. But the Krugle team had specific goals: Position itself as the most formidable player in the market, attract beta testers, and secure additional investment. With its VCs in tow, Krugle came to the show, trumpeted $1.2 million in funding, and wowed everyone with its polished demo. The result? The company signed up more than 35,000 beta testers, landed another $5 million in funding, and is now recognized as the market leader.

Step 3

Open an Office (Objective: Bring Everyone Under One Roof as Cheaply as Possible.)

Although seasoned entrepreneurs recommend toiling in your proverbial garage as long as possible, there comes a time when working remotely begins to take a toll on productivity—typically when your company has more than 10 full-time employees. In theory, opening an office should be cause for celebration: It's an opportunity to hang your

| 1 | | 2 | 3 | 4 | 5 | | 1 | | 2 | | 3 | | 1 | | 2 | | 3 | | 4 | | 1 | | 2 | | 3 | **4** |

ESTABLISH　　　　PROTOTYPE　　　　BETA　　　　LAUNCH

shingle over an actual front door. In practice, it's perilous: Many young companies go belly-up after locking themselves into expensive real estate deals. Treat your first office as a temporary expedient. Figure out the minimum total square footage you need today, and how much you might need in the next 12 months. (Assume 80 to 100 square feet of floor space per worker.) Executive suites aren't prestigious, but the leases are flexible, and most come with high-speed Internet connections, phone systems, printers, and copiers. (Searchofficespace.com is a good one-stop resource.) Another option is to share space with another startup or sublease space from a more well-established company—moves that can reduce leasing costs by as much as 50 percent.

Things to Avoid
The Four Deadly Sins of Office Real Estate

1. **Overpayment.** Rent should be no more than 4 to 6 percent of total operating costs.
2. **Overimprovement.** Resist the temptation to renovate an existing space or splurge on furniture and fixtures.
3. **Overcommitment.** Assume that your first office is temporary. Try to avoid signing a lease for longer than 12 months.
4. **Overoptimism.** Plan conservatively. Short-term overcrowding is less troublesome than paying for unused space.

Step 4

Hit the Market (Objective: Stop Fiddling and Start Selling!)

There are two ways to bring a new product into the world. With the quiet approach, a price tag is attached and beta customers transition into paying customers. That's great if you have a clear notion of who your customers are and your sales team has a comprehensive list of them. More likely, however, you need to attract a little attention. Industry trade shows are a common way to introduce yourself, but the best reason to launch at a show has nothing to do with making a grand entrance: It's the hard deadline a trade show creates. A public launch imposes a drop-dead completion timeline for everything your team is working on, and that counteracts the impulse to keep tinkering. Set specific but realistic publicity goals: a short list of journalists to reach, the number of blog mentions you want, a target for website hits and registrations. Treat early customers like VIPs. (Each early adopter is typically in a position to shape the buying behavior of 10 prospective customers.) Then pause for a moment to appreciate all that you've accomplished. It's probably too soon to know what happens next, but you've successfully reached the end of the beginning. Good luck!

Tip
Building Buzz on the Cheap

No money for an elaborate marketing campaign? Here are three relatively inexpensive ways to jump-start sales.

Give It Away. If you're selling a physical product or fee-based service, compile a list of the people you'd most like to have as customers. Then give them the product for free. That's how Brondell built buzz for the launch of its Japanese-style electronic toilet seats. Everyone on a marketing agency's list of "the 100 most influential people in Silicon Valley" received one of Brondell's seats for free, and the product is now sold in Home Depot and Bed Bath & Beyond.

Think Like a Blog. Weblogs are the obvious guerrilla route to publicity, but don't treat them like other media outlets. Online, it's essential to hone your message to an easy-to-digest length and keep it consistent. For example, Krugle's "Find code. Find answers." Says marketing consultant Don Thorson, "Three words is ideal, seven is OK. If it's 15, you're screwed."

Create A Clever Gimmick. A simple stunt can generate a major splash if it's surprising, focused, and well targeted. In the early days, Salesforce.com employees "picketed" competitors at industry events, marching and carrying signs emblazoned with the hosted application provider's battle cry: "No more software."

MICHAEL V. COPELAND (mcopeland@business2.com) and **OM MALIK** (omalik@business2.com) are senior writers at *Business 2.0*.

Market Research on the Cheap

There's no need to spend a bundle on professionals when you can do Internet surveys, mine government data, or even take a clipboard to the mall.

JOHN TOZZI

Large corporations spend millions on sophisticated surveys and focus groups from established researchers such as Harris Interactive (HPOL) and Survey Sampling to determine whether their products or services will appeal to customers at a price they're willing to pay. But for entrepreneurs operating on a shoestring budget, there are ways to gather key information about your customers and prospects without hiring an outside firm. Here are five practical suggestions to keep in mind.

1. Research the Same Way You Sell

While "market research" may bring to mind spreadsheets and pie charts, your first step before introducing a new product or launching a business should be to interview your potential customers the same way you plan to sell to them, according to Rob Adams, director of the Moot Corp Business Plan Competition at the University of Texas, Austin and author of *A Good Hard Kick in the Ass: Basic Training for Entrepreneurs.*

"If you sell in person, survey in person. If you sell over the phone, survey over the phone," he says. And for entrepreneurs who plan to sell primarily online, a Web survey can gauge interest. "If you get no results, that should tell you something," says Adams. If you're not sure who to talk to, he says, take a clipboard to the mall (BusinessWeek.com, 11/19/07) on Saturday morning.

Above all, you must have a direct interaction with the people you imagine will buy your product, marketing experts say. John Hauser, a marketing professor at MIT's Sloan School of Management, says his students are astonished when they actually talk to members of their target market, because reality can be so different from their expectations. "I force them to go out and talk to customers. They come back and say, 'Wow, what an experience.' They're just overwhelmed," says Hauser.

2. Mine Public Data

You've already paid for some of the most expensive market research available—with your taxes. The U.S. Census Bureau Web site contains demographic information you can use, often broken down to the neighborhood level. The census data is far more detailed than just population and income levels. Trying to reach customers during their morning commute? Find out what time most people in your county leave for work. Starting a baby clothing company? Check how many women gave birth in the last year.

Beyond the census, you can search federal databases on banking, labor, housing, agriculture, and imports and exports, all without paying a cent. "You don't have to do primary research, you can do secondary research," says Tom Miller, president of Research Publishers in Madison, Wis., and a former market research professor. "Those data are free." To get started, visit this government site.

3. Recruit B-School Students

You may not be able to afford professional researchers, but you can call a local business school and see if a marketing class can help you with your research needs. Many professors are eager to create assignments from projects for small business owners, and students benefit from real-world experience. "The business owner's obligation is to provide the time, share information about the company, and give feedback to the students when it's all over," Miller says.

A marketing class won't match the depth or access to specialized sample groups that professional firms offer, but you'll get a rigorous study at little, if any, cost. "The MBA students learn very systematically all the methods. We teach them survey, focus groups, in-depth interviews," says Hai Che, marketing professor at UC Berkeley's Haas School of Business. "That can be a high-quality but low-cost method."

4. Survey online

You can select from an array of Internet survey companies to get a quick take on a product or service. Some online polls are free for a limited number of responses. The premium version from Zoomerang, at $599 a year, allows unlimited surveys of your existing customer lists. For extra fees, you can tap into the company's global panel of 2.5 million people and tailor your survey to specific niches. "We offer the ability for companies of any size to select samples of a particular group," says Pam Kramer, chief marketing officer of Zoomerang's parent company, MarketTools. Kramer says purchasing a sample runs around $1,500, but the narrower the group you want to sample, the more you'll pay.

Vizu, which places survey questions in banner ad spaces on blogs and Web sites, can target polls based on the audiences of those sites. "If they want to access business people or tech enthusiasts, we'll limit where we place the poll," says Vizu Chief Executive Dan Beltramo. Marketing experts caution that using online samples may not be as accurate as professionally selected panels. But Beltramo says Vizu's results line up with national polls. For entrepreneurs looking to test a concept before acting on it, online surveys can provide a quick and cheap solution.

5. Create an Online Community

Web-based businesses in particular can set up and moderate panels online to glean insight from customers. Forums or live chats reveal customers' experience with your product or perception of your brand. If you already have a database of customer information, you can handpick which customers to invite to the forum to get the sample you want.

"Community management is less expensive than traditional market research consulting," says Barry Libert, co-CEO of Mzinga, which creates and moderates customer communities. The company's self-service option, in which the client moderates the community, costs $1,000 per month. Another player in the customer community space, Networked Insights, charges several thousand per month, based on the number of interactions users have in the forum.

Dan Neely, Networked Insights' founder, says companies value being able to gather information directly from their communities. "It's not just small businesses, but businesses all over are looking for tools to let them do the research themselves," he says. The online community provides that tool, he says. "It's like having 500 of your customers standing in a room chatting and you just get to stand there and listen."

Most survey companies like Vizu or Zoomerang offer templates for questions, and marketers suggest asking several iterations of your question to get a sense of how reliable your data are. Even with do-it-yourself solutions available, hiring a professional market research firm can be worth the price. You might test an idea with some homespun queries, but formal surveys provide more precise data to inform a potentially costly decision. Adams, of the Moot Corp competition, advises companies to budget 5% to 10% of their startup costs for market research before making a bigger investment. "I'd rather find out after spending $10,000 that nothing's there, than find out after I personally guaranteed a lease," he says.

Tozzi covers small business for BusinessWeek.com.

20 Reasons Why You Need a Business Plan

PETE KENNEDY

1. To Prove that You're Serious about Your Business

A formal business plan is necessary to show all interested parties—employees, investors, partners and *yourself*—that you are committed to building the business.

2. To Establish Business Milestones

The business plan should clearly lay out the long-term milestones that are most important to the success of your business. To paraphrase Guy Kawasaki, a milestone is something significant enough to come home and tell your spouse about (without boring him or her to death). Would you tell your spouse that you tweaked the company brochure? Probably not. But you'd certainly share the news that you launched your new website or reached $1M in annual revenues.

3. To Better Understand Your Competition

Creating the business plan forces you to analyze the competition. All companies have competition in the form of either direct or indirect competitors, and it is critical to understand your company's competitive advantages.

4. To Better Understand Your Customer

Why do they buy when they buy? Why don't they when they don't? An in-depth customer analysis is essential to an effective business plan and to a successful business.

5. To Enunciate Previously Unstated Assumptions

The process of actually writing the business plan helps to bring previously "hidden" assumptions to the foreground. By writing them down and assessing them, you can test them and analyze their validity.

6. To Assess the Feasibility of Your Venture

How good is this opportunity? The business plan process involves researching your target market, as well as the competitive landscape, and serves as a feasibility study for the success of your venture.

7. To Document Your Revenue Model

How exactly will your business make money? This is a critical question to answer in writing, for yourself and your investors. Documenting the revenue model helps to address challenges and assumptions associated with the model.

8. To Determine Your Financial Needs

Does your business need to raise capital? How much? The business plan creation process helps you to determine exactly how much capital you need and what you will use it for. This process is essential for raising capital and for effectively employing the capital.

9. To Attract Investors

A formal business plan is the basis for financing proposals. The business plan answers investors' questions such as: Is there a need for this product/service? What are the financial projections? What is the company's exit strategy?

10. To Reduce the Risk of Pursuing the Wrong Opportunity

The process of creating the business plan helps to minimize opportunity costs. Writing the business plan helps you assess the attractiveness of this particular opportunity, versus other opportunities.

11. To Force You to Research and Really Know Your Market

What are the most important trends in your industry? What are the greatest threats to your industry? Is the market growing or shrinking? What is the size of the target market for your product/service? Creating the business plan will help you to gain a wider, deeper, and more nuanced understanding of your marketplace.

12. To Attract Employees and a Management Team

To attract and retain top quality talent, a business plan is necessary. The business plan inspires employees and management that the idea is sound and that the business is poised to achieve its strategic goals.

13. To Plot Your Course and Focus Your Efforts

The business plan provides a roadmap from which to operate, and to look to for direction in times of doubt. Without a business plan, you may shift your short-term strategies constantly without a view to your long-term milestones.

14. To Attract Partners

Partners also want to see a business plan, in order to determine whether it is worth partnering with your business. Establishing partnerships often requires time and capital, and companies will be more likely to partner with your venture if they can read a detailed explanation of your company.

15. To Position Your Brand

Creating the business plan helps to define your company's role in the marketplace. This definition allows you to succinctly describe the business and position the brand to customers, investors, and partners.

16. To Judge the Success of Your Business

A formal business plan allows you to compare actual operational results versus the business plan itself. In this way, it allows you to clearly see whether you have achieved your strategic, financing, and operational goals (and why you have or have not).

17. To Reposition Your Business to Deal with Changing Conditions

For example, during difficult economic conditions, if your current sales and operational models aren't working, you can rewrite your business plan to define, try, and validate new ideas and strategies.

18. To Document Your Marketing Plan

How are you going to reach your customers? How will you retain them? What is your advertising budget? What price will you charge? A well-documented marketing plan is essential to the growth of a business.

19. To Understand and Forecast Your Company's Staffing Needs

After completing your business plan, you will not be surprised when you are suddenly short-handed. Rather, your business plan provides a roadmap for your staffing needs, and thus helps to ensure smoother expansion.

20. To Uncover New Opportunities

Through the process of brainstorming, white-boarding and creative interviewing, you will likely see your business in a different light. As a result, you will often come up with new ideas for marketing your product/service and running your business.

Since 1999, Growthink's business plan experts have assisted more than 1,500 clients in launching and growing their businesses, and raising more than $1 billion in growth financing.

How to Write a Great Business Plan

Which information belongs—and which doesn't—may surprise you.

WILLIAM A. SAHLMAN

Few areas of business attract as much attention as new ventures, and few aspects of new-venture creation attract as much attention as the business plan. Countless books and articles in the popular press dissect the topic. A growing number of annual business-plan contests are springing up across the United States and, increasingly, in other countries. Both graduate and undergraduate schools devote entire courses to the subject. Indeed, judging by all the hoopla surrounding business plans, you would think that the only things standing between a would-be entrepreneur and spectacular success are glossy five-color charts, a bundle of meticulous-looking spreadsheets, and a decade of month-by-month financial projections.

Nothing could be further from the truth. In my experience with hundreds of entrepreneurial start-ups, business plans rank no higher than 2—on a scale from 1 to 10—as a predictor of a new venture's success. And sometimes, in fact, the more elaborately crafted the document, the more likely the venture is to, well, flop, for lack of a more euphemistic word.

What's wrong with most business plans? The answer is relatively straightforward. Most waste too much ink on numbers and devote too little to the information that really matters to intelligent investors. As every seasoned investor knows, financial projections for a new company—especially detailed, month-by-month projections that stretch out for more than a year—are an act of imagination. An entrepreneurial venture faces far too many unknowns to predict revenues, let alone profits. Moreover, few if any entrepreneurs correctly anticipate how much capital and time will be required to accomplish their objectives. Typically, they are wildly optimistic, padding their projections. Investors know about the padding effect and therefore discount the figures in business plans. These maneuvers create a vicious circle of inaccuracy that benefits no one.

Don't misunderstand me: business plans should include some numbers. But those numbers should appear mainly in the form of a business model that shows the entrepreneurial team has thought through the key drivers of the venture's success or failure. In manufacturing, such a driver might be the yield on a production process; in magazine publishing, the anticipated renewal rate; or in software, the impact of using various distribution channels. The model should also address the break-even issue: At what level of sales does the business begin to make a profit? And even more important, When does cash flow turn positive? Without a doubt, these questions deserve a few pages in any business plan. Near the back.

What goes at the front? What information does a good business plan contain?

If you want to speak the language of investors—and also make sure you have asked yourself the right questions before setting out on the most daunting journey of a businessperson's career—I recommend basing your business plan on the framework that follows. It does not provide the kind of "winning" formula touted by some current how-to books and software programs for entrepreneurs. Nor is it a guide to brain surgery. Rather, the framework systematically assesses the four interdependent factors critical to every new venture:

The People. The men and women starting and running the venture, as well as the outside parties providing key services or important resources for it, such as its lawyers, accountants, and suppliers.

The Opportunity. A profile of the business itself—what it will sell and to whom, whether the business can grow and how fast, what its economics are, who and what stand in the way of success.

The Context. The big picture—the regulatory environment, interest rates, demographic trends, inflation, and the like—basically, factors that inevitably change but cannot be controlled by the entrepreneur.

Risk and Reward. An assessment of everything that can go wrong and right, and a discussion of how the entrepreneurial team can respond.

The assumption behind the framework is that great businesses have attributes that are easy to identify but hard to assemble. They have an experienced, energetic managerial team from the top to the bottom. The team's members have skills and experiences directly relevant to the opportunity they are pursuing. Ideally, they will have worked successfully together in the past. The opportunity has an attractive, sustainable business model; it is possible to create a competitive edge and defend it. Many options exist for expanding the scale and scope of the business, and these options are unique to the enterprise and its team.

Business Plans: For Entrepreneurs Only?

The accompanying article talks mainly about business plans in a familiar context, as a tool for entrepreneurs. But quite often, start-ups are launched within established companies. Do those new ventures require business plans? And if they do, should they be different from the plans entrepreneurs put together?

The answer to the first question is an emphatic yes; the answer to the second, an equally emphatic no. All new ventures—whether they are funded by venture capitalists or, as is the case with intrapreneurial businesses, by shareholders—need to pass the same acid tests. After all, the marketplace does not differentiate between products or services based on who is pouring money into them behind the scenes.

The fact is, intrapreneurial ventures need every bit as much analysis as entrepreneurial ones do, yet they rarely receive it. Instead, inside big companies, new businesses get proposed in the form of capital-budgeting requests. These faceless documents are subject to detailed financial scrutiny and a consensus-building process, as the project wends its way through the chain of command, what I call the "neutron bomb model of project governance." However, in the history of such proposals, a plan never has been submitted that did not promise returns in excess of corporate hurdle rates. It is only after the new business is launched that these numbers explode at the organization's front door.

That problem could be avoided in large part if intrapreneurial ventures followed the guidelines set out in the accompanying article. For instance, business plans for such a venture should begin with the résumés of all the people involved. What has the team done in the past that would suggest it would be successful in the future, and so on? In addition, the new venture's product or service should be fully analyzed in terms of its opportunity and context. Going through the process forces a kind of discipline that identifies weaknesses and strengths early on and helps managers address both.

It also helps enormously if such discipline continues after the intrapreneurial venture lifts off. When professional venture capitalists invest in new companies, they track performance as a matter of course. But in large companies, scrutiny of a new venture is often inconsistent. That shouldn't or needn't be the case. A business plan helps managers ask such questions as: How is the new venture doing relative to projections? What decisions has the team made in response to new information? Have changes in the context made additional funding necessary? How could the team have predicted those changes? Such questions not only keep a new venture running smoothly but also help an organization learn from its mistakes and triumphs.

Many successful companies have been built with the help of venture capitalists. Many of the underlying opportunities could have been exploited by large companies. Why weren't they? Perhaps useful lessons can be learned by studying the world of independent ventures, one lesson being: Write a great business plan.

Value can be extracted from the business in a number of ways either through a positive harvest event—a sale—or by scaling down or liquidating. The context is favorable with respect to both the regulatory and the macroeconomic environments. Risk is understood, and the team has considered ways to mitigate the impact of difficult events. In short, great businesses have the four parts of the framework completely covered. If only reality were so neat.

The People

When I receive a business plan, I always read the résumé section first. Not because the people part of the new venture is the most important, but because without the right team, none of the other parts really matters.

I read the résumés of the venture's team with a list of questions in mind. (See the insert "Who Are These People, Anyway?") All these questions get at the same three issues about the venture's team members: What do they know? Whom do they know? and How well are they known?

What and whom they know are matters of insight and experience. How familiar are the team members with industry players and dynamics? Investors, not surprisingly, value managers who have been around the block a few times. A business plan

should candidly describe each team member's knowledge of the new venture's type of product or service; its production processes; and the market itself, from competitors to customers. It also helps to indicate whether the team members have worked together before. Not played—as in roomed together in college—but *worked*.

Investors also look favorably on a team that is known because the real world often prefers not to deal with start-ups. They're too unpredictable. That changes, however, when the new company is run by people well known to suppliers, customers, and employees. Their enterprise may be brand new, but they aren't. The surprise element of working with a start-up is somewhat ameliorated.

Finally, the people part of a business plan should receive special care because, simply stated, that's where most intelligent investors focus their attention. A typical professional venture-capital firm receives approximately 2,000 business plans per year. These plans are filled with tantalizing ideas for new products and services that will change the world and reap billions in the process—or so they say. But the fact is, most venture capitalists believe that ideas are a dime a dozen: only execution skills count. As Arthur Rock, a venture capital legend associated with the formation of such companies as Apple, Intel, and Teledyne, states, "I invest in people, not ideas." Rock also has said, "If you can find good people, if they're wrong about the product, they'll make a switch, so what good is it to understand the product that they're talking about in the first place?"

Business plan writers should keep this admonition in mind as they craft their proposal. Talk about the people—exhaustively. And if there is nothing solid about their experience and abilities to herald, then the entrepreneurial team should think again about launching the venture.

The Opportunity

When it comes to the opportunity itself, a good business plan begins by focusing on two questions: Is the total market for the venture's product or service large, rapidly growing, or both? Is the industry now, or can it become, structurally attractive? Entrepreneurs and investors look for large or rapidly growing markets mainly because it is often easier to obtain a share of a growing market than to fight with entrenched competitors for a share of a mature or stagnant market. Smart investors, in fact, try hard to identify high-growth-potential markets early in their evolution: that's where the big payoffs are. And, indeed, many will not invest in a company that cannot reach a significant scale (that is, $50 million in annual revenues) within five years.

As for attractiveness, investors are obviously looking for markets that actually allow businesses to make some money. But that's not the no-brainer it seems. In the late 1970s, the computer disk-drive business looked very attractive. The technology was new and exciting. Dozens of companies jumped into the fray, aided by an army of professional investors. Twenty years later, however, the thrill is gone for managers and investors alike. Disk-drive companies must design products to meet the perceived needs of original equipment manufacturers (OEMs) and end users. Selling a product to OEMs is complicated. The customers are large relative to most of their suppliers. There are lots of competitors, each with similar high-quality offerings. Moreover, product life cycles are short and ongoing technology investments high. The industry is subject to major shifts in technology and customer needs. Intense rivalry leads to lower prices and, hence, lower margins. In short, the disk-drive industry is simply not set up to make people a lot of money; it's a structural disaster area.

The information services industry, by contrast, is paradise. Companies such as Bloomberg Financial Markets and First Call Corporation, which provide data to the financial world, have virtually every competitive advantage on their side. First, they can assemble or create *proprietary* content—content that, by the way, is like life's blood to thousands of money managers and stock analysts around the world. And although it is often expensive to develop the service and to acquire initial customers, once up and running, these companies can deliver content to customers very cheaply. Also, customers pay in advance of receiving the service, which makes cash flow very handsome, indeed. In short, the structure of the information services industry is beyond attractive: it's gorgeous. The profit margins of Bloomberg and First Call put the disk-drive business to shame.

Thus, the first step for entrepreneurs is to make sure they are entering an industry that is large and/or growing, and one

that's structurally attractive. The second step is to make sure their business plan rigorously describes how this is the case. And if it isn't the case, their business plan needs to specify how the venture will still manage to make enough of a profit that investors (or potential employees or suppliers, for that matter) will want to participate.

Once it examines the new venture's industry, a business plan must describe in detail how the company will build and launch its product or service into the marketplace. Again, a series of questions should guide the discussion. (See the insert "The Opportunity of a Lifetime—or Is It?")

Often the answers to these questions reveal a fatal flaw in the business. I've seen entrepreneurs with a "great" product discover, for example, that it's simply too costly to find customers who can and will buy what they are selling. Economically viable access to customers is the key to business, yet many entrepreneurs take the *Field of Dreams* approach to this notion: build it, and they will come. That strategy works in the movies but is not very sensible in the real world.

The market is as fickle as it is unpredictable. Who would have guessed that plug-in room deodorizers would sell?

It is not always easy to answer questions about the likely consumer response to new products or services. The market is as fickle as it is unpredictable. (Who would have guessed that plug-in room deodorizers would sell?) One entrepreneur I know proposed to introduce an electronic newsclipping service. He made his pitch to a prospective venture-capital investor who rejected the plan, stating, "I just don't think the dogs will eat the dog food." Later, when the entrepreneur's company went public, he sent the venture capitalist an anonymous package containing an empty can of dog food and a copy of his prospectus. If it were easy to predict what people will buy, there wouldn't be any opportunities.

Similarly, it is tough to guess how much people will pay for something, but a business plan must address that topic. Sometimes, the dogs will eat the dog food, but only at a price less than cost. Investors always look for opportunities for value pricing— that is, markets in which the costs to produce the product are low, but consumers will still pay a lot for it. No one is dying to invest in a company when margins are skinny. Still, there is money to be made in inexpensive products and services—even in commodities. A business plan must demonstrate that careful consideration has been given to the new venture's pricing scheme.

The list of questions about the new venture's opportunity focuses on the direct revenues and the costs of producing and marketing a product. That's fine, as far as it goes. A sensible proposal, however, also involves assessing the business model from a perspective that takes into account the investment required— that is, the balance sheet side of the equation. The following questions should also be addressed so that investors can understand the cash flow implications of pursuing an opportunity:

- When does the business have to buy resources, such as supplies, raw materials, and people?
- When does the business have to pay for them?
- How long does it take to acquire a customer?

- How long before the customer sends the business a check?
- How much capital equipment is required to support a dollar of sales?

Investors, of course, are looking for businesses in which management can buy low, sell high, collect early, and pay late. The business plan needs to spell out how close to that ideal the new venture is expected to come. Even if the answer is "not very"— and it usually is—at least the truth is out there to discuss.

The opportunity section of a business plan must also bring a few other issues to the surface. First, it must demonstrate and analyze how an opportunity can grow—in other words, how the new venture can expand its range of products or services, customer base, or geographic scope. Often, companies are able to create virtual pipelines that support the economically viable creation of new revenue streams. In the publishing business, for example, *Inc.* magazine has expanded its product line to include seminars, books, and videos about entrepreneurship. Similarly, building on the success of its personal-finance software program Quicken, Intuit now sells software for electronic banking, small-business accounting, and tax preparation, as well as personal-printing supplies and on-line information services—to name just a few of its highly profitable ancillary spin-offs.

Now, lots of business plans runneth over on the subject of the new venture's potential for growth and expansion. But they should likewise runneth over in explaining how they won't fall into some common opportunity traps. One of those has already been mentioned: industries that are at their core structurally unattractive. But there are others. The world of invention, for example, is fraught with danger. Over the past 15 years, I have seen scores of individuals who have devised a better mousetrap—newfangled creations from inflatable pillows for use on airplanes to automated car-parking systems. Few of these idea-driven companies have really taken off, however. I'm not entirely sure why. Sometimes, the inventor refuses to spend the money required by, or share the rewards sufficiently with, the business side of the company. Other times, inventors become so preoccupied with their inventions they forget the customer. Whatever the reason, better-mousetrap businesses have an uncanny way of malfunctioning.

Whatever the reason, better-mousetrap businesses have an uncanny way of malfunctioning.

Another opportunity trap that business plans—and entrepreneurs in general—need to pay attention to is the tricky business of arbitrage. Basically, arbitrage ventures are created to take advantage of some pricing disparity in the marketplace. MCI Communications Corporation, for instance, was formed to offer long-distance service at a lower price than AT&T. Some of the industry consolidations going on today reflect a different kind of arbitrage—the ability to buy small businesses at a wholesale price, roll them up together into a larger package, and take them public at a retail price, all without necessarily adding value in the process.

Taking advantage of arbitrage opportunities is a viable and potentially profitable way to enter a business. In the final analysis, however, all arbitrage opportunities evaporate. It is not a question of whether, only when. The trick in these businesses is to use the arbitrage profits to build a more enduring business model, and business plans must explain how and when that will occur.

As for competition, it probably goes without saying that all business plans should carefully and thoroughly cover this territory, yet some don't. That is a glaring omission. For starters, every business plan should answer the following questions about the competition:

- Who are the new venture's current competitors?
- What resources do they control? What are their strengths and weaknesses?
- How will they respond to the new venture's decision to enter the business?
- How can the new venture respond to its competitors' response?
- Who else might be able to observe and exploit the same opportunity?
- Are there ways to co-opt potential or actual competitors by forming alliances?

Business is like chess: to be successful, you must anticipate several moves in advance. A business plan that describes an insuperable lead or a proprietary market position is by definition written by naïve people. That goes not just for the competition section of the business plan but for the entire discussion of the opportunity. All opportunities have promise; all have vulnerabilities. A good business plan doesn't whitewash the latter. Rather, it proves that the entrepreneurial team knows the good, the bad, and the ugly that the venture faces ahead.

The Context

Opportunities exist in a context. At one level is the macroeconomic environment, including the level of economic activity, inflation, exchange rates, and interest rates. At another level are the wide range of government rules and regulations that affect the opportunity and how resources are marshaled to exploit it. Examples extend from tax policy to the rules about raising capital for a private or public company. And at yet another level are factors like technology that define the limits of what a business or its competitors can accomplish.

Context often has a tremendous impact on every aspect of the entrepreneurial process, from identification of opportunity to harvest. In some cases, changes in some contextual factor create opportunity. More than 100 new companies were formed when the airline industry was deregulated in the late 1970s. The context for financing was also favorable, enabling new entrants like People Express to go to the public market for capital even before starting operations.

Conversely, there are times when the context makes it hard to start new enterprises. The recession of the early 1990s combined with a difficult financing environment for new companies: venture capital disbursements were low, as was the amount of capital raised in the public markets. (Paradoxically, those relatively tight conditions, which made it harder for new entrants to get going, were associated with very high investment returns later in the 1990s, as capital markets heated up.)

Sometimes, a shift in context turns an unattractive business into an attractive one, and vice versa. Consider the case of a packaging company some years ago that was performing so poorly it was about to be put on the block. Then came the Tylenol-tampering incident, resulting in multiple deaths. The packaging company happened to have an efficient mechanism for installing tamper-proof seals, and in a matter of weeks its financial performance could have been called spectacular. Conversely, U.S. tax reforms enacted in 1986 created havoc for companies in the real estate business, eliminating almost every positive incentive to invest. Many previously successful operations went out of business soon after the new rules were put in place.

Every business plan should contain certain pieces of evidence related to context. First, the entrepreneurs should show a heightened awareness of the new venture's context and how it helps or hinders their specific proposal. Second, and more important, they should demonstrate that they know the venture's context will inevitably change and describe how those changes might affect the business. Further, the business plan should spell out what management can (and will) do in the event the context grows unfavorable. Finally, the business plan should explain the ways (if any) in which management can affect context in a positive way. For example, management might be able to have an impact on regulations or on industry standards through lobbying efforts.

Risk and Reward

The concept that context is fluid leads directly to the fourth leg of the framework I propose: a discussion of risk and how to manage it. I've come to think of a good business plan as a snapshot of an event in the future. That's quite a feat to begin with—taking a picture of the unknown. But the best business plans go beyond that; they are like movies of the future. They show the people, the opportunity, and the context from multiple angles. They offer a plausible, coherent story of what lies ahead. They unfold possibilities of action and reaction.

Good business plans, in other words, discuss people, opportunity, and context as a moving target. All three factors (and the relationship among them) are likely to change over time as a company evolves from start-up to ongoing enterprise. Therefore, any business plan worth the time it takes to write or read needs to focus attention on the dynamic aspects of the entrepreneurial process.

Of course, the future is hard to predict. Still, it is possible to give potential investors a sense of the kind and class of risk and reward they are assuming with a new venture. All it takes is a pencil and two simple drawings. (See the insert "Visualizing Risk

Visualizing Risk and Reward

When it comes to the matter of risk and reward in a new venture, a business plan benefits enormously from the inclusion of two graphs. Perhaps *graphs* is the wrong word; these are really just schematic pictures that illustrate the most likely relationship between risk and reward, that is, the relationship between the opportunity and its economics. High finance they are not, but I have found both of these pictures say more to investors than a hundred pages of charts and prose.

The first picture depicts the amount of money needed to launch the new venture, time to positive cash flow, and the expected magnitude of the payoff.

This image helps the investor understand the depth and duration of negative cash flow, as well as the relationship between the investment and the possible return. The ideal, needless to say, is to have cash flow early and often. But most investors are intrigued by the picture even when the cash outflow is high and long—as long as the cash inflow is more so.

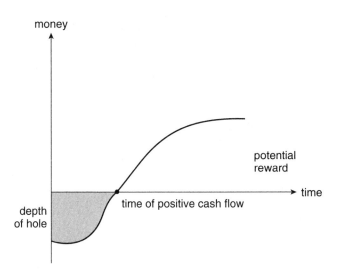

Of course, since the world of new ventures is populated by wild-eyed optimists, you might expect the picture to display a shallower hole and a steeper reward slope than it should. It usually does. But to be honest, even that kind of picture belongs in the business plan because it is a fair warning to investors that the new venture's team is completely out of touch with reality and should be avoided at all costs.

The second picture complements the first. It shows investors the range of possible returns and the likelihood of achieving them. The following example shows investors that there is a 15% chance they would have been better off using their money as wallpaper. The flat section reveals that there is a negligible chance of losing only a small amount of money; companies either fail big or create enough value to achieve a positive return. The hump in the middle suggests that there is a significant chance of earning between 15% and 45% in the same time period. And finally, there is a small chance that the initial outlay of cash will spawn a 200% internal rate of return, which might have occurred if you had happened to invest in Microsoft when it was a private company.

Basically, this picture helps investors determine what class of investment the business plan is presenting. Is the new venture drilling for North Sea oil—highly risky with potentially big payoffs—or is it digging development wells in Texas, which happens to be less of a geological gamble and probably less lucrative, too? This image answers that kind of question. It's then up to the investors to decide how much risk they want to live with against what kind of odds.

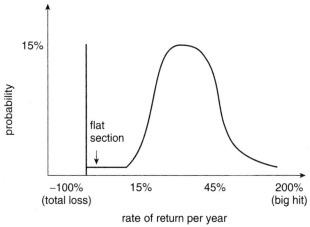

Again, the people who write business plans might be inclined to skew the picture to make it look as if the probability of a significant return is downright huge and the possibility of loss is negligible. And, again, I would say therein lies the picture's beauty. What it claims, checked against the investor's sense of reality and experience, should serve as a simple pictorial caveat emptor.

and Reward.") But even with these drawings, risk is, well, risky. In reality, there are no immutable distributions of outcomes. It is ultimately the responsibility of management to change the distribution, to increase the likelihood and consequences of success, and to decrease the likelihood and implications of problems.

One of the great myths about entrepreneurs is that they are risk seekers. All sane people want to avoid risk.

One of the great myths about entrepreneurs is that they are risk seekers. All sane people want to avoid risk. As Harvard Business School professor (and venture capitalist) Howard Stevenson says, true entrepreneurs want to capture all the reward and give all the risk to others. The best business is a post office box to which people send cashier's checks. Yet risk is unavoidable. So what does that mean for a business plan?

The best business is a post office box to which people send cashier's checks.

It means that the plan must unflinchingly confront the risks Ahead—in terms of people, opportunity, and context. What happens if one of the new venture's leaders leaves? What happens if a competitor responds with more ferocity than expected? What happens if there is a revolution in Namibia, the source of a key raw material? What will management actually *do?*

Those are hard questions for an entrepreneur to pose, especially when seeking capital. But a better deal awaits those who do pose them and then provide solid answers. A new venture, for example, might be highly leveraged and therefore very sensitive to interest rates. Its business plan would benefit enormously by stating that management intends to hedge its exposure through the financial-futures market by purchasing a contract that does well when interest rates go up. That is the equivalent of offering investors insurance. (It also makes sense for the business itself.)

Finally, one important area in the realm of risk/reward management relates to harvesting. Venture capitalists often ask if a company is "IPOable," by which they mean, Can the company be taken public at some point in the future? Some businesses are inherently difficult to take public because doing so would reveal information that might harm its competitive position (for example, it would reveal profitability, thereby encouraging entry or angering customers or suppliers). Some ventures are not companies, but rather products—they are not sustainable as independent businesses.

Therefore, the business plan should talk candidly about the end of the process. How will the investor eventually get money out of the business, assuming it is successful, even if only marginally so? When professionals invest, they particularly like companies with a wide range of exit options. They like companies that work hard to preserve and enhance those options along the way; companies that don't, for example, unthinkingly form alliances with big corporations that could someday actually *buy* them. Investors feel a lot better about risk if the venture's endgame is discussed up front. There is an old saying, "If you don't know where you are going, any road will get you there." In crafting sensible entrepreneurial strategies, just the opposite is true: you had better know where you might end up and have a map for getting there. A business plan should be the place where that map is drawn, for, as every traveler knows, a journey is a lot less risky when you have directions.

The Deal and Beyond

Once a business plan is written, of course, the goal is to land a deal. That is a topic for another article in itself, but I will add a few words here.

When I talk to young (and old) entrepreneurs looking to finance their ventures, they obsess about the valuation and terms of the deal they will receive. Their explicit goal seems to be to minimize the dilution they will suffer in raising capital. Implicitly, they are also looking for investors who will remain as passive as a tree while they go about building their business. On the food chain of investors, it seems, doctors and dentists are best and venture capitalists are worst because of the degree to which the latter group demands control and a large share of the returns.

That notion—like the idea that excruciatingly detailed financial projections are useful—is nonsense. From whom you raise capital is often more important than the terms. New ventures are inherently risky, as I've noted; what can go wrong will. When that happens, unsophisticated investors panic, get angry, and often refuse to advance the company more money. Sophisticated investors, by contrast, roll up their sleeves and help the company solve its problems. Often, they've had lots of experience saving sinking ships. They are typically process literate. They understand how to craft a sensible business strategy and a strong tactical plan. They know how to recruit, compensate, and motivate team members. They are also familiar with the Byzantine ins and outs of going public—an event most entrepreneurs face but once in a lifetime. This kind of know-how is worth the money needed to buy it.

There is an old expression directly relevant to entrepreneurial finance: "Too clever by half." Often, deal makers get very creative, crafting all sorts of payoff and option schemes. That usually backfires. My experience has proven again and again that sensible deals have the following six characteristics:

- They are simple.
- They are fair.
- They emphasize trust rather than legal ties.
- They do not blow apart if actual differs slightly from plan.
- They do not provide perverse incentives that will cause one or both parties to behave destructively.
- They are written on a pile of papers no greater than one-quarter inch thick.

But even these six simple rules miss an important point. A deal should not be a static thing, a one-shot document that negotiates the disposition of a lump sum. Instead, it is incumbent upon entrepreneurs, before they go searching for funding, to think about capital acquisition as a dynamic process—to figure out how much money they will need and when they will need it.

How is that accomplished? The trick is for the entrepreneurial team to treat the new venture as a series of experiments. Before launching the whole show, launch a little piece of it. Convene a focus group to test the product, build a prototype and watch it perform, conduct a regional or local rollout of a service. Such an exercise reveals the true economics of the business and can help enormously in determining how much money the new venture actually requires

A Glossary of Business Plan Terms

What They Say . . .	and What They Really Mean
We conservatively project . . .	We read a book that said we had to be a $50 million company in five years, and we reverse-engineered the numbers.
We took our best guess and divided by 2.	We accidentally divided by 0.5.
We project a 10% margin.	We did not modify any of the assumptions in the business plan template that we downloaded from the Internet.
The project is 98% complete.	To complete the remaining 2% will take as long as it took to create the initial 98% but will cost twice as much.
Our business model is proven . . .	If you take the evidence from the past week for the best of our 50 locations and extrapolate it for all the others.
We have a six-month lead.	We tried not to find out how many other people have a six-month lead.
We only need a 10% market share.	So do the other 50 entrants getting funded.
Customers are clamoring for our product.	We have not yet asked them to pay for it. Also, all of our current customers are relatives.
We are the low-cost producer.	We have not produced anything yet, but we are confident that we will be able to.
We have no competition.	Only IBM, Microsoft, Netscape, and Sun have announced plans to enter the business.
Our management team has a great deal of experience . . .	Consuming the product or service.
A select group of investors is considering the plan.	We mailed a copy of the plan to everyone in *Pratt's Guide*.
We seek a value-added investor.	We are looking for a passive, dumb-as-rocks investor.
If you invest on your terms, you will earn a 68% internal rate of return.	If everything that could ever conceivably go right does go right, you might get your money back.

and in what stages. Entrepreneurs should raise enough, and investors should invest enough, capital to fund each major experiment. Experiments, of course, can feel expensive and risky. But I've seen them prevent disasters and help create successes. I consider it a prerequisite of putting together a winning deal.

Beware the Albatross

Among the many sins committed by business plan writers is arrogance. In today's economy, few ideas are truly proprietary. Moreover, there has never been a time in recorded history when the supply of capital did not outrace the supply of opportunity. The true half-life of opportunity is decreasing with the passage of time.

A business plan must not be an albatross that hangs around the neck of the entrepreneurial team, dragging it into oblivion. Instead, a business plan must be a call for action, one that recognizes management's responsibility to fix what is broken proactively and in real time. Risk is inevitable, avoiding risk impossible. Risk management is the key, always tilting the venture in favor of reward and away from risk.

A plan must demonstrate mastery of the entire entrepreneurial process, from identification of opportunity to harvest. It is not a way to separate unsuspecting investors from their money by hiding the fatal flaw. For in the final analysis, the only one being fooled is the entrepreneur.

We live today in the golden age of entrepreneurship. Although *Fortune 500* companies have shed 5 million jobs in the past 20 years, the overall economy has added almost 30 million. Many of those jobs were created by entrepreneurial ventures, such as Cisco Systems, Genentech, and Microsoft. Each of those companies started with a business plan. Is that why they succeeded? There is no knowing for sure. But there is little doubt that crafting a business plan so that it thoroughly and candidly addresses the ingredients of success—people, opportunity, context, and the risk/reward picture—is vitally important. In the absence of a crystal ball, in fact, a business plan built of the *right* information and analysis can only be called indispensable.

WILLIAM A. SAHLMAN is Dimitri V. d'Arbeloff Professor of Business Administration at the Harvard Business School in Boston, Massachusetts. He has been closely connected with more than 50 entrepreneurial ventures as an adviser, investor, or director. He teaches a second-year course at the Harvard Business School called "Entrepreneurial Finance," for which he has developed more than 100 cases and notes.

Outline for a Business Plan
A Proven Approach for Entrepreneurs Only

. . . a written representation of where a company is going, how it will get there, and what it will look like once it arrives.

Ernst and Young LLP

Business plans are the preferred mode of communication between entrepreneurs and potential investors. Experienced owners and managers of closely held businesses know that business plans can also be an indispensable management tool. Many have found that just completing the steps required to develop a business plan forces them to introduce discipline and a logical thought process into all of their planning activities. They have found that a properly prepared business plan can greatly improve their company's ability to consistently establish and meet goals and objectives in a way that best serves the company's owners, employees, and investors.

A business plan can take many forms, from a glossy, professionally produced document to a handwritten manuscript in a three-ring binder that serves as the documentation for the goals, objectives, strategies, and tactics of a company.

In any form, a business plan is simply a written representation of where a company is going, how it will get there, and what it will look like once it arrives.

Uses of a Business Plan

A business plan is a valuable management tool that can be utilized in a wide variety of situations.

In most companies, business plans are used at a minimum to:

- Set the goals and objectives for the company's performance.
- Provide a basis for evaluating and controlling the company's performance.

- Communicate a company's message to middle managers, outside directors, lenders, and potential investors.

When utilized most efficiently, the same business plan, with slight modification, can be used for all three actions.

Setting Goals and Objectives

The business plan for an early-stage company is, in many ways, a first attempt at strategic planning. An entrepreneur should use a business plan as a tool for setting the direction of a company over the next several years, and a plan should set the action steps and processes to guide the company through this period. Many entrepreneurs say that the pressures of the day-to-day management of a company leave them little time for planning, and this is unfortunate because, without it, an owner runs the risks of proceeding blindly through the rapidly changing business environment. Of course, writing a business plan is not a guarantee that problems will not arise. But, with a thoroughly thought-out plan, a business owner can better anticipate a crisis situation and deal with it up front. Further, a well-constructed plan can help avoid certain problems altogether. All in all, business planning is probably more important to the survival of a small and growing company than a larger, more mature one.

Performance Benchmarks

A business plan can also be used to develop and document milestones along your business's path to success. In the heat of daily operations, you may find that taking an objective look at the performance of your business is difficult. Often, the trees encountered daily obscure your view of the forest in which your company operates. A business plan can provide you and your management team with an objective basis for determining if the business is on track to meet the goals and objectives you have set.

Internal and External Communications

Your company's story must be told and retold many times to prospective investors, potential and new employees, outside advisors, and potential customers. And the most important part of the story is the part about the future, the part featured in a business plan.

Your business plan should show how all the pieces of your company fit together to create a vibrant organization capable of meeting its goals and objectives. It must be able to communicate your company's distinctive competence to anyone who might have an interest.

Steps in Preparing Your Business Plan

This booklet presents a generalized outline for writing a business plan. The outline is intended to be used with *Ernst & Young's Business Plan Guide,* published by John Wiley & Sons. The Guide can be purchased at many bookstores. . . .

Listed below are the steps you should follow in preparing your business plan, whether you are writing it for the first time or rewriting it for the twentieth.

Step 1—Identify Your Objectives

Before you can write a successful business plan you must determine who will read the plan, what they already know about your company, what they want to know about your company, and how they intend to use the information they will find in the plan. The needs of your target audience must be combined with your communication objectives—what you want the reader to know. Once you have identified and resolved any conflicts between what your target audience wants to know and what you want them to know, you are ready to begin preparing a useful business plan.

Step 2—Outline Your Business Plan

Once you have identified the objectives for your business plan, and you know the areas that you want to emphasize, you should prepare an outline based on these special requirements. The outline can be as general or detailed as you wish, but typically a detailed outline will be more useful to you while you are writing your plan.

Step 3—Review Your Outline

Review your outline to identify the areas that, based on your readers and objectives, should be presented in detail or summary form in your business plan. Keep in mind that your business plan should describe your company at a high level and that extremely detailed descriptions are to be avoided in most cases. However, you must be prepared to provide detailed support for your statements and assumptions apart from your business plan if necessary.

Step 4—Write Your Plan

The order in which the specific elements of the plan are developed will vary depending on the age of your company and your experience in preparing business plans.

You will probably find it necessary to research many areas before you have enough information to write about them. Most people begin by collecting historical financial information about their company and/or industry, and completing their market research before beginning to write any part of their plan. Even though you may do extensive research before you begin to develop your plan, you may find that additional research is required before you complete it. You should take the time to complete the required research because many of the assumptions and strategies described in the plan will be based on the findings and analysis of your research.

Initial drafts of prospective financial statements are often prepared next, after the basic financial and market research and analysis are completed.

By preparing these statements at this time, you will have a good idea which strategies will work from a financial perspective before investing many hours in writing a detailed description of them. As you develop your prospective statements, be certain that you keep detailed notes on the assumptions you make to facilitate preparation of the footnotes that must accompany the statements, as well as the composition of other business plan elements.

The last element of a business plan to be prepared is the Executive Summary. Since it is a summary of the plan, its contents are contingent on the rest of the document, and it cannot be written properly until the other components of the plan are essentially complete.

While preparing each element of your plan, refer to the outline in this booklet to be certain that you have covered each area thoroughly.

Step 5—Have Your Plan Reviewed

Once you have completed and reviewed a draft of your plan, have someone familiar with business management and the planning process review it for completeness (by referring to the outline in this publication), objectivity, logic, presentation, and effectiveness as a communications tool. Then, modify your plan based on your reviewer's comments.

Step 6—Update Your Plan

Business plans are "living" documents and must be periodically updated, or they become useless. As your environment and your objectives—and those of your readers—change, update your plan to reflect these changes. Refer to this booklet each time your plan is updated to be certain that all areas are properly covered.

Outline for a Business Plan
I. Executive Summary

The Executive Summary should not be a mere listing of topics contained in the body of your business plan but should emphasize the key issues presented.

A critical point that must be communicated in the Executive Summary is your company's distinctive competence—the factors that will make your business successful in a competitive market.

> If your company is new, you could be sending your business plan to potential investors who review hundreds of them each year. More often than not, these individuals do not get past the Executive Summary of the plans they receive. Your Executive Summary must therefore give the reader a useful understanding of your business and make the point of most interest to them: "What is in it for the investor?"

A. The Purpose of the Plan

1. Attract investors
2. Document an operational plan for controlling the business

B. Market Analysis

1. The characteristics of your target market (demographic, geographic, etc.)
2. The products or services you will offer to satisfy those needs

C. The Company

1. The needs your company will satisfy
2. The products or services you will offer to satisfy those needs

D. Marketing and Sales Activities

1. Marketing strategy
2. Sales strategy
3. Keys to success in your competitive environment

E. Product or Service Research and Development

1. Major milestones
2. Ongoing efforts

F. Organization and Personnel

1. Key managers and owners
2. Key operations employees

G. Financial Data

1. Funds required and their use
2. Historical financial summary
3. Prospective financial summary (including a brief justification for prospective sales levels)

Note—In total, your Executive Summary should be less than three pages in length and provide the reader with a succinct overview of your entire business plan.

The Executive Summary should be followed by a brief table of contents designed to assist readers in locating specific sections in the plan. Detailed descriptions of the plan's contents should be avoided in the table of contents.

II. Market Analysis

The Market Analysis section should reflect your knowledge of your industry, and present highlights and analysis of your market research. Detailed market research studies, however, should be presented as appendices to your plan.

A. Industry Description and Outlook

1. Description of your primary industry
2. Size of the industry
   a. *Historically*
   b. *Currently*
   c. *In five years*
   d. *In ten years*
3. Industry characteristics and trends (Where is company in its life cycle?)
   a. *Historically*
   b. *Currently*
   c. *In the future*
4. Major customer groups
   a. *Businesses*
   b. *Governments*
   c. *Consumers*

B. Target Markets

1. Distinguishing characteristics of your primary target markets and market segments. Narrow your target markets to a manageable size. Efforts to penetrate target markets that are too broad are often ineffective.
   a. *Critical needs*
   b. *Extent to which those needs are currently being met*
   c. *Demographics*
   d. *Geographic location*
   e. *Purchasing decision-makers and influencers*
   f. *Seasonal/cyclical trends*
2. Primary/target market size
   a. *Number of prospective customers*
   b. *Annual purchases of products or services meeting the same or similar needs as your products or services*
   c. *Geographic area*
   d. *Anticipated market growth*
3. Market penetration—indicate the extent to which you anticipate penetrating your market and demonstrate why you feel that level of penetration is achievable based on your market research
   a. *Market share*
   b. *Number of customers*
   c. *Geographic coverage*
   d. *Rationale for market penetration estimates*
4. Pricing/gross margin targets
   a. *Price levels*
   b. *Gross margin levels*
   c. *Discount structure (volume, prompt payment, etc.)*

5. Methods by which specific members of your target market can be identified
   a. *Directories*
   b. *Trade association publications*
   c. *Government documents*
6. Media through which you can communicate with specific members of your target market
   a. *Publications*
   b. *Radio/television broadcasts*
   c. *Sources of influence/advice*
7. Purchasing cycle of potential customers
   a. *Needs identification*
   b. *Research for solutions to needs*
   c. *Solution evaluation process*
   d. *Final solution selection responsibility and authority (executives, purchasing agents, engineers, etc.)*
8. Key trends and anticipated changes within your primary target markets
9. Secondary target markets and key attributes
   a. *Needs*
   b. *Demographics*
   c. *Significant future trends*

C. Market Test Results

1. Potential customers contacted
2. Information/demonstrations given to potential customers
3. Reaction of potential customers
4. Importance of satisfaction of targeted needs
5. Test group's willingness to purchase products/services at various price levels

D. Lead Times (Amount of Time between Customer Order Placement and Product/ Service Delivery)

1. Initial orders
2. Reorders
3. Volume purchases

E. Competition

1. Identification (by product line or service and market segment)
   a. *Existing*
   b. *Market share*
   c. *Potential (How long will your "window of opportunity" be open before your initial success breeds new competition? Who will your new competitors likely be?)*
   d. *Direct*
   e. *Indirect*
2. Strengths (competitive advantages)
   a. *Ability to satisfy customer needs*
   b. *Market penetration*

> As your market analysis provides the only basis for your prospective sales and pricing estimates, make sure that this section clearly demonstrates that there is a market need for your product or service, that you as owner not only understand this need but can meet it, and that you can sell at a profit. This section should also include an estimate of your market penetration annually for the next five years.

c. *Track record and reputation*
d. *Staying power (financial resources)*
e. *Key personnel*
3. Weaknesses (competitive disadvantages)
   a. *Ability to satisfy customer needs*
   b. *Market penetration*
   c. *Track record and reputation*
   d. *Staying power (financial resources)*
   e. *Key personnel*
4. Importance of your target market to your competition
5. Barriers to entry into the market
   a. *Cost (investment)*
   b. *Time*
   c. *Technology*
   d. *Key personnel*
   e. *Customer inertia (brand loyalty, existing relationships, etc.)*
   f. *Existing patents and trademarks*

F. Regulatory Restrictions

1. Customer or governmental regulatory requirements
   a. *Methods for meeting the requirements*
   b. *Timing involved*
   c. *Cost*
2. Anticipated changes in regulatory requirements

III. Company Description

The Company Description section must provide an overview of how all of the elements of your company fit together without going into detail, since most of the subjects will be covered in depth elsewhere in the plan.

A. Nature of Your Business

1. Marketplace needs to be satisfied
2. Method(s) of need satisfaction (products and services)
3. Individuals/organizations with the needs

B. Your Distinctive Competencies (Primary Factors That Will Lead to Your Success)

1. Superior customer need satisfaction
2. Production/service delivery efficiencies
3. Personnel
4. Geographic location

Writing this section is the first real test of your ability to communicate the essence of your business. The lack of a clear description of the key concepts of your company will indicate to the reader that you have not yet clearly defined it in your own mind. Therefore, you must be certain that this section concisely and accurately describes the substance of your new business.

Do not underestimate the importance of presenting a well-conceived sales strategy here. Without an efficient approach to beating a path to the doors of potential customers, companies with very good products and services often fail.

IV. Marketing and Sales Activities

Both general and specific information must be included in this part of your plan. Your objective here is to describe the activities that will allow you to meet the sales and margin levels indicated in your prospective financial statements.

A. Overall Marketing Strategy

1. Marketing penetration strategy
2. Growth strategy
   a. *Internal*
   b. *Acquisition*
   c. *Franchise*
   d. *Horizontal (providing similar products to different users)*
   e. *Vertical (providing the products at different levels of the distribution chain)*
3. Distribution channels (include discount/profitability levels at each stage)
   a. *Original equipment manufacturers*
   b. *Internal sales force*
   c. *Distributors*
   d. *Retailers*
4. Communication
   a. *Promotion*
   b. *Advertising*
   c. *Public relations*
   d. *Personal selling*
   e. *Printed materials (catalogues, brochures, etc.)*

B. Sales Strategies

1. Sales force
   a. *Internal vs. independent representatives (advantages and disadvantages of your strategy)*
   b. *Size*
   c. *Recruitment and training*
   d. *Compensation*
2. Sales activities
   a. *Identifying prospects*
   b. *Prioritizing prospects*
   c. *Number of sales calls made per period*
   d. *Average number of sales calls per sale*
   e. *Average dollar size per sale*
   f. *Average dollar size per reorder*

V. Products and Services

Special attention should be paid to the users of your business plan as you develop this section. Too much detail will have a negative impact on most external users of the plan. Avoid turning this section of your business plan into a policies and procedures manual for your employees.

A. Detailed Product/Service Description (From the User's Perspective)

1. Specific benefits of product/service
2. Ability to meet needs
3. Competitive advantages
4. Present stage (idea, prototype, small production runs, etc.)

B. Product Life Cycle

1. Description of the product/service's current position within its life cycle
2. Factors that might change the anticipated life cycle
   a. *Lengthen it*
   b. *Shorten it*

C. Copyrights, Patents, and Trade Secrets

1. Existing or pending copyrights or patents
2. Anticipated copyright and patent filings
3. Key aspects of your products or services that cannot be patented or copyrighted
4. Key aspects of your products or services that qualify as trade secrets
5. Existing legal agreements with owners and employees
   a. *Nondisclosure agreements*
   b. *Noncompete agreements*

D. Research and Development Activities

1. Activities in process
2. Future activities (include milestones)
3. Anticipated results of future research and development activities
   a. *New products or services*
   b. *New generations of existing products or services*
   c. *Complementary products or services*
   d. *Replacement products or services*
4. Research and development activities of others in your industry
   a. *Direct competitors*
   b. *Indirect competitors*
   c. *Suppliers*
   d. *Customers*

VI. Operations

Here again, too much detail can detract from the rest of your plan. Be certain that the level of detail included fits the specific needs of the plan's users.

A. Production and Service Delivery Procedures

1. Internal
2. External (subcontractors)

B. Production and Service Delivery Capability

1. Internal
2. External (subcontractors)
3. Anticipated increases in capacity
   a. *Investment*
   b. *New cost factors (direct and indirect)*
   c. *Timing*

C. Operating Competitive Advantages

1. Techniques
2. Experience
3. Economies of scale
4. Lower direct costs

D. Suppliers

1. Identification of the suppliers of critical elements of production
   a. *Primary*
   b. *Secondary*
2. Lead-time requirements
3. Evaluation of the risks of critical element shortages
4. Description of the existing and anticipated contractual relationships with suppliers

VII. Management and Ownership

Your management team's talents and skills are some of the few truly unique aspects of your company. If you are going to use your plan to attract investors, this section must emphasize your management's talents and skills, and indicate why they are a part of your company's distinctive competence that cannot easily be replicated by your competition. Remember that individuals invest in people, not ideas.

Do not use this section of the plan to negotiate future ownership of the company with potential investors. Simply explain the current ownership.

A. Management Staff Structure

1. Management staff organization chart
2. Narrative description of the chart

> The emphasis in this section should be on your company's unique ability to satisfy the needs of the marketplace. Avoid criticizing your competition's products too severely in this section, because the natural tendency of a reader who is not part of your organization will be to empathize with the unrepresented party—your competition.
>
> Concentrate on the positive aspects of your product's ability to meet existing market needs and allow your readers to come to their own conclusions about your competition based on the objective information presented here and in the Market Analysis section.

B. Key Managers (Complete Resumes Should Be Presented in an Appendix to the Business Plan)

1. Name
2. Position
3. Brief position description, including primary duties
4. Primary responsibilities and authority
5. Unique skills and experiences that add to your company's distinctive competencies
6. Compensation basis and levels (be sure they are reasonable—not too high and not too low)

C. Planned Additions to the Current Management Team

1. Position
2. Primary responsibilities and authority
3. Requisite skills and experience
4. Recruitment process
5. Timing of employment
6. Anticipated contribution to the company's success
7. Compensation basis and levels (be sure they are in line with the market)

D. Legal Structure of the Business

1. Corporation
   a. *C corporation*
   b. *S corporation*
2. Partnership
   a. *General*
   b. *Limited*
3. Proprietorship

E. Owners

1. Names
2. Percentage ownership
3. Extent of involvement with the company
4. Form of ownership
   a. *Common stock*
   b. *Preferred stock*
   c. *General partner*
   d. *Limited partner*

> Because many of the aspects of your new business are still theoretical at this point, special care must be taken to be sure the specifics of your operations do not conflict with the information included in your prospective financial statements. Any inconsistencies between those two areas will result in some unpleasant surprises as your company begins operations.

5. Outstanding equity equivalents
    a. *Options*
    b. *Warrants*
    c. *Convertible debt*
6. Common stock
    a. *Authorized*
    b. *Issued*

F. Board of Directors

1. Names
2. Position on the board
3. Extent of involvement with the company
4. Background
5. Contribution to the company's success
    a. *Historically*
    b. *In the future*

VIII. Funds Required and Their Uses

Any new or additional funding reflected in your prospective financial statements should be discussed here. Alternative funding scenarios can be presented if appropriate, and corresponding prospective financial statements are presented in subsequent sections of your plan.

A. Current Funding Requirements

1. Amount
2. Timing
3. Type
    a. *Equity*
    b. *Debt*
    c. *Mezzanine*
4. Terms

B. Funding Requirements over the Next Five Years

1. Amount
2. Timing
3. Type
    a. *Equity*
    b. *Debt*
    c. *Mezzanine*
4. Terms

C. Use of Funds

1. Capital expenditures
2. Working capital
3. Debt retirement
4. Acquisitions

D. Long-Range Financial Strategies (Liquidating Investors' Positions)

1. Going public
2. Leveraged buyout
3. Acquisition by another company
4. Debt service levels and timing
5. Liquidation of the venture

Note—Ernst & Young's Guide to Financing for Growth contains a detailed discussion of various alternatives for raising capital and may provide you with some of the ideas and information you may need to write this portion of your business plan. The Guide, written by E&Y partners and published by John Wiley & Sons, can be purchased at many bookstores.

IX. Financial Data

The Financial Data section contains the financial representation of all the information presented in the other sections. Various prospective scenarios can be included, if appropriate.

A. Historical Financial Data (Past Three to Five Years, If Applicable)

1. Annual statements
    a. *Income*
    b. *Balance sheet*
    c. *Cash flows*
2. Level of CPA involvement (and name of firm)
    a. *Audit*
    b. *Review*
    c. *Compilation*

B. Prospective Financial Data (Next Five Years)

1. Next year (by month or quarter)
    a. *Income*
    b. *Balance sheet*
    c. *Cash flows*
    d. *Capital expenditure budget*
2. Final four years (by quarter and/or year)
    a. *Income*
    b. *Balance sheet*
    c. *Cash flows*
    d. *Capital expenditure budget*
3. Summary of significant assumptions
4. Type of prospective financial data
    a. *Forecast (management's best estimate)*
    b. *Projection ("what-if" scenarios)*

> Because your management team is unique, make sure that you stress members' backgrounds and skills, and how they will contribute to the success of your product/service and business. This is especially important to emphasize when you are looking for financing.

> The Financial Data section of your business plan is another area where specialized knowledge can be invaluable. If you do not have someone with sufficient financial expertise on your management team, you will probably need to utilize an outside advisor.

> Remember that because the rate of return is their most important consideration—and that the initial public offering market is sometimes not available—investors will be looking for alternative exit strategies. Therefore, be flexible and creative in developing these opportunities, taking into consideration such recent trends as merger/acquisitions and strategic partnering. Although details can be worked out later, investors need to know that you understand their primary objectives as you develop your overall business strategy.

> In some instances, the thicker the business plan, the less likely a potential investor is to read it thoroughly. However, you do want to be able to demonstrate to potential funding sources that you have done a complete job in preparing your plan and that the comments made within it are well documented. By properly utilizing appendices and exhibits, you can keep the size of your business plan palatable to its users and still have the additional information they may require readily available.

5. Level of CPA involvement
   a. *Assembly*
   b. *Agreed-upon procedures*
   c. *Review*
   d. *Examination*

C. Analysis

1. Historical financial statements
   a. *Ratio analysis*
   b. *Trend analysis with graphic presentation*
2. Prospective financial statements
   a. *Ratio analysis*
   b. *Trend analysis with graphic presentation*

X. Appendices or Exhibits

Any additional detailed or confidential information that could be useful to the readers of the business plan but is not appropriate for distribution to everyone receiving the body of the plan can be presented here. Accordingly, appendices and exhibits should be bound separately from the other sections of the plan and provided on an as-needed basis to readers.

A. Resumes of Key Managers

B. Pictures of Products

C. Professional References

D. Market Studies

E. Pertinent Published Information

1. Magazine articles
2. References to books

F. Patents

G. Significant Contracts

1. Leases
2. Sales contracts
3. Purchase contracts
4. Partnership/ownership agreements
5. Stock option agreements
6. Employment/compensation agreements
7. Noncompete agreements
8. Insurance
   a. *Product Liability*
   b. *Officers' and directors' liability*
   c. *General liability*

Administrative Considerations

The copies of your plan should be controlled, and a distribution record should be kept. This process will allow you to update your distributed plans as needed and help to ensure that your plan is not more widely distributed than you intend. In fact, many plans include ethical disclaimers that limit the ability of individuals distributing or otherwise copying the plan without the consent of the company's owners. Remember too that an appropriate private placement disclaimer should be included if the plan is being used to raise capital.

The 10 Biggest Business Plan Mistakes

Former venture capitalist and angel investor Christine Comaford-Lynch has reviewed hundreds of business plans. She explains where many entrepreneurs go wrong.

CHRISTINE COMAFORD-LYNCH

It's a crime to work so hard on writing a business plan only to sabotage your chances of getting funded by omitting or shortchanging the key components. When a financier, board member, or key executive assesses your plan, they want to see the 10 topics listed below. The problem is, many businesses plans I've read make the same mistakes. Getting it right conveys that you know where your business is going, and you know how to get there. The following advice applies to a traditional business plan:

1. Company Overview

The Goal: A few concise and compelling sentences describing your company's purpose/goal.

The Mistake: More often than not, the company's purpose/objective is vague, common, not compelling. I stop reading here.

2. Pain

The Goal: Identify the specific market pain you will reduce or remove. At the same time, explain why your product or service is crucial.

The Mistake: Some entrepreneurs feel they don't need to include this topic, but you always have to make a case to convince readers unfamiliar with your product or service.

3. Solution

The Goal: Explain as completely as possible what your solution is to the market pain—and exactly how it works.

The Mistake: Not fully explaining your solution and exactly how it works.

4. Company Information

The Goal: While no one expects you to have a fully fleshed-out team in the early days, you should at least have a skeletal team supplemented with advisers.

The Mistake: One- and two-person teams simply don't demonstrate your ability to enroll others in your vision. As a general rule of thumb, list as many key players as possible in this section.

5. Financial Information

The Goal: Describe your funding history (if you have any), the total amount of money sought, the source, the anticipated use of funds, last year's revenue, a five-year revenue forecast, monthly burn rate, projected cash-flow positive date. Entrepreneurs always ask me why five years of fictitious revenue estimates matter. The answer is because financiers want to know how ambitious you are.

The Mistake: Pie-in-the-sky financials. Be sure to back up your projections with how you expect to achieve them.

6. Product

The Goal: A short paragraph explaining the status of your product. It's okay if you're in early trials or even if you have a killer demo.

The Mistake: Not helping the reader understand how you're going to get to a full-fledged product and when.

7. Defensibility

The Goal: Explain how your intellectual property or market position will be protected from competitors and how you'll mitigate risk for financiers. You also need to answer these questions: Do you have patents in process? What are the key risks with your company? How will you help to mitigate them?

The Mistake: Not demonstrating that you've considered these topics, and have thoughtful answers.

8. Competition

The Goal: Name your competitors, both now and in the future.

The Mistake: Saying you have no competitors—you do. Even inertia is a competitor, and a formidable one at that. A security company I recently met with listed all of their competitors to me, and one by one explained how their solution was better. I love honest acknowledgment coupled with doing your homework. It's rare and compelling.

9. Business Model

The Goal: Show how you'll make money and grow your business. By considering all the angles, you could end up discovering secondary and tertiary revenue streams that you've given cursory thought to. Don't hold back.

The Mistake: Not explaining exactly how your business will make money, when, and what the new revenue streams will be over time.

10. Key Milestones

The Goal: Show the deals/achievements that are accelerating/will accelerate your company's growth—be specific in stating the stage of these deals/achievements. This is where the rubber hits the road.

The Mistake: Not explaining specifically what you have accomplished within a time frame, and what you plan to achieve within a future time frame.

UNIT 3

Financing a New Business Venture

Unit Selections

Key Points to Consider

- Why do entrepreneurs need to raise money to grow?

- How does a startup venture determine how much capital is required to get going?

- What is the difference between debt and equity financing?

- Why is an executive summary important to the potential investor?

- What are some of the problems with personal and family loans to entrepreneurs?

- What is an angel investor? How do they decide and consider their investments?

- What is venture capital? What impact does venture capital have on the economy?

- How does angel investing differ from venture capital?

- What do venture capitalists provide entrepreneurs, other than money?

- What are some important "deal-points" to an entrepreneur? To an investor?

Student Website
www.mhcls.com

Internet References

Angel Capital Association
http://www.angelcapitalassociation.org/

Center for Private Equity and Entrepreneurship
http://mba.tuck.dartmouth.edu/pecenter/

Center for Venture Research
http://wsbe.unh.edu/cvr

National Association of Small Business Investment Companies (NASBIC)
http://www.nasbic.org

National Venture Capital Association (NVCA)
http://www.nvca.org/

Private Equity Hub
http://www.pehub.com/

Small Business Investment Companies (SBIC)
http://www.sba.gov/aboutsba/sbaprograms/inv/index.html

Venture Capital Institute
http://www.vcinstitute.org

How do entrepreneurs finance their new ventures? The most successful entrepreneurs turn to the venture capital industry. The entrepreneur brings fresh ideas, management skills, and personal commitment while the venture capitalists (VCs) bring cash. Venture capital is provided by professionals who invest alongside management in young, rapidly growing companies that have the potential to develop into significant ventures.

The venture capital industry in the United States has grown to a size that could only be imagined in years past. The venture capital contribution to U. S. jobs, economic growth, and technological progress has climbed steadily over the last few years. Questions of how to raise money, when to raise money, and how to work with venture capitalists are frequent topics of concern with entrepreneurs today. This unit will describe some common sources of capital, provide information about the venture capital market, and offer guidance in approaching the venture capitalists and presenting the business plan.

Growth is an unavoidable fact of successful businesses. Growth due to an increase in sales requires product; in turn, additional product requires inputs like labor, inventory, raw materials, plant, property, and equipment. Because internally generated funds typically won't meet all expansion needs, most startups depend on outside capital to finance growth. In some instances, the entrepreneur may find that the new business does not begin to earn a profit until two or three years down the road. The job of the entrepreneur, therefore, revolves around securing the necessary capital to pioneer a new venture through the "financial Death Valley" and sustain the desired growth rate of the venture.

Financing the fast-growing venture tends be a time-consuming, complex task for the entrepreneur—who is most likely working heads-down on the daily needs. Typically, financing a new venture employs a combination of debt and equity financing. Debt is presumed to be lower-risk capital because it is repaid according to a set schedule of principal and interest. Debt financing involves an interest-bearing instrument usually called a loan. The payment is only indirectly related to the sales and profits of the new venture and typically, debt financing (also known as asset-based financing) requires some asset—for instance a vehicle, house, or other property/land—that will be used as collateral. Generally, lenders will allow ventures to borrow against their expected ability to generate the cash to repay the loan.

The entrepreneur with a new idea for launching a business, and when turned down by a bank, will often turn to a wealthy individual or several friends to back the business venture. In the United States these "angel investors" commit some $30–60 billion per year to small businesses. But before receiving such "angelic support" many questions must first be answered. Certain critical elements must be present in a business plan before the venture will receive financing. And those who wish to be successful in dealing with outside investors should spend the time and effort to understand the objectives of their potential investors. Academic research on this topic has shown that, in all too many cases, startups don't get financed because the

© Steven Puetzer/Getty Images

entrepreneur is not familiar with an investor's industry preferences, requirements, and specialization; risks, protection against losses; participation in management; or with the investor's "harvesting options" or "exit goals."

A good relationship between the entrepreneur and the venture capitalist is a vital element in a successful venture. Understanding this partnership is a necessary first step for the prospective entrepreneur. The entrepreneur must be prepared to compete successfully for the venture capitalists' dollars. It will be the task of the entrepreneur to select and approach the VC, most often with a complete business plan and strategic focus that supports an oral presentation. The presentation must demonstrate management's competence in knowing the following: (1) earning power/operating cash flows of the venture, (2) the potential terminal value of the business at exiting, (3) the value of the business model underlying the venture, (4) industry competitors and competitive advantages, and (5) how the management team intends to assess risks and create contingency plans.

When meeting with VCs, the entrepreneurs need to be well prepared and "know their business numbers cold." Few analytical terms are more widely used and, at the same time, more poorly understood than the term *cash flow*. The cash flowing into a business venture is not the same as accounting profit. It is important for entrepreneurs to make weekly and monthly projections of cash received and disbursed. Such financial forecasts that relate to the future are called financial pro formas. This forecasting procedure is very difficult and perhaps that is why most entrepreneurs avoid it. As Mark Twain once said: "The art of prophecy is very difficult, especially with respect to the future."

Financial management is the cornerstone of the scorekeeping system for these investing and profit-making activities. A cash flow statement can help the entrepreneur come up with realistic estimates, determine financial requirements, understand the financial strategy framework, and craft a fund-raising strategy. The *cash flow statement,* also known as the statement of cash flows, is one of the most important financial planning tools that a startup venture can prepare for the business plan. It is used to provide the entrepreneur with a clearer insight into the venture's cash management strategy: where funds come from and how they are disbursed; the amount of cash available; the amount of additional funds needed (AFN) to grow; and the general financial well-being of the new venture.

Finally, a well-prepared cash flow statement should also track the company's *burn rate* and top line revenue flow of cash into the business venture, which helps the investors recognize the true value of the venture. They prefer to see positive cash flows from operations, not just continual injections of cash and/or equity. A good financial plan for investors should not only show profit and cash flows; it should show how the business will pay back the money and make more money in the future. A comprehensive, investor-oriented business plan with complete financials will not guarantee success to the entrepreneur in raising funds for growing, but the lack of such financials will ensure failure.

Writing a Compelling Executive Summary

WILLIAM M. REICHERT

By now, you've probably already read several articles, web pages—even books—about writing the perfect executive summary. Most of them offer a wealth of well-intended suggestions about all the stuff you need to include in the executive summary. They provide a helpful list of the forty-two critical items you should cover, and then they tell you to be concise. Most guides to writing an executive summary miss the key point: The job of the executive summary is to sell, not to describe.

The executive summary is often your initial face to a potential investor, so it is critically important that you create the right first impression. Contrary to the advice in articles on the topic, you do not need to explain the entire business plan in 250 words. You need to convey its essence, and its energy. You have about 30 seconds to grab an investor's interest. You want to be clear and compelling.

Forget what everyone else has been telling you. Here are the key components that should be part of your executive summary:

1. The Grab

You should lead with the most compelling statement of why you have a really big idea. This sentence (or two) sets the tone for the rest of the executive summary. Usually, this is a concise statement of the unique solution you have developed to a big problem. It should be direct and specific, not abstract and conceptual. If you can drop some impressive names in the first paragraph you should—world-class advisors, companies you are already working with, a brand name founding investor. Don't expect an investor to discover that you have two Nobel laureates on your advisory board six paragraphs later. He or she may never get that far.

2. The Problem

You need to make it clear that there is a big, important problem (current or emerging) that you are going to solve, or opportunity you are going to exploit. In this context you are establishing your Value Proposition—there is enormous pain and opportunity out there, and you are going to increase revenues, reduce costs, increase speed, expand reach, eliminate inefficiency, increase effectiveness, whatever. Don't confuse your statement of the problem with the size of the opportunity (see below).

3. The Solution

What specifically are you offering to whom? Software, hardware, service, combination? Use commonly used terms to state concretely what you have, or what you do, that solves the problem you've identified. Avoid acronyms and don't try to use these precious few words to create and trademark a bunch of terms that won't mean anything to most people. You might need to clarify where you fit in the value chain or distribution channels—who do you work with in the ecosystem of your sector, and why will they be eager to work with you. If you have customers and revenues, make it clear. If not, tell the investor when you will.

4. The Opportunity

Spend a few more sentences providing the basic market segmentation, size, growth and dynamics—how many people or companies, how many dollars, how fast the growth, and what is driving the segment. You will be better off targeting a meaningful percentage of a smaller, well-defined, growing market than claiming a microscopic percentage of a huge, heterogeneous, mature market. Don't claim you are addressing the $24 billion widget market, when you are really addressing the $85 million market for specialized arc-widgets used in the emerging wocket sector.

5. Your Competitive Advantage

No matter what you might think, you have competition. At a minimum, you compete with the current way of doing business. Most likely, there is a near competitor, or a direct competitor that is about to emerge (are you sufficiently paranoid yet??). So, understand what your real, sustainable competitive advantage is, and state it clearly. Do not try to convince investors that your key competitive asset is your "first mover advantage." Here is where you can articulate your unique benefits and advantages. Believe it or not, in most cases, you should be able to make this point in one or two sentences.

6. The Model

How specifically are you going to generate revenues, and from whom? Why is your model leverageable and scaleable? Why will it be capital efficient? What are the critical metrics on which you will be evaluated—customers, licenses, units, revenues, margin? Whatever it is, what impressive levels will you reach within three to five years?

7. The Team

Why is your team uniquely qualified to win? Don't tell us you have 48 combined years of expertise in widget development; tell us your CTO was the lead widget developer for Intel, and she was on the original IEEE standards committee for arc-widgets. Don't just regurgitate a shortened form of each founder's resume; explain why the background of each team member fits. If you can, state the names of brand name companies your team has worked for. Don't drop a name if it's an unknown name, and don't drop a name if you aren't happy to give the contact as a reference at a later date.

8. The Promise

When you are pitching to investors, your fundamental promise is that you are going to make them a boatload of money. The only way you can do that is if you can achieve a level of success that far exceeds the capital required to do that. Your Summary Financial Projections should clearly show that. But if they are not believable, then all of your work is for naught. You should show five years of revenues, expenses, losses/profits, cash and headcount. You should also show a key driver or two, such as number of customers and units shipped each year.

9. The Ask

This is the amount of funding you are asking for now. This should generally be the minimum amount of equity you need to reach the next major milestone. You can always take more if investors are willing to make more available, but it is hard to take less. If you expect to be raising another round of financing later, make that clear, and state the expected amount.

You should be able to do all this in six to eight paragraphs, possibly a few more if there is a particular point that needs emphasis. You should be able to make each point in just two or three simple, clear, specific sentences.

This means your executive summary should be about two pages, maybe three. Some people say it should be one page. They're wrong. (The only reason investors ask for one page summaries is that they are usually so bad the investors just want the suffering to be over sooner.) Most investors find that there is not enough information in one page to understand and evaluate a company.

Please remember that the outline above should not be applied rigidly or religiously. There is no template that fits all companies, but make sure you touch on each key issue. You need to think through what points are most important in your particular case, what points are irrelevant, what points need emphasis, and what points require no elaboration.

Some other general points:

- Do not lead with broad, sweeping statements about the market opportunity. What matters is not market size, but rather compelling pain. Investors would rather invest in a company solving a desperate problem for a small growing market, than a company providing an incremental improvement for a large established market.

- Don't acronym your own name. Sun Microsystems did not build its brand by calling itself "SMI." (Of course, if you know where the name Sun came from, you understand this is an inside joke.)

- Drop names, if they are real; don't drop names if they are smoke. If you have a real partnership with a brand name company, don't hide your lantern under a bushel basket. If you consulted for Cisco's HR department one week, don't say you worked for Cisco.

- Avoid "purple farts"—phrases and adjectives that sound impressive but carry no substance. "Next generation" and "dynamic" probably don't mean anything to your readers (unless you are talking about DRAM) and tend to be irritating. Everybody thinks their software is "intelligent" and "easy-to-use," and everyone thinks their financial projections are "conservative." Explain your company the way you would to a friend at a cocktail party (after one drink, not five).

- State your value proposition and competitive advantage in positive terms, not negative terms. It is what you can do that is important, not what others cannot do. With the one or two most obvious competitors, however, you may need to be very explicit: "Unlike Cisco's firewall solution, our software can operate . . ."

- Use simple sentences, not multi-tiered compound sentences.

- Use analogies, as long as you are clarifying rather than hyping. You can say you are using the Google model for generating revenues, as long as you don't say you expect to be the next Google.

- Don't lie. You would think this goes without saying, but too many entrepreneurs cross over the line between passionate enthusiasm and fraudulent misrepresentation. On a lighter note, check out "The Top Ten Lies of Entrepreneurs" on the Garage website.

- Go back and reread each sentence when you think you're done: Is each sentence clear, concise and compelling?

If you are looking for help developing your slide presentation for investors, you can read "Perfecting Your Pitch" on the Garage website.

Finally, one of the most important sentences you write will not even be in the executive summary—it is the sentence that introduces your company in the email that you or a friend uses to send the executive summary. Your summary might not even get read if this sentence is not well-crafted. Again, it should be specific and compelling. It should sell your company, not just describe it.

Venture investors are predisposed to like entrepreneurs. Many of us were entrepreneurs in our prior lives, and all of us enjoy the challenge and excitement of starting up companies. We are on your side. So please help us get to know you better by telling your story clearly and concisely.

Good luck!

If you have any questions about this article, or about *Garage Technology* Ventures, you can contact Bill Reichert, Managing Director of Garage Technology Ventures (email: reichert@garage.com).

The People's Bank

How to borrow from the people who love you without making them hate you.

ANDREW PARK

Restaurateur Artie Bucco asked a friend to loan him $50,000 so he could go into business with an importer of French liquor. The friend said no, explaining that he'd have no recourse if Bucco didn't pay him back. The problem was that Bucco just happened to have another friend—mob boss Tony Soprano. The friend's worry: "If you don't pay me back, I ain't gonna be able to hurt you."

You don't have to be a character on *The Sopranos* to know that going to family and friends for business capital can be a dicey proposition. Admonitions against mixing love and money may be as old as currency itself. "Neither a borrower nor a lender be," warned Shakespeare. "For loan oft loses both itself and friend." And a Punjabi proverb cautions: "When there is affection, never go into business together." But when your savings well runs dry and you can't snag a bank loan or are horrified by the rate you're offered, who better to turn to than the friends and family who believe in you and your dreams? Informal investment—money from friends, family, neighbors, colleagues, and the like—totaled $92.7 billion in 2005, according to the Global Entrepreneurship Monitor, an annual survey of entrepreneurial activity around the world.

That's not surprising, considering the many advantages of raising capital close to home. Friends and family often give you more favorable terms than a bank or a professional investor will, such as a higher estimate of your company's value or a lower interest rate on a loan. They are predisposed to trust you, so you likely won't have to jump through as many hoops to win their investment. And they may be more forgiving if your company goes south.

But Shakespeare knew a thing or two about human nature, and entrepreneurs would be wise to keep his words in mind. Your investors may feel entitled to a say in how you run your company, whether or not you want their opinions. If they don't reap the return they expected or you can't make payments on a loan, holiday get-togethers could be mighty awkward. "The fallout can be pretty ugly if you don't turn out to be the star you thought you were or the market isn't right for what you want to do," says Susan Newman, a social psychologist in Metuchen, N.J.

The key, Newman says, is to tread carefully. Your investors may have known you since you were in diapers, but this is business. From the start, give the process of raising money the attention it deserves. Figure out how much you really need, and whether debt or equity would be better for your company (though investors may get a bigger say in that than you'd like). Terms, of course, have to be fair to both parties. Perhaps most important, you'll need to take great care with the emotional aspects of the financial relationship: How will Aunt Jane feel if you go bankrupt and can't pay her back? Does Mom want a seat on the board? Talk it all through, and then write it down, in detail. Says Newman: "If family members keep focused on what's important—important being the relationship—it can work."

For most startups, debt makes more sense than equity, says Asheesh Advani, chief executive officer and founder of CircleLending, a Waltham (Mass.) company that administers loans between friends and family online. With equity, it can be difficult to get your investors' money out of the company unless you sell or go public. Equity deals are also more complicated to set up, and having a lawyer to guide you is essential. You'll first need to put a value on your company, taking into account its assets and potential to generate revenue and profits, and then multiplying that total by an amount common for companies in your industry. You probably will also want to structure the company as an S-Corporation or a limited liability company, both of which allow your investors to deduct corporate losses on their personal income taxes. Above all, you'll want to make sure you're complying with federal and state securities laws. A common mistake is not properly disclosing risks to nonaccredited investors, defined by the Securities & Exchange Commission as those having a net worth of less than $1 million or an annual income of less than $200,000. The amount you're raising might be small enough to fall under de minimis exemptions, which the federal government caps at $1 million (state exemptions vary), but ask your lawyer to check.

If you plan to go to angel investors or venture capitalists for additional rounds of financing, be aware that they will look closely at how you valued the equity you gave your friends and family. Likewise, professional investors might shy away if your so-called friends and family round hasn't been handled properly—if you've failed to document investments or have investors who could pose a legal liability by claiming they weren't informed of risks or were promised special rights. "It's much more cumbersome having a lot of small shareholders," says Jeff Harder, managing shareholder of business law firm Winstead in The Woodlands, Tex.

Equity investors often expect more of a say in how you run the company. In 2003, Heather Battey wanted to expand Spiritual Fitness Wear, her Mission Viejo (Calif.) workout apparel company. She brought in an investor who got a 5% stake. Although the investment agreement spelled out that Battey retained control of the company, the investor fought to have her way. After seven months, and with the woman threatening to sue, Battey bought her out. "It is hard to find people to invest without having to give up a huge percentage of your company or the rights, especially being small," says Battey. "You want the money, but you don't want to give up control." Battey has since turned down other friends who asked about an equity stake. She eventually took $30,000 from a friend—as a loan.

Still, entrepreneurs optimistic enough to foresee a relatively quick exit from their company may still prefer equity. When Shawn Harris started SkyWire Media in November, 2005, he eschewed loans. "I didn't want to consider debt," says Harris. After all, he anticipated an initial public offering or acquisition within a few years. To help finance the Las Vegas-based startup, which provides cell-phone ads and other mobile marketing services to businesses, Harris had planned to keep his job as a sales and business development executive at InfoGenesis, a technology company. But over Thanksgiving dinner at Harris' house, his father-in-law, Gerald Cunningham, a serial entrepreneur himself, grilled him about the company. Harris explained that he'd spoken with a potential customer whose enthusiasm for SkyWire's technology made him realize the company could be bigger than he initially thought. On the spot, Cunningham offered to invest. "I was just talking," says Harris. "I didn't ask him. I didn't volunteer anything. He saw the potential." Cunningham put in $44,000 and received less than 1% of SkyWire's common stock. Harris brought in 10 other investors, raising $250,000. He left his job to become CEO of the company, now with 11 employees, in March, 2006.

Rifling the Rolodex

Once you have some idea of which type of financing you're looking for and how much you might need, finding the right investors is all about who you know. Start by pulling out your address book or BlackBerry and listing potential investors. Include Mom and Dad, of course, but don't overlook the cousins you haven't visited in years or friends you see only in church on Sundays. Ask friends and neighbors if they know anyone who might be interested. But skip anyone with whom you have a shaky relationship or unresolved emotional issues, or for whom making an investment might be too risky, such as a grandparent on a fixed income or a friend who says he will tap his 401(k) for you.

No matter what form of financing you're seeking, be clear with potential investors about your expectations for the business, the risks of investing in it, what will happen if you can't repay them, and what role, if any, they are to play in operating the company. "The most common mistake is thinking that friends and family are easy targets, so you don't need a great pitch for a great business idea," says Guy Kawasaki, managing director of Garage Technology Ventures in Palo Alto, Calif. "The best model is to pretend you are meeting with [venture capital firms] Kleiner Perkins or Sequoia and give a great presentation." Go ahead and ditch the PowerPoint, but be prepared with a business plan and financial projections. Be direct and be passionate about your business. Better yet, show potential investors a tangible representation of your company, such as a prototype of your invention or the blueprint for your restaurant. "You want to bring the business to life," says Advani. "When family and friends feel they're helping you build something, they feel much happier about getting involved."

But every investment has its risks, and leavening your confidence with a bit of realism might prevent discord down the road. For Lisa and James Clunie, being frank made it easier to borrow from relatives to launch Rhombus Wear, which makes "studious but not stuffy," casual clothes. At first the Clunies worried borrowing might damage their relationships, and they didn't want any help. Says Lisa, the company's president: "We've really wanted to do things on our own terms and in our own way and show up at Thanksgiving and say 'Look what we've done!'" But as family members got wind of their plans, some asked if they could help. The Clunies gave potential investors a formal request for a five-year loan that included a business plan and three years of financial projections. They were careful to explain that they needed money to manufacture the clothes even before they knew if they would sell. Then it came time to negotiate terms. Clunie asked the relative who would likely make the largest loan what it would take to get him involved. She then worked with an accountant and determined, based on Rhombus' projected cash flow, that the company could handle payments at his requested rate of 8%. Two other family members then made loans under similar terms, and the Clunies had the $200,000 they expect to need to fill their first orders this spring. "It turns out that raising money from friends and family was a lot harder than we thought," says Lisa. "The lenders are so generous and so considerate. This was kind of a test to see if you can handle something like this, see if you can negotiate with somebody you care about."

To prepare for negotiations, first consult the Internal Revenue Service's applicable federal rates, which are the minimum rates Uncle Sam will allow you to charge to avoid classifying a loan as a gift. Then check the average rates your investors could get elsewhere, such as in a certificate of deposit, stock, or bond. Often, you'll have to match those rates, but some investors, particularly relatives, will give you a break. CircleLending's Advani says the current average interest for loans from a family member is 6.1%, compared with 8.2% for those from nonfamily members.

Consider asking investors for a grace period, perhaps six months or a year, to give you some breathing room. Clunie negotiated that first-year payments would be interest-only. Another option: a graduated repayment schedule that allows you to start with smaller payments. Balloon repayments also keep payments low but require a lump-sum payment at the end of the loan period.

Share the Wealth

Profit sharing is another way to reward your investors if your business is successful, with no risk to you if it is not. The Clunies promised their largest investor a bonus equal to 2% of net sales in the year that the loan is paid off, provided that the company's gross margin that year is at least 40%. Says Advani: "It is a great idea. It aligns everyone's interests and could also influence the behavior of your investors to really help you." Still, creating a profit-sharing plan can be tricky. The definition of profit varies, and it is difficult for a startup to project profits five or ten years down the line. A simpler option is to set a milestone, such as reaching $1 million in sales, and give your lenders a bonus payment or increase the interest rate on their loans when you reach the goal.

Once final terms have been nailed down, be sure to document them. "Far and away the biggest error entrepreneurs make is not stipulating the form of financing," says Bill Payne, entrepreneur-in-residence at the Kauffman Foundation and an angel investor. "They tend to be so grateful for Grandma's ten grand to get their business started that neither Grandma nor the entrepreneur document it." A promissory note is all that is needed for an unsecured loan. A secured loan requires a security agreement stating that, in the event of default, the lender has a claim on some property belonging to the borrower. For equity deals, your attorney will draw up term sheets and stock purchase agreements that indicate the number of shares an investor receives and the rights they carry.

Plan on being just as diligent about managing your investors once their money is in the bank. Whether they're lenders or shareholders, your investors will likely expect you to keep them informed about your progress. A quarterly letter or annual report can do this. Better yet, create a section of your company's Web site exclusively for investors, where they can get updates—and you can trumpet your successes—at any time.

Angel Investment Criteria

RICHARD SUDEK

Introduction

This study examines what business angel investors consider when reviewing an investment opportunity, and how they prioritize their investment criteria. Angel investors, who are often wealthy individuals with experience building a business, provide early stage financing, called seed capital, for start-up ventures. Venture capitalists (VCs) typically provide later stage financing, after the angels' investment.

Many start-up businesses need external financing to grow (Tyebjee & Bruno, 1984; Hisrich & Jankowicz, 1990). If these new ventures anticipate quick and aggressive growth, they often turn to angel or venture capital investors for capital. Angels invest more funds in more firms than any other source of outside financing (Freear, Sohl, & Wetzel, 1992). Although it is hard to estimate the exact size of angel investment due to its highly fragmented nature, in 2004 it was reported to total $22.5 billion (Sohl, 2005). This estimate puts total angel investments higher than formal venture capital investing for 2004 (Sohl, 2005).

Angel investing has provided seed capital for some famous U.S. businesses such as Bell Telephone in 1874, Ford Motor Company in 1903, and Apple Computer in 1977 (Van Osnabrugge & Robinson, 2000). Entrepreneurial ventures dramatically affect the U.S. economy and are the primary job-creating engine of our economy, providing three out of four new jobs (Ojala, 2002). To put this in perspective, it is estimated that new business start-ups averaged approximately 550,000 per month between 1996 and 2004 (Kauffman Foundation, 2005). The Small Business Administration estimates that 51 percent of private sector output is from small business (Van Osnabrugge & Robinson, 2000). Between 1995 to 1999, the *Inc.* 500 (the 500 fastest growing privately held companies in the U.S. reported by *Inc.* magazine) created 6 million of 7.7 million new jobs (Van Osnabrugge & Robinson, 2000). Clearly entrepreneurial businesses are a powerhouse in the U.S. economy.

Literature Review

Most of the literature which addresses the start-up investment decision process has focused on how VCs make investment decisions. (Elitzur & Gavious, 2003; Mason & Harrison, 2002). There has been little attention given to angel investors in the literature due to its private, fragmented nature. In fact, to the author's knowledge, this is the first empirical study addressing

U.S. angel investment criteria. It has been difficult to locate and survey angels (Mason & Harrison, 2002). However, since the late 1990s, angels have started to form organizations that help coordinate their efforts (Kauffman Foundation, 2002). Also, we can draw from the venture capital literature for angel investors due to some similarity of the investment process by angels and VCs. However, let us start with the differences between angel and VCs.

An important difference in the process between how angels and VCs invest is that VCs perform more due diligence than angels: "a recent study found that 71 percent of venture capitalists, but only eight percent of business angels, take three or more references, with the two groups averaging around four and one respectively" (Van Osnabrugge, 1998). Angels perform less professional due diligence than VCs, invest more opportunistically, rely more on instincts, and do not calculate internal rates of return (Timmons, 1990; Baty, 1991; Mason & Harrison, 1996; Van Osnabrugge & Robinson, 2000). VCs may have a staff of people to perform due diligence or may hire professional firms to perform all or portions of the due diligence process (Van Osnabrugge & Robinson, 2000). Since angel investors invest their own money (Benjamin & Margulis, 2000), they are less accountable than VCs, and their lack of rigor can lead to poorer investment decisions.

Angels and VCs also differ in their motives, their entrepreneurial experience, and their expected involvement (Van Osnabrugge & Robinson, 2000). In general, angel investors are much more involved with the companies in which they invest than VCs, and are often involved more in day-to-day operations than VCs (Benjamin & Margulis, 2000). In the United States, 87 percent of angels have operating experience (Freear and Wetzel, 1991), while a typical VC has little or no operating experience (Van Osnabrugge & Robinson, 2000). Angels typically have more entrepreneurial experience than VCs; research has shown that 75 to 83 percent of angels have start-up experience as compared to approximately 33 percent for VCs (Van Osnabrugge & Robinson, 2000). Often, angels will work part-time, with periods of full-time commitment, to help entrepreneurs through challenging issues (Van Osnabrugge & Robinson, 2000). In fact, some angels are looking to work on a regular basis at their investments, whereas VCs rarely have the intention of being involved in operations (Benjamin & Margulis, 2000). For these reasons, the angel investment often becomes more personal to both the investor and the entrepreneur. An angel investor is typically motivated beyond return on investment (ROI) (Benjamin & Margulis, 2000; Van Osnabrugge & Robinson, 2000), while VCs primary reason for existence is ROI. VCs are in business to return a profit on the partners' investment, while angels enjoy helping another entrepreneur build a business and giving back to the entrepreneurial community (Benjamin & Margulis, 2000; Van Osnabrugge & Robinson, 2000). In summary, VCs are more objective with regards to financial return, less emotionally attached, and more interested in ROI.

The literature suggests that the entrepreneur is the most important factor when evaluating a start-up (MacMillan, Siegel, & SubbaNarasimha, 1985, MacMillan, Zemann, & SubbaNarasimha, 1987; Van Osnabrugge & Robinson, 2000). Arthur Rock, a legendary venture capitalist, once said, "Nearly every mistake I've made has been in picking the wrong people, not the wrong idea" (Bygrave & Timmons, 1992, p. 6). Both angels and VCs feel that the entrepreneur and the management team (Van Osnabrugge, 1998; MacMillan et al., 1987; Van Osnabrugge & Robinson 2000) are the two factors that attract them to most deals. Macmillan, et al., (1985), for example, found that for VCs the quality of the entrepreneur ultimately determines the funding decision. Some literature suggests that angels are more attracted to the entrepreneur while VCs might be slightly more attracted to the idea (Van Osnabrugge & Robinson, 2000). VCs, for instance, often feel they can attract better management to a deal if the deal is fundamentally sound (Van Osnabrugge & Robinson, 2000; Ehrlich, Noble, Moore, & Weaver, 1994; Harrison & Mason, 1992; Freear, Sohl, & Wetzel, 1997; Macmillan et al.). Timmons and Spinelli (2004) stated that the management team can make the difference in venture success.

Some literature suggests the management team is the most important factor (Shepherd, 1999; Dixon, 1991; Macmillan et al., 1987). Carter and Van Auken (1992) found the management team second only to the entrepreneur in a survey of VCs consisting of 27 investment criteria. Clearly, the entrepreneur and the management team are very important criteria for the investment decision for both angels and VCs. Understanding the entrepreneur and the team are important in evaluating how angels and VCs prioritize their investment criteria. Understanding what characteristics angel investors look for in the entrepreneur is the next step to understand the investment decision process.

Carter and Van Auken (1992) found that out of 27 investment criteria, VCs found entrepreneur's honesty ranked first, and entrepreneur's commitment ranked second. Van Osnabrugge and Robinson (2000) performed a study of European start-up investments that showed enthusiasm and trustworthiness were ranked first and second, respectively out of twenty-seven investment criteria for angels—see Table 1.

Although VCs are more focused on a ROI for their limited partners, they still rank trustworthiness and enthusiasm higher than ROI. Coveney (1996) found that lack of trust reduces investment by angels. Timmons and Spinelli (2004) stated that the entrepreneur's commitment and determination are more important than any other factor when looking for successful entrepreneurs. Benjamin and Margulis (2000) stated that "Some investors are motivated by the passionate commitment of the entrepreneur. People committed to a venture can be persuasive;

Table 1 Van Osnabrugge Angel Investment Criteria

Selected Investment Criteria	Ranking
Enthusiasm of the entrepreneur(s)	1
Trustworthiness of the entrepreneur(s)	2
Sales potential of the product	3
Expertise of the entrepreneur(s)	4
Investor liked the entrepreneur(s) upon meeting	5
Growth potential of the market	6
Quality of product	7
Perceived financial rewards (for investors)	8
Niche market	9
Track record of the entrepreneur	10
Expected rate of return	11
Product's informal competitive protection	12
Investor's involvement possible (contribute skills)	13
Investor's strengths fills gaps in business	14
High margins of business	15
Low overheads	16
Nature of competition	17
Ability to reach break-even without further funding	18
Low initial capital expenditures needed (on assets)	19
Size of the investment	20
Product's overall competitive protection	21
Low initial cost to test the market	22
Venture is local	23
Investor understands the business/industry	24
Potential exit routes (liquidity)	24
Presence of (potential) co-investors	26
Formal competitive protection of product (patents)	27

they have enthusiasm and solid entrepreneurial vision [p. 95]" Benjamin and Margulis (2000) combined the themes of passion, commitment, and enthusiasm.

The themes of passion, commitment, and enthusiasm are used interchangeably throughout the literature (Coveney, 1996; Timmons & Spinelli, 2004, Benjamin & Margulis, 2000, Van Osnabrugge, 1998). Hence, this study treats them as the same construct relative to characteristics of the entrepreneur.

In addition, Van Osnabrugge and Robinson (2000) found that expertise of the entrepreneur, liking the entrepreneur upon meeting, and track record were important characteristics of the entrepreneur.

Integration and Research Question

With little literature focusing on the angel investment process, and an estimated $22.5 billion (Sohl, 2005) invested in 2005, it seems important to pursue empirical research in this area. A logical place to start is the understanding of how angel investors make their investment decision. Numerous studies have provided this same empirical research for VC investors, thus, the next step is to provide similar studies in the angel investment area. Therefore, this study will focus on providing empirical data regarding the U.S. angel investor decision process. To the author's knowledge, this is the first study to provide empirical data on how U.S. angel investors rank investment criteria. Van Osnabrugge (1998) provided empirical insight into the angel investment process in the U.K. Accordingly, the present study builds directly on the work of Van Osnabrugge. As such, the research objective for this study is to identify U.S. angel investment decision criteria. A secondary objective of this study is to understand how U.S. angel investors prioritize their investment criteria. Thus:

[**Research Question**]: How do U.S. angel investors prioritize their investment criteria?

Study Overview

There has been little research on how angel investors select their investments (Elitzur & Gavious, 2003). Understanding how angel investors rank investment criteria and the relative importance of their perceptions will help us understand the investment process better. The better we understand this process, the more likely we can improve the angel investment process.

This study utilized a two-phase approach to understanding how angels make their investment decisions. This two-phase approach consisted of a qualitative first phase and a quantitative second phase. The results of the first phase were intended to help inform the second phase and develop the quantitative instrument. (Miles & Huberman, 1994; Greene, Caracelli, & Graham, 1989). A participant-observer methodology was utilized in the first phase to collect data. In this case, the participant-observer methodology involved the researcher personally observing and experiencing the angel organization as a member. Patton (2002) discussed six key advantages of the participant-observer methodology. First, direct observation allows the observer to understand and capture interaction between people in context. Second, it allows the observer to be open to new information and be more inductive, relying less on prior conceptualizations. Third, one can see things unfold that may routinely escape the people involved in the process. Fourth, the opportunity to learn things while observing that might not be uncovered in interviews: sometimes, people are less likely to discuss sensitive topics in a direct interview that may be observed in the natural setting. Fifth, the ability to gather data that is not biased by an interviewer's selective perceptions. Finally, the process of the observations allows the observer to draw on firsthand experiences during the formal interpretations stage of analysis and discussion.

In the case of the current study, another advantage of the participant-observer methodology was complete access to the angel organization that the investors afforded to the investigator. This allowed a more natural observation versus an outsider to the organization. An outsider's results would not have been as accurate as members tend to modify their comments when outsiders

are present. In addition, outsiders are not allowed access to certain portions of organization meetings due to legal issues related to disclosure of information. Accordingly the qualitative phase was intended to create understanding of how angels go about their investment process, what they discuss, what seems important in evaluating a start-up, and how they prioritize their investment criteria. Collecting data through this process helped to build the survey for the second phase of the study.

The second phase was quantitative and consisted of surveying angels on what criteria they use to make an investment and how these criteria are prioritized. Existing literature was reviewed to identify any previously used questionnaires on angel investment criteria. This search identified one such instrument (Van Osnabrugge, 1998). Accordingly, in the phase two quantitative investigation, a quantitative questionnaire was developed based on the phase one qualitative results and the Van Osnabrugge (1998) instrument.

Method

This study was based on observation and survey of members of Tech Coast Angels (TCA). TCA is the largest angel organization in the U.S. consisting of 173 angels, as of August 2004. TCA is located in Southern California.

TCA members bring extensive and diverse experience and networking resources to the angel investment process. Since most of the members have been entrepreneurs, they can provide more than just a financial perspective to start-up companies. As an example, many can offer operating, marketing, sales, and engineering experience to the start-up company.

TCA does not invest as a whole but, rather, each angel decides whether to independently invest. The typical minimum investment per angel is $25,000, although some deals allow for lower amounts. As a whole, TCA typically provides funding in the range of $250,000 to $1,000,000 per venture. This financing garners from 10 to 40 percent ownership of the company. The terms of the transactions vary, but normally include preferred stock, automatic conversion to common stock at IPO, antidilution provisions, voting rights, and a board seat. As of August 2004, TCA had funded 81 companies with $52,707,836. In addition, these companies have received additional financing in excess of $536,633,332 from other sources.

The decision to invest in a company is often affected by the impression the investor forms of the entrepreneur and the company in the initial meeting. This initial meeting is often called a screening. At a screening, the entrepreneur presents the company plan and answers questions for potential investors. The screenings consist of two distinct sections. The first section is the public portion which normally consists of the entrepreneur presenting a PowerPoint slide show for 15 minutes; the next 15 minutes are dedicated to open question and answers. The public section typically consists of four presentations by four different entrepreneurs.

The second section consists of a private discussion where the angels discuss each presentation. This private portion provides the most enlightening observations. The angels effectively let down their guard during this discussion and speak freely about their perceptions of, concerns about, doubts about, and interest in the project. Two-hundred fifty-nine companies were observed at TCA screenings prior to the survey in August 2004. The qualitative phase was drawn from these screening observations.

The quantitative phase consisted of a survey instrument that was developed to survey TCA members on how they rank their investment criteria. The instrument was developed based on themes that emerged during the qualitative phase and the Van Osnabrugge instrument.

In reviewing the Van Osnabrugge instrument, there were many items that appeared appropriate to retain. Items discussed in the TCA meetings that were already on the Van Osnabrugge instrument were retained.

The next step was to delete items that did not seem appropriate for the TCA instrument. Based on the qualitative phase of the study, items were deleted based on their rarely being discussed in the screenings. In addition, some items were ambiguous, redundant, or did not apply. In addition, item terminology was modified to be more aligned with U.S. angel culture. These items were only edited, not removed.

The last step was to add items that emerged in phase one of the study but were not on the Van Osnabrugge instrument. The most important item that was added was that of the "management team". In addition, "barrier for entry of competitors", and "advisors currently involved" were added. The instrument consisted of a Likert scale with 5 being very important, and 1 being not important.

A survey pilot was tested with a handful of TCA members in July of 2004. After minor modifications for clarification, the survey was announced by the author at a monthly dinner meeting in August 2004. The survey was handed out to the dinner attendees and 30 members filled out the survey at the dinner and handed it back upon exiting. Two emails regarding the survey were sent to the membership after the dinner to encourage more participation. The total sample size for the survey was 173. In total, 73 members responded, a response rate of 42 percent. One survey was eliminated due to the member not having made any investments, therefore final sample size was 72.

Results
Qualitative Results

The purpose of the qualitative phase was to identify important decision criteria of angels that would be subsequently used in the quantitative phase. Common themes emerged from the observed screenings and associated discussions. The angels consciously focus most of their time and energy on four main themes. These themes are: the passion of the lead entrepreneur; the trustworthiness of the lead entrepreneur; the quality of the management team; and the existence of an exit strategy or liquidity potential for the investor.

Passion

Passion and commitment of the entrepreneur emerged as the most important criterion. Investors look for entrepreneurs who show passion. Entrepreneurs who demonstrated this quality typically received more interest than ones who may have had

a better business model or product but lacked passion. If the entrepreneur lacked passion or enthusiasm, investors appeared to be less interested. This may be due to the perception that start-up success is so difficult that entrepreneurs without great commitment and enthusiasm might be less likely to succeed. In the angel's mind, it appeared that commitment and passion would translate into business success.

Angels seemed particularly interested in whether the entrepreneur was passionate and committed to do whatever it takes to work through all of the problems of a start-up to succeed. Angels found entrepreneurs with passion and commitment more engaging and interesting. One entrepreneur that embodied this kind of passion was a financial services start-up that provided prepaid credit cards. While the entrepreneur did not have any actual financial services experience, he showed high energy enthusiasm that impressed the angels. In addition, he had made reasonable money in past careers and had put up most of his money, including mortgaging his house, to start the company. The passion and perceived commitment of this financial services entrepreneur garnered excitement from the investors.

Trustworthiness

From the angels' perspective, each interaction between the entrepreneur and the angels is an opportunity to build or break down trust. The richest content on this point surfaced when the entrepreneurs were out of the room. Some entrepreneurs benefited when they admitted that they did not have an answer to a specific question but would get the answer later. Others appeared to obfuscate, giving the angels sly answers. Generally, the angels agreed that if the entrepreneur was avoiding the question, he or she might not be able to be trusted. The entrepreneur failing to listen to the question was problematic in its own right. In addition, entrepreneurs who appeared to provide contradictory answers lost credibility and trust. Some angels clearly stated they did not trust a particular entrepreneur based on their answers to questions and had no further interest no matter how appealing the business proposition was. A lack of trust would often cancel out any of the business idea's merits, growth potential, or ROI potential in the minds of the angel investors. The entrepreneur has to be trustworthy.

Management Team

In the private portion of the discussion, questions would often emerge as to whether the management team was appropriate for the project. This discussion typically centered on whether all of the pieces of the management team were in place. The entrepreneur was not expected to be able to do everything. However, the angels did expect the entrepreneur to know what the shortcomings of the current team were, and what team members needed to be added.

As they did with the entrepreneur, the angels looked for passion and commitment in the team. A team that appeared to have passion, commitment, and an understanding of their individual roles was a plus. In addition, on a few occasions, a team that was part of a previous successful team was a highly regarded characteristic. For instance, a team that had success building a product and was then acquired by a large company was perceived as a winning combination.

While angels were less concerned about the team being in place for start-ups that were not very far along, they often asked questions to uncover whether the entrepreneur knew what type of team was needed for success. Accepting that the management team is an important attribute, the next step is to understand what characteristics of the management team are important to the angel investor. Coachablity of the team was one primary theme that was discussed. Teams that were perceived as not coachable were less likely to advance to due diligence phase of the process. Another aspect that was commonly discussed was the commitment of the team. This was often described as survivability. Investors liked teams that struggled through hard times and kept pursuing the venture. An example of a team that was considered to have high survivability was one that had been working their venture out of the garage for a long time to keep overhead low. The perception by the angels was that the team would do whatever it took to succeed. As with the entrepreneur, passion was discussed in relation to the team. Investors found that passion was not just necessary in the entrepreneur but in the team as a whole. Other themes that emerged were: experience of advisors, complementary skills of the advisors, track record of the individuals on the team, and experience of the team working together.

Exit

Angels primarily invest to receive a return on their money. Since angel investments usually have a 4–6 year horizon (Mason & Harrison, 2002), and return is typically only attained through an exit or liquidity event, angels seek ventures that will grow and be attractive to acquirers or have the possibility of an initial public offering (IPO). Since IPO's are rare, angels are very interested in learning who the potential acquirers may be for a particular venture. While observing entrepreneur presentations at TCA, it was not uncommon to observe a start-up that had already demonstrated profitability, had a solid business plan, and was led by an entrepreneur with a proven track record but did not garner much interest due to an unclear exit path.

In one example, a company had clearly identified potential acquirers and a potential sale price of the firm. Included in this were the potential returns the investors could receive from various acquirers upon liquidation. In addition, this entrepreneur had been part of a company that was built and sold within the industry, so he understood who would be interested, why they would want to purchase a company, and approximately how much they would invest. Again, since angels can only attain a return on their investment through a liquidity event, there is often a focus on who and why someone would want to purchase the start-up. The main theme for angels was seeing how the start-up reached an exit. The general feeling was if there is good growth in the company and there are likely exit paths, then the ROI will come.

In yet another example, a company did not have any information on exit in their presentation. When the entrepreneur was asked about their exit path, he responded "I believe we can do an IPO". This statement yielded strong feelings in the post-presentation discussion among angels. An IPO is such a rare event, that it caused angels to feel that the entrepreneur had not thought about a viable exit plan. Watching this process helped make it clear that the best business plan or idea might not be perceived as the best investment.

Other Themes Identified

Throughout observation of the screenings, many other themes emerged. These included: barrier to entry of competitors; intellectual property; growth potential; competition; profitability; what advisors were involved; domain knowledge of the investor similar to the start-up; and ROI. However, these themes were not as consistent nor did they carry the intensity of the four themes mentioned above. Also, some investors focused on specific criteria across all screening candidates. For instance, one investor asked nearly every entrepreneur how much of their own money was invested. When this investor was absent from a screening, this question was not consistently asked. Some investors often focused on functional areas of the business such as finance, marketing or on intellectual property. This was often due to their professional background. For example, someone who had a finance background might focus on issues related to the financial projections. In addition, through interviews, it was uncovered that some investors were biased towards certain criteria based on previous investment success or failure. For instance, one investor focused on understanding the competition, since he had previous investments fail due to competitor issues.

Quantitative Results

The results of the quantitative phase confirm the results in the qualitative phase, with trustworthiness (4.81), management team (4.64), enthusiasm (4.63), and exit (4.53) ranking as the top four criteria (5 being very important, 1 being not important). These results were expected based on the qualitative phase, however, there were no significant differences between the top 4 items and the next items in the survey.

With the exception of the "management team" item which was added for the purposes of this study, the results are similar to those of Van Osnabrugge (1998) which found enthusiasm ranked first, and trustworthiness ranked second. This study's results showed enthusiasm ranked third, and trustworthiness ranked first. The management team ranked second in this study. In addition, exit, which emerged as a top theme in the qualitative portion of the study, ranked fourth in the survey. Van Osnabrugge found exit to be twenty-fourth. Table 2 shows the ranking of the survey items.

Most venture capital literature shows the management team ranking high in investment criteria. This study shows the management team ranked second and, thus, is an important investment criterion. The literature lacks detail on which attributes of the management team are important. This study shows passion (4.71), survivability (4.42), and openness (4.33) of the team are the top 3 criteria for the management team. Table 3 shows the items and ranking of the management team.

The sample was predominately male (males = 68, females = 4). Since there were only four females in the study, no analysis

Table 2   Results of Investment Criteria (N = 72)

Investment Criteria	Rank of Current Study	Mean	STD	Rank of Van Onsabrugge
Trustworthiness/honesty of the entrepreneur(s)	1	4.81	.399	2
Management Team	2	4.64	.657	N/A
Enthusiasm/commitment of the entrepreneur(s)	3	4.63	.592	1
Potential exit routes (potential liquidity)	4	4.53	.712	24
Revenue potential	5	4.47	.581	3
Domain expertise of the entrepreneur(s)	6	4.44	.603	4
Growth potential of the market	7	4.29	.701	6
Return on Investment (ROI)	8	4.26	.805	11
Barrier for entry for competitors	9	4.19	.781	N/A
Product's overall competitive protection (in market segment)	10	4.11	.815	21
Profit margin of the business	11	4.08	.746	15
Track record of the entrepreneur(s)	12	4.00	.839	10
Competition of market segment	13	3.94	.785	17
Liked entrepreneur(s) upon meeting	14	3.90	.922	5
Product's formal competitive protection (patents)	15	3.56	.933	27
Your personal knowledge of the business/industry	16	3.53	.822	27
Ability to maintain low overhead	17	3.46	1.020	18
Potential of co-investors present	18	3.44	1.033	18
Advisors currently involved	19	3.40	.899	N/A
Niche market	20	3.31	1.121	9
Size of the investment	21	3.26	.769	20
Ability to reach break-even without further funding	22	3.24	1.000	18
Low initial capital expenditures needed (i.e. on assets)	23	3.22	.996	22
Investor's (your) strengths fill gaps in business	24	2.92	1.017	20
Ability for involvement possible (contribute skills)	25	2.85	.914	13

Table 3   Results of Management Team Criteria (N = 72)

Item	Rank	Mean	STD
Passion of the team	1	4.71	.568
Perceived sense of survivability of the team (how persistence they will be without giving up)	2	4.42	.707
Openness of team for mentoring (coachabilty)	3	4.33	.628
Track record of individual team members	4	4.04	.759
How complementary the skills of the team are	5	3.87	.691
Experience of the advisors	6	3.67	.888
How much experience the team has working together	7	3.22	.826

was performed related to gender differences. The mean age of the investors was 53.7 (N = 70). Forty-nine angels had started a business with a minimum of five employees and stayed in business for at least three years (N = 69). The mean level of education was 2.83 (N = 72, 1 = high school diploma, 2 = bachelors degree, 3 = masters degree, 4 = PhD). The distribution of the highest degree completed were as follows: 11 PhDs, 41 Masters, 17 bachelors, and three high school diplomas. The mean number of face to face meetings the angels have with the entrepreneurs before making an investment were 6.02 (N = 66). Angels were asked in what percentage of investments do they have domain expertise. The results show that they have domain expertise in 54 percent of their investments (N = 66, low = 10%, high = 100%). The mean number of investments made were 10.54 (N = 72, low = 1, high = 50). Of those investments, 48% had no exit yet, 32% had a negative return, and 20% had a positive return (N = 71). Analysis was performed to see if there was a relationship between investment experience (based on number of investments) and criteria rankings. This analysis showed no significant relationship between investor experience and criteria rankings. However, if we group number of investments by least experience (up to 5 investments), medium experience (6–15 investments), and most experience (over 15 investments), "honesty" was rated as very important by 71 percent of least experienced investors, 82 percent of those with medium experience, and 93 percent of those with the most investing experience. Only 58 percent of least experienced investors rated enthusiasm as highly important criterion, compared to 71 percent for investors with more than five investments. The mean year for starting investing was 1991 (oldest 1971, most recent 2004, N = 72). The mean total investment amount per angel was $1,610,363 (N = 69). However, there were three total investment amounts of $25,000,000, $20,000,000, and $18,000,000, which were angels who also do VC investing. If we remove these investments, the mean total investment amount per investor was $729,015 (N = 66). Again, analysis was performed to see if there was a relationship between investment experience (based on investment amount) and criteria rankings. This analysis also showed no significant relationship between investor experience and criteria rankings. The mean years to expected liquidity were 5.25 years (N = 72). Angels were asked to weight the importance of motivation based on three categories. The means were 62.85% for return on investment, 21.70% for helping build companies, and 15.45% for mentoring entrepreneurs (N = 71).

Discussion

The primary focus of this study was to identify U.S. angel investment decision criteria. Secondary focus was to understand how U.S. angel investors prioritize investment criteria. There has been little empirical research that provides insight on how U.S. angel investors rank their investment criteria (Wetzel, 1987; Harr, Starr, & MacMillan, 1988).

Confirming the results of the qualitative phase of the research, the most important findings in the quantitative phase were that TCA Angel investors rank trustworthiness, enthusiasm, and the management team high in their investment criteria. As such, this study showed results similar to the Van Osnabrugge (1998) survey. Greater understanding of how investors prioritize their investment criteria will allow us to build better due diligence processes and potentially improve the overall investment process and resulting outcomes.

This study brings new information to light with regard to how important the management team is to the investor. There is much research which has focused on the entrepreneur. It seems logical that the entrepreneur may be the single most important member of the management team. However, the team is usually very important to the success of a new venture. Understanding more about how investors perceive a good management team will help us understand the investment process in more depth. This study showed that the combination of passion and commitment was the most important ingredient for the management team from the investor point of view. This result makes sense since enthusiasm of the entrepreneur ranked third in the investment criteria. Clearly, investors feel that passion is necessary to attain success. This can be explained by the often grueling and difficult process entrepreneurs go through to build a company. A management team without strong passion may not have enough drive to go the long haul. The second attribute for a management team is survivability. This goes hand-in-hand with passion. A successful management team of a start-up needs to

have passion for what they are doing and a strong drive to survive the challenges they will encounter. This finding supports the need to further understand the soft side of the investment process. Trustworthiness, enthusiasm, passion of the team, and sense of team survivability are all qualitative aspects of investment criteria.

The results of this study differ from the Van Osnabrugge (1998) survey in a number of ways. Since there is little literature comparing U.S. and U.K. angel investors, we cannot draw any clear conclusion regarding the distinctions. However, a few differences between this study and the Van Osnabrugge (1998) survey should be noted. Although this survey consisted of only 72 angels from one angel organization, it is the first U.S.-based angel investment criteria survey. It might not be possible to generalize this organization to all U.S. angels; however, since the angels of this organization invest independently of each other and are from diverse backgrounds, some generalizabilty may be suggested. Two items which were rated near opposite ends of the scale by U.S. and U.K. angels were "Potential exit routes" and "Liked entrepreneur upon meeting". U.S. angels rated "Potential exit routes" at fourth, while U.K. angels rated it twenty-fourth. A potential explanation for this may be a focus by U.S. investors on success in the investment process. If a new venture does not have a clear exit path, it is unlikely to be successful and bring any return to the investor. This may also explain why U.S. angels rated "Liked entrepreneur upon meeting" fourteenth, while U.K. angels rated it fifth. The perception of TCA investors is that almost all of the deals funded are expected to need venture capital investment. The venture capital model typically allows for the entrepreneur to be replaced. It is possible that TCA investors are not concerned whether they like the entrepreneurs but whether they can be trusted and if the venture is likely to be successful. In addition, angels who are part of a formalized investment association may be more likely motivated by ROI rather than mentoring entrepreneurs or building companies. Additional, albeit weaker, support for this assertion is that this study showed ROI ranked eighth by U.S. angels and eleventh by U.K. angels.

There are many potential logical steps beyond this study. First, a larger sample could be attained to verify the findings here. Second, the top criteria could be studied in more depth. Understanding how investors form their perceptions of these top criteria may allow us to develop a better process in evaluating these constructs. Third, a longitudinal study could be initiated that tracks investments and how investors rank these criteria to see if there are any correlations with the investment criteria and success in the venture. Due to many external forces that may lead to start-up failure such as market shifts, government regulations changes, and unanticipated competitor moves, developing a high correlation between investment criteria and success may prove to be difficult.

Practical Implications

There are practical implications for both entrepreneurs and investors in this study. First, entrepreneurs need to realize that a good idea alone is not enough to obtain funding. How an entrepreneur manages the presentation to investors, answers questions, and facilitates the relationship through the process will have an impact on securing funding. Second, entrepreneurs need to build a management team that investors are willing to trust and invest in. It is important that the entrepreneur communicate about the team to the investors. Third, entrepreneurs need to clearly communicate an exit strategy for investors so that they can see an eventual return on their investment. Fourth, investors need to be aware how faulty first impressions can be in the initial stages of meeting an entrepreneur. Jumping to conclusions on how trustworthy and passionate the entrepreneur is needs to be evaluated through the due diligence process. Angels tend to spend most of their time in the due diligence process evaluating the quantitative side of the deal; more time spent on the qualitative side, or soft side, might lead to better investments. Angel investors should consider utilizing new techniques to evaluate the soft side of the deal rather than just their gut feeling. Effective human capital assessment tools appear not to be prevalent in the start-up area, therefore, more rigorous interview techniques and entrepreneur background reviews may be helpful.

Limitations

The major limitation of this study is the fact that only one angel investing organization was surveyed. Although TCA is one of the largest angel organizations in the country and, therefore, may be a good sample for predicting the behavior of the U.S. angel population, extending the survey to other organizations and individual angel investors would increase the power of the study. Also, inherent in any self-reported survey is the issue of accuracy and bias. It is possible that some investors may have biased their answers to a more socially acceptable orientation. As with any self-reporting survey there is no opportunity to verify the accuracy of the responses. In addition, the participant-observer process utilized in the qualitative phase can be susceptible to bias, inaccurate perceptions, and selective perceptions.

Conclusion

This study addresses an important gap in current academic literature on angel investors. This study surveyed U.S. angel investors to help understand how they evaluate and prioritize their investment criteria. This study highlights the importance of the passion of the lead entrepreneur, the management team, trustworthiness of the lead entrepreneur, and a reasonable exit strategy as the most important ingredients for angel investors. This study takes the next step in understanding what angel investors are looking for from the management team. Passion, survivability, and openness to mentoring are the top three ingredients for the management team.

A greater understanding of how angel investors make their investment decisions will allow them to review how their due diligence processes align with their investment decisions. This in turn will lead to a better investment process. Additionally, entrepreneurs will have a better understanding of what angel investors are looking for.

References

Baty, G.B. (1991). *Entrepreneurship for the 1990s*. Englewood Cliffs, NJ: Prentice Hall.

Benjamin, G.A. & Margulis, J. (2000). *Angel Financing: How to Find and Invest in Private Equity*. New York: John Wiley & Sons.

Bygrave, W.D. & Timmons, J.A. (1992). *Venture Capital at the Crossroads*. Boston, MA: Harvard Business School Press.

Carter, R.B. & Van Auken, H.E. (1992). Effect of professional background on venture capital proposal evaluation. *Journal of Small Business Strategy, 3*(1): 45–55.

Coveney, P. (1996). *Informal Investment in Britain: An Examination of the Behaviors, Characteristics, Motives and Preferences of British Business Angels*. Unpublished doctoral dissertation, Univeristy of Oxford.

Dixon, R. (1991). VCs and the appraisal of investments. *OMEGA International Journal of Management Science,19,* 333–344.

Elitzur, R. & Gavious, A. (2003). Contracting, signaling, and moral hazard: a model of entrepreneurs, angels, and venture capitalists. *Journal of Business Venturing, 18,* 709–725.

Ehrlich, S.B., Noble, A.F., Moore, T., & Weaver, R.R. (1994). After the cash arrives: a comparative study of venture capital firms and private investor involvement in entrepreneurial firms. *Journal of Business Venturing, 9,* 67–82.

Freear, J. & Wetzel, W.E. (1991, April). *The informal venture capital market in the year 2000.* Paper presented at the Third Annual International Research Symposium on Small Business Research, Florida State University.

Freear, J., Sohl, J.E., & Wetzel, W.E. (1992). *The truth about angels more than a myth.* Working Paper, Center for Venture Research, University of New Hampshire.

Freear, J., Sohl, J.E., & Wetzel, W.E. (1997). "The informal venture capital market: milestones passed and the road ahead." In D. Sexton and R. Smilor (eds) *Entrepreneurship 2000* (Chicago: Upstart Publishing Company), 47–70.

Greene, J.C., Caracelli, V.J., & Graham, W.F. (1989). Toward a conceptual framework for mixed-method evaluation designs. *Educational Evaluation and Policy Analysis, 11*(2), 255–274.

Harr, N.E., Starr, J., & MacMillan, I.C. (1988). Informal risk capital investors: investment patterns on the east coast of the U.S.A. *Journal of Business Venturing, 3,* 11–29.

Harrison, R.T. & Mason, C.M. (1992). International perspectives on the supply of informal venture capital. *Journal of Business Venturing, 7,* 459–475.

Hisrich, R. & Jankowicz, A. (1990). Intuition in venture capital decisions: an exploratory study using a new technique. *Journal of Business Venturing, 5,* 49–62.

Kauffman Foundation. (2002). *Business angel investing groups growing in North America.* Retrieved April 10, 2006, from http://www.kauffman.org/pdf/angel_summit_report.pdf.

Kauffman Foundation. (2005). *Kauffman index of entrepreneurial activity.* Retrieved April 10, 2006, from http://research.kauffman.org/cwp/Show Property/webCacheRepository/Documents/2005.Fairlie.KauffmanIndex.pdf.

MacMillan, I.C., Sigel, R., & SubbaNarashimha, P.N. (1985). Criteria used by venture capitalists to evaluate new venture proposals. *Journal of Business Venturing, 1,* 119–128.

MacMillan, I.C., Zemann, L., & SubbaNarashimha, P.N. (1987). Criteria distinguishing successful from unsuccessful ventures in the venture screening process. *Journal of Business Venturing, 2,* 123–137.

Mason, C.M. & Harrison, R.T. (1996). Why 'business angels' say no: a case study of opportunities rejected by an informal investor syndicate. *International Small Business Journal, 14*(2), 35–51.

Mason, C.M. & Harrison, R.T. (2002). Is it worth it? The rates of return from informal venture capital investments. *Journal of Business Venturing, 17,* 211–236.

Miles, M.B. & Huberman, A.M. (1994). *Qualitative Data Analysis: An Expanded Sourcebook.* Thousand Oaks, CA: Sage.

Ojala, M. (2002). Researching Small Business Concerns. *Online, 26*(6), 55–57.

Patton, M.Q. (2002). *Qualitative Research and Evaluation Methods.* Thousand Oaks, CA: Sage Publications.

Shepherd, D.A. (1999). Venture capitalists' assessment of new venture survival. *Management Science, 45*(5), 621–632.

Sohl, J. (n.d.). *The angel investor market 2004: the angel market sustains the modest recovery.* Retrieved April 8, 2006 from University of New Hampshire Web site: http://www.unh.edu/news/docs/cvr2004.pdf

Timmons, J.A. (1990). *Planning and Financing the New Venture.* Acton, MA: Brick House Publishing Co.

Timmons, J.A.& Spinelli, S. (2004). *New Venture Creation: Entrepreneurship for the 21st Century.* New York, NY: McGrawHill/Irwin.

Tyebjee, T. & Bruno, A. (1984). A model of venture capitalist investment activity. *Management Science, 30*(9), 1051–1066.

Van Osnabrugge, M. (1998). *The Financing of Entrepreneurial Firms in the UK.* Unpublished doctoral dissertation, Univeristy of Oxford.

Van Osnabrugge, M. & Robinson, R. J. (2000). *Angel investing: matching start-up funds with start-up companies: the guide for entrepreneurs, individual investors, and venture capitalist.* San Francisco: Jossey-Bass.

Wetzel, W.E. (1987). The informal venture capital market: aspects of scale and market efficiency. *Journal of Business Venturing, 2,* 299–313.

Venture Capital 101: What Is Venture Capital?

Venture capital has enabled the United States to support its entrepreneurial talent and appetite by turning ideas and basic science into products and services that are the envy of the world. Venture capital funds and builds companies from the simplest form—perhaps just the entrepreneur and an idea expressed as a business plan—to freestanding, mature organizations.

Risk Capital for Business

Venture capital firms are professional, institutional managers of risk capital that enables and supports the most innovative and promising companies. This money funds new ideas that could not be financed with traditional bank financing, that threaten established products and services in a corporation, and that typically require five to eight years to be launched.

Venture capital firms are professional, institutional managers of risk capital that enables and supports the most innovative and promising companies.

Venture capital is quite unique as an institutional investor asset class. When an investment is made in a company, it is an equity investment in a company whose stock is essentially illiquid and worthless until a company matures five to eight years down the road. Follow-on investment provides additional funding as the company grows. These "rounds," typically occurring every year or two, are also equity investment, with the shares allocated among the investors and management team based on an agreed "valuation." But, unless a company is acquired or goes public, there is little actual value. Venture capital is a long-term investment.

More Than Money

The U.S. venture industry provides the capital to create some of the most innovative and successful companies. But venture capital is more than money. Venture capital

Venture Capital Backed Companies Known for Innovative Technology and Products 2000 and 2006 Employment

Company	2000	2006	# Change
Intel Corporation	86,100	103,200	17,100
Microsoft	39,100	71,000	31,900
Medtronic, Inc.	21,490	36,000	14,510
Apple Inc.	8,568	17,100	8,532
Google	—	10,600	10,600

Source: Hoover's

Venture Capital Backed Companies Known for Innovative Business Models 2000 and 2006 Employment

Company	2000	2006	# Change
The Home Depot	201,000	345,000	144,000
Starbucks Corporation	47,000	116,700	69,700
Staples	49,993	68,500	18,507
Whole Foods Market, Inc.	18,500	38,600	20,100
PetSmart, Inc.	19,825	30,300	10,475
eBay	1,927	12,800	10,873

Source: Hoover's

partners become actively engaged with a company, typically taking a board seat. With a startup, daily interaction with the management team is common. This limits the number of startups in which any one fund can invest. Few entrepreneurs approaching venture capital firms for money are aware that they essentially are asking for 1/6 of a person!

Yet that active engagement is critical to the success of the fledgling company. Many one- and two-person companies have received funding but no one- or two-person company has ever gone public! Along the way, talent must be recruited and the company scaled up. Ask any venture capitalist who has had an ultra-successful investment and he or she will tell you that the company that broke through the gravity evolved from the original business plan concept with the careful input of an experienced hand.

Deal Flows—Where the Buys Are

For every 100 business plans that come to a venture capital firm for funding, usually only 10 or so get a serious look, and only one ends up being funded. The venture capital firm looks at the management team, the concept, the marketplace, fit to the fund's objectives, the value-added potential for the firm, and the capital needed to build a successful business. A busy venture capital professional's most precious asset is time. These days, a business concept needs to address world markets, have superb scalability, be made successful in a reasonable timeframe, and be truly innovative. A concept that promises a 10 or 20 percent improvement on something that already exists is not likely to get a close look.

Many technologies currently under development by venture capital firms are truly disruptive technologies that do not lend themselves to being embraced by larger companies whose current products could be cannibalized by this. Also, with the increased emphasis on public company quarterly results, many larger organizations tend to reduce spending on research and development and product development when things get tight. Many talented teams have come to the venture capital process when their projects were turned down by their companies.

Common Structure—Unique Results

While the legal and economic structures used to create a venture capital fund are similar to those used by other alternative investment asset classes, venture capital itself is unique. Typically, a venture capital firm will create a Limited Partnership with the investors as LPs and the firm itself as the General Partner. Each "fund," or portfolio, is a separate partnership. A new fund is established when the venture capital firm obtains necessary commitments from its investors, say $100 million. The money is taken from investors as the investments are made. Typically, an initial funding of a company will cause the venture fund to reserve three or four times that first investment for follow-on financing. Over the next three to eight or so years, the venture firm works with the founding entrepreneur to grow the company. The payoff comes after the company is acquired or goes public.

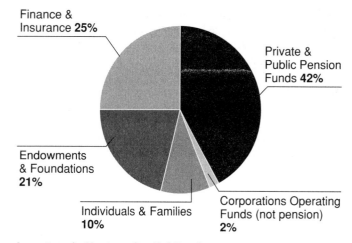

Investors in Venture Capital Funds

Source: 2004 NVCA Yearbook prepared by Thomson Financial using 2003 data

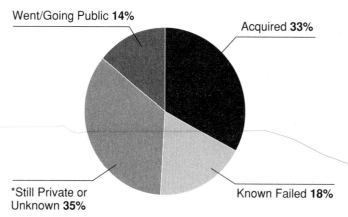

The Exit Funnel—Outcomes of the 11,686 Companies First Funded 1991 to 2000

* Of these, most have quietly failed

Although the investor has high hopes for any company getting funded, only one in six ever goes public and one in three is acquired.

Economic Alignment of All Stakeholders—An American Success Story

Venture capital is rare among asset classes in that success is truly shared. It is not driven by quick returns or transaction fees. Economic success occurs when the stock price increases above the purchase price. When a company is successful and has a strong public stock offering, or is acquired, the stock price of the company reflects its success. The entrepreneur benefits from appreciated stock and stock options. The rank and file employees throughout the organization historically also do well with their stock options. The venture capital fund and its investors split the capital gains per a pre-agreed formula. Many college endowments, pension funds, charities, individuals, and corporations have benefited far beyond the risk-adjusted returns of the public markets.

What's Ahead

Much of venture capital's success has come from the entrepreneurial spirit pervasive in the American culture, financial recognition of success, access to good science, and fair and open capital markets. It is dependent upon a good flow of science, motivated entrepreneurs, protection of intellectual property, and a skilled workforce.

The nascent deployment of venture capital in other countries is gated by a country's or region's cultural fit, tolerance for failure, services infrastructure that supports developing companies, intellectual property protection, efficient capital markets, and the willingness of big business to purchase from small companies.

Pursuing Venture Capital

WILLIAM J. LINK

Seventeen years ago, I worked with a stellar team to build Chiron Vision, a company I founded in 1986. It took several long months and hundreds of edits before we felt our business plan was ready to be presented to potential investors. Our goal was to focus the company on ophthalmic surgical products primarily for cataract and refractive surgery and position it for an eventual sale.

These days, I am a venture capitalist. Some 10 to 20 entrepreneurs as hopeful as I was at Chiron approach me every week, and I read more than 50 business plans and executive summaries a month. Despite all the news about venture capital shrinking, I see that investors are still making deals. In fact, the most knowledgeable entrepreneurs with the best deals still receive multiple competitive offers from financiers vying for the chance to invest in their companies.

Based on my venture capital experience, I now recognize more of the major elements of building a business and approaching investors that could have helped me at Chiron. Securing venture capital—the major source of money for growth—is a matter of entrepreneurs understanding that they need to approach this market as both sellers and buyers. What follows is a look at the steps necessary on each side.

You, the Seller

As an entrepreneur seeking venture capital, you are, at the most fundamental level, a seller. You are selling your business idea and your ability to execute on that idea. Securing the funding you need is a matter of taking specific steps, namely the following:

Gain Access

One of the biggest challenges entrepreneurs face when pursuing funding is gaining access to venture capitalists. Submitting your business plan is not as simple as shooting off a few dozen e-mails. In most situations, it is crucial that you begin by networking with the right people. Most venture capitalists are looking for new business ideas that have been endorsed by people they know and trust, such as other entrepreneurs, lawyers and accountants who understand the funding business. Unfortunately, due to the number of plans we need to review, an unannounced e-mail from an entrepreneur may not get our attention.

Endorsement is a critical part of beginning the venture capital relationship, and gaining the respect of well-connected professionals should be a major first step for any entrepreneur looking for capital.

Prepare an Arresting Executive Summary

Once you have an introduction to a venture capitalist, your executive summary is the second door to open in the process. Your summary should be brief—no more than three pages—but should encapsulate the thrust of your full plan without going too deeply into the details. A good executive summary includes an overview of your company's goals, the market you will be targeting, the competitive advantage the company has, the people involved in the business, the projected timeline, and financial projections and cash requirements.

The bottom line is that if you want to get someone to spend time reviewing your lengthy business plan, you need to hook the reader with this essential first document.

Write an Excellent Business Plan

Once you're in the door and the venture capitalists have recognized your executive summary as exciting enough for consideration, you need to begin the true selling portion of your relationship. Selling your ideas to a virtual stranger is not exactly comfortable, but it is crucial that you explain your business model thoroughly and passionately. That said, do not think that a good business plan is a long business plan. Complete information communicated thoroughly but with brevity is more important to success than extraneous information added for no reason other than increasing length.

To be truly excellent, your business plan needs to demonstrate the market for your product or service, including information about the competitive landscape. It must also clearly outline the necessary research and development and the risks involved.

The plans that stand out in my experience are those that raise a question in the reader's mind and then go on to answer it. For example, if there are some major risks related to the competition, mention them and then address them directly. Remember, the venture capitalist reading your plan will conduct independent research to make sure your information is accurate, and you can consider the deal over if you have left out any significant details or failed to address them completely.

Address Financial Needs in the Plan

Your financial needs are another important element of the plan. It is essential that the venture capitalist know how much money is required to fund the project to self-sufficiency, which is the ultimate goal. You should also align those needs with timing goals and valuation expectations. Again, we will figure it out if it's not there, so it's better to answer the questions before we notice that you did not do so. Your financial needs should be clearly laid out on a year-by-year basis.

Venture capitalists will conduct extensive risk assessment—we will independently evaluate opportunities and risks. Personal references are a crucial part of this fact-checking period, so make sure you have credible sources that will vouch for you. Also note that we will conduct independent research by speaking with our contacts in the industry to determine their take on your market and potential.

Sell Your Most Important Element: You

When approaching venture capitalists, you need to demonstrate the passion and dedication to your venture that you undoubtedly feel. Hopefully, the investors will recognize your ability to build a company based on your plan and your proficiency and extend an offer.

Venture capitalists look for entrepreneurs with experience leading a management team in the chosen market, as well as proven expertise in operations, research and development, finances and marketing, or a solid plan to attract top talent to those positions. The investor is betting on you just as much as the business opportunity, so don't sell yourself short when presenting your capabilities.

You, the Buyer

Once you have garnered the interest of the venture capitalists, remember that you are a buyer of their services as well as a seller of your dreams to them. So turn the tables and make sure you see the passion in their eyes and feel that your company will be an important addition to their stable of investments.

At the most fundamental level, you should not look just for the highest bidder or the biggest name—you should look for a partner who can help build your company. This is a relationship that needs to be productive for years, so seek out investors with a strong understanding of your market and domain, proven track records, and references that will speak to their skills in financial and strategic contributions.

There is no doubt that venture capitalists must assess risks and financial rewards, and that legalities and negotiations will be uncomfortable and distressing, but you should not enter a relationship with a venture capitalist that you do not trust on some level. Remember, this person could very well hold an active and high-ranking seat on your board and add significant direction to your company, so chemistry and trust are crucial. To determine if the investor is right for you, consider the following checklist:

Request References

The references you ask for should relate directly to your market sector and the lead investor in your company. Call the references—you can bet that the investors are calling your references, so make sure you do your own due diligence. Ask them carefully planned questions about the negotiation process, the first few months into the deal, and the ongoing relationship. Listen carefully for hidden clues. You should expect some level of discontent—almost every type of business deal has faults, but the overall feeling should be of confidence and respect.

Check the Passion Quotient

Does the lead investor appear sincerely passionate about your company, or is the person just going through the sales motions? You should be very careful to ensure that the investors feel an affinity for your product or service, since they will likely be actively directing your company.

Consider Experience

Have the venture capitalists you are working with ever built companies on their own? Do they have the experience of securing financing for their own companies, or are they straight from business school? Look for people who recognize entrepreneurial spirit and respect it.

Evaluate Interim Expectations

Many current venture capital deals are made with built-in "milestones," which predetermine steps that your company needs to take prior to receiving portions of money. Determine whether the milestones that you will be forced to meet are reasonable. Do not get stuck in a no-win situation in which you cannot possibly make the sales goals outlined.

In 1997, I achieved my goal of selling my own company, Chiron Vision, which was bought for $310 million by Bausch & Lomb, a global eye care company that had made the strategic decision to enter the ophthalmic surgical field and saw the potential for the products we developed.

Such an end game is within reach for entrepreneurs who secure venture capital, the type of funding most likely to position a company for substantial growth. So pursue these critical financiers, keeping in mind that you are both a seller of your dream and buyer of their services. Ask a lot of questions, do all your homework and choose carefully.

WILLIAM J. ("Bill") **LINK,** 56, co-founded Versant Ventures, a venture capital firm based in Newport Beach, California, in 1999.

Evaluating a Venture Capital Firm to Meet Your Company's Needs

What is the best way to approach and work with a venture capital firm? What do venture firms look for in evaluating a new company? How should the entrepreneur go about evaluating that firm and any financing it might provide his company? Venture firms are as different as entrepreneurs. There is thus a wide range among these firms in terms of their industry expertise, business experience and, most importantly, their ability to work effectively with you.

Your process of selecting a venture firm is, therefore, much more analogous to the selection of key managers in your company than it is to the selection of a bank for a loan. With a banker, the appropriate question is How much money will he give me? With a venture firm, the right question is How much money will he make me?

This is because your venture firm, if used effectively, will be an important element in the continuous decision making process of your company. The venture capitalist can bring a broad perspective of experience to your corporate problems based on multiple other corporate situations in your industry with which he has been involved. This experience enables him to recognize patterns within your company and industry niche which may be invisible to you. For example, he would be aware of external factors beyond your control which are already influencing other market niches in your industry and which your company will either capitalize on or be limited by.

When you select a venture firm, you are likely to be embarking on a relationship that will last five to ten years or more and which can be a pivotal factor in turning your company into a major enterprise. Because of the rate at which a high growth venture company encounters new challenges, decision making times can be greatly shortened. Therefore, the relationship with your venture firm can be critical.

A talented venture firm reinforces management's naturally good instincts on solving corporate problems and discerning industry directions. The less experience you have in some matters, the more you may need to rely on your venture firm's advice. The more experience you have, the more you will appreciate the quality of the advice.

The venture firm's investment makes it uniquely dedicated to your success. Venture firms only succeed if you succeed and this frequently depends on their ability to persuade you to do what is in your own self-interest. Therefore, the key question to ask in evaluating a venture firm is: do you believe that you can develop a relationship with the firm such that your confidence in it will accelerate your problem solving and decision making to enable you to emerge as a world class competitor in your industry?

How Venture Firms Evaluate You

This is a two way process: you should be evaluating venture firms and how well they understand your market at the same time they are evaluating you. Unless you have previously known and worked with a venture firm, you should expect to have a number of intensive meetings with the firm's principals to develop a personal relationship. Remember, the venture firm is backing you and your team as individuals. A new start-up is like a marriage—both parties must get to know one another well before any long term plans can be made.

The Business Plan

The business plan you present to a venture capital firm will likely be the single most important written document in the early years of your firm. Investigation of this plan by the venture firm will account for much of the discussion you have with the venture firm. It is the vehicle around which you get to know each other.

The plan should contain the business concept, the marketing, production and technology elements, the backgrounds of the principal founders and how much money will be required. The more specific the plan, the better—both for the venture capitalist now and you later on. Ironically, experience has shown that the longer the plan, the lower the likelihood of success. The concise articulation of a simple but powerful concept for an innovative solution to an emerging but important unmet customer need is the hallmark of a good business plan.

As every business has different needs and goals, one really cannot be much more specific about what should be included in a plan. However, there are some general principles that can be followed, both in developing the plan and in the subsequent dealings with the venture firm. You can keep these principles in mind and assess your own plans and discussions against them.

Defining Your Contribution

It may seem self-evident to say that a new company must make a true contribution to prosper, but attention to this fundamental discipline of a free market system is often lost in the enthusiasm to start a new company in a growth market. Unfortunately, despite that growth, market share will only go to a new company if it is adding value by solving unmet customer needs.

A simple formula venture capitalists tend to use in evaluating the potential size of your company is:

Market Size × Market Growth × Your Contribution = Size
Naturally, the more experienced the venture capitalist is in your industry, the more readily he is likely to grasp the significance of your contribution to the target customers.

In defining your company's contribution, a balance must be struck between biting off too much too soon and not having adequate value-added to justify starting the company. If the definition of served customer needs is too narrow, the company will tend to be vulnerable, small and potentially trapped in a limited growth path. On the other hand, too broad a definition requires resources beyond what the company will have for years.

Ideally, a company should initially serve highly specific customer needs that lie within a broader generic category of needs of the same customers or industry. The company can then execute profitably in the short-term as well as grow smoothly through a coherent product line and market expansion. To grow continuously, a company must constantly and more broadly redefine its contribution to the market. Last years' contribution must become next year's feature within a broader definition.

Independent Verification of Key Plan Assumptions

Every business plan rests on certain key assumptions. These often include the technological expertise of the founders, production techniques and marketing strategies. The analytical role of the venture firm is to identify these key assumptions and then independently correlate them with both independent sources of information and the venture firm's own experience. Time can easily be wasted performing due diligence on irrelevancies.

You can help this process, and thus speed up decision making, by clearly stating key assumptions on which your new firm's success will be based and identifying independent sources—customers, former employers, or industry experts—for verification. Of course, the more knowledgeable a venture firm is in your industry, the easier it will be for them to recognize the key assumptions and independently verify them with their own sources.

Risk Identification

Venture firms approach the venture business as much from the standpoint of risk reduction as from opportunity maximization. That is, the operating assumption is that opportunities can be realized by eliminating the risks (impediments) to their achievement. Almost by definition, the companies in which venture firms invest will be standing in the middle of enormous opportunities. The practical problem then becomes how to eliminate the impediments to achieve this success.

Thus, your plan and your discussions with the venture firm must address the question of risk reduction: how much money will it take to eliminate each major risk, and what will be the milestones in measuring whether that goal is being achieved?

Obviously, risk can never be fully eliminated; however, there are definite benchmarks in technical and marketing accomplishments that represent the lowering of risk levels. Performing an analysis with respect to risk reduction will put you on the same wavelength as your potential venture investors. You can evaluate in this process whether the venture firm really appreciates the risks particular to your industry.

Of course, each milestone of risk reduction achieved is the basis for raising additional money for the company.

Competitive Analysis

The absence of good analysis and lack of and appreciation for the competition are probably the most common mistakes made by new entrepreneurs. Therefore, one way to distinguish yourself and your business plan from the many others a venture firm is reviewing is through the quality and completeness of your analysis of the competition. If you have done such an analysis, you will be able to easily convince the venture firm that your key assumptions are realistic and reasonable. Furthermore, in the process of describing the competition, you will accelerate the education of the venture firm vis-à-vis your relative position in the market. You will find that this relative information is very important to the venture firm in reaching a decision.

Insightful understanding of the competition in your marketplace by the venture firm can be critical to obtaining their initial backing. Usually, new technology driven markets emerge at the intersection of two or more established markets. A subtle grasp of why the traditional suppliers will be slow to cross into this emerging product market category is critical to comprehending the opportunity for a new company. Of course, when it comes to assisting in future product strategy and money raising, this competitive understanding by your venture firm is critical.

Openness

Entrepreneurs often worry that venture firms will be frightened off if they know how many risks are really involved in accomplishing the business plan of a new venture. This can be a fatal mistake for the entrepreneur, because an experienced venture capitalist is not likely to make a positive decision until these questions have been answered.

Your objective, assuming you want to do business with a particular venture firm, is to get the venture capitalist comfortable with the project and management team. The venture firm must not be made to feel there are unknowns lurking in the background yet to be discovered. In your first meetings with a venture capitalist, it may appear that his limited knowledge about your particular industry niche makes it unnecessary or unwise to tell him all the problems that your company will face. This is a serious error to make. When a venture capitalist doesn't know what the right questions are, he won't make a positive decision. Rather, he will just keep asking questions until he feels he has asked the right ones. Since your objective is to get the venture capitalist to make a quick, positive decision, you may as well identify what all the problems are up front.

Remember: a venture firm is in the business of working with the problems you foresee in your company's growth, so you need not be concerned that identifying these will frighten off the firm. Dealing with risks and uncertainties is a venture capitalist's business, and you need to get him quickly to the point of feeling he knows what those uncertainties are.

Most venture firms also realize that every management team will initially have significant gaps in its experience. Often the team has the technical expertise necessary to build the product but only limited marketing and general management experience. Actually, this can be a positive and low-cost approach to getting started.

The best way to protect against easily frightened—or worse, less-than-capable—venture capitalists is to be open about the problems. If they are frightened off, don't regret it. When a venture capitalist only wants to hear about the opportunities and not the problems, then you should be nervous.

Objective Standards

Evaluate a venture capital firm the same way you would evaluate any key management team member. That is, look at the firm's record of experience, external contacts and accomplishments. How directly relevant to your company's challenges is this record? Has the firm done it before? If you don't feel comfortable with first hand impressions, check with other entrepreneurs with whom the firm has worked. Some specific areas about which you might inquire include:

- What companies has the firm been involved with in the past, and how does the history of those companies compare with the future you envision for your company?
- What was the firm's relationship with those companies? Was it as a passive investor, or did it make a constructive contribution?
- What do the entrepreneurs in those companies say about the firm's contribution?
- What industries is the firm investing in? Does the firm have sufficient experience in your industry to understand and contribute to your potential?

- How helpful is the firm going to be in the future financing of the company? What has it done for other companies along this line in the past? Has it stuck by its companies in difficult times?
- Does it have a reputation that will attract other financial sources? Does it know how to handle investment banks and other financial sources to minimize the future dilution?
- You should get to know as many as possible of the principals and consultants of any firm since they all represent potential resources available to you in the future.
- Will the firm be helpful in establishing overseas sales and distribution for you? For technology companies, overseas sales can be key to a company's financial success
- Will the firm be helpful in finding and attracting key managers when needed by your company? Do the firm's historical associations suggest: access to high quality technology managers in your industry, a reputation that will help attract them to an embryonic company, and experience in evaluating such managers?
- The answers to these questions will be infinitely more important to the eventual value of your company than the terms or amount of your initial financing. Indeed, while every entrepreneur's first objective must be to get a good price for his company, a common mistake among first time entrepreneurs is to be overly concerned with this goal.
- Excessive preoccupation with achieving the best deal can result in a delayed project or, worse, becoming over shopped to the point of not being able to be financed. In practice, the price will not vary much from firm to firm— after all, venture financings are a free and competitive market. No venture firm will remain in business long if its pricing is not essentially competitive and fair.
- New companies should add to their management team the highest quality people who can be found. Never compromise in favor of someone who can be added for a little less salary or equity. The higher the quality of the individuals, the more likely they are to make key contributions.
- The same advice holds in evaluating and selecting a venture firm: aim for the very best.

Perfecting Your Pitch

William M. Reichert

Endless articles, books, and blogs have been written on the topic of business plan presentations and pitching to investors. In spite of this wealth of advice, almost every entrepreneur gets it wrong. Why? Because most guides to pitching your company miss the central point: The purpose of your pitch is to *sell,* not to teach. Your job is to excite, not to educate.

Pitching is about understanding what your customer (the investor) is most interested in, and developing a dialog that enables you to connect with the head, the heart, and the gut of the investor. If you want advice about pitching, you can ask a venture capitalist, but you probably won't get a very good answer. Most VCs are analytic types, and so they will give you a laundry list of topics you should cover. They won't tell you what really floats their boat, mainly because they themselves can't articulate it in useful terms. "I know it when I see it," is about the best answer you'll get.

What is the investor most interested in? Contrary to popular belief, the venture capitalist sitting at the other end of the table glaring inscrutably at the presenting entrepreneur is *not* thinking, "Is this company going to make a lot of money?" That is the simple question that most entrepreneurs think they are answering, but they are missing the crux of the venture capital process. What the investor is really thinking is, "Is this company the best next investment for me and my fund?" That is a much more complex question, but that is what the entrepreneur has to answer.

To win over the hearts and minds of investors, your pitch has to accomplish three things:

- Tell a good, clear, easy-to-repeat story—the story of an exciting new startup.
- Position your company as a perfect fit with other investments the investors have made and their firm is chartered to make.
- Beat out the other new investments the firm is currently considering.

These latter two issues are beyond the scope of this modest guide. So for now, let's just concentrate on telling a good story.

Tell a Good Story

Most of the articles on pitching are generally right about the topics, even if they miss the nuance (sell, don't explain). But don't take any template as graven in stone. Your story may require a moderate or even a dramatic variation on the list of slides below.

You may need to explain the solution before you can explain the market; or if you are in a crowded space you may need to explain why you are different than everyone else early on in the conversation; or you may want to drop some very impressive brand-name customers before you explain your product or your market. The one thing *you may not do* is expand the number of slides to 20 (or 30 or 50)! Other than that, let the specifics of your situation dictate the flow of your slides.

Nevertheless, it is useful to have a guide. With the caveats above in mind, here is a basic outline for your pitch:

Cover slide: Company name, location, tagline, presenter's name and title. If there are multiple team members participating in the pitch, put names on the next slide instead. Key objective: Everyone in the room should know the basic idea and value proposition of the company, including the target market, before the next slide is shown. All the words should not be on this slide, but with one or two sentences orally, reinforcing and extending the tagline, everyone should have a foundation for what is to come. Cardinal sin: Launching into your presentation with an investor at the table thinking, "I wonder what these guys do?"

Intro slide: Team. The three or four key players in the company. For some reason, everyone puts the team slide at the end, but investors almost always want to know this at the beginning, and it is just common courtesy to make sure everyone is introduced. But make this short, crisp and relevant. This is not the time to share everyone's life story, or detail the resumes of all six members of the advisory board. Focus on a significant, relevant accomplishment for each person that identifies that person as a winner. In 10 to 15 seconds, you should be able to say three or four sentences about your CTO that says everything the investors want to know about him or her at that moment. Key objective: Investors should be confident that there is a good credible core group of talent that believe in the company and can execute the next set of milestones. One of those milestones may be filling out the team, and so it is important to convey that the initial team knows how to attract great talent, as well as having great domain skills. If there is a gap in the team, address it explicitly, before investors have to ask about it.

Slide 1: Company overview. The best way to give an overview of your company is to state concisely your core value proposition: What unique benefit will you provide to what set of customers to address what particular need? Then you can add three or four additional dot points to clarify your target markets, your unique technology/solution, and your status (launch date, current customers, revenue rate, pipeline, funding needed). Key objective: Flesh out the foundation you established at the beginning. At this point, no one should have any question about what it is that your company does, or plans to do. The only questions that should remain are the details of how you are going to do it. Another key objective you should have achieved by this point in your presentation is to make sure that if there are some compelling brand names associated with your company (customers, partners, investors, advisors), your audience knows about them. Feel free to drop names early and often—starting with your first email introduction to the investor. Brand name relationships build your credibility, but do not overstate them if they are tenuous.

Slide 2: Problem/Opportunity.

You need to make it clear that there is a big, important problem (current or emerging) that you are going to solve, or opportunity you are going to exploit, and that you understand the market dynamics surrounding the opportunity—why does this situation exist and persist, and why is it only now that it can be addressed? Show that you really understand the very particular market segment you are targeting, and frame your market analysis according to the specific problem and solution you are laying out. In some cases, however, the problem you are attacking is so obvious and clear that you can drop this slide altogether. You do not have to tell investors that there are a lot of cell phones out there, or that teenagers like to socialize. Save yourself, and the investors, the pain of restating the obvious.

Slide 2.1: Problem/Opportunity size.

Even if your market opportunity is not obvious, in most cases you can assert the size of your opportunity on slide 2. But sometimes you may need a dedicated slide to clarify the factors that define the size and scope of the opportunity, particularly if you are going after multiple market segments. Or there may be a unique emerging trend that requires explanation. Do not use this slide to quote the Gartner Group or Frost & Sullivan; show that you really understand where your prospective customers are from the ground up.

Slide 3: Solution.

What specifically are you offering to whom? Software, hardware, services, a combination? Use common terms to state concretely what you have, or what you do, that solves the problem you've identified. Avoid acronyms and don't try to use these precious few words to create and trademark a bunch of terms that won't mean anything to most people, and don't use this as an opportunity to showcase your insider status and facility with the idiomatic lingo of the industry. If you can demonstrate your solution (briefly) in a meeting, this is the place to do it.

Slide 3.1: Delivering the solution.

You might need an extra slide to show how your solution fits in the value chain or ecosystem of your target market. Do you complement commonly used technologies, or do you displace them? Do you change the way certain business processes get executed, or do you just do them the same way, but faster, better and cheaper? Do you disrupt the current value chain, or do you fit into established channels? Who exactly is the buyer, and is that person different than the user?

Slide 4: Benefits/Value.

State clearly and quantify to the extent possible the three or four key benefits you provide, and who specifically realizes these benefits. Do some constituents benefit more than others, or earlier than others? These dynamics should inform your go-to-market strategy, and your product/service roadmap, which you will discuss later.

Slide 5: Secret sauce/Intellectual property.

Depending on your solution, you might need a separate slide to convince investors that no one else can easily duplicate or surpass your solution (assuming that's actually true). If you are in a business sector in which intellectual property is important, this is where you drill down into your secret sauce. This is usually some combination of proprietary technology, unique team domain expertise, and unique partnership. Boil this down to simple elements and terms, devoid of jargon. Do not walk the audience through a detailed tour of your product architecture. Instead, highlight the elements of your technology that give you unique potential for leverage and scale as you grow. If you do slides 4 and 5 well, it will be easy to make the case for your . . .

Slide 6: Competitive advantage.

You may be good, but are you really better than everyone else? Most entrepreneurs misunderstand the objective of this slide, which is not to enumerate all the deficiencies of the competition (as much fun as that may be). Just because you have really cool technology does not mean you will win. You need to convince the investor that lots of folks will buy your product or service, even though they have several alternatives. And don't forget that the toughest competitor is often the status quo—most prospective customers can muddle on without buying your solution or your competitor's solution. The best way to convince an investor that you really do have a better mousetrap is to have referenceable customers or prospects articulate in their own words why they bought or will buy your offering over the alternatives. Use this slide to summarize the three or four key reasons why customers prefer your solution to other solutions. Many entrepreneurs have been coached to use a four-square matrix that shows that they are in the upper right-hand quadrant, but this has become a joke in the venture community. Check-boxes are better, if they are not abused. Make sure your check-box criteria reflect the market's requirements, not just your product's features.

Slide 6.1: Competitive advantage matrix.

Depending on how important the analysis of competitive players is in your market segment, you may need a detailed list of competitors by category with their strengths and weaknesses in comparison with your company. Preferably, you develop this as a "pocket slide" to be used for Q&A, if necessary. Whether or not you present this slide, it is important that you do your homework on the competition, and that you don't misrepresent their strengths or their weaknesses.

Slide 7: Go to market strategy.

The single most compelling slide in any pitch is a pipeline of customers and strategic partners that have already expressed some interest in your solution—if they haven't already joined your beta program. Too often this slide is, instead, a bland laundry list of standard sales and marketing tactics. You should focus on articulating the non-obvious, potentially disruptive elements of your strategy. Even better, frame your comments in terms of the critical hurdles you need to get over, and how you are going to jump them. If you don't have a pipeline, and there is nothing unique or innovative about your strategy, then drop this slide and make the elements of your sales model clear in the discussion of your business model (next slide).

Slide 8: Business model. How do you make money? Usually by selling something for a certain price to certain customers. But there are lots of variations on the standard theme. Explain your pricing, your costs, and why you are going to be especially profitable. Make sure you understand the key assumptions underlying your planned success and be prepared to defend them. What if you can't sustain the price? What if it takes twice as long to make each sale? What if your costs don't decline over time? Many investors will want to test the depth of your understanding of your business model. Be ready to articulate the sensitivity of your business to variations in your assumptions.

Slide 9: Financial projections. The two previous slides above should come together neatly in your five-year financial projections. You should show the two or three key metrics that drive revenues, expenses and growth (such as customers, unit sales, new products, expansion sales, new markets), as well as the revenue, expense, profit, cash balance, and headcount lines. The most important thing to convey on this slide is that you really understand the economics and evolution of a growing, dynamic company, and that your vision is grounded in an understanding of practical reality. Your financials should tell your story in numbers as clearly as you are telling your story in words. Investors are not focused on the precision of your numbers; they're focused on the coherence and integrity of your thought process.

Slide 10: Financing requirements/milestones. It should be clear from your financials what your capital requirements will be. On this slide you should outline how you plan to take in funding—how big each round will be, and the timing of each—and map the funding against your key near-term and medium-term milestones. You should also include your key achievements to date. These milestones should tie to the key metrics in your financial projections, and they should provide a clear, crisp picture of your product introduction and market expansion roadmap. In essence, this is your operating plan for the funds you are raising. Do not spend time presenting a "use of funds" table. Investors want to see measures of accomplishment, not measures of activity. And they want to know that you are asking for the right amount of money to get the company to a meaningful milestone.

Summary slide. This slide is almost always wasted. Most entrepreneurs just put up three or four dot points about how wonderful their investment opportunity is. Generally the words are the same words that investors hear from scores of other entrepreneurs, such as, "We have a huge opportunity, and we

will be the winners!" Your key objective on this slide is to solidify the core value proposition of your company in words that are memorable and unique to your company. If the venture investor in the room has to give a short description of your company to his partners, these are the words you want used. This is a good place to reinforce your tagline, or mantra—the short phrase that captures the essence of your message to investors. The best solution to creating your summary slide is to imagine that this is the only slide you will ever be able to present. If you had to do your whole pitch in one slide (with 30 point font), this is that slide.

So here we have a good general outline for pitching your company. But remember, it's about selling your investment proposition, not about covering points. Don't get fixated on using this or any other template. You should know the issues about your company that investors are most concerned about. Those are the issues you need to concentrate on. Make sure you address all the predictable "burning questions" as early as you can in your presentation, even if it means violating the sequence above.

Tips on Effective Pitching

How do you turn a pitch from a monolog to a sale? Make sure every point you make connects with your audience. Keep your text very, very short. Really. Please. Use charts and pictures if you can. And engage your prospect. Ask questions. "Do you think this market opportunity is interesting?" "Have you seen anyone else addressing this problem?" "Do you think CIOs would be interested in a solution like this?" You may get some tough responses, but you will know a lot more about what is going on in the investor's mind, and you will be engaging them in your story—instead of letting them play with their Blackberries under the table.

Some additional tips to improve the effectiveness of your pitch:

- Make sure that everyone in the room is introduced. Rarely do entrepreneurs ask the investors in the room to introduce themselves. While it is appropriate to be familiar with each investor's bio (assuming it is on the web), it's fair to ask something like, "What investments have you been looking at recently?" And if there are some other faces in the room, you should absolutely have them introduce themselves and provide a little background.

- Don't use a feel-good, visionary "Mission Statement" on your overview slide. Mission statements have also become a joke in the venture industry. It's like saying, "Our projections are conservative." Focus on making sure your statement of your company's value proposition is crisp, clear, and unique.

- Prepare good use cases. Sometimes, no matter how simple and clear the description of a product, what the investor really needs is a concrete example of how people will actually use it. In some cases there will be multiple different use cases. You may need to explain these to get your point across.

- Drop names, early and often. If you really have some brand names involved in your company—as customers, as partners, as members of the team—don't keep them a secret for the first nine slides; make sure the investor knows about them early in the presentation. But be prepared for the investor to contact every single name you drop—whether it's a person or a company. If you are going to drop names, they had better be real.

- Make sure you can tell the entire story in 10 to 15 minutes. Even if you have time, your total presentation should be no longer than 20 minutes. You want to have time to engage the investors and discuss their questions or concerns. If you think you have additional critical points that have to be made, prepare "pocket slides" that you can put up if the topic arises.

- Average entrepreneur pitch: 38 slides. Average VC attention span/cranial capacity: 10 slides. Do the math.

- Learn how to control the flow of the meeting, without seeming inflexible or anxious. Watch and listen. Body language and questions will tell you if you are okay deferring a point or if you need to address it immediately. If you let your audience take over the flow, you will probably wind up creating a confusing, incomplete impression of your company. But if you don't address the "burning questions" early and effectively, the investors won't hear anything else you say.

- Don't lie. You would think this goes without saying, but in their enthusiasm for their creations, entrepreneurs tend to slip across the line all too often. Please do not interpret our exhortation to "sell" as an endorsement of hype, exaggeration, misrepresentation, spin, or lying. The best salespeople are credible and trustworthy. It is more important that investors trust you than that they understand every nuance of your business.

- Pitching investors is different than pitching customers. If you have a sales presentation for customers, do not think you can simply modify it slightly for pitching to VCs. Start from scratch, keeping in mind with every slide that an investor has a very different perspective than a customer.

- You don't have to be "conservative," but you do have to be realistic. Almost every entrepreneur fails to be realistic about how long things take in the real world (vs. the spreadsheet world). Whether it's the time to complete product development, or the time to close the next ten sales, entrepreneurs are pathologically optimistic. As with your financials, find examples of comparable challenges addressed by other companies, and use that data in your model.

- Never ever put so much text on a page that the investor has to read it. Everything should be short, content-rich bullets in a font large enough to read without squinting. The words are simply reinforcement of the points you are making orally. Pictures, graphs, and charts should be uncluttered and make clear, compelling points. If they have to be deconstructed and explained piece by piece, you will lose focus and momentum.

- And never use your presentation stack as a standalone document. It is perfectly okay if it is not readable when you are not around. That's the job of your executive summary or your business plan.

A good pitch is very rare. It is so hard executing on everything else that has to be done to build a successful company, pitching often suffers. But the ability to pitch is a key indicator for investors—if the entrepreneur doesn't know how to sell, how can he or she build a great company?

At Garage Technology Ventures, we appreciate how hard you have worked to get to where you are, and how hard you have worked to craft your investor presentation. We wish we could work with all the great entrepreneurs we meet, but unfortunately we can't. Please help us get to know you better by telling your story clearly and concisely.

If you are looking for a guide to writing an executive summary, you can find our version online: "Writing a Compelling Executive Summary."

If you have any questions about this article, or about Garage, you can contact Bill Reichert, Managing Director of Garage Technology Ventures (email: reichert@garage.com).

From *Garage Technology Ventures*, 2006, pp. 1–9. Copyright © 2006 by Garage Technology Ventures. Reprinted by permission.

Writing and Negotiating Term Sheets with a View toward Success

PETER M. ROSENBLUM

A good term sheet sets up the business for success. While we do include a variety of terms that may be useful at various times, everyone needs to recognize that the principal reason for a term sheet is to outline the participants' understanding, not necessarily to set up a plan to enforce in court every right at every time.

When it comes time to negotiate terms, I encourage angel investors and entrepreneurs to keep these points in mind:

1. How is everyone going to make money from the deal?
2. How do you want to do the next round of financing because there will almost certainly be another round?
3. What is your exit strategy?

Success and prosperity is a good theme; there are ways to draft the documents along those lines.

For purposes of this discussion, I will exclude valuation as a separate topic, recognizing its extreme importance and complexity and that it is more a business than legal issue.

Standard Documents

Early stage deals need a term sheet that is credible but doesn't get in the way of future financing by having terms that can't be waived or will be unpalatable to future investors. I like to start with a standard, middle of the road set of documents that are fairly standard in the venture capital community.

This sets a tone, and I find that sometimes the VCs will simply add their deal-specific terms to the documents as written. If the terms look like what the VCs are expecting, they will tend to do minor amending and then their deal will move forward. Even when they want to negotiate or change some of the terms, we don't have to go back to square one.

Board Provisions

The ability to set strategy and move the company in the proper direction is a very important thing. The terms that define the composition of the board of directors are among the most strategically important conditions of the deal and should be based on significant dialogue between the company and the angel investors.

For all but the smallest deals, it probably isn't appropriate to allow the founders and existing management team to control the board. This does not necessarily mean that the angels control the board, just that the founders and management cannot overwhelm them.

On smaller rounds (say, $250,000 and under), angels might take one seat or an observer position; for larger rounds they should seek significant angel representation on the board. An effective angel group is not just contributing money; they also provide perspective, expertise, and assistance. The place where that is most easily expressed and applied is at the board level.

My preference is to have a five-person board with two angels; the CEO; one other representative of the common stock, and then an independent member from the industry who can add perspective.

Preferred Stock

Other than for very small deals, I recommend preferred stock and tend to avoid any form of convertible debt. Using a debt instrument postpones the time that that the company can show any stockholders equity and leaves the company with an insolvent balance sheet from day one, which can create a variety of legal issues at unfortunate times, as the law treats an insolvent company differently than it treats a solvent one. An unintended and difficult consequence is that every time a third party views the company's balance sheet, all they see is debt because there is no equity. This will discourage risk-adverse third parties.

Preferred stock is useful for all of the usual reasons that people choose preferred over common. There is also a more subtle reason. If the angel investors buy common stock, that will set the company's stock option price at that level—usually too high. If they take a preferred stock, there will be opportunities for better option pricing.

In terms of the preferred stock itself, the question is: how is it preferred? I like it to look like a middle of the road Series A preferred. It doesn't cost more to use a standard form as opposed to tinkering, and, as mentioned, I believe there can be a real advantage to standard terms when you reach subsequent rounds.

We do like to put in a provision allowing two-thirds of the preferred stock (or other majority) to waive provisions that would otherwise favor the preferred. The idea is that if you have to do something quickly, you have a way to do it. If someone is unavailable to vote (for example, they might be having surgery or be visiting Antarctica), or if one or two small holders are adverse, it will not frustrate necessary corporate action. We want documents to be protective but not to get in the way of making money for the company and all of its stockholders.

Employee Option Pool

Assume that the pre-money valuation of a particular deal is $1 million and that the angels are putting up $500,000. If there is no option pool, the angels receive equity reflecting one-third of the $1.5 million post-money valuation.

Now suppose you want to create a 10 percent (or larger) option pool for managers and employees (not founders)—a very important thing to do if you want to attract the right talent to the enterprise. What percent of the company do the angels get now?

The angels will prefer that the option pool comes out of the founders' shares. If this approach is followed, the angels will retain one-third of the stock, while the founders' percentage of ownership drops from two-thirds to 56 2/3 percent because 10 percent of the founders' shares go into the option pool.

The founders might respond by asserting that if the company had made all of its key hires and allocated the option pool to them, the company would have a higher valuation.

Split responsibility for the pool reflects the company reality. The founders then negotiate for responsibility for the pool to be split in proportion to allocated pre-money valuation—producing 30 percent of the equity going to the angels, 60 percent to the founders, and 10 percent to the pool.

How this finally settles out depends on who has the most bargaining power.

Here's why the allocation of the pool is important. If you think of a company going public at a $100 million pre-money valuation, every one percent is worth $1 million to someone. By the time a company has an IPO, even if the initial capitalization is diluted by four to one, the 10 percent which is retained by the angels from the founders is worth about $2.5 million—which is real money and worth negotiation.

In the next round with the VCs, there may be a substantial fight over the same issues. Many VCs view the option pool as the responsibility of the management team and the angel group, and they won't take responsibility for any part of it. Consistency in approach may help, but then again the VCs may not care about what went before.

Anti-Dilution Terms

For most term sheets, angels are better served with weighted-average than full-ratchet anti-dilution. Even though full-ratchet terms may appear more beneficial by effectively adjusting the price of previously issued shares to the price of a new issuance, they set a precedent for the VCs and may produce very undesirable results in future rounds.

Investments in certain industries (biotech comes to mind) lend themselves particularly to a full-ratchet approach.

Liquidation Preferences, Cumulative Dividends, Warrants, Registration, and Conversion Rights

I'm not a big fan of cumulative dividends, warrants, or participating preferred stock that has liquidation preference and then participates with common stock on a share per share basis. When I include any of these terms in a deal, I keep in mind that I'm setting a baseline for subsequent rounds.

The VCs are going to ask for whatever the angels have (and more) and any participating preferred the VCs have will drain away a substantial amount of money from the founders and angels. Cumulative dividends are seldom, if ever, paid. Practically speaking, angels will only receive them to the extent that the VCs decide not to require that the angels give them up.

The same goes for warrants. If they survive, they complicate the balance sheet, and VCs often ask for additional consideration to permit the warrants to remain outstanding. That said, business considerations may suggest that cumulative dividends and warrants are important for future positioning of the investment.

Registration rights raise a variety of complex issues, but also should receive a practical approach. The important registration rights are piggy back (granting the investor the right to register unregistered stock when either the company or another investor initiates a registration) and so-called S-3 registration rights (which allow use of a short-form registration on Form S-3 after the company is already public).

In over 30 years of practice, I think I've only done one demand registration (where the investors can initiate the registration process) that was not an S-3 registration.

Protective Covenants

Protective covenants become more important depending on board composition. They matter more if angels don't have a significant role on the board. I try to think of the protective covenants in two groups.

The first category consists of actions which relate to the operations of the company, such as changes to the stock option pool, incurrence of debt, and certain kinds of licensing. These should require only a vote of the board including angel directors to authorize them. Once the board has spoken, why appeal to the stockholders?

The second category includes actions which fundamentally affect the angels' investment and should go back to them for authorization—for example amendments to the charter or bylaws or mergers and acquisitions.

The term sheet also should have tag-along rights which are integrated with the basic rights of first refusal in the documents. Tag-along rights (also called co-sale rights) allow the angels to sell their shares if the management team is selling. If management has the right to sell shares, then you want the passive investors to be able to participate, too.

The deal should also provide for drag-along rights, which compel people to sell their shares if a specified group decides the company should be sold and prevent an attempt by minority stockholders from obstructing the sale.

Such rights can be a particularly good idea in angel deals because frequently there is a large group of people investing and some of them develop a very close relationship with the company founders. You need the drag-along rights to be able to profit from the success of the company, and you don't want one or two hold-outs on the founder or angel side to be able to halt a deal that is advantageous.

This goes back to my original themes of future financing, success, and exit. When a good exit shows up, you want to be able to grab hold and run with it.

Sometimes founders will worry that drag-along rights will allow someone to steal the company. One way to address this concern is to require a reasonably high threshold of approval to trigger the drag-along rights.

For example, if the board (which has a fiduciary duty) and some reasonably substantial percentage of the stockholders (perhaps 75 percent of the total or two-thirds of each class) vote "yes," then everyone has to go along.

An anti-circumvention clause, a charter provision that says the company and other investors will not undertake a merger or any other transaction which would have the effect of depriving investors of their rights, is designed to prevent a cram-down without consent and can be useful. It doesn't necessarily have to go into the term sheet but can be part of the deal documents.

Vesting

Many times the founders will argue that they should be fully vested in their equity in the company when the deal closes because of all the work they've done before the closing. However, from an investor's point of view, the day the deal closes is day one and there is considerable work to be done for the founders to earn their shares and justify the claims that induced the investment. A variety of compromises are possible.

I frequently see management with 20 to 25 percent of their equity vested at closing and the balance vesting over four years. Many investors favor a one-year cliff and then monthly or quarterly vesting after that.

I resist acceleration of vesting because of an IPO or sale of the company for a number of reasons. Equity is typically provided to founders and management to assure that they will remain with the company for a period of time. Performance triggers to vesting can be used but raise a host of other independent issues. In fact, the time of an IPO is precisely the time when continuing "golden handcuffs" is most important. Public investors and underwriters want to make certain that management remains in place after their investment.

Many sophisticated acquirers feel the same way about a post-sale period and penalize companies and their selling stockholders if there is acceleration of vesting at the time of sale. Indeed, there is no guarantee that a sale is a "success" and mandatory acceleration might be providing a reward for failure. Finally, there are a number of venture capitalists who have policies precluding so-called single trigger acceleration, and this could become an issue in a later round.

Termination for Cause

Termination for cause and the definition of "cause" seem to have become flash points in negotiations in recent years, if not at the term sheet phase then in the negotiations of basic documents. In the real world after all the lawyers get done, almost no one admits that they have been fired for cause. That being said, there is no reason not to have a good, tight definition of cause in a transaction.

At a minimum, it will shape negotiations on termination, but it also will set forth the company's expectations of its employees. The way we typically handle this issue in negotiation is to ask the CEO to take off the CEO's employee hat and consider how he or she as CEO wants to manage these issues with every other person employed by the company. Most CEOs get it after that.

Conclusion: There Is No Perfect Term Sheet, Just as There Is No Perfect Deal

The term sheet is simply a manifestation of the deal prepared against the background of expectations of both parties. A lot of the terms have to be worked out on a person-to-person basis to achieve the basic business understanding that underpins the deal and shapes the parties' future relationship. I'm one of those lawyers who think that the best documents are the ones that I draft, that people sign, and that never come out of the drawer.

PETER ROSENBLUM, a partner at Foley Hoag, LLP, counsels clients in diverse industries concerning business and regulatory matters, financing strategies and structuring of corporate transactions. He is actively involved in the firm's corporate and corporate finance practices, with an emphasis on public and private offerings of debt and equity, mergers and acquisitions, joint ventures and venture capital. Rosenblum has broad experience structuring and executing mergers and acquisitions for public and private clients. He represents numerous registered investment advisors and managers of private investment funds and hedge funds, both onshore and offshore. He may be reached at PMR@foleyhoag.com.

UNIT 4

Managing and Growing a New Business Venture

Unit Selections

Key Points to Consider

- Why is having a competitive advantage so important?

- What are the different legal forms an entrepreneur can use for organizing a startup?

- What are the key entrepreneurial management functions?

- What is the difference between entrepreneurial management and professional management?

- Why do so many small companies fail to escape their initial entrepreneurial phase?

- How can a business plan aid in the transition from entrepreneurial doers to entrepreneurial leaders and coaches?

- What motivates entrepreneurs? How do entrepreneurs motivate their employees?

- What are the characteristics of a successful entrepreneurial management team?

- How should companies approach the process for tailoring a board of directors to fit their needs?

- Why do startups fail? How can the entrepreneur use strategic planning to reduce risks?

Student Website

www.mhcls.com

Internet References

Association for Corporate Growth (ACG)
http://www.acg.org/

CalPERS Shareowner Forum
http://www.calpers-governance.org/

Entrepreneur Magazine
http://www.entrepreneurmag.com

Foundation for Enterprise Development/Beyster Institute
http://www.fed.org

Inc.com
http://www.inc.com/

Moot Corp.
http://www.mootcorp.org/

National Federation of Independent Business (NFIB)
http://www.nfib.org/

Service Corps of Retired Executives (SCORE)
http://www.score.org/

© Flying Colours Ltd/Getty Images

When combined, goals and strategies define the scope of operations and the relationship with employees, customers, competitors, and other stakeholders. The term "strategy" is widely used in the business world today. It is one of those words that people define in one way and often use in another, without realizing the difference. It is derived from the ancient Greek word meaning "the art and science of the general deploying of forces for battle."

Winning business strategies are grounded in a sustainable competitive advantage. A new business venture has a competitive advantage whenever it has an edge over rivals in attracting customers, attracting investors, and defending against competitive forces and industry risks. With a competitive advantage a new business venture has good prospects for above-average survivability, long-term profitability, and success in the industry. Without one, a new business venture risks being outcompeted by strong rivals and locked into poor, to at best, average performance.

A business model is a consistent, economically sound configuration of the elements comprising a venture's goals, strategies, processes, technologies, and organizational structure, conceived to create and consistently add value for the customers identified. In other words, it is the entire system that allows a business venture to capture and deliver value to targeted customers in a profitable business activity.

But it takes little time to destroy a high growth-potential venture with a sound business model. One turn-around expert says,

"Ninety-five percent of the failures are due to internal problems. I can't tell you how many companies I've been to that have the fast-growing-company plaque on the wall and are about to go under. They don't have the systems and the people in place. Accounting is lagging. Purchasing is not done in the most efficient manner. Inventory gets out of control. All of a sudden, all these mistakes compound, and the least little burp kills them."

Michael Dell of Dell Computers discovered this: "As success followed on success, it was hard to imagine that growth would at some point become our greatest vulnerability. We didn't understand that with every new growth opportunity came a commensurate level of risk—a lesson we learned the hard way."

This unit looks at what happens after startup, such as managing rapid growth and establishing formal management practices. The set of changes that startups need to make as they rapidly grow is often termed the transition from entrepreneurial to professional management. This unit only begins to address the issues that startups must deal with in making the transition.

The growth of any new business venture is a product of both the opportunity selection and management factors. The true mark of a good venture is how it manages growth and whether it can sustain it. Centralized decision making and informal controls characterize entrepreneurial management. In startups, one person can comprehend all the information required for decision making and there is little need for formal procedures. The venture is small enough that business activity can be monitored via the supervision of the entrepreneur. The ventures that survive the growth phase have a disciplined team with intellectual honesty; they know what they know and do not know. Their honesty prevents a myopic vision that might be intoxicated by current success. They are also quick to delegate decision-making responsibility.

The entrepreneurial challenges of leadership and the job of management in a fast-growing venture can be complex and difficult. Entrepreneurs new at leadership often feel that they must have all the answers and must dictate policy or they will be seen as weak. But breaking through the growth wall requires an organization-wide transition from a culture of entrepreneurial doers and managers to entrepreneurial coaches and team leaders. Leadership is about knowing when to lead and when to step aside. Leaders should manage through directions, discussion, and suggestions.

The selection of stakeholders and organizational structure for any business venture requires some major decisions that will affect long-term effectiveness and profitability. When it comes to successful entrepreneurs and entrepreneurial teams, most investors will agree that they prefer a grade A entrepreneur with a grade B business idea to a grade B entrepreneur with a grade A idea. In other words, they prefer to bet on the jockey and not the horse. Since no one individual can possess all the attributes that venture capitalists and academics say are important for success, it is generally a strong entrepreneurial management team, not the lone entrepreneur, which investors will back. Regardless of how great the opportunity may seem to be, it will not become a successful venture unless a venture team with strong entrepreneurial and management skills develops it.

Coordinating profitable, rapid growth requires a detailed plan and budget. Also, employees who are capable of delivering the desired outcomes in the growth plan must be hired. Entrepreneurs of startups should know that it is never too late to start developing smart tactics/practices for finding workers. Startups must be prepared, as they enter the battle for talented workers, with a plan, creative compensation packages, capital budgets with room for human capital investment, and other powerful strategic weaponry. Just as the most successful startup ventures have business plans, operational or manufacturing plans, and financial plans, companies that grow to the next level, breaking through the growth wall, also have internal plans for expansion.

How Entrepreneurs Craft Strategies That Work

Entrepreneurs adopt the approaches that work—and they're quick, cheap and timely.

Amar Bhidé

However popular it may be in the corporate world, a comprehensive analytical approach to planning doesn't suit most start-ups. Entrepreneurs typically lack the time and money to interview a representative cross section of potential customers, let alone analyze substitutes, reconstruct competitors' cost structures, or project alternative technology scenarios. In fact, too much analysis can be harmful; by the time an opportunity is investigated fully, it may no longer exist. A city map and restaurant guide on a CD may be a winner in January but worthless if delayed until December.

By the time an opportunity is investigated fully, it may no longer exist.

Interviews with the founders of 100 companies on the 1989 *Inc.* "500" list of the fastest growing private companies in the United States and recent research on more than 100 other thriving ventures by my MBA students suggest that many successful entrepreneurs spend little time researching and analyzing. [See the box, "Does Planning Pay?"] And those who do often have to scrap their strategies and start over. Furthermore, a 1990 National Federation of Independent Business study of 2,994 start-ups showed that founders who spent a long time in study, reflection, and planning were no more likely to survive their first three years than people who seized opportunities without planning. In fact, many corporations that revere comprehensive analysis develop a refined incapacity for seizing opportunities. Analysis can delay entry until it's too late or kill ideas by identifying numerous problems.

Yet all ventures merit some analysis and planning. Appearances to the contrary, successful entrepreneurs don't take risks blindly. Rather, they use a quick, cheap approach that represents a middle ground between planning paralysis and no planning at all. They don't expect perfection—even the most astute entrepreneurs have their share of false starts. Compared to typical corporate practice, however, the entrepreneurial approach is more economical and timely.

What are the critical elements of winning entrepreneurial approaches? Our evidence suggests three general guidelines for aspiring founders:

1. Screen opportunities quickly to weed out unpromising ventures.
2. Analyze ideas parsimoniously. Focus on a few important issues.
3. Integrate action and analysis. Don't wait for all the answers, and be ready to change course.

Screening out Losers

Individuals who seek entrepreneurial opportunities usually generate lots of ideas. Quickly discarding those that have low potential frees aspirants to concentrate on the few ideas that merit refinement and study.

Screening out unpromising ventures requires judgment and reflection, not new data. The entrepreneur should already be familiar with the facts needed to determine whether an idea has prima facie merit. Our evidence suggests that new ventures are usually started to solve problems the founders have grappled with personally as customers or employees. (See the diagram "Where Do Entrepreneurs Get Their Ideas?") Companies like Federal Express, which grew out of a paper its founder wrote in college, are rare.

Profitable survival requires an edge derived from some combination of a creative idea and a superior capacity for execution. (See the diagram "Tipping the Competitive Balance.") The entrepreneur's creativity may involve an innovative product or a process that changes the existing order. Or the entrepreneur may have a unique insight about the course or consequence of an external change: the California gold rush, for example, made paupers of the thousands caught in the frenzy, but Levi Strauss started a company—and a legend—by recognizing the opportunity to supply rugged canvas and later denim trousers to prospectors.

But entrepreneurs cannot rely on just inventing new products or anticipating a trend. They must also execute well, especially if their concepts can be copied easily. For example, if an innovation cannot be patented or kept secret, entrepreneurs must acquire and manage the resources needed to build a brand name or other barrier that will deter imitators. Superior execution can also compensate for a me-too concept in emerging or rapidly growing industries where doing it quickly and doing it right are more important than brilliant strategy.

Ventures that obviously lack a creative concept or any special capacity to execute—the ex-consultant's scheme to exploit grandmother's cookie recipe, for instance—can be discarded without much thought. In other cases, entrepreneurs must reflect on the adequacy of their ideas and their capacities to execute them.

Successful start-ups don't need an edge on every front. The creativity of successful entrepreneurs varies considerably. Some implement a radical idea, some modify, and some show no originality. Capacity for execution also varies among entrepreneurs. Selling an industrial niche product doesn't call for the charisma that's required to pitch trinkets through infomercials. Our evidence suggests that there is no ideal entrepreneurial profile either: successful founders can be gregarious or taciturn, analytical or intuitive, good or terrible with details, risk averse or thrill seeking. They can be delegators or control freaks, pillars of the community or outsiders. In assessing the viability of a potential venture, therefore, each aspiring entrepreneur should consider three interacting factors:

There is no ideal profile. Entrepreneurs can be gregarious or taciturn, analytical or intuitive, cautious or daring.

1. Objectives of the Venture

Is the entrepreneur's goal to build a large, enduring enterprise, carve out a niche, or merely turn a quick profit? Ambitious goals require great creativity. Building a large enterprise quickly, either by seizing a significant share of an

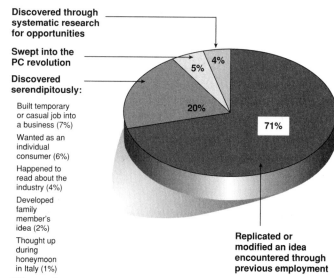

Discovered through systematic research for opportunities

Swept into the PC revolution

Discovered serendipitously:

Built temporary or casual job into a business (7%)

Wanted as an individual consumer (6%)

Happened to read about the industry (4%)

Developed family member's idea (2%)

Thought up during honeymoon in Italy (1%)

Replicated or modified an idea encountered through previous employment

Where do entrepreneurs get their ideas?
Source: 100 founders of the 1989 inc. "500" fastest growing private companies

existing market or by creating a large new market, usually calls for a revolutionary idea. Launching Home Depot, for example, called for a new retailing concept of immense proportions; opening a traditional hardware store does not. Revolutionary enterprises usually require new processes or manufacturing techniques; competitive markets rarely fail to provide valuable products or services unless providing them involves serious technological problems.

Requirements for execution are also still. Big ideas often necessitate big money and strong organizations. Successful entrepreneurs, therefore, require an evangelical ability to attract, retain, and balance the interests of investors, customers, employees, and suppliers for a seemingly outlandish vision, as well as the organizational and leadership skills to build a large, complex company quickly. In addition, the entrepreneur may require considerable technical know-how in deal making, strategic planning, managing overhead, and other business skills. The revolutionary entrepreneur, in other words, would appear to require almost superhuman qualities: ordinary mortals need not apply.

Consider Federal Express founder Fred Smith. His creativity lay in recognizing that customers would pay a significant premium for reliable overnight delivery and in figuring out a way to provide the service for them. Smith ruled out using existing commercial flights, whose schedules were designed to serve passenger traffic. Instead, he had the audacious idea of acquiring a dedicated fleet of jets and shipping all packages through a central hub that was located in Memphis.

As with most big ideas, the concept was difficult to execute. Smith, 28 years old at the time, had to raise $91 million in venture funding. The jets, the hub, operations in 25 states, and several hundred trained employees had to be in place before the company could open for business. And Smith

Does Planning Pay?

Interviews with the founders of 100 companies on the 1989 *Inc.* "500" list of the fastest growing companies in the United States revealed that entrepreneurs spent little effort on their initial business plan:

- 41% had no business plan at all.
- 26% had just a rudimentary, back-of-the-envelope type of plan.
- 5% worked up financial projections for investors.
- 28% wrote up a full-blown plan.

Many entrepreneurs, the interviews suggested, don't bother with well-formulated plans for good reasons. They thrive in rapidly changing industries and niches that tend to deter established companies. And under these fluid conditions, an ability to roll with the punches is much more important than careful planning.

The experiences of two *Inc.* "500" companies, Attronica Computers and Bohdan Associates, illustrate the limitations of planning in entrepreneurial ventures. Carol Sosdian and Atul Tucker, who had worked together in a large corporation, started Attronica in 1983 to retail personal computers in Washington, D.C. Carol recalls that Atul "wrote a one-paragraph business plan and brought it to me, and I turned it into a real business plan. It took about one month, and then we bantered back and forth over the next three months. We got to where we thought it might work, and then we showed it to some friends. It passed the 'friends test.'"

Heartened, Carol and Atul conducted almost two years of market research, which led them to purchase a Byte franchise for $150,000. Soon after they opened their first store, however, Byte folded. They then signed on as a franchisee of World of Computers, which also folded, and in 1985, Attronica began to operate as an independent, direct dealer for AT&T's computers. This partnership clicked, and Attronica soon became one of AT&T's best dealers. Attronica also changed its customer focus from people off the street to corporate and government clients. They found large clients much more profitable because they valued Attronica's technical expertise and service.

Peter Zacharkiw founded Bohdan Associates in a Washington, D.C., suburb in the same year that Atul and Carol launched Attronica. Peter did not conduct any research, however. He was employed by Bechtel and invested in tax shelters on the side. He bought a computer for his tax shelter calculations, expecting to deduct the cost of the machine

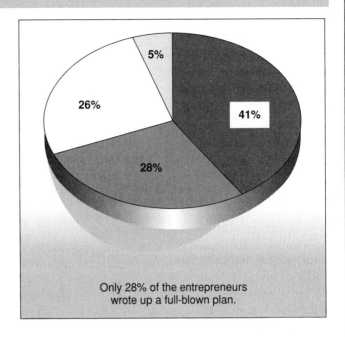

Only 28% of the entrepreneurs wrote up a full-blown plan.

from his income. When Peter discovered that he was overdeducted for the year, he placed an ad in the *Washington Post* to sell his computer. He got over 50 responses and sold his machine for a profit. Peter figured that if he had had 50 machines, he could have sold them all and decided to begin selling computers from his home. "At first, I just wanted to earn a little extra Christmas money," he recalls. "My wife put systems together during the day, and I delivered them at night. We grew to $300,000 per month, and I was still working full-time. I made more then than I would have made the entire year at Bechtel."

Like Attronica, Bohdan evolved into serving corporate clients. "First, we sold to individuals responding to ads. But these people were working for companies, and they would tell their purchasing agents, 'Hey, I know where you can get these.' It was an all-referral business. I gave better service than anyone else. I would deliver them, install them, and spend time teaching buyers how to use them." In 1985, after customers started asking for Compaq machines, Bohdan became a Compaq dealer, and the business really took off. "We're very reactive, not proactive," Peter observes. "Business comes to us, and we react. I've never had a business plan."

needed great fortitude and skill to prevent the fledgling enterprise from going under: Federal Express lost over $40 million in its first three years. Some investors tried to remove Smith, and creditors tried to seize assets. Yet Smith somehow preserved morale and mollified investors and lenders while the company expanded its operations and launched national advertising and direct-mail campaigns to build market share.

In contrast, ventures that seek to capture a market niche, not transform or create an industry, don't need extraordinary ideas. Some ingenuity is necessary to design a product that will draw customers away from mainstream offerings and overcome the cost penalty of serving a small market. But features that are too novel can be a hindrance; a niche market will rarely justify the investment required to educate customers and distributors about the benefits

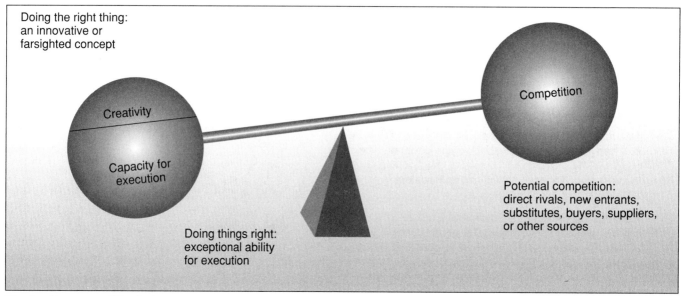

Doing the right thing:
an innovative or
farsighted concept

Creativity

Capacity for
execution

Doing things right:
exceptional ability
for execution

Competition

Potential competition:
direct rivals, new entrants,
substitutes, buyers, suppliers,
or other sources

Tipping the competitive balance.

of a radically new product. Similarly, a niche venture cannot support too much production or distribution innovation; unlike Federal Express, the Cape Cod Potato Chip Company, for example, must work within the limits of its distributors and truckers.

And since niche markets cannot support much investment or overhead, entrepreneurs do not need the revolutionary's ability to raise capital and build large organizations. Rather, the entrepreneur must be able to secure others' resources on favorable terms and make do with less, building brand awareness through guerrilla marketing and word of mouth instead of national advertising, for example.

Jay Boberg and Miles Copeland, who launched International Record Syndicate (IRS) in 1979, used a niche strategy, my students Elisabeth Bentel and Victoria Hackett found, to create one of the most successful new music labels in North America. Lacking the funds or a great innovation to compete against the major labels, Boberg and Miles promoted "alternative" music—undiscovered British groups like the Buzzcocks and Skafish—which the major labels were ignoring because their potential sales were too small. And IRS used low-cost, alternative marketing methods to promote their alternative music. At the time, the major record labels had not yet realized that music videos on television could be used effectively to promote their products. Boberg, however, jumped at the opportunity to produce a rock show, "The Cutting Edge," for MTV. The show proved to be a hit with fans and an effective promotional tool for IRS. Before "The Cutting Edge," Boberg had to plead with radio stations to play his songs. Afterward, the MTV audience demanded that disc jockeys play the songs they had heard on the show.

2. Leverage Provided by External Change

Exploiting opportunities in a new or changing industry is generally easier than making waves in a mature industry. Enormous creativity, experience, and contacts are needed to take business away from competitors in a mature industry, where market forces have long shaken out weak technologies, strategies, and organizations.

But new markets are different. There start-ups often face rough-around-the-edges rivals, customers who tolerate inexperienced vendors and imperfect products, and opportunities to profit from shortages. Small insights and marginal innovations, a little skill or expertise (in the land of the blind, the one-eyed person is king), and the willingness to act quickly can go a long way. In fact, with great external uncertainty, customers and investors may be hesitant to back a radical product and technology until the environment settles down. Strategic choices in a new industry are often very limited; entrepreneurs have to adhere to the emerging standards for product features, components, or distribution channels.

The leverage provided by external change is illustrated by the success of numerous start-ups in hardware, software, training, retailing, and systems integration that emerged from the personal computer revolution of the 1980s. Installing or fixing a computer system is probably easier than repairing a car; but because people with the initiative or foresight to acquire the skill were scarce, entrepreneurs like Bohdan's Peter Zacharkiw built successful dealerships by providing what customers saw as exceptional service (see "Does Planning Pay?"). As one Midwestern dealer told me, "We have a joke slogan around here: We aren't as incompetent as our competitors!"

Bill Gates turned Microsoft into a multibillion-dollar company without a breakthrough product by showing up in the industry early and capitalizing on the opportunities that came his way. Gates, then 19, and his partner Paul Allen, 21, launched Microsoft in 1975 to sell software they had created. By 1979, Microsoft had grown to 25 employees and $2.5 million in sales. Then in November 1980, IBM chose Microsoft to provide an operating system for its personal computer. Microsoft thereupon bought an operating system from Seattle Computer Products, which it modified into the now ubiquitous MS-DOS. The IBM name and the huge success of the 1–2–3 spreadsheet, which only ran on DOS computers, soon helped make Microsoft the dominant supplier of operating systems.

Microsoft's Bill Gates built a multibillion-dollar business without a breakthrough product.

Microsoft won the operating system battle without clockwork execution and amidst considerable organizational turmoil. According to author Scott Lewis, during the early 1980s, "The firm was doubling in size every year and had not yet adapted to being a large company. Gates, whose volatile temperament was well-known in the computer industry, had exacerbated Microsoft's chaos by abruptly changing product specifications and moving developers around."[1]

External changes can provide great leverage for creative and nimble entrepreneurs.

External changes, such as collapses in the price of real estate or energy, also create opportunities for entrepreneurs who speculate in out-of-favor assets. Sam Zell, the self-described "grave dancer," and his now deceased partner, Robert Lurie, built a multibillion-dollar real estate and industrial empire through such opportunities. Their first big success followed the collapse of the real estate investment trusts in the early 1970s. Later they picked up millions of square feet of office space and shopping centers and tens of thousands of apartments and trailer-park spaces for mobile homes. During the early 1980s, the partners sold a number of buildings in the booming Southwest and invested in Rust Belt cities like Buffalo and Chicago.

His approach, Zell concedes, doesn't call for the sort of creativity that's involved in building a business.[2] Contrarian speculators don't innovate much; the entrepreneur merely anticipates that the confusion or panic that has depressed prices will pass. Nor does successful execution require much managerial capacity. Organizational development, engineering, or marketing abilities add little value when an entrepreneur buys assets at a low price, expecting to sell them at a high price. Rather, good execution requires the ability to move quickly, negotiate astutely, and raise funds under favorable terms.

3. Basis of Competition: Proprietary Assets versus Hustle

In some industries, such as pharmaceuticals, luxury hotels, and consumer goods, a company's profitability depends significantly on the assets it owns or controls—patents, location, or brands, for example. Good management practices like listening to customers, maintaining quality, and paying attention to costs, which can improve the profits of a going business, cannot propel a start-up over such structural barriers. Here a creative new technology, product, or strategy is a must.

Companies in fragmented service industries, such as investment management, investment banking, head hunting, or consulting cannot establish proprietary advantages easily but can nonetheless enjoy high profits by providing exceptional service tailored to client demands. Start-ups in those fields rely mainly on their hustle.[3] Successful entrepreneurs depend on personal selling skills, contacts, their reputations for expertise, and their ability to convince clients of the value of the services rendered. They also have the capacity for institution building—skills such as recruiting and motivating stellar professionals and articulating and reinforcing company values. Where there are few natural economies of scale, an entrepreneur cannot create a going concern out of a one-man-brand or ad hoc ensemble without a lot of expertise in organizational development.

McKinsey & Company grew out of a simple idea: high-quality advice for top managers.

Marvin Bower, who cofounded McKinsey & Company in 1939, created a premier management consulting firm through the relentless execution of a simple idea: providing high-quality business advice to the top managers of large companies. Bower was very skilled in developing and serving his clients and was dogged in building organizational capabilities. He preached constantly the virtues of putting clients' interests first. Under his leadership, McKinsey started recruiting from top business schools, adopted an up-or-out policy to eliminate employees who didn't make the mark, declined studies that didn't fit the firm's mission of serving top management, and opened international offices to better serve chosen clientele. Bower didn't dictate policy, however, and had the patience to work on bringing partners around to his point of view. Also, he was willing to sell his stock at book value so that the equity of the firm was shared widely.[4]

Gauging Attractiveness

Entrepreneurs should also screen potential ventures for their attractiveness—their risks and rewards—compared to other opportunities. Several factors should be considered. Capital requirements, for example, matter to the entrepreneur who lacks easy access to financial markets. An unexpected need for cash because, say, one large customer is unable to make a timely payment may shut down a venture or force a fire sale of the founder's equity. Therefore, entrepreneurs should favor ventures that aren't capital intensive and have the profit margins to sustain rapid growth with internally generated funds. In a similar fashion, entrepreneurs should look for a high margin for error, ventures with simple operations and low fixed costs that are less likely to face a cash crunch because of factors such as technical delays, cost overruns, and slow buildup of sales.

Other criteria reflect the typical entrepreneur's inability to undertake multiple projects: an attractive venture should provide a substantial enough reward to compensate the entrepreneur's exclusive commitment to it. Shut-down costs should be low: the payback should be quick, or failure soon recognized so that the venture can be terminated without a significant loss of time, money, or reputation. And the entrepreneur should have the option to cash in, for example, by selling all or part of the equity. An entrepreneur locked into an illiquid business cannot easily pursue other opportunities and risks fatigue and burnout.

These criteria cannot be applied mechanically like, say, a textbook rule of backing all projects with positive net present value (NPV). Ventures that shine by one measure are often questionable by another. For example, a successful biotech venture whose parents provide sustainable advantages can be taken public more easily than an advertising agency. But biotech entrepreneurs need to raise significant capital and may be locked into a venture whose success can't be ascertained for many years.

Surviving the inevitable disappointments on the rough road to success requires passion for the chosen business.

Ventures must also fit what the individual entrepreneur values and wants to do. Surviving the inevitable disappointments and near disasters one encounters on the rough road to success requires a passion for the chosen business. Entrepreneurs should evaluate a potential new venture against what they're looking for and the sacrifices they're willing to make. Do they want to make a fortune, or will a small profit be sufficient? Do they seek public recognition? Is the stimulation of working with exciting technologies, customers, or colleagues important to them? Are they prepared to devote their lives to a business, or do they want to cash out quickly? Can they tolerate working in an industry that has questionable ethical standards? Or an industry where there is high uncertainty? What financial and career risks are they prepared to take and for how long?

These deeply personal preferences determine the types of ventures that will enthuse and fortify an entrepreneur. For example, ambitious undertakings like Federal Express fit people who are ready to win or lose on a grand scale. Success can create dynastic fortunes and turn the entrepreneur into a near-cult figure. But the risks also are substantial. Visionary schemes may fail for any number of reasons: the product is flawed, cannot be made or distributed cost-effectively, serves no compelling need, or requires customers to incur unacceptable switching costs. Worse, the failure may not be apparent for several years, locking the entrepreneur into an extended period of frustrating endeavor. Even businesses that succeed may not be financially rewarding for their founders, especially if they encounter delays en route. Investors may dump the visionary founders or demand a high share of the equity for additional financing. The entrepreneur must therefore anticipate recurring disappointments and a high probability that years of toil may come to naught. Unless entrepreneurs have a burning desire to change the world, they should not undertake revolutionary ventures.

Surprisingly, small endeavors often hold more financial promise than large ones. Often the founders can keep a larger share of the profits because they don't dilute their equity interest through multiple rounds of financings. But entrepreneurs must be willing to prosper in a backwater; dominating a neglected market segment is sometimes more profitable than intellectually stimulating or glamorous. Niche enterprises can also enter the "land of the living dead" because their market is too small for the business to thrive but the entrepreneur has invested too much effort to be willing to quit.

Speculators like Zell, who don't build a company or introduce an innovation to the world, can take pleasure from showing up the crowd. Their financial risks and returns depend on the terms of the deal, the capital at risk, the conditions and amount of borrowing, and, or course, the price of the asset acquired. Risks are generally not staged; the entrepreneur is fully exposed when the asset is acquired. Liquidity or exit options often turn on the success of the speculation: if, as hoped, prices rise, the speculator can expect many buyers for the asset owned, but if prices decline or stay depressed, market liquidity for the asset will be generally poor. All things considered, such ventures appeal most to entrepreneurs who enjoy making deals and rolling the dice.

A new company that is based on hustle in, say, consulting or advertising can provide the satisfaction of working with talented colleagues in a dynamic and competitive market. Capital requirements are low, and investments can be staged as the business grows. Entrepreneurs can therefore avoid significant personal risk and meddling by outside investors. But although such businesses can provide attractive current income, great wealth in those situations is elusive: hustle businesses, which lack a sustainable franchise, cannot be easily sold or taken public at a high multiple of earnings. The entrepreneur must therefore savor the venture enough to make a long-term career of it rather than enjoy the fruits of a quick harvest.

Parsimonious Planning and Analysis

To conserve time and money, successful entrepreneurs minimize the resources they devote to researching their ideas. Unlike the corporate world, where foil mastery and completed staff work can make a career, the entrepreneur only does as much planning and analysis as seems useful and makes subjective judgment calls when necessary.

As Harvard's Michael Porter has pointed out, a start-up faces competition not only from rivals offering the same goods but also potentially from substitutes, suppliers, buyers, and other new entrants. A start-up even competes with companies outside its industry for employees and capital. A complete analysis, therefore, would cover many industry participants and probe internal core competencies and weaknesses. But the astute entrepreneur isn't interested in completeness. He or she understands that returns from additional analysis diminish rapidly and avoids using spreadsheet software to churn out detailed but not particularly insightful analyses of a project's break-even point, capital requirements, payback period, or NPV.

Entrepreneurs must be smart enough to recognize mistakes and change strategies.

In setting their analytical priorities, entrepreneurs must recognize that some critical uncertainties cannot be resolved through more research. For example, focus groups and surveys often have little value in predicting demand for products that are truly novel. At first, consumers had dismissed the need for copiers, for instance, and told researchers they were satisfied with using carbon paper. With issues like this, entrepreneurs have to resist the temptation of endless investigation and trust their judgment.

The parsimonious analyst should also avoid research that he or she can't act on. For example, understanding broad market trends and the strategies of the industry leaders is unlikely to affect what a start-up in a hustle business like advertising does and therefore isn't worth bothering with. Entrepreneurs should concentrate instead on issues that they can reasonably expect to resolve through analysis and that determine whether and how they will proceed. Resolving a few big questions—understanding what things *must* go right and anticipating the venture-destroying pitfalls, for instance—is more important than investigating many nice-to-know matters.

Standard checklists or one-size-fits-all approaches don't work. The appropriate analytical priorities vary for each venture.

Standard checklists or one-size-fits-all approaches don't work for entrepreneurs. The appropriate analytical budget and the issues that are most worthy of research and analysis depend on the characteristics of each venture.

Ambitious endeavors like Federal Express, for example, require significant capital and must be better researched and documented than ventures that can be self-financed. Professional investors usually ask for a written business plan because it provides clues about the entrepreneur's seriousness of purpose, concern for investors, and competence. So entrepreneurs must write a detailed plan even if they are skeptical about its relationship to the subsequent outcomes.

Revenues are notoriously difficult to predict. At best, entrepreneurs may satisfy themselves that their novel product or service delivers considerably greater value than current offerings do; how quickly the product catches on is a blind guess. Leverage may be obtained, however, from analyzing how customers might buy and use the product or service. Understanding the purchase process can help identify the right decision makers for the new offering. With Federal Express, for instance, it was important to go beyond the mail-room managers who traditionally bought delivery services. Understanding how products are used can also help by revealing obstacles that must be overcome before consumers can benefit from a new offering.

Visionary entrepreneurs must guard against making competitors rich from their work. Many concepts are difficult to prove but, once proven, easy to imitate. Unless the pioneer is protected by sustainable barriers to entry, the benefits of a hard-fought revolution can become a public good rather than a boon to the innovator. Sun

Microsystems and Apple, for example, won big from path-breaking innovations that had been developed at Xerox's Palo Alto Research Center.

Entrepreneurs who hope to secure a niche face different problems: they often fail because the costs of serving a specialized segment exceed the benefits to customers. Entrepreneurs should therefore analyze carefully the incremental costs of serving a niche and take into account their lack of scale and the difficulty of marketing to a small, diffused segment. And especially if the cost disadvantage is significant, entrepreneurs should determine whether their offering provides a significant performance benefit. Whereas established companies can vie for share through line extensions or marginal tailoring of their products and services, the start-up must really wow its target customers. A marginally tastier cereal won't knock Kellogg's Cornflakes off supermarket shelves.

Start-ups with powerful competitors must wow their customers. A marginally tastier cereal won't knock Kellogg's Cornflakes off supermarket shelves.

Inadequate payoffs also pose a risk for ventures that address small markets. For example, a niche venture that can't support a direct sales force may not generate enough commissions to attract an independent broker or manufacturers' rep. Entrepreneurs will eventually lose interest too if the rewards aren't commensurate with their efforts. Therefore, the entrepreneur should make sure that everyone who contributes can expect a high, quick, or sustainable return even if the venture's total profits are small.

Entrepreneurs who seek to leverage factors like changing technologies, customer preferences, or regulations should avoid extensive analysis. Research conducted under conditions of such turbulence isn't reliable, and the importance of a quick response precludes spending the time to make sure every detail is covered.

The entrepreneur has to live with critical uncertainties, such as the relative competencies of rivals or the preferences of strategic customers, which are not easy to analyze. Who could have forecast, for example, that Sun Microsystems's four 27-year-old founders, who had virtually no business or industry experience, would beat more than a dozen start-ups, including Apollo, a textbook venture launched by industry superstars? Or that IBM would turn to Microsoft for an operating system, gain dominance for its hardware, and go on to dethrone Digital Research's entrenched CP/M operating system? Entering a race requires faith in one's ability to finish ahead of whoever else might happen to play.

Analyzing whether or not the rewards for winning are commensurate with the risks, however, can be a more feasible and worthwhile exercise. In some technology races, success is predictably short-lived. In the disk-drive industry, for example, companies that succeed with one generation of products are often leap-frogged when the next generation arrives. In engineering workstations, however Sun enjoyed long-term gains from its early success because it established a durable architectural standard. If success is unlikely to be sustained, entrepreneurs should have a plan for making a good return while it lasts.

Ventures in fast-changing markets are more likely to fold because they can't design, produce, or sell a timely, cost-effective product that works than because they pursued a poor strategy. Successful entrepreneurs, therefore, usually devote more attention to operational analysis and planning than strategic planning. Sun's business plan, one founder recalls, was mainly an operating plan, containing specific timetables for product development, opening sales and service offices, and hiring engineers.

For speculators like Zell who seek to purchase assets at depressed prices, two sets of analysis are crucial. One relates to the market dynamics for the asset being acquired or, more specifically, why the prices of the asset may be expected to rise. Entrepreneurs should try to determine whether prices are temporarily low (due to, say, an irrational panic or a temporary surge in supply), in secular decline because of permanent changes in supply or demand, or merely correcting after an irrational prior surge. Also important to analyze is the entrepreneur's ability to hold or carry the asset until it can be sold at a profit because it is difficult to predict when temporarily depressed prices will return to normal. Carrying capacity depends on the extent of borrowing used to purchase the asset, the conditions under which financing may be revoked, and the income produced by the asset. Rental properties or a producing well that provides ongoing income, for example, can be carried more easily than raw land or drilling rights. For certain kinds of assets, mines and urban rental properties, for example, the entrepreneur should also consider the risks of expropriation (through, for example, rent control) and windfall taxation.

In ventures based on hustle rather than proprietary advantages, a detailed analysis of competitors and industry structure is rarely of much value. The ability to seize short-lived opportunities and execute them brilliantly is of far more importance than a long-term competitive strategy. Analysis of specific clients and relationships dominates general market surveys. Partnership agreements, terms for offering equity to later employees, performance measurement criteria, and bonus plans are important determinants of company success and are best thought through before launch rather than hastily improvised later on. And although projections of long-term cash flows are not meaningful, back-of-the-envelope, short-term cash forecasts and analyses of breakevens can keep the entrepreneur out of trouble. Overall, though, the analytical preparation required for such ventures is modest.

Integrating Action and Analysis

Standard operating procedure in large corporations usually makes a clear distinction between analysis and execution. In contemplating a new venture, managers in established companies face issues about its fit with ongoing activities: Does the proposed venture leverage corporate strengths? Will the resources and attention it requires reduce the company's ability to build customer loyalty and improve quality of core markets? These concerns dictate a deliberate, "trustee" approach: before they can launch a venture, managers must investigate an opportunity extensively, seek the counsel of people higher up, submit a formal plan, respond to criticisms by bosses and corporate staff, and secure a headcount and capital allocation.[5]

Entrepreneurs who start with a clean slate, however, don't have to know all the answers before they act. In fact, they often can't easily separate action and analysis. The attractiveness of a new restaurant, for example, may depend on the terms of the lease; low rents can change the venture from a mediocre proposition into a money machine. But an entrepreneur's ability to negotiate a good lease cannot be easily determined from general prior analysis; he or she must enter into a serious negotiation with a specific landlord for a specific property.

Acting before an opportunity is fully analyzed has many benefits. Doing something concrete builds confidence in oneself and in others. Key employees and investors will often follow the individual who has committed to action, for instance, by quitting a job, incorporating, or signing a lease. By taking a personal risk, the entrepreneur convinces other people that the venture *will* proceed, and they may believe that if they don't sign up, they could be left behind.

Early action can generate more robust better informed strategies too. Extensive surveys and focus-groups research about a concept can produce misleading evidence: slippage can arise between research and reality because the potential customers interviewed are not representative of the market, their enthusiasm for the concept wanes when they see the actual product, or they lack the authority to sign purchase orders. More robust strategies may be developed by first building a working prototype and asking customers to use it before conducting extensive market research.

The ability of individual entrepreneurs to execute quickly will naturally vary. Trial and error is less feasible with large-scale, capital-intensive ventures like Orbital Sciences, which had to raise over $50 million to build rockets for NASA, than with a consulting firm start-up. Nevertheless, some characteristics are common to an approach that integrates action and analysis:

- *Handling Analytical Tasks in Stages.* Rather than resolve all issues at once, the entrepreneur does only enough research to justify the next action or investment. For example, an individual who has developed a new medical technology may first obtain crude estimates of market demand to determined whether it's worth seeing a patent lawyer. If the estimates and lawyer are encouraging, the individual may do more analysis to investigate the wisdom of spending money to obtain a patent. Several more iterations of analysis and action will follow before the entrepreneur prepares and circulates a formal business plan to venture capitalists.

- *Plugging Holes Quickly.* As soon as any problems or risks show up, the entrepreneur begins looking for solutions. For example, suppose that an entrepreneur sees it will be difficult to raise capital. Rather than kill the idea, he or she thinks creatively about solving the problem. Perhaps the investment can be reduced by modifying technology to use more standard equipment that can be rented instead of bought. Or under the right terms, a customer might underwrite the risk by providing a large initial order. Or expectations and goals for growth might be scaled down, and a niche market could be tackled first. Except with obviously unviable ideas that can be ruled out through elementary logic, the purpose of analysis is not to find fault with new ventures or find reasons for abandoning them. Analysis is an exercise in what to do next more than what not to do.

- *Evangelical Investigation.* Entrepreneurs often blur the line between research and selling. As one founder recalls, "My market research consisted of taking a prototype to a trade show and seeing if I could write orders." Software industry "beta sites" provide another example of simultaneous research and selling; customers actually pay to help vendors test early versions of their software and will often place larger orders if they are satisfied with the product.

From the beginning, entrepreneurs don't just seek opinions and information, they also look for commitment from other people. Entrepreneurs treat everyone whom they talk to as a potential customer, investor, employee, or supplier, or at least as a possible source of leads down the road. Even if they don't actually ask for an order, they take the time to build enough interest and rapport so they can come back later. This simultaneous listening and selling approach may not produce truly objective market research and statistically significant results. But the resource-constrained entrepreneur doesn't have much choice in the matter. Besides, in the initial stages, the deep knowledge and support of a few is often more valuable than broad, impersonal data.

- *Smart Arrogance.* An entrepreneur's willingness to act on sketchy plans and inconclusive data is often sustained by an almost arrogant self-confidence. One successful high-tech entrepreneur likens his kind to "gamblers in a casino who know they are good at craps and are therefore likely to win. They believe: 'I'm smarter, more creative, and harder working than most people. With my unique and rare skills, I'm doing investors a favor by taking their money.'" Moreover, the entrepreneur's arrogance must stand the test of adversity. Entrepreneurs must have great confidence in their talent and ideas to persevere as customers stay away in droves, the product doesn't work, or the business runs out of cash.

But entrepreneurs who believe they are more capable or venturesome than others must also have the smarts to recognize their mistakes and to change their strategies as events unfold. Successful ventures don't always proceed in the direction on which they initially set out. A significant proportion develop entirely new markets, products, and sources of competitive advantage. Therefore, although perseverance and tenacity are valuable entrepreneurial trails, they must be complemented with flexibility and a willingness to learn. If prospects who were expected to place orders don't, the entrepreneur should consider reworking the concept. Similarly, the entrepreneur should also be prepared to exploit opportunities that didn't figure in the initial plan.

The evolution of Silton-Bookman Systems illustrates the importance of keeping an open mind. The venture's original plan was to sell general-purpose, PC-based software for human resource development. But established competitors who already sold similar software on mainframes were beginning to develop products for PCs. So the company adopted a niche strategy and developed a training registration product. And although the founders had initially targeted small companies that couldn't afford mainframe solutions, their first customer was someone from IBM who happened to respond to an ad. Thereafter, Silton-Bookman concentrated its efforts on large companies, where they had considerable success. "The world gives you lots and lots of feedback," cofounder Phil Bookman observes. "The challenge is to take advantage of the feedback you get."

The apparently sketchy planning and haphazard evolution of many successful ventures like Silton-Bookman doesn't mean that entrepreneurs should follow a ready-fire-aim approach. Despite appearances, astute entrepreneurs do analyze and strategize extensively. They realize, however, that businesses cannot be launched like space shuttles, with every detail of the mission planned in advance. Initial analyses only provide plausible hypotheses, which must be tested and modified. Entrepreneurs should play with and explore ideas, letting their strategies evolve through a seamless process of guesswork, analysis, and action.

References

1. Scott Lewis, "Microsoft Corporation," in *International Directory of Company Histories,* ed. Paula Kepos (Detroit, Michigan: St. James Press, 1992), p. 258.
2. Erik Ipsen, "Real Estate: Will Success Spoil Sam Zell?" *Institutional Investor,* April 1989, pp. 90–99.
3. See Amar Bhidé, "Hustle as Strategy," HBR September–October 1986.
4. See "McKinsey & Company [A]: 1956," Harvard Business School Case No. 393–066, 1992.
5. See Howard Stevenson and David Gumpert, "The Heart of Entrepreneurship," HBR March–April 1985.

AMAR BHIDÉ teaches entrepreneurship at the Harvard Business School, where he is associate professor. His last HBR article was "Bootstrap Finance: The Art of Start-ups" (November–December 1992).

Seven Keys to Shaping the Entrepreneurial Organization

MICHIE P. SLAUGHTER

Background

The Kauffman Center for Entrepreneurial Leadership is one of a very few national not-for-profit organizations with significant resources devoted to accelerating entrepreneurship (and job growth) in America. The Center has become a trusted resource, promoting opportunities for entrepreneurs, educators and youth nationwide. The Center is a legacy of the late Ewing Marion Kauffman, and is funded by the Foundation which bears his name.

The Kauffman Center is located in Kansas City, Missouri, the birthplace of Marion Laboratories, Inc. The company was founded by Mr. Kauffman in 1950 in the basement of his home. At the time of its merger in 1989 with the Merrell Dow arm of the Dow Chemical Co., Marion had sales of $1 billion and employment of 3,400. The firm now operates as a major part of Hoechst Marion Roussel, a worldwide healthcare firm with revenues exceeding $9 billion and employing more than 40,000 people.

Michie P. Slaughter was involved in the original conceptual design of the Kauffman Center for Entrepreneurial Leadership, was named its first president in February 1992 and served in that role until 1998. Slaughter continues to serve as chairman of the Kauffman Center. During his 17-year career as vice president of human resources and member of the board of directors of Marion Laboratories, Slaughter was a key influence in helping the founder and chairman, Ewing M. Kauffman, institutionalize his basic business philosophies: that we should "treat others as we want to be treated," and that "those who produce should share." He was one of the primary architects of the leadership, organization and management development strategies employed by Marion during its most dramatic growth period.

Many businesses are similar with respect to products, services, and markets. Yet some seem to grow rapidly, passing through higher and higher levels of complexity in the firm while others do not achieve significant growth. For the growth-oriented firms, barriers to transitions that the firm must overcome in the pursuit of growth appear to be only minor disturbances. When this occurs, it is not the result of action of the "lone ranger" entrepreneur, but the action of a purpose-driven team and organization that is committed to the goals and directions established for the firm. When this purpose-driven attitude or entrepreneurial spirit has been established, the transition from the entrepreneurial leader to entrepreneurial organization has been achieved. The entrepreneurial organization may look like any other firm. Yet it thrives on an attitude toward growth that exists only when a team spirit is fostered among the associates and with the suppliers and customers of the firm.

Shaping the entrepreneurial organization is not a difficult process when growth, strongly supported by the founders and the top management team, is well planned and constantly reinforced. When these conditions exist, a seven-step approach can be used to implement the process and achieve the desired results.

These seven steps are: 1) hire self-motivated people; 2) help others be successful; 3) create clarity in the organization—clarification of purpose, direction, structure, and measurement; 4) determine and communicate your own values and philosophies; 5) provide appropriate reward systems; 6) create an experimental learning attitude; and 7) celebrate your victories.

The key to the success of most growing organizations is that the entrepreneur has put together a team of highly qualified people who are committed to the goals and objectives of the firm. This does not minimize the importance of identifying opportunities in the marketplace, and developing products or services that satisfy the opportunity or need while producing a profit. Nor does it mean that the judicious use of resources to achieve growth is not a necessary criterion for success. What it does mean is that the successful entrepreneur has expanded his or her capabilities by delegating responsibilities for various functions to a team of motivated people who share the goals and objectives of the entrepreneur leading the firm.

The successful entrepreneurs we read about in the national press are not "Lone Rangers" who have accomplished their greatness through individual achievement. Rather, they are skilled, motivated individuals with a dream who have been able to gather around them similarly skilled people who share their dreams and make them come true! The ability to build an entrepreneurial organization is, therefore, essential to entrepreneurial success.

Fortunately, many successful entrepreneurs are willing to share the secrets of building effective, entrepreneurial organizations. I have had the good fortune to be associated with a number of these "master" entrepreneurs and have learned many of their secrets. Most notable among this list of masters were two who shared as mentors and teachers to me while, together, we built several successful entrepreneurial teams.

In 1950, Ewing Marion Kauffman founded Marion Laboratories, Inc. in the basement of his home in Kansas City. By the time of his death in 1993, "Mr. K," as he was known throughout the Midwest, had built Marion into a company of 3,400 dedicated people with $1 billion in sales and valued at more than $6 billion on the New York Stock Exchange. When the company merged with the Merrell Dow arm of Dow Chemical in 1989, more than 300 of his "associates" became millionaires as a result of his unique philosophy of sharing with those who produced the dramatic growth and profitability of the company.

Gerald W. Holder retired as senior vice president and chief administrative officer of Marion Laboratories in 1985. He had joined Mr. K in 1973 to help him build an executive team capable of doing $100 million in business. At that time, the company had sales of just over $50 million. Prior to 1973, Mr. Holder had enjoyed a successful career building growth-creating organizations for pharmaceutical and chemical firms such as Abbott and Union Carbide. At the time of his death in 1992, Mr. Holder was still teaching entrepreneurs how to build the capacity for growth into their companies.

Much of what I have learned about building entrepreneurial organizations came at the elbows of these two great men or through exposure to other teachers they enabled me to meet. Our goal now at the Kauffman Center for Entrepreneurial Leadership is to find effective ways to teach the entrepreneurial skills learned from these and other successful entrepreneurs to emerging entrepreneurs so that they might continue the legacy of economic vitality that is so essential to the growth of our nation. This chapter is an abbreviated version of the seven keys to building entrepreneurial organizations. While you may recognize some of these keys as practical applications of organization research you have read about in the past, others will strike you as an "obvious" practical application of what we know about human nature to building entrepreneurial teams.

Several books have been written on this topic, some of which are included in the bibliography. But there is no substitute for experience and the information we learn from our mentors.

These seven keys are by no means the only things you need to do in building entrepreneurial success, but they will give you a head start in understanding the ingredients necessary to build an effective entrepreneurial team.

Hire Self-Motivated People

Anyone who is a sports fan understands that the key to winning is having a talented, motivated team. But in business, we too often settle for talent that's "just good enough," talent that we feel we can afford. When we do that, we compromise what our company can become. Entrepreneurs need to hire the very best people they can find—people who bring their motivation with them. In addition to people with great technical skill, you need people who will share your dream with you and work with you to make it become reality. This means you need people with inner drive who give off energy of their own. Avoid people who constantly need to be motivated by you or others.

People who can motivate others have an ability to draw on those who are already strongly motivated from within. They will work hard to find ways to tap into that motivation and avoid actions that turn it off. When trying to build a solid business, most of us don't have the time or skills to create motivation in others where it doesn't already exist, so we need to structure our selection process to find those who are self-motivated. The most effective way to do this is to learn what has been the source of a candidate's motivation in the past. Since past behavior is still the most reliable predictor of future behavior, we can learn about this directly from the candidate by asking "why" he or she did certain things in their lives. You often have to probe to understand real reasons for an action, but by doing so you will gain insight into how they think and what things guided them in making key decisions in their lives. In each case, you will be looking for signs that tell you whether these people look to others for these elements. As entrepreneurs, we need people who can guide themselves.

In addition to asking the candidate why he or she took certain actions, you can learn more about how the person actually behaves by asking for real life examples of how they handled certain situations in the past. For example, ask for a specific example of how the candidate responded to a major setback ("What was the setback and how did you deal with it?") rather than posing a hypothetical question such as "How would you deal with a setback?" This requires the candidate to speak from experience and gives you some past behavior to evaluate. You can then use the example as a window into the person's motivation by asking the follow-up question, "Why did you choose that course of action?"

Remember, each of us puts our best foot forward in interview situations. To get the most information from an interview, we must probe for details and examples. You can then confirm these examples and the candidate's version of them when you call the references the candidate has given you. Having real examples to discuss with the reference will get you past the tendency to obtain only dates of employment and job titles, limited information which has become the norm in today's litigious society.

Ewing Kauffman offered his own personal twist to the talent equation with the advice to entrepreneurs to "Hire people who are smarter than you! In doing so, you prevent limiting the organization to the level of your own ability . . . and you grow the capabilities of your company." Kauffman said, "Someone has to be the smartest guy in the room. Never invest in that man! Put your bets on those who hire the best and smartest people they can find." He further explained, "If you hire people you consider smarter than you, you are more likely to listen to their thoughts and ideas, and this is the best way to expand on your own capabilities and build the strength of your company."

Help Each Other Be Successful

To build Marion Laboratories, Ewing Kauffman worked hard to create ways his associates could realize their own dreams by helping him realize the dreams he had for the company. His "treat others as you would be treated" philosophy and belief that "those who produce should share in the profits" are excellent examples of establishing the climate for such a partnership mentality. MacGregor (1985) referred to this as an "integration of individual and organizational goals." In the South, it is often referred to as "the way folks are." An old Southern saw says, "Given the opportunity, people will tend to act in their own best interest . . . Not given the opportunity, people will still tend to act in their own best interest." Clearly one good way to build a successful organization is to find ways to have your own interests be in concert with those you employ.

If you want a "we're all in this together" mentality, you must create one! To do so, you must find out the goals, dreams, and aspirations of your people. This means taking the time to ask and listen. This becomes more difficult as the organization grows in size, but if you establish the concept early in the process, supervisors and managers will sustain it as the company grows. Indeed, it is essential that you encourage the management team to follow this practice. Only by requiring team to do so can you demonstrate your own commitment to the principle. People often watch how we treat others (and how we allow them to treat others) as true signs of how we will treat them!

This process will help you learn what is important to those who will determine your success. For some, the motivator will be money; for others, it will be recognition, achievement, growth, freedom, and autonomy, or even time to be with their children. The important thing to remember is that motivations vary greatly from person to person. The key is to find out what motivates the person you want to motivate.

Responding to the interests and dreams of your people requires that you treat them as distinct and separate individuals. This flies in the face of the cliché that "the only way to be fair is to treat everyone the same." We have all experienced examples of the illogical behavior required when an organization "treats everybody the same." Responding to individual needs will make it possible to create conditions in which individuals' dreams will mesh with yours.

Create Clarity in the Organization—Clarity of Purpose, Direction, Structure, and Measurement

In his analysis of the successful growth of Marion Laboratories, Gerald W. Holder attributed much of the organization's strength to an entrepreneurial leadership team that focused significant energy on creating clarity throughout the work force. This enabled people to operate with a commonality of understanding and the assurance that everyone was working together. Holder believed strongly that creating clarity in the organization was the most important role for leadership. It required that leaders first establish clarity for themselves, then implement a major communications and reinforcement effort to create it for the organization. He acknowledged that complete clarity is never attained in a growing organization; however, the changes that come with growth only increase the importance of clear thinking and clear communications. Following are the four clarities Holder identified as critical to the success of Marion Laboratories.

Clarity of Purpose

It is important that people know why the organization exists. People need a reason to give you their enthusiastic support. Do not expect anyone but your family (and often not even them) to get excited about "making you rich." Most people will not mind if you make lots of money if they share in the gain with you. But most still need a purpose that is grander than money. Becoming the first or becoming the best or even doing what no one else has ever done in a given business or industry are challenges which excite people.

Helping people solve problems or lead better, safer, healthier, and more productive lives are the kinds of things that call upon the best of human values and stir people to committed action. Since no product or service will survive unless it meets a true need in the marketplace, opportunity to meet that need better, more quickly, or less expensively often provides the real purpose for an organization.

The people with entrepreneurial spirit who you want in your company will enjoy the opportunity to build and create a business where none has existed before. Give them the opportunity to share in the excitement of this building process by communicating why you are willing to make your own personal sacrifice to make it happen. If after deep personal reflection your only reason is to "get rich," reconsider the whole thing. Your customers, employees, suppliers, and investors will want you to have a purpose beyond personal wealth before they will share the risk with you. You must realize that each of them must share your risk in order for you to succeed.

Clarity of Direction

Without careful thought and communication, people often wonder "Where are we headed with this business?" or "What kinds of skills and talent do we need to bring into the company?" This does not mean that the direction is set in concrete and is unchangeable; rather, it means that the current direction often results in the diffusion of scarce resources in areas of minimal or even counterproductive return.

Clarity of Structure

The next key challenge in a growing business is the co-ordination of "Who's going to do what?" and "What part of the job is mine and what is yours?" and "Whose responsibility is it?" When you are the sole employee, this is not a problem. But when the company begins to grow beyond what you can do alone, it becomes a consuming task of leadership. I am not referring to the dreaded organizational chart here, but rather to the process of thinking through and communicating to your team the roles, responsibilities, and accountabilities of each so they can devote their efforts fully and confidently to doing their part.

We all watch with admiration when a shortstop and second baseman turn a double play, when an alley-oop pass results in a slam dunk basket, or when a trap block springs a runner free for a touchdown. The same level of knowledge, forethought, planning, and practice are required in the entrepreneurial firm in creating, recognizing, and capitalizing on opportunities. In each sports case cited above, the players must know and have confidence in the roles and responsibilities of their teammates, in addition to their own roles and responsibilities. This knowledge and confidence allows them to concentrate on their own job and give it their full energy while recognizing the interdependence of the players. No less is necessary for the growing firm. Deciding who will do what is sometimes difficult. But not deciding will always create difficulty. The entrepreneur must stay alert to the evolutionary changes in the organization that can bring about confusion related to who is to do what and work to keep it clear.

Clarity of Measurement

Knowing how to measure the results in a business is as essential as knowing how to score in an athletic event. Too often, though, we assume that everyone understands and fail to make it clear. Sometimes even the entrepreneur misunderstands how the customer or the investor will measure performance and is surprised when one or both withdraw their support. As businesses become increasingly complex, it becomes more difficult to determine what the key measures of success are. In many cases, there is a significant time lag between initial action and the end result. Careful thought to interim milestones in the development of the business is essential to making changes in direction, allocation of resources, rewarding people, and a variety of critical decisions the entrepreneur must make. Americans are great "measurers." We equate changes in measurements with achievement. We have more statistics on every aspect of both individual and team performance in sports such as baseball and basketball than the inventors of the games ever imagined, but we often overlook the importance of similar measurements in our business. Since people often pay more attention to the things they know you are going to measure, it is important that you make sure you are measuring the things that you have decided are important to you. Your people should have access to the information that will allow them to measure these things, too. If these things are sensitive financial information and you are reluctant to share it, consider how long you would exert your energy in a game, such as bowling, where you couldn't keep score and didn't know how well you were doing or if someone else was keeping score and wouldn't tell you how you were doing. If you still have that reluctance, please read Jack Stack's book, *The Great Game of Business,* which describes how he used open-book management to turn a dying business into an exciting entrepreneurial venture.

Determine and Communicate Your Own Values and Philosophies

The importance of values and philosophy has received a great deal of attention during the last few years. Much of that attention, however, has been focused on the quality of the values and their goodness, or lack thereof. While very important, the quality of the values is not enough. Your values must be clearly communicated and consistent with your actions to have a positive impact on your business. They must be reinforced by both your words and your actions. Ewing Kauffman's philosophies of "treat others as you would be treated" and "those who produce should share in the results" would have little impact on his business had he not constantly expressed them in both word and deed.

Values and philosophies are also important in providing a basis for making decisions and a basis for teaching people in the organization how to make decisions. Clearly stated, consistent values provide a framework within which people can make the myriad of major and minor decisions required daily in their jobs. Large bureaucratic organizations try to communicate direction through often complicated and voluminous policies and procedures, sometimes presented in multiple volumes of three-ring binders. Creating such manuals requires an impossible ability to know in advance all circumstances in any situation, or the result is illogical action "just because that's our policy!"

A clearly communicated set of values allows people at various levels in an organization to know what is important to the leadership and how those leaders would go about making a decision. Understanding the stated values helps people make decisions appropriate to the organization and its leaders. The internalization of values can help expand capacity, because that understanding clears the way for delegating more decisions to others. Since associates will often have more current and complete information than the leader, such delegation can reduce your risk while expanding your capacity. Every entrepreneur knows that reducing risk while expanding capacity is as elusive as cold fusion. Achieving clarity of values is a very effective way to do just that.

Provide Appropriate Reward Systems

Most entrepreneurs think of "rewards" in the narrow context of compensation, namely bonus plans. There is great power, however, in a broader interpretation of the term. Effective reward systems include all forms of compensation, plus the wide variety of other things that are important to people in a work setting, such as job assignment, recognition, growth and learning, additional responsibility, authority, and autonomy. Mr. Kauffman was a firm believer in the simple, but powerful concept of appreciation as a reward and motivator. The effectiveness of any reward system is a function of two primary factors: whether or not the recipient perceives the reward as a positive, and whether the reward actually encourages the desired behavior. A third factor, judicious use, preserves the value of a reward and recognizes that any reward given indiscriminately loses value quickly.

Our assumption that something we would consider a reward would be viewed in the same way by an associate often results in the use of rewards that disappoint. Some rewards actually represent punishment to the recipient. For example, early in my career I once received an award for having done an outstanding job leading a fundraising campaign, a project which I found to be an unpleasant experience. The reward was being named to head the campaign again the following year. It is no surprise that the best way to find out what an associate values as reward is to ASK!

In order for the reward to be effective, it must encourage the desired behavior, and the desired behavior must be consistent with the strategy you have designed for your business. I have often seen sales bonuses used as rewards for opening new accounts, at the same time a key element in the marketing strategy is maintaining and servicing current accounts. In one case, the sales bonus plan actually took off points for time spent prospecting new accounts when "growing the customer base" was an essential part of the company strategy. The key here, of course, is that there is no right or wrong. Just be sure you are rewarding the behavior you really want. Ideally, people should be able to look at their pay and other rewards to learn the keys to good performance. It is the leader's responsibility to make sure the reward system is set up to support the business strategy.

Create an Experimental, Learning Attitude

One of the biggest failings of our education system at every level is the process of teaching that there is always ONE right answer (and it's in the back of the book!). In most entrepreneurial settings, it is clear that, "No one has ever done what you have set out to do!" In almost every case, there will be several good ways—some will be better than others and some will be truly untried. The wise entrepreneur will take advantage of this dynamic and encourage associates to experiment, to look for and try different ways to do a task better, to come up with novel solutions. Acknowledging that you don't know all of the answers yourself can free up your team to help find solutions, and it presents an opportunity for them to contribute to your

success. An enthusiastic, "we're making this up as we go along" attitude can do wonders to keep people looking for better ways to improve your product or service.

In these days of continuous improvement, it is critical to establish an experimental attitude to create the freedom to try new things. Such an attitude also sets the stage for change when an experiment doesn't work out. Rather than spending great energy trying to prove you are right, you can more easily say, "That's not working, let's try another way!" Or as Stevenson (1985) said, "The best entrepreneurs are the ones who 'fail quickly' and get on with learning how to do it better." Establishing an "experimental, learning attitude" can turn early failures into success.

Celebrate Your Victories!

Good people want to be associated with a winner! We see sports fans in cities large and small engage in totally irrational behavior just to establish their affiliation with a winning team. Yet we often fail to give our associates an opportunity to celebrate their association with the victories we enjoy in our business. We see kids and adults give each other "high five's" when they get a hit, sink a putt, or make a touchdown. Why not when you make a big sale, secure that new account, or get that "nice job" from an important customer? Simple, spontaneous joy can be great motivational fuel for that next challenge.

References

Holder, G. W., and Kenneth McKensie. *A Theory of Marion.* Marion Laboratories, Inc. Internal Publication, 1986.

MacGregor, Douglas. *The Human Side of Enterprise.* New York: McGraw Hill, 1985.

Mintzburg, H. *Power in and Around Organizations.* Englewood Cliffs, N.J.: Prentice-Hall, 1983.

Pascarella, P., and M. A. Frogman. *The Purpose Driven Organization.* San Francisco: Josey-Bass, 1989.

Rosen, Robert H. *The Healthy Company.* New York: Putnam Publishing Co., 1991.

Stack, John P. *The Great Game of Business.* New York: Currency Books, 1992.

Stevenson, Howard, and D. E. Gumpert. "The Heart of Entrepreneurship," *Harvard Business Review 63,* no. 2 (1985):85–94.

Characteristics of a Successful Entrepreneurial Management Team

Alexander L. M. Dingee, Brian Haslett, and Leonard E. Smollen

What are the personal characteristics required to be a successful entrepreneur? Before making the personal sacrifices required to start and build a major enterprise, would-be entrepreneurs should engage in serious soul-searching to be sure they have what it takes to thrive in the toughest jungle of the business world.

To assist in this introspection, the following guidelines have been prepared by principals of Venture Founders Corporation (VFC). Founded in 1970 to design and apply new approaches to venture development and financing, VFC serves investor clients both in the United States and in the United Kingdom. These clients have committed capital to funds that finance new and young ventures that are found, evaluated and assisted by VFC.

Venture capitalists say they prefer a grade A entrepreneur with a grade B business idea to a grade B entrepreneur with a grade A idea. And it is generally a strong management team, not a lone entrepreneur that they back.

With that in mind, there are some initial questions that would-be entrepreneurs must consider: Do I have adequate *commitment, motivation* and *skills* to start and build a major business—to be a successful entrepreneur? Does my management team have the necessary skills to enable us to succeed in building a particular venture? And finally, do I have a viable idea?

If these questions can be answered affirmatively, then it may be wise to consider developing a business plan and beginning a search for venture capital. This, however, is only the first step of the entrepreneurial self-examination process.

Am I an Entrepreneur?

A good way to answer this question is by objectively comparing yourself to a successful entrepreneur. Begin by studying the following characteristics that successful entrepreneurs, venture capitalists and behavioral scientists say are important for success.

Drive and energy level: A successful entrepreneur must have the ability to work long hours for sustained periods with less than the normal amount of sleep.

Self-confidence: A belief in yourself and your ability to achieve your goals and a sense that events in your life are self-determined is essential.

Setting challenging but realistic goals: The ability to set clear goals and objectives that are challenging, yet realistic and attainable.

Long-term involvement: A commitment to projects that will reach completion in five to seven years and to work towards distant goals. This means total dedication to the business and to attaining these goals.

Using money as a performance measure: Money, in the form of salary, profits, or capital gains, should be viewed more as a measure of how the company is doing rather than as an end in itself.

Persistent problem solving: You must have an intense and determined desire to solve problems toward the completion of tasks.

Taking moderate risks: Entrepreneurial success is generally the result of calculated risk-taking that provides a reasonable and challenging chance of success.

Learning from failure: Understanding your role in a failure can be instrumental in avoiding similar problems in the future. A failure may be disappointing, but should not be discouraging.

Using criticism: You need to be able to seek and use criticism of the style and substance of your performance.

Taking initiative and seeking personal responsibility: You need to seize opportunities and put yourself in situations where you are personally responsible for success or failure. You should be able to take the initiative to solve problems or fill leadership vacuums. You should enjoy being involved in situations where your impact on a problem can be measured.

Making good use of resources: Can you identify and use expertise and assistance that is relevant to the accomplishment of your goals? You should not be so involved in the achievement of your goals and in independent accomplishment that you will not let anyone help you.

Competing against self-imposed standards: Do you tend to establish your own standard of performance, which is high yet realistic, and then compete with yourself?

No one individual possesses all these attributes. Weaknesses can be compensated for in other members of your management team. Do remember, though, *you* are the *most* critical risk. Rate yourself on each of these key characteristics "strong," "average," or "weak" compared with others you know and respect. Be as honest and accurate as you can. If you think you are average or weak on most of them, then do yourself, your family, and your would-be business associates a favor—do not start a business.

If you rate yourself high on most traits, this may be unrealistic and therefore you should review these ratings with people who know you well. Spouses, teachers, peers, and professional advisors are all likely to view you differently, both in terms of your past accomplishments and your potential. Take time with each reviewer to explain *why* you rate yourself as you do. Be prepared to alter your ratings in light of their opinions. If people you know tell you that you are likely to fail as an entrepreneur, they may be right. But both of you should be aware that making such an evaluation realistically is no quick-and-dirty task.

Once you believe you have an adequate assessment of yourself, think back on personal experiences that demanded entrepreneurial strengths. Reflect on these incidences and see if you acted in a manner consistent with your rating.

If you are convinced that you have the entrepreneurial wherewithal to start and build a business, you must now evaluate your management skills to determine your abilities and those that your management team must have. To this end, you should systematically audit your managerial experience and accomplishments in marketing and sales; operations; research, development, and engineering; finance and accounting; general management and administration; personnel; and the legal and tax aspects of business. To rate yourself, we suggest the following standards.

> Strong = Know thoroughly and have proven ability
> Average = Have limited knowledge and accomplishments
>   and will need backup perhaps part-time
> Weak = Unfamiliar and need someone's full-time skills

The different nature of each element makes it unlikely for individuals to be equally strong in all elements of these seven functions. For example, a powerful direct salesperson probably will not show equal strength in market research and evaluation.

Before giving yourself an overall rating on each of these functions, we suggest that you break them down to the principal elements and rate yourself on each element. Note that the critical elements of any function may vary with each venture: the marketing and sales function includes market research and evaluation and marketing planning as well as sales management and merchandising, direct selling, service, and distribution. The latter will not be critical if you market through distributors.

A listing and brief description of representative elements of all seven functions is presented at the end of this article.

For a more objective evaluation, you may want to review your management skills with former and current supervisors, peers and subordinates, who may all see a different side of you. After thoroughly evaluating your entrepreneurial traits and your management skills, you should be able to determine the personal risks you will run if you try to create a business.

If your dream is to build a multimillion-dollar business, it might also be wise to check your evaluation with one or more of the professionals who are active and respected in the fields of career counseling and entrepreneurial behavior. A man with a weak heart may only ask his wife about taking a gentle stroll up a small grassy hill, but he would be wise to consult a doctor before trying to climb a mountain.[1]

Does My Team Have the Necessary Complementary Skills?

Research into successful ventures shows that teams perform better than one individual. Knowing this, venture capitalists always look for a balanced team. So your next task is to analyze the business you are contemplating and determine what abilities and skills are critical to its success in the first two to three years. Then set about building a management team that includes people who are strong where you are weak.

In a new company, you may not want or be able to afford full-time staff to perform all functions. It is, however, important to choose part-time people carefully, since you may want some of them to come on board later. Avoid teaming up with a school friend whom you only know in casual situations or a colleague in the lab or office whose skills match your own. Although these collaborations are tempting, they rarely work out, and venture capitalists may be put off by a team that is made up of all engineers, salespeople or relatives.[2]

Do I Have a Viable Idea?

Imaging yourself a venture capitalist who has just analyzed the few hundred business proposals examined last year. Your analysis shows that you handled the various proposals in these ways.

1. Sixty percent were rejected after a 20- to 30-minute scanning.
2. Another quarter were discarded after a lengthier review.
3. About 15% were investigated in depth and two-thirds of those were dismissed because of serious flaws in the management team or the business plan that could not be easily resolved.
4. Of the 5% that were viable investment opportunities, terms acceptable to the entrepreneur(s) and other existing stock holders were negotiated in only 3%.

The 15% that were investigated in depth were presented by strong, well-balanced management teams who were able to show you relevant accomplishments in marketing, finance and operations and had developed (perhaps with some prodding by you) a comprehensive business plan.

As an entrepreneur, think what that venture capitalist's analysis means to you: there is a three-in-one-hundred chance of securing capital from any one source on terms acceptable to you and the investor and only a 15% chance of being considered seriously for investment, and a comprehensive business plan is usually required to qualify for such consideration.

So if you are really serious about going into business for yourself, you should start to develop a comprehensive business plan. If the plan is done properly and completely, it will probably take you 150 to 300 hours of intense work. Even when it is done, there is no guarantee that you will raise enough investment capital.

Is there any way to avoid going to all this effort only to have your plan rejected after a 20-minute perusal? Try seeing your business idea through the objective, critical eyes of a venture capitalist.

Before developing a business plan, it is important to answer the questions that venture capitalists may have on their minds when they review a plan to determine if it is worth studying and calling a meeting to discuss. The first question: What exactly will be sold to whom? Other key market questions are:

- Why will the customer buy your product?
- Who are the ultimate users and what influences on their purchasing habits are beyond your control?
- Who is the competition? Are they profitable now? Why do you think you can successfully compete with them?
- Is the market large and growing? Does it offer a multi-million-dollar potential for your company?
- Are you or will you be in a recognized growth industry?

You should then answer several questions about the other major aspects of the business you contemplate, questions about your team, your financial needs and the risks you are running. Such questions may include:

- What is the *maximum* amount of dollars and length of time that will be needed before your product is ready for market?
- What is the depth of your team's knowledge and extent of their reputations in the types of markets, technologies and operations in which you will be active?
- What are your team's management skills in the three key areas of marketing, finance and operations?
- How many unproven marketing, technical and manufacturing approaches do you contemplate?
- What are the strengths, weaknesses and major risks of your venture?

Careful thought about these areas should enable you to take a reasonable first look at your own venture ideas and to evaluate the potential for success as well as the major risks. The risks in any entrepreneurial venture are you, the entrepreneur, your team

and any fundamental flaws in your venture idea. You should then be able to put together a business plan and avoid many of the early errors (for example, team inadequacies; underpricing; weak cash management) that so often cripple new ventures. You should also be able to improve your chances of securing financing and launching a successful venture.

Representative Elements of Seven Management Functions
1. Marketing and Sales

a. *Market research and evaluation:* Ability to design and conduct market research studies and to analyze and interpret study results; familiarity with questionnaire design and sampling techniques.

b. *Strategic sales:* Experience in developing marketing strategies and establishing forces and then planning appropriate sales, advertising and promotional programs and setting up an effective network distributor or sales representative organization.

c. *Sales management and merchandising:* Ability in organizing, supervising, motivating and providing merchandising support to a direct sales force; analyzing territory and sales potential; and managing a sales force to obtain a target share of the market.

d. *Direct sales:* Experience in identifying, meeting and developing new customers, demonstrated success in closing sales.

e. *Service:* Experience in identifying service needs of particular products and in determining service and spare parts requirements, handling customer complaints, and managing a service organization.

f. *Distribution management:* Ability to organize and manage the flow of the product from manufacturing through distribution channels to the ultimate customer, including familiarity with shipping costs, scheduling techniques, carriers, etc.

g. *Overall marketing skills:* Give yourself a combined rating reflecting your skill level across all of the above marketing areas.

2. Operations

a. *Manufacturing management:* Knowledge of the production processes, machines, manpower, and space requirements to produce the product; experience in managing production to produce products within time, cost, and quality constraints.

b. *Inventory control:* Familiarity with techniques of controlling in-process and finished goods inventories of materials.

c. *Quality control:* Ability to set up inspection systems and standards for effective control of quality in incoming, in-process and finished materials.

d. *Purchasing:* Ability to identify appropriate sources of supply, the amount of material in inventory, familiarity with economical order quantities and discount advantage.

e. *Overall operations skills:* Give yourself a combined rating reflecting your skill level across all of the above operations areas.

3. Research, Development and Engineering

a. *Direction and management of applied research:* Ability to distinguish and keep a prudent balance between long-range projects at the frontiers of your technology, which attract the most creative individuals, and shorter range research in support of current product development activity.

b. *Management of development:* Ability to plan and direct work of development engineers and to use time and cost budgets so that perfectionists do not ruin you and yet product performance, appearance, and production engineering needs can be met; ability to distinguish between bread-board, field and pre-production prototype programs.

c. *Management of engineering:* Ability to plan and direct engineers in the final design of a new product for manufacture and in the engineering and testing of the production process to manufacture that new product.

d. *Technical know-how:* Ability to contribute personally to research, development, and/or engineering because of up-to-date in-depth knowledge of the technologies in which your company is involved.

e. *Overall research, development, and engineering skills:* Give yourself a combined rating reflecting your skill level across the above areas.

4. Financial Management

a. *Raising capital:* Ability to decide how best to acquire funds for startup and growth; ability to forecast the need for funds and to prepare budgets; familiarity with sources and vehicles of short- and long-term financing.

b. *Money management:* Ability to design, install, maintain, use financial controls; familiarity with accounting and control systems needed to manage; ability to set up a project cost control system, analyze overhead/contribution/absorption, prepare profit and loss and balance sheets, and manage a bookkeeper.

c. *Specific skills:* Cash flow analysis; break-even analysis; contribution analysis; budgeting and profit-planning techniques; profit and loss, balance sheet, and present value analysis of return on investment and payback.

d. *Overall financial skills:* Give yourself a combined rating reflecting your skill level across all of the above financial areas.

5. General Management and Administration

a. *Problem solving:* Ability to anticipate potential problems and plan to avoid them; ability to gather facts about problems, analyze them for real causes, and plan effective action to solve problems; thoroughness in dealing with the details of particular problems and in follow-through.

b. *Communications:* Ability to communicate effectively and clearly, both in speech and in writing, to the media, the public, customers, peers, and subordinates.

c. *Planning:* Ability to set realistic and attainable goals, identify obstacles to achieving the goals and develop detailed action plans to achieve those goals; ability to schedule own time very systematically.

d. *Decision making:* Ability to make decisions on your best analysis of incomplete data.

e. *Project management:* Skill in organizing project teams, setting project goals, defining project tasks, and monitoring task completion in the face of problems and cost/quality constraints.

f. *Negotiating:* Ability to work effectively in a negotiating situation; ability to quickly balance value given and value received.

g. *Personnel administration:* Ability to set up payroll, hiring, compensation, and training functions.

h. *Overall administrative skills:* Give yourself a combined rating reflecting your skill level across all of the above administrative areas.

6. Personnel Management

a. *Leadership:* Ability to understand the relationships between tasks, the leader, and the followers; ability to lead in situations where it is appropriate; willingness to manage actively, supervise, and control activities of others through directions, suggestions, inspiration, and other techniques.

b. *Listening:* Ability to listen to and understand without interrupting or mentally preparing your own rebuttal at the expense of hearing the message.

c. *Helping:* Ability to ask for and provide help and to determine situations where assistance is warranted.

d. *Criticism:* Ability to provide performance and interpersonal criticism to others that they find useful; ability to receive feedback from others without becoming defensive or argumentative.

e. *Conflict resolution:* Ability to confront differences openly and to deal with them until resolution is obtained.

f. *Teamwork:* Ability to work well with others in pursuing common goals.

g. *Selecting and developing subordinates:* Ability to select and delegate responsibility to subordinates and to coach them in the development of their managerial capabilities.

h. *Climate building:* Ability to create, by the way you manage, a climate and spirit conducive to high performance; ability to press for higher performance while rewarding work well done.

i. *Overall interpersonal skills:* Give yourself a combined rating reflecting your skill level across all of the above personnel management areas.

7. Legal and Tax Aspects

a. *Corporate law:* Familiarity with legal issues relating to stock issues, incorporation, distribution agreements, leases, etc.

b. *Contract law:* Familiarity with contract procedures and requirements (government and commercial), including default, warranty, and incentive provisions; fee structures; overhead, general and administrative expenses allowable, and so forth.

c. *Patent law:* Experience with preparation and revision of patent applications; ability to recognize a strong patent; familiarity with claim requirements.

d. *Tax Law:* Familiarity with general state and federal reporting requirements for businesses and with special provisions concerning Subchapter S corporations, tax shelters, fringe benefits, etc.

e. *Overall legal and tax skills:* Give yourself a combined rating reflecting your skill level across all of the above legal and tax areas.

Notes

1. For a discussion and appraisal of such evaluations, see "Business Leadership Training: A Six-Month Evaluation," a paper by Jeffry A. Timmons, D.B.A., and John L. Hayes.
2. For further discussion, see "The Entrepreneurial Team: Formation and Development" by Jeffry A. Timmons, D.B.A., a competitive paper presented at the annual Academy of Management meeting in 1973.

ALEXANDER L. M. DINGEE is a cofounder and chairman of Venture Founders Corporation, Lexington, Massachusetts, which manages venture capital funds dedicated to creating and investing in seed, startup and first-stage situations. Previously he had successfully started two companies and now he also continues to cofound new ventures, Network Inc., a terabit router company, Marlboro, Massachusetts, and Cortec Inc., turnkey coinjection systems, Beverly, Massachusetts, for his own account. **BRIAN HASLETT** was a cofounder of Venture Founders Corporation and played a lead role in establishing its U.K. subsidiary and in helping many American and British entrepreneurs create and finance their new enterprises. He subsequently was a contributor to Venture Capital Journal. Mr. Haslett died in 1985. **LEONARD E. SMOLLEN** was executive vice president and a cofounder of Venture Founders Corporation, a private company that manages venture capital funds. Currently Mr. Smollen provides consulting services to new ventures and venture capital partnerships.

Managing Growth

The set of changes that smaller, younger firms need to make as they grow is often termed *the transition from entrepreneurial to professional management.* This [article] addresses the issues that firms must deal with in making the transition:

- What is entrepreneurial management and how does it differ from professional management?
- What pressures force the firm to make the transition?
- How can entrepreneurs and their firms make the transition with a greater chance of success?

MICHAEL J. ROBERTS

Entrepreneurial and Professional Management

The terms *entrepreneurial* and *professional management* mean very different things to different people. To some, *entrepreneurial management* suggests creative people and an innovative and successful organization, while *professional management* implies a stifling bureaucracy. To others, entrepreneurs are associated with disorganization, and professional management offers efficiency and effectiveness. For the sake of this [article], however, *entrepreneurial* and *professional management* are merely descriptive terms and imply nothing about the creativity, innovation, or success of the organization.

Entrepreneurial Management

Entrepreneurial management is a style of management that is typically used when the firm is young and small. It is characterized by a number of features, including:

- *Centralized decision making:* In a small organization, the general manager can usually make most of the decisions required to manage the firm. The business is sufficiently small and simple enough that one person can comprehend all the information required for decision making.
- *Informal control:* The entrepreneurial firm is typically informal. There is little need for formal procedures, systems, and structures because the firm is small enough that activity can be monitored via the personal supervision of the entrepreneur. Moreover, the firm is young and inexperienced and has not yet learned the routines required for success.

The entrepreneur's own ability to collect information, make decisions, and monitor their implementation reduces the need for formal structure, policies, and procedures.

Professional Management

Professional management is characterized by:

- *Delegation of decision-making responsibility:* Larger firms are sufficiently complex that one individual cannot make all of the decisions required to manage the firm. Therefore, the general manager must delegate responsibility to a hierarchy of middle managers. This pattern of delegation both determines and is determined by the firm's structure.
- *Use of formal control systems:* In response to the delegation of decision-making responsibility, formal systems are introduced. Because the general manager does not *personally* make all of the firm's decisions, there is a need for systems to guide and evaluate the performance of those who *are* making those decisions. These systems usually include a mechanism for setting objectives, monitoring performance against those objectives, and rewarding desired performance. In addition, general managers also develop policies and standard procedures to guide the actions of those below.

The "Strategy of Coordination"

Just as the firm has an (explicit or implicit) strategy for its actions in the competitive marketplace, it also has an internal strategy for coordinating its efforts. Essentially, the dimensions of organization that we have been discussing are all elements of the way in which the firm chooses to coordinate its efforts.

There are two key dimensions to the strategy of coordination:

- The delegation of responsibility: whether the general manager makes the day-to-day operating decisions personally or delegates that decision-making responsibility to a hierarchy of middle managers.

- The use of formal control systems: whether the firm uses formal systems to set objectives, monitor performance, and control the activities of organization members.

These two dimensions describe a broad range of approaches to coordinating the firm's efforts. If we simply think in terms of the two-by-two matrix defined by these two dimensions, we can see that there are four archetypical strategies of coordination:

- Entrepreneurial management, which relies on centralized decision making and informal, personal control.
- Professional management, which utilizes the delegation of responsibility and extensive formal controls.
- Laissez-faire management, in which responsibilities are delegated, but control remains informal.
- Bureaucratic management, in which centralized decision making is supplemented with formal control.

	Use of Formal Control Mechanisms	
	Low	**High**
Delegation of Responsibility **High**	Laissez-faire management	Professional management
Low	Entrepreneurial management	Bureaucratic management

A *fundamental proposition* that underlies these ideas is that decisions regarding delegation and control have a strong influence on the firm's performance along two critical dimensions:

- Efficiency: the firm's ability to achieve its goals with a minimum of resources.
- Effectiveness: the firm's ability to adapt its goals and innovate to meet the changing needs of its environment.

Moreover, these two performance dimensions—and the decisions regarding delegation and control that underlie them—are fundamentally in *opposition*. Broadly speaking, choices that favor delegation have the potential to increase effectiveness, but simultaneously decrease efficiency; and the use of formal controls increases efficiency while reducing effectiveness. *Thus, the general manager's choices regarding delegation and control determine how these critical trade-offs are made.*

Making the Transition to Professional Management

When properly implemented, professional management offers an approach to coordinating the activities of a larger, more complex organization while avoiding the problems inherent in laissez-faire or bureaucratic management. There are several steps required for a successful transition to professional management.

Recognizing the Need for Change

The first step in the transition process is a recognition of the need for change. This is often extremely difficult because it is a by-product of success. Success reinforces beliefs and behavior that are appropriate to the entrepreneurial mode but that may not fit the needs of a larger, more complex firm.

Frequently, it is a crisis of some sort that highlights the need for change. Fortunately, knowledgeable outsiders can often help the entrepreneur see the need for such change before a crisis. Experienced board members or consultants can spot the early warning signs: lack of follow-up on details, incredible stress on the individual entrepreneur, and a sense of organizational disarray.

Once the entrepreneur has recognized the need for change, it is often difficult to know what to change *to*. Those who have successfully made the transition report that it requires a fundamental change in orientation: The manager must shift from getting personal satisfaction from direct action to a mode where that sense of accomplishment comes from achieving results *through others*.

Developing the Human Resources

Given this change of personal role in the organization, the entrepreneur needs to develop the human resources required to implement that model. Often, individuals who can accept and execute responsibility are not present in the entrepreneurial organization. The entrepreneur's style has made it difficult for aggressive, independent employees to survive. Moreover, many young firms simply lack the resources to attract and hire managerial talent.

In order to develop a competent managerial team, the entrepreneur must overcome personal loyalties that threaten the organization. In virtually every firm, the entrepreneur has a "right-hand person" without whom the business would not have survived in the early years. Unfortunately, many of these employees are unable to develop the more specialized skills needed to grow with the company. Entrepreneurs must overcome their personal loyalties and find more suitable employees for critical positions.

Delegating Responsibility

Once the entrepreneur has perceived the need for change and developed a management team, real delegation of responsibility can begin. The power of professional management lies in placing the responsibility close to the source of information required for sound decision making. Typically, this means delegating responsibility to managers who are close to customers, suppliers, and competitors. In the process of delegating, the general manager must be careful *not* to give up responsibility for key policy issues that require personal perspective. Moreover, delegation does not mean that the entrepreneur loses the opportunity to have *input* into the decision-making process; surely, the benefit of that experience should not be lost.

Developing Formal Controls

A final step in the transition process is the development of formal control mechanisms. Successful entrepreneurs realize that, with the onset of delegation, they can no longer control the behavior of individuals in the organization. It is important that the focus of the control system shifts to performance rather than behavior. In addition, successful firms realize the danger in simply adapting policies and procedures that are used at other firms. Firms that customize policies ensure that the practice makes sense for the organization. The process of devoting time and effort often inspires creative solutions, and builds commitment.

Conclusion

The reason why the transition to professional management is often so difficult is that it requires *far more* than changes in organizational systems and structures. It requires a *fundamental change in the attitudes and behaviors of the entrepreneur.* Merely creating organizational structures and systems accomplishes little if the entrepreneur is unwilling to truly delegate. Control systems are meaningless if the entrepreneur fails to use them. It is this need to fundamentally change the individual general manager's self-concept behavior that makes the transition process so difficult.

Three Strategies for Managing Fast Growth

Managers can't leave growth to chance. They should have a strategy for growing as well as for applying new knowledge faster than their competitors.

GEORGE VON KROGH AND MICHAEL A. CUSUMANO

Many companies approach growth management with no strategy other than to do what they did when they were new. New companies begin with a flourish. They have certain capabilities and knowledge. As they get caught up in short-term survival, they may cling to the same capabilities and knowledge. Or they may acquire the wrong kind of new knowledge and fail to grow the right capabilities. In the end, they may pour on new capabilities and knowledge—when it's too late.

The key to a long, healthy corporate life is steady growth. According to a 1998 survey, of the companies that enjoyed greater than 10% sales growth per year, about 78% were still around six years after starting. Of the companies with flat or decreasing sales, only 27.5% survived for six years.[1]

Growing Strategically

To grow steadily and avoid stagnation, a company must learn how to scale up and extend its business, lengthen its expansion phase, and accumulate and apply new knowledge to new products and markets faster than competitors.

Managers can't leave growth to chance. They must choose a plan that renders consistent sales growth for years, not just in short bursts. A good growth plan captures the vision for expanding the company. It addresses the product and market combinations the company intends to pursue, the size it hopes to achieve in a particular time frame, and most important, the know-how and organizational structures that will support expansion or diversification.

Such planning has an internal focus—rather than a focus on what competitors might do or what type of technological change might transform an industry. It is designed to help a company exert more control over its fate as it tackles outside challenges.[2] Implementation is easier for startup companies but possible for established enterprises, too. Company size should not drive the growth plan. Companies of all sizes need systems

for creating, acquiring and sharing knowledge. Consider Netigy, a San Jose-based e-commerce service provider. Netigy has only 650 employees, but it already has invested in a chief knowledge officer and a knowledge-management system for 20,000 people. Netigy is prepared to handle its vision for growth.[3]

What does drive the growth plan is the company's set of capabilities. Managers must choose a plan that fits with the knowledge, learning skills and assets that the organization possesses or plans to develop. On the basis of the literature and our personal knowledge of fast-growing companies, we conclude that companies grow using three basic strategies: scaling, duplication and granulation. (See "About the Research.") There is no one best strategy. A growth plan may end up tapping more than one. The important thing is to include principles of organizational learning, knowledge acquisition and knowledge transfer.

Scaling: Doing More of What You're Good At

Scaling starts with a coherent vision of products, technologies and customers. The vision is the foundation for growth, at least until circumstances change significantly. The vision should reflect the company's commitment to growth, be brief and clear, and be understood by all employees. The focus should be on a concrete product, technology and customer segment.[4]

Netscape's founders believed that the Interact would revolutionize the way people worked and interacted.[5] Their vision was to build infrastructure software that would put the company at the heart of the new, networked world and let it ride the Internet wave while experimenting with new products, technologies and markets.

Scaling requires a company to implement its vision quickly. As co-founder Jim Clark observed, "An axiom of motorcycle racing applies precisely to the technology business: Move fast, keep going—or end up on your butt. Slow down on the throttle

About the Research

We began our inquiry into growth strategies and capabilities by reflecting on cases of rapidly growing companies we knew. Michael Cusumano has written about Nissan, Toyota, Microsoft and Netscape.* Georg von Krogh has addressed learning, capability building and application of knowledge management in companies such as Skandia AFS, Sencorp, Shiseido, Sony, Siemens, Gemini Consulting, General Electric and Phonak AG.[†]

We also considered what authors in management and organization studies had to say about expansion strategies, the management of startups and young firms, the processes of knowledge creation and knowledge sharing—and organizational learning in general. We found that very few authors addressed the topics in combination and none attempted to integrate ideas about growth strategy, knowledge management, capabilities and organizational learning.

We concluded that companies must combine strategies for growth with explicit strategies for learning. They must base their growth strategies on their capabilities and market opportunities, then prepare their organizations to acquire or create specific knowledge about new technologies, customers and industries.

* M A. Cusumano, "The Japanese Automobile industry Technology and Management at Nissan and Toyota," Harvard East Asian Monographs no. 122 (Cambridge, Massachusetts: Council on East Asian Studies, Harvard University, 1989), M.A. Cusumano and R.W. Selby, "Microsoft Secrets" (New York. Free Press/Simon & Schuster, 1995); and M.A. Cusumano and D B. Yoffie, "Competing on Internet Time" (New York Free Press/Simon & Schuster. 1998).

[†] G. von Krogh, K. Ichijo and I. Nonaka, "Enabling Knowledge Creation: How To Unlock the Mystery of Tact Knowledge and Release the Power of Innovation" (New York. Oxford University Press. 2000); and G. von Krogh and J Roos, "Organizational Epistemology" (London MacMillan, 1995).

Netscape

1994: Founded by Jim Clark and Marc Andreessen
1995: $80 million in sales
1998: Approximately $500 million in revenues and more than 3,000 employees

Is Scaling the Right Strategy?

Growth by scaling works best when:
* the market is potentially large enough for rapid growth in a focused product line.
* the product creates unique value in the customers' view.
* the company can distribute products widely at low cost. Netscape used the Internet to overcome traditional entry barriers that software producers faced, such as bundling software with hardware or relying on software retail stores. Customers simply downloaded software from the Netscape Web site.

Scaling requires a company to learn about mass manufacturing and new manufacturing techniques. If the product is related to software or services, the company must become expert in the latest relevant technologies and standards, information systems and hardware trends. Knowledge of mass marketing is important, but when competition intensifies, individualized customer information becomes the strategic weapon. Learning how to offer technical support for an increasing customer group is critical for companies that are scaling. So are new routines (for procedures, quality standards, planning, milestones and goals), without which a company can become increasingly chaotic and unprofessional—and ultimately hurt product quality and service.

IKEA

1954: Starts as a small, domestic furniture manufacturer and retailer in Sweden with sales of 2 million Dutch guilder.
1984: Sales grow to 2,679 billion guilder.
1999: Sales grow to 16,954 billion guilder. Is franchiser and direct owner of many stores; operates out of Denmark. Has a presence in 25 countries, with 50,000 employees worldwide; 80% of sales are in Europe and 14% in the United States.

and you'll be off the road and into the trees."[6] In two years, Netscape went from a basic browser for surfing the Internet to more sophisticated browsers for corporate customers. It kept up the momentum by quickly adding a variety of servers, then opening up new markets for corporate intranets and extranets (the latter being intranets extended to select customers or suppliers). Next it moved to electronic commerce, adding new servers and applications tools and creating Netcenter.com—all within four years of starting. When America Online acquired it in fall 1998, Netscape had a value of more than $10 billion.

Invest Aggressively

To grow by scaling, a company expands product development around core technologies and offerings, expands product lines and increases the intensity of marketing by using existing distribution channels to reach new customer groups with related needs. It must increase manufacturing capacity and enlarge corporate infrastructure—for example, by building bigger and better information systems and setting up central human-resource-management systems to recruit and train employees quickly. (See "Is Scaling the Right Strategy?")

Companies must pursue aggressive investment—often *before* sales growth becomes apparent. Netscape invested in growth, knowing that without growth, it would face far more serious problems than overinvesting. And Netscape grew—even more quickly than it anticipated.

Specialize and Standardize

Companies that grow fast often centralize and standardize administrative areas such as finance and accounting to handle the increased transactions. Initially, they have simple functional structures, with manufacturing, marketing, sales, product development, finance and accounting all separate. As they grow, they duplicate the functional departments within divisions tied to particular products or geographic markets. Smaller teams then focus on specific customer segments and control the resources they need. Netscape moved from one small research-and-development group to separate R&D divisions for its browser and server products—and later for its e-commerce tools and Web site.

Hire the Right Mix

To refine and exploit existing products, processes and market know-how, key people must learn quickly and share their insights and technical knowledge. Netscape co-founder Mark Andreessen and a core group of programmers gained invaluable design experience and market insights from working at the University of Illinois on Mosaic, Navigator's predecessor. They distributed 2 million copies of Mosaic and learned how the networked world of the Internet could function, with hot links potentially connecting every computer and database worldwide.[7]

But although Andreessen and the other programmers had most of the essential concepts and technical skills, they lacked the money, managerial insights and organizational skills needed. Jim Clark, who had founded Silicon Graphics a few years earlier and knew how to make a technology, into a viable business, served as a Pied Piper in attracting other talent and resources.[8]

Netscape had to learn quickly. Its customers changed from savvy Internet users of a single product—the browser—to more-conservative corporate users who wanted an array of products that were rock-solid reliable. Netscape had to figure out how to design, document, test, sell and support mission-critical products in a more professional way.

At the same time, it had to absorb many new people. Clark hired young programmers who had worked on Web browsers and added seasoned managers, engineers, and sales and marketing experts from computer and telecommunications industries. Recruiting from a veritable Who's Who of U.S. high-tech companies, Netscape leveraged the experts' knowledge to train the less seasoned.

Adapt the Structures

For knowledge to be shared, a company must set up the right organizational structures, processes and culture. As Netscape grew, it sought to maintain the creativity and innovative capabilities typical of small organizations; in late 1996, it reorganized the product divisions into minidivisions, or *divlets.* Each divlet reported to its own general manager and worked on a specific product release or server product.

The arrangement had certain flaws: poor cooperation, redundant work and mistakes that could have been avoided through collective brainstorming. In 1997, after Netscape failed to rewrite Navigator/Communicator in Java, Barksdale decided to make the divlets report directly to Andreessen. As chief technology officer, Andreessen had been without formal product responsibilities. Barksdale's move effectively centralized product planning and gave Andreessen authority to cancel projects and to force more knowledge sharing among the browser and server teams.

Find Ways to Learn from Customers Early

Netscape discovered the intranet market by learning from its customers. A major bank in Switzerland had begun using Netscape's browser and server technology for its internal corporate network to allow employees to share information easily by using the Internet communications protocols. Netscape quickly identified intranets as a new opportunity and extended the idea to create extranets.

Netscape also learned to cultivate lead users and to have them test early versions of its products and give rapid feedback to developers. It started internal initiatives to find new ways to apply its technology to corporate markets. It used its own technology to create extranets that linked Netscape engineers, sales, marketing and support personnel to independent software vendors, content providers, Internet-service providers and computer manufacturers.

Duplication: Repeat the Business Model in New Regions

Like scaling, duplication starts with a coherent vision of products, technologies and customer segments. But unlike scaling, the vision must include goals for geographical expansion. The vision of IKEA founder Ingvard Kamprad was to go beyond Sweden and democratize the furniture industry throughout Europe by making new products affordable to the masses. Kamprad's vision relied on Swedish design skills and a store ambiance that could communicate an appealing lifestyle to young people everywhere. (See "Is Duplication the Right Strategy?")

Balance Standardization and Adaptation

Duplication typically involves packaging the company's entrepreneurial know-how for new geographic areas—for example, by setting up overseas subsidiaries or franchising a business concept.[9] A carefully orchestrated tension balances standardization (keeping processes and organizational details close to the way they are done in the original location) and adaptation (changing the organization and processes to address the needs of the local region).

Duplicating marketing in overseas markets is important, but responsiveness to local market conditions is key to long-term success. In new geographic areas, companies may choose to centralize manufacturing and administrative functions, duplicate the functions or both. Centralized manufacturing reduces manufacturing case, but duplicated manufacturing increases flexibility.

Duplicated businesses should follow similar human-resource-management practices. By standardizing staffing, training and remuneration plans, a company can rotate employees among subsidiaries instead of having to hire and train new people when work in one locale increases. With HR duplication, employees also share new ideas and experience smoothly while providing consistent service to customers.

Hire Flexible, Independent Managers

Companies must give managers the independence they need to balance adaptation to local markets with preserving what made the original business successful. IKEA did that well, although its senior country and regional managers often were Swedish or familiar with the Swedish language. Eventually, however, a truly global company must train foreign managers in its practices and values, as IKEA has been doing gradually in the United States and China.

Duplicate Keys Parts of the Infrastructure

Geographical expansion calls for simple procedures and for work processes robust enough to handle varied employee backgrounds. During expansion, informal sharing of experience usually is not the best learning mechanism. Senior managers have less control over local recruiting and human-resource development than those using scaling. Growing by duplication requires that a company externalize, or transfer, key elements of its infrastructure.[10] Some companies use *black-boxing*—whatever mechanism they can set up to share their *black boxes* (critical data at various levels of detail in ready-to-use form, such as written or online manuals or video presentations).

Black boxes must be available at a moment's notice to help employees and managers worldwide to accomplish important tasks. A single black box at one level of detail may help in establishing a new subsidiary in a new territory. It might include checklists on choosing a site, using legal counsel, selecting and training personnel, laying out a store and purchasing manuals. A box at another level might include detailed instructions on how to service clients outside business hours or how to set up a store-maintenance program.

IKEA used black-boxing. The European expansion group it organized to jump-start its duplication in Switzerland, Germany, France, Italy, Denmark, Norway and Austria bought land, hired people, constructed furniture outlets and decided on the new outlets' decor. Two months before opening a new store, a first-year operations group would move in while the expansion group moved on to the next site. The first-year group would take charge, train people, arrange the store opening and set up the operations. Then IKEA would establish a local country organization to run the operations. The international expansion group, IKEA's "Knowledge Marines," represented the ideal mechanism for accumulating know-how from each new site and spreading the knowledge to newer operations.

Duplicate Entrepreneurial Knowledge

IKEA learned how to black-box entrepreneurial knowledge, too. The preferred site for new stores was always relatively cheap land on the outskirts of a city. The stores were simple and functional, most often two-story buildings with displays on the second floor and warehousing on the first. IKEA standardized and documented products, catalog format, logo use (although in Norway the company used red and white instead

of the traditional blue and yellow), and personnel selection and training. The custodian of the entrepreneurial knowledge was the international expansion group.

IKEA also used *devoted practice* to duplicate its corporate vision. Local employees would devote themselves to learning certain tasks by studying manuals and attending training courses. Kamprad acted like a field commander, communicating the vision to new employees, visiting new stores, taking notes on store operations and discussing procedures and improvements directly with employees. Through such attention to detail, the black box can become a local routine. Employees then use it as a foundation for devising new and better solutions.

Be Aware of the Limitations

It would be naive to expect black-boxing to be consistently successful. Customer tastes and employee backgrounds are too diverse for one set of processes and programs to fit all situations. When IKEA expanded to the United States in 1986, it found that U.S. customers had subtle but important differences in tastes and shopping habits from Europeans. They wanted shelves, but for televisions, not books. European sheets did not fit American beds. European cups, plates and drawers seemed small to Americans.[11]

In addition, black boxes may not be sensitive to new requirements. A company that grows through duplication must be able to learn quickly, fixing procedures and products that don't work and making the people who created them aware of the new requirements. That is especially true of young high-growth companies expanding abroad in highly competitive markets. Senior executives and central-management systems must have the openness and flexibility necessary for modifying a formula that was a winner back home.

IKEA had a slow start in the United States, but it learned quickly.[12] The company now adapts fully one-third of its product designs to U.S. tastes. Combining black-boxing and local learning has helped IKEA improve duplication of its business and remain competitive over time in many markets.

SAP

1972: Is founded by former IBM software engineers in Mannheim, Germany.

1992: Launches resource-planning software R/3 and makes its name.

1996: Begins developing industry-specific solutions. Introduces AcceleratedSAP methodology.

1998: Delivers services map for complete life-cycle solutions and support. Has 22,000 employees in more than 50 countries. Hires 2,400 employees in this year alone.

1999: Delivers mySAP.com. Reports total sales of $5 billion, a one-year increase of 18%.

Is Duplications the Right Strategy?

Growth by duplication works best when:
- the business requires physical presence and the company can repeat its business model in new geographic markers. Home furnishings, for example, include items that customers want to see before purchasing. For services such as consulting, architecture and customized software development, personal contact and trust building are essential.
- there is a need for better distribution. A company might shift from a scaling to a duplicating strategy when distribution channels are underdeveloped or when it can build up a unique set of local distributors that would be costly for potential competitors to imitate.
- the company can adapt its experience in product development, manufacturing and marketing approaches fairly easily. Unique information about local customers and new trends from foreign markets may lead to better market segmentation and targeted marketing than smaller local companies can offer.

Duplication requires several kinds of learning. To set up new subsidiaries abroad, a company must learn about local market conditions and apply the knowledge in adapting products, marketing and operations. Duplicating, like scaling, may require learning about mass manufacturing or mass marketing, but it is also likely to need individualized communication flowing between central management and local management, product-development staff, local marketing staff, sales staff and customers. Duplicating involves learning about new competitors, regulatory differences, the best ways to handle logistics and currency-related risks. Alliances with local companies can expand knowledge because they provide access to local insights about marketing, manufacturing capacity and product development. Acquisitions are an option, but integration into the existing organization may be problematic, especially if the acquired company is in another country.

Granulation: Growing Select Business Cells

There are limits to scaling and duplicating. A company's product line may run out of steam, too many low-cost competitors may copy it, or there may be no new foreign markets to conquer. At that point, the best strategy could be granulation—distinguishing the cells, or smaller granules, of the business and growing them aggressively.

SAP, now one of the largest software companies in the world, went through both scaling and duplication before attempting granulation. The company initially specialized in enterprise-resource-planning (ERP) systems that let clients track and plan financial and ether resource flows. Its early product, R/1, supported only a few resource flows. In 1989, SAP launched R/2, which offered new features and more than doubled the company's sales ever the next three years. In 1992, it launched R/3, which integrated resource planning across functions and customer-suppliers, allowing customers to manage more than 1,500 business processes. R/3 made SAP a global name in software.

Toward the end of 1997, SAP embarked on duplication. In 1998 it reorganized into industry business units, with a core development unit for new technologies and services plus a global sales-and-marketing unit. As custodians of specialized know-how in industry-specific resource planning, the units transformed SAP from a one-product company to a multiple-product company. SAP now builds on the R/3 platform whatever the customer needs, while integrating component software from other suppliers.[13] It continues to improve R/3 and shares knowledge by training in-house personnel and representatives from local IT consultancies. Approximately 150 instructors now teach more than 200 courses at 85 training centers worldwide. SAP is adding remote training programs, too. Such enhancements and SAP's extensive implementation expertise have enabled it to add Chevron, Eastman Chemical and Microsoft to its long customer list.

Balance the Old and New

Granulation is like the other strategies in starting with a strong, coherent vision for growth, but its focus is on developing unique capabilities and creating new businesses. A company uses its resources and knowledge to explore new territory with new, autonomous business units, independent subsidiaries or corporate spinoffs. Granulation is risky; business units may not leverage fully the company's existing knowledge and asset base. Although individual entrepreneurs learn from working on local technologies with local customers and local staff, they work better when they have access to information, expertise and resources from other parts of the company.[14] Each new cell, therefore, should reuse existing product technologies, manufacturing processes, organizational processes and consumer information but combine those assets in new ways. (See "Is Granulation the Right Strategy?")

In 1996, SAP released R/3 Version 3.1, which had Web interfaces. The launch inspired further exploration of e-business solutions at SAP and led to a new growth strategy. The company began developing new business groups to create technologies for both individuals and small to midsize firms. It then launched mySAP.com, a portal-based marketplace that facilitates transactions among customers with different transaction volumes. In March 2000, SAP formed SAPMarkets, a separate venture for electronic market activities.

Balance the Informal and Formal

Both informal and formal methods are required for knowledge to flow between entrepreneurial cells. Informal personal ties help people in different groups establish trust and share experiences. SAP favors a "football team" style of work over hierarchies. Communication frequently occurs spontaneously, making SAP seem almost like a university.[15]

However, informal ties generally center on short-term issues.[16] Fast-growing companies need to complement informal mechanisms with more-formal knowledge sharing, such as strategic-planning processes that encourage regular discussions among managers and employees from different cells. Companies also can hold periodic conferences or rotate experienced personnel among company units.

Evaluate and Monitor

Companies benefit from selectively evaluating and monitoring new business opportunities the way venture capitalists do. First, local entrepreneurs conceive business ideas, draft business plans, organize a venture team and form entrepreneurial cells. Then senior-management representatives act as investors, with both a monitoring and advising role. The entrepreneurial model also lets companies invest successfully in outside enterprises with attractive technologies, products, services or customer bases.

Learn from Customers, Partners and Competitors

At SAP, the business units' chore is to dig up industry knowledge. Often knowledge comes from customer feedback or lead users. SAP has gathered interested customers to work with company developers on some 50 projects. A strategic alliance with Nokia—to extend mySAP.com to a wireless mobile work force—is likely to generate useful learning, too.

When a company grows through granulation, its competitors may be unknown, but they are probably not inactive. The company must establish systems to gather and analyze intelligence on existing and potential competitors—and speed it to decision makers.

Acquiring smaller companies with expertise in the new technology and forming alliances are two ways to acquire external knowledge. Both need routines for sharing knowledge between the acquisition or alliance partner and the rest of the company. Sharing mechanisms may include integration teams (for acquisitions), shared management responsibilities, periodic conferences and meetings, or shared access to databases and knowledge bases.

Combining Strategies

To identify the strategy with the best fit, a company should start with a bird's eye view of the comparative strengths of scaling, duplicating and granulating. (See "Strategies for Growing and Learning.") The scaling strategy is simplest: A company merely learns how to do more of what it already does. Duplication is more complex, requiring a company to learn how to apply what it knows to new geographical markets. The most demanding in terms of knowledge acquisition, granulation requires a company to gather substantial information about new competitors and new product and market opportunities. But it also enables gradual diversification from related businesses into unrelated technologies, products and markets.

Johnson & Johnson, with its emphasis on creating subsidiaries, is a classic example of granulation.[17] Founded to provide surgical supplies to doctors, the company grew by expanding

---

Is Granulation the Right Strategy?

Growth by granulation works best when:
- growth through scaling and duplicating has clear limits. The company has conquered all relevant markets, product demand is flattening out, customers are changing their preferences, or increasing competition for market share makes further growth too expensive.
- a new technology is flourishing that could become a substitute for the company's products or a new business opportunity. Companies must explore and experiment with new technologies that are adjacent but outside current knowledge areas, routines and capabilities.
- the company is sufficiently mature to monitor new business activities, share knowledge internally and learn effectively about new markets and competitive scenarios.

Granulation requires that a company obtain knowledge outside itself and its operations, especially about its industry. Initially, a new cell, or business unit, might benefit from employees' internal experiences, but as it ventures into an unknown market with new products and learns from the experience available to the industry at large, it will move away from the parent company's core know-how.* Skill at acquiring industry experience rapidly should become a generic skill for entrepreneurs throughout a company.

* P. Ingram and J.A.C. Baum "Opportunity Constraint: Organizations' Learning From Operating and Competitive Experiences of Industries," *Strategic Management* Journal 18 (1997): 75–98.

---

into related healthcare markets for hospitals and home consumers. Early on, management created separate companies (usually wholly owned by J&J) for each distinct market and allowed them considerable independence. When necessary, the separate companies collaborate—for example, in providing joint distribution services to the hospital industry. By 1999, the company had 190 subsidiaries, 98,000 employees, operations in 51 countries and approximately $24 billion in sales (divided among the hospital, pharmaceutical and consumer health-care sectors). It remains one of the fastest-growing large companies in the world.[18]

Large companies with business units or subsidiaries in different growth stages may want to tackle scaling, duplication and granulation simultaneously. For most early-stage companies, though, it is best if managers implement the three growth strategies sequentially, with some overlapping, as SAP did. A successful firm might first try scaling up its basic business. As it reaches the limits of scaling, it might start duplicating its successful business model abroad, while still emphasizing scaling as much as possible. Eventually the company should be able to pursue granulation, using new business units or spinoffs to diversify in its home market and, later, abroad.

Strategies for Growing and Learning

Means of Learning	Scaling Netscape	Duplicating IKEA	Granulating SAP
Experience sharing	Sharing the core business knowledge	Sharing the know-how of selecting entrepreneurs and managers	Sharing entrepreneurial knowledge new business cells for new markets
Externalization: Making experiences explicit	Making entrepreneurial know-how in product development, manufacturing, marketing and sales explicit	Black-boxing entrepreneurial know-how and applying it across new markets	Making the knowledge of entrepreneurs in new cells explicit
Formal sharing of knowledge	Sharing within and between functions, such as product development or marketing	Sharing knowledge about procedures that work and those that don't work	Building on and recombining explicit knowledge across cells in order to enhance creativity and generate new business
Devoted practice: Learning by doing	Developing different routines, practices, functions and disciplines	Applying black-box procedures and knowledge	Devoting attention to evaluation and monitoring of new business opportunities
External knowledge acquisition	Establishing formal market connections to ensure customer feedback to product development	Acquiring knowledge about the appropriateness of products, services and processes in the local context	Developing procedures for industry learning

The road will not always be smooth. SAP learned from early customer feedback that it had overengineered R/3: Implementation at customer sites required considerable time, effort and money. The company responded by launching its Accelerated-SAP rapid-implementation technology, which speeds up the introduction and use of its software systems. It also started to provide best-practice cases of business processes so that its clients could benchmark and improve their own operations.[19]

For most early-stage companies, through, it is best if managers implement the three growth strategies sequentially, with some overlapping.

Managing and sharing knowledge is vital. Both IKEA, with its Knowledge Marines, and SAP, with its aggressive training program, worked hard to mobilize local staff to sell and implement products in different markets. But however a company chooses to apply its knowledge and whatever strategy it chooses, it must be committed to continued growth. It can't afford to become complacent. Companies that aren't steadily growing might very well be on their way to steadily dying.

Additional Resources

Many companies have deep corporate knowledge but are not sure how to use it to competitive advantage. "Working Knowledge: How Organizations Manage What They Know." by Thomas Davenport and Lawrence Prusak (Cambridge, Massachusetts: Harvard Business School Press, 1997), and "Enabling Knowledge Creation: How To Unlock the Mystery of Tacit Knowledge and Release the Power of Innovation," by Georg von Krogh, Kazuo Ichijo and Ikujiro Nonaka (New York: Oxford University Press, 2000), provide ample guidelines. The KnowledgeSource Web site (http://www.knowledgesource.org/) offers additional links and information.

Reading about lessons learned from successful companies is a good way to avoid pitfalls and duplicate what works. "Competing on Internet Time: Lessons From Netscape and Its Battle With Microsoft," by Michael Cusumano and David Yoffie (New York: Free Press, 1998), and "Microsoft Secrets: How the World's Most Powerful Software Company Creates Technology, Shapes Markets and Manages People," by Michael Cusumano and Richard Selby (New York: Free Press/Simon & Schuster, 1995), capture lessons from rapidly growing companies. Robert Spector tells Amason.com's story in "Amazon.com—Get Big Fast: Inside the Revolutionary Business Model That Changed the World" (New York: Harper Business, 2000).

John Nesheim's "High Tech Start Up: The Complete Handbook for Creating Successful New High Tech Companies" (New York: Free Press, 2000) gives good pointers, particularly on how to deal with risk.

References

1. J. Timmons, "New Venture Creation" (Burr Ridge, Illinois: Irwin, 1998), 14.
2. We concur with S.L. Brown and K.M. Eisenhardt's notion in "Competing on the Edge: Strategy as Structured Chaos"

(Boston: Harvard Business School Press, 1998) that growth should be organically driven by the internal pace of the company rather than external factors.

3. Chuck Salter, "Built To Scale," Fast Company, July 2000, 348–354.

4. J.R. Baum, E.A. Locke and S.A. Kirkpatrick, "A Longitudinal Study of the Relation of Vision and Vision Communication to Venture Growth in Entrepreneurial Firms," *Journal of Applied Psychology* 83, no. 1 (1998): 43–54.

5. M. Cusumano and D. Yoffie, "Competing on Internet Time: Lessons From Netscape and Its Battle With Microsoft" (New York: Free Press, 1998).

6. J. Clark, "Netscape Time: The Making of the Billion-Dollar Start-Up That Took on Microsoft" (New York: St. Martin's Press, 1999), 60.

7. Marc Andreessen often jumped from one topic to another during conversations but showed a remarkable ability to connect seemingly diverse ideas. As chief legal counsel of Netscape, Roberta Katz, commented. "The browser is a map of his brain." Cusumano and Yoffie, "Competing on Internet Time," 18.

8. Clark, "Netscape Time."

9. S.G. Winter and G. Szulanski, "Replication as Strategy," working paper 98.10, Wharton School, Philadelphia, Pennsylvania, 1999.

10. G. von Krogh, K. Ichijo and I. Nonaka, "Enabling Knowledge Creation: How To Unlock the Mystery of Tacit Knowledge and Release the Power of Innovation" (New York: Oxford University Press, 2000); and M. Boisot, "Knowledge Assets: Securing Competitive Advantage in the Information Economy" (New York: Oxford University Press, 1998).

11. "IKEA: Furnishing the World," *The Economist* (Nov. 19, 1994): 79–80; and also see C.A. Bartlett and A. Nada, "Inguardkamprad and IKEA," Harvard Business School case 390–132 (Boston: Harvard Business School Publishing Corp., 1990).

12. www.ikea.com/about_ikea/timeline/fullstory.asp.

13. J. Rieker, "Die drei von der Baustelle," *Manager Magazin,* April 1998, 114–126.

14. R.N. Yeaple, "Why Are Small Research and Development Organizations More Productive?" *IEEE Transactions on Engineering Management* 39, no. 4 (1992): 332–346.

15. "Die Regeln der SAP," *Manager Magazin,* May 1998, 238.

16. M.W.H. Weenig, "Communication Networks in the Diffusion of an Innovation in an Organization," *Journal of Applied Social Psychology* 25, no. 5 (1999): 1072–1092.

17. Another is Thermo Electron, whose growth is described in C.Y. Baldwin and J. Forsyth, "Thermo Electron," Harvard Business School case no. 9-292-104 (Boston: Harvard Business School Publishing Corp., 1992). Unlike Johnson & Johnson, Thermo Electron generally sold public stock in its subsidiaries to take advantage of the capital markets—an important tactic for raising money.

18. "Dusting the Opposition," *The Economist,* April 29, 1995, 71–72: and www.jnj.com/annual/99_annual/jj_99_ar.pdf.

19. www.sap.com/service/asap_rm.htm; and A. Seufert, "SAP: The German Software Giant" (presentation at the MIT Sloan School of Management, Cambridge, Massachusetts, Nov. 5, 1999).

GEORG VON KROGH is a professor of management at the University of St. Gallen in Switzerland and director of its Institute of Management. **MICHAEL A. CUSUMANO** is a professor of management at the MIT Sloan School of Management in Cambridge, Massachusetts. Contact the authors at georg.vonkrogh@unisg.ch *and* cusumano@mit.edu.

Acknowledgments—For their helpful comments, we wish to thank three anonymous reviewers; also Simon Grand, Peter Gomez. Yvonne Wicki and Mark Macus of the University of St. Gallen, and Harbir Singh of the University of Pennsylvania's Wharton School. In addition, we thank participants at the Conference on Knowledge and Innovation (Helsinki School of Economics and Business Administration, Helsinki, Finland, May 26–27, 2000), including James G. March, Ikujiro Nonaka, Patrick Reinmoeller and Giovanni Dosi. Andreas Seufert at the University of St. Gallen assisted in the research on SAP.

The Zappos Way of Managing

How Tony Hsieh uses relentless innovation, stellar customer service, and a staff of believers to make Zappos.com an e-commerce juggernaut— and one of the most blissed-out businesses in America.

Max Chafkin

"What would make you happier in your life?" Tony Hsieh asks me this question as we sit at a booth with half a dozen young people in one of those absurdly lavish lounges that can be found only in Las Vegas. It's called Lavo, setting of recent Paris Hilton and Nelly sightings and the city's newest hot spot. The theme is an ancient Roman bathhouse, and so, in addition to the normal nightclub features—thumping bass, low tables, dim lighting—there's the distracting aspect of two scantily clad women performing a risqué bathing routine, complete with damp sponges and music.

It's a strange setting for an interview—especially for an interview with Hsieh (pronounced *Shay*). He's a thoughtful, low-key fellow who seems out of place in such a louche setting. Indeed, he seems oddly oblivious to his surroundings, which makes sense, given that he runs what is arguably the decade's most innovative start-up, Zappos.com. Hsieh helped start Zappos in 1999 as an online shoe store, and the company has since expanded to all manner of goods. Zappos booked $1 billion in gross sales in 2008, 20 percent better than the year before. It has been profitable since 2006.

At a time when most business leaders are retrenching, Hsieh is thinking big. In late 2006, he launched an outsourcing program to handle selling, customer service, and shipping for other companies, and last December, he started an educational website for small businesses that charges them $39.95 a month to tap Zappos executives for advice. Hsieh has said Zappos will eventually move beyond retail to businesses such as hotels and banking—anything where customer service is paramount. "I wouldn't rule out a Zappos airline that's just about the best customer service," he announced at the Web 2.0 conference last fall.

But Hsieh, 35, isn't interested in talking about any of this right now. He's still on the happiness thing. "On a scale of 1 to 10, how happy are you right now?" he asks, informing me that, right now, he's at about an 8.

I think for a second and then respond, "Maybe a 7?"

This isn't polite conversation for Hsieh. "I've been doing a lot of research into the science of happiness," he says. In addition to

asking everyone he meets what makes him or her happy, he has also been studying books on the subject, especially Jonathan Haidt's *The Happiness Hypothesis,* which uses social psychology experiments to evaluate the world's great religions and philosophies and concludes that ancient wisdom and science are both useful tools in the quest for contentment. Hsieh is working on a system to supersede both. "I've been trying to come up with a unified theory for happiness," he says.

Unlike the world's great religions, the Tony Hsieh Unified Happiness Theory is not entirely settled. It involves establishing balance among four basic human needs: perceived progress, perceived control, relatedness, and a connection to a larger vision. And because Hsieh's life is his company, the test subjects are Zappos employees. "I've got a few different frameworks, and I'm just figuring out how to combine them," he says without irony or even a smile. "I think I'm pretty close."

Hsieh is widely regarded as one of the most innovative Internet marketers of all time. The Web entrepreneur and marketing guru Seth Godin has likened Hsieh's ability to use technology to connect with his customers to the Beatles' ability to animate their teenage fans. The blog Search Engine Land calls Zappos "the poster child for how to connect with customers online." And Hsieh's mastery isn't limited to marketing. Zappos's warehouse boasts a fleet of 70 brand-new robots that allows it to ship a pair of shoes in as little as eight minutes, earning reams of praise from logistics-industry trade publications.

But Hsieh has a hard time getting excited about any of this. What he really cares about is making Zappos's employees and customers feel really, really good. This is not because Hsieh is a nice guy (though he is a very nice guy), but because he has decided that his entire business revolves around one thing: happiness. Everything at Zappos serves that single end. Other business innovators work with software code or circuit boards or molecular formulas. Hsieh prefers to work with something altogether more complex and volatile: human beings themselves.

That single-minded focus on happiness has led to plenty of accolades for the company, which routinely scores high on lists of the best places to work. But Zappos's approach to workplace bliss differs significantly from that of other employee-friendly businesses. For one thing, Zappos pays salaries that are often below market rates—the average hourly worker makes just over $23,000 a year. Though the company covers 100 percent of health care costs, employees are not offered perks found at many companies, such as on-site child care, tuition reimbursement, and a 401(k) match. Zappos does offer free food to its employees, but the pile of cold cuts in the small cafeteria loses its allure faster than you can say *Googleplex*. Instead of buying his employees' loyalty, Hsieh has managed to design a corporate culture that challenges our conception of that tired phrase.

Hsieh's accomplishments are all the more impressive when you consider Zappos's origins. The idea of selling shoes on the Web may seem merely unoriginal today, but it seemed truly wrong-headed in 1999. "There wasn't an ounce of evidence to suggest it would work," says Michael Moritz, a partner with Sequoia Capital and the guy who backed Yahoo, Google—and, after initially passing on the company in 2001, Zappos. And yet, as Hsieh turned that daft idea into a business, his company transformed. Zappos now boasts systems that are breathlessly praised by academics, entrepreneurs, and, of course, the customers who seem eternally tickled by the company's free shipping and unbelievably responsive service. At many companies, talk of corporate culture dulls the luster, inducing cynicism among employees and creating hours of busywork for managers. At Zappos, the culture is the luster. And Hsieh—softspoken, deliberate, awkward—has emerged as a most unlikely business guru.

I first met Hsieh three years ago at a cocktail hour at the *Inc.* 500 conference. (Zappos had landed at No. 23, with revenue of $135 million.) We spoke for 10 minutes or so, and I remember being struck by the scope of his achievement. But I was even more impressed by the oddness of Hsieh's mannerisms.

Hsieh is hard to know and even harder to read. He's generous and smart, but so subdued in one-on-one conversation that it's easy to mistake his reticence for rudeness. When he does speak, it's in full paragraphs that sound as if they have been formulated in advance. He sometimes smiles—as he does when he's explaining the clever way Zappos manages its call center—but he doesn't laugh at other people's jokes and seldom tells his own.

And yet, this mild-mannered fellow leads a company that is entirely uninhibited. Interviews are held over vodka shots, bathrooms are plastered with "urine color" charts (ostensibly to ensure that employees are hydrated but also just to be weird and funny), and managers are encouraged to goof off with the people they manage. Zappos's 1,300 employees talk about the place with a religious fervor. The phrase *core values* can prompt emotional soliloquies, and the CEO is held with a regard typically afforded rock stars and cult leaders.

Hsieh tries his best to keep up with the goofy, libertine culture. Every day, he blasts a steady stream of playful messages to 350,000 people on Twitter. (Before taking the stage at a conference earlier this year, he posted this missive: "Spilled Coke on left leg of jeans, so poured some water on right leg so looks like the denim fade.") He has also become an accomplished public speaker who spends a good chunk of his time on the road giving talks, which are delivered without notes.

What most of Hsieh's admirers—and even some Zappos employees—don't know is that this openness doesn't come naturally. Hsieh has been exceptionally shy all his life and finds meeting strangers exhausting. (His trick to get over his shyness is to pretend he's interviewing you for a job.) Those seemingly off-the-cuff Twitter missives? He spends 10 minutes or so carefully composing each one. He takes his employees out to restaurants and bars not because he loves nightlife but because he thinks it sets a good example. "I just want to have a company where people can hang out together," he says, "and then come in to work the next day and not worry about whether they've done something stupid." Most CEOs make their companies in their own image; Hsieh seems to have designed his company to behave the way he wishes he could.

Hsieh has always been a little different. He grew up in San Rafael, California, and excelled from an almost creepily young age. In first grade, he taught himself to program, playing with a Radio Shack microcomputer that his father, Richard—a Chinese-born chemical engineer with a Ph.D., an M.B.A., and 29 patents to his name—brought home. The next year, Richard blew a month's salary and bought his son an IBM XT personal computer. By third grade, Hsieh's bedroom was littered with pages of software code for a bulletin board system—a precursor to today's Internet message boards, accessed by dial-up modem—that he ran for several years, tying up the household phone line and mystifying his parents. "He stayed in his room for hours at a time," says Richard Hsieh.

Hsieh started his first company, LinkExchange, shortly after graduating from Harvard with a degree in computer science. The company allowed amateur Web publishers to barter for advertising by agreeing to publish one another's ads. "It was just something to keep busy," he says. "But within a week, we knew we were onto something." In three months, Hsieh signed up 20,000 websites; he decided that the site could make money by selling ads as well as trading them. Though Link-Exchange was unprofitable, the idea had enough steam to pick up a $3 million investment from Sequoia Capital—Moritz led the investment. By 1998, the company, which had revenue of about $10 million, would be sold to Microsoft for a staggering $265 million. Hsieh was just 24 years old.

And yet, despite this success, Hsieh found himself depressed. "The easiest way to explain it was that going into the office started to feel like work," he says. He felt increasingly that the people he had hired were not committed to the venture's long-term growth. "The Silicon Valley culture is, 'I'm going to work hard for four years and make millions of dollars and then retire,'" he says. Work, which once had felt liberating, had become a chore. He resolved that his next company would not be about a short-term payday. It would be about long-term growth, about creating a place to which he and his employees would want to come every day.

When you visit Zappos's headquarters in Henderson, Nevada, it's easy to miss Hsieh's desk. Not only is it tucked into a row of cubicles in the middle of the floor, but it's also smaller and more cluttered than any CEO's desk I have ever seen. There are stacks of unopened mail, empty Styrofoam cups, several unopened liquor bottles, and a sizable collection of self-help books—titles include *Mastering the Rockefeller Habits, The Time Paradox: The New Psychology of Time That Will Change Your Life,* and *14,000 Things to Be Happy About.* There are a few science titles—part of Hsieh's quest for a happiness framework—a few on food and wine, and one on marathon running, which he recently took up.

Hsieh is a relentless self-improver, which may help explain why, after selling LinkExchange, he didn't start a new company. Instead, he started 27. In 1999, he and Alfred Lin, a Harvard classmate, launched something called Venture Frogs. Though structured as a venture capital fund, it was more ambitious. Hsieh and Lin leased 15,000 square feet of office space in the same San Francisco building in which they both owned lofts, and they gave the space to the start-ups in which they invested.

Hsieh's involvement in Zappos started with a voice mail from a young man named Nick Swinmurn, who said he wanted to start an online shoe company. Hsieh had never been particularly taken with the idea of online retail, but when Swinmurn mentioned that catalog companies sold $2 billion a year worth of shoes, Hsieh got interested. In 1999, Venture Frogs agreed to invest $500,000, if Zappos—the name is a play on *zapatos,* the Spanish word for *shoes*—could recruit someone with shoe experience. Swinmurn found Fred Mossler, then a Nordstrom buyer.

Six months later, Swinmurn was out of money, and the site offered only three shoe brands. (Most orders were initially filled by a few local retailers.) "We were down to the last day, essentially," says Mossler. "And Tony called." Hsieh said he would keep the company afloat and offered to help. By the summer of 2000, Hsieh and Swinmurn were co-CEOs, and Zappos was operating out of Hsieh's living room. Says Hsieh: "It was the most interesting opportunity, and the people were the most fun."

This is also a delicate way of saying that Hsieh was not especially happy as an investor. A few of Venture Frogs' investments succeeded—notably the search engine Ask.com and the restaurant reservation system OpenTable—but as the dot-com bubble burst, most struggled to survive, and some were shuttered. Hsieh had been attracted to investing because it seemed to bring all the fun of start-ups on a larger scale; instead, it became a treadmill of meetings full of bad news. "I think it was much harder than he first imagined," says Moritz. What Hsieh wanted, he realized, was the unstructured fun of a new company. As he puts it, "I wanted to be involved in building something."

Zappos's early years were a scramble. Footwear brands, which associated the Web with heavy discounting, resisted putting their merchandise on Zappos. Still, Mossler succeeded in signing up about 50 companies in the first year and a half. Hsieh wrote software code and focused on financing—he bankrolled the company until he secured a line of credit with Wells Fargo in 2003. Nobody had set jobs, nobody cared about titles, and everybody hung out with everybody else after work. The economy was falling apart around them, but somehow, even the struggle was fun.

The defining aspect of the Zappos customer experience— free shipping and free returns—was concocted out of necessity. Hsieh figured that there was no other way to get people to try

the site. He also added a prominently displayed toll-free customer support number, a personal buying service, free socks— anything to help put skeptical customers at ease. Because the company could not afford to spend money on marketing, the sales strategy involved making customers so happy that they bought again or told their friends or both.

Though shoemakers were initially reluctant to sell to Zappos—Nike held out for more than seven years—by 2002, Mossler had lined up more than 100 brands, including Steve Madden and Converse, and the company was beginning to do a brisk business. Sales hit $32 million in 2002, up from $8.6 million the previous year. At the time, 25 percent of orders were shipped from manufacturers' warehouses; these orders were often delayed for days. Hsieh decided to stop listing these items on Zappos and opened a warehouse outside of Louisville.

A few months later, Hsieh moved the company from San Francisco to Las Vegas—70 of the company's 100 employees made the trip. The move made sense for lots of reasons, chief among them lower taxes and a lower cost of living. Hsieh also wanted to be in a city where restaurants and stores are open 24 hours a day, to accommodate call center reps who work the graveyard shift. The move corresponded with yet another jump in sales and helped put an end to any financial worries. In late 2004, the company, which sold $184 million worth of goods that year, landed $20 million from Sequoia Capital.

Such rapid growth was exciting. But it also led Hsieh to wonder how he could preserve Zappos's radical dedication to customer service and its fun, loose work environment. "We always hired for culture fit," he says. "But we were growing so quickly that managers who hadn't been around for very long might not know what our culture was." He wrote an e-mail to the entire company asking for help, and he distilled the responses into a list of 10 core values, including "Be humble," "Create fun and a little weirdness," and "Deliver WOW through service." Then he assigned and collected short essays from every employee on the subject of the company's culture and published them, unedited, in a book that he distributed to the staff.

Every year, all employees, both new and old, contribute a fresh essay to the book, which has grown to 480 pages. Hsieh uses it as a way not only to get employees thinking about the meaning of their work but also to show the outside world what he has built. Talk to Hsieh for five minutes, and he will inevitably try to get your address so he can mail you a copy. The book is painfully earnest and yet affecting nonetheless. There are all the clichés one might expect—acronyms, ridiculous overstatement (one call center rep compared Zappos to China's Ming Dynasty), and a fondness for the word *Zapponians.* It often goes way over the top. "Could you imagine if Zappos was more than an online retailer, or the job that pays the bills, but actually became a way of life?" wrote Donavon Roberson, a pastor who left the ministry before joining Zappos.

Most Zappos employees are familiar with all this history. In fact, despite all the research I did before heading to Las Vegas, I didn't know that Nike had spurned Zappos until I sat in on a two-hour Zappos history class—part of a four-week course on the subject—and watched as employees called out various milestones: 2002, $32 million in gross sales! 2006, the year the company recorded its first $3 million day! 2007, the year Nike joined Zappos!

This mastery isn't accidental. It's required. All new Zappos employees receive two weeks of classroom training. Then they spend two weeks learning how to answer customer calls. At the conclusion of the program, trainees are famously offered $2,000, plus time worked, to quit. The practice, Hsieh's idea, began in 2005, with a $100 offer. "Our training team had gotten good at figuring out who wasn't going to make it, and we were thinking, How do you get rid of those people?" says Hsieh. Paying them to quit saves the company money by weeding out people who would jump ship anyway and allows those who remain to make a public statement of commitment to their new employer.

More recently, Hsieh has overseen the development of an even more comprehensive curriculum. The first course, intended for employees who have worked at Zappos for two years or less, involves more than 200 hours of class time (during work hours) and mandates that students read nine business books. Topics include Sarbanes-Oxley compliance and Twitter use. Advanced students can take classes in public speaking and financial planning. "The vision is that three years from now, almost all our hires will be entry-level people," Hsieh says. "We'll provide them with training and mentorship, so that within five to seven years, they can become senior leaders within the company."

The Zappos headquarters takes up three modest buildings in a nondescript office park about a 20-minute drive from the Las Vegas Strip. Walk in, and it becomes immediately clear why for some entrepreneurs, visiting Zappos is of a piece with the buffet at the Bellagio or a trip to the top of the (replica) Eiffel Tower. In fact, Zappos hosts a tour of its headquarters every couple of hours, an operation that is staffed by 12 people and includes two SUVs and a bus with custom Zappos paint jobs. Call the company from your hotel, and someone will pick you up and ferry you to Henderson.

My tour is led by Roberson, the former pastor, who wears jeans and a maroon polo shirt and carries a giant Zappos flag. We are joined by four consultants from Deloitte. In the lobby, Roberson points out the Reply to All Hat—a sort of dunce cap for employees who commit that venial office sin of the inadvertent mass e-mail—and takes us past the nap room, where three employees are stretched out on couches. At the office of the company's staff life coach, who also happens to be Hsieh's former chiropractor, we are each photographed while sitting on a throne.

But the most striking thing about the tour is the extent to which the company's long-term plan is on display. A sales chart in the lobby informs everyone in the building that the day before—March 4, 2009—Zappos sold $2.5 million worth of merchandise. A computer printout in the hallway notes that there are currently 4.1 million items, mostly shoes, in stock in the warehouse in Kentucky. At the conclusion of the tour, we are invited to peruse the company library, which is filled with multiple copies of two dozen business and self-help books. We are urged to take whatever grabs our fancy, a policy that applies to employees as well. Roberson explains that one of Zappos's core values is personal growth and that books are given out to help employees grow with the company.

When I tell Hsieh that Zappos strikes me as not unlike a religious cult, he doesn't disagree. "I think there's a lot you can learn from religion," he says. "This is not just a company. It's like a way of life."

Of course, nobody except Hsieh works at Zappos to save his or her soul. It's a job—and not a particularly glamorous one. Customer service reps start at $11 an hour, warehouse workers at $8.25. But even in its hiring process, Zappos creates wildly different expectations than do most companies. Prospective hires must pass an hourlong "culture interview" before being handed off to whatever department they are applying to. Questions include, "On a scale of 1—10, how weird are you?" and "What was your last position called? Was that an appropriate title?" (The first question makes sure that employees are sufficiently weird; the second, in which the interviewer is trying to goad the applicant into grumbling about his or her title, tests for humility.)

If there is a disagreement between HR and the manager doing the hiring, Hsieh personally interviews the candidate and makes the final call. His strategy is to get the applicant into a social situation to see if they can connect emotionally. Alcohol often figures in the hiring process. "I had three vodka shots with Tony during my interview," says Rebecca Ratner, Zappos's head of human resources. "And I'm not atypical." I asked Hsieh if this wasn't exposing the company to unnecessary risks. "It's a risk," he says. "But if we're building a culture where everyone is friends with everyone else, it's worth the risk."

After my tour, I spend a few minutes sitting in the Zappos call center with Grace Hale, a bubbly young woman with dyed black hair and a lip piercing. Unlike most call center operators, Zappos does not keep track of call times or require operators to read from scripts. Hale has a penchant for offering unsolicited commentary on customers' shoe selections—"They *are* beautiful," she coos during one call, as she pulls up a picture of a pair of Dr. Scholl's Asana heels that a customer found uncomfortable. Not only are reps encouraged to make decisions on their own—for instance, offering a refund on a defective item—they are supposed to send a dozen or so personal notes to customers every day. "It's all about P-E-C," Hale explains to me. "Personal Emotional Connection with the customer." (After a few hours at Zappos, you actually stop noticing this argot.)

All of this is designed to impress customers—or as Hale would have it, "wow them." Last year, Zappos stopped promising free overnight shipping on its website, but not because of the cost. In fact, the company *still* ships almost every order overnight, but Hsieh wanted customers to be surprised when they got the item the next day. According to Patti Freeman Evans, an analyst with Forrester Research, this has helped Zappos fend off challenges from copycat sites such as Amazon's Endless.com and IAC's Shoebuy.com, which offer similar perks and even lower prices. "A lot of companies talk about service. Zappos really does it," Evans says.

During Zappos's early days, long workdays would often spill into late-night socializing. Hsieh enjoyed this so much that he formalized it at Zappos: Managers are now required to spend 10 percent to 20 percent of their time goofing off with the people they manage. "It's just kind of a random number we made up,"

Hsieh concedes. "But part of the way you build company culture is hanging out outside of the office."

On my last night in Las Vegas, Hsieh offers to take me out and show me what he is talking about. We are joined by a couple of his friends and six Zappos employees and bounce from a bar to a lounge to a nightclub. By the time I beg out, at 2 a.m., Hsieh and a few others are heading to a dive bar to grab a late-night bite to eat. Though Hsieh seems to enjoy himself—and though he does indulge in a few shots of Grey Goose—he never really lets loose. For the first half of the evening, we chat seriously about happiness. Then he withdraws, eventually sitting down, playing with his BlackBerry, and watching the party with what looks like a smile.

In his speeches, Hsieh likes to point out that Zappos does not have specific policies for dealing with each customer service situation. He claims that the company's culture allows it to do extraordinary things. I saw him make this point earlier this year in New York City, when he told a story about a woman whose husband died in a car accident after she had ordered boots for him from Zappos. The day after she called to ask for help with the return, she received a flower delivery. The call center rep had ordered the flowers without checking with a supervisor and billed them to the company. "At the funeral, the widow told her friends and family about the experience," Hsieh said, his voice cracking and his eyes tearing up ever so slightly. "Not only was she a customer for life, but so were those 30 or 40 people at the funeral."

Hsieh paused to compose himself. "Stories like these are being created every single day, thousands and thousands of times," he said. "It's just an example that if you get the culture right, then most of the other stuff follows."

MAX CHAFKIN is *Inc.'s* senior writer.

Give Me the Bad News: Successful Entrepreneurs Need Negative Feedback

Kerri Susan Smith

Tom Blondi has been involved with several start-up companies, and he's learned there are two essential ingredients every successful venture needs.

First, someone needs to come up with a good idea. Second, the founder needs to hear negative feedback about that idea. In fact, the negative feedback may be the more important element in the formula for success.

You'll Need a Mentor, Not a Fan

"Very few of us can create the perfect idea without feedback," Blondi told a breakout session at the Spark 2008 IT Invitational this fall. "If you've got a great idea and you present it to someone, and they immediately like it with no reservations—it's not a good idea."

Entrepreneurs need people who will ask tough, specific questions about how the business will function. Friends and relatives generally are not the best people to act as a sounding board for the company's founder.

But hearing something other than "brilliant" or "you'll make a fortune" can be tough for a prospective entrepreneur. People who want to start companies and are willing to risk the time and effort on a startup are often personally attached to their idea and their vision for the business.

It takes a dialogue with "a real live human being who is willing to write a check" before you know you're getting the right kind of feedback, he said. To truly consider yourself an entrepreneur, Blondi said, you need someone to invest in your idea.

Blondi said he used to feel the sting when he heard his ideas questioned. "I thought the person was in some way jealous of me," he said. "Later I realized this was just constructive criticism."

The best person to mentor an entrepreneur through that start-up process is someone who has a track record of success and failure, he said. Knowing what works is important. First-hand experience with what doesn't work is just as important.

An Entrepreneur's Trail

Blondi has experienced both since he began running start-up companies 18 years ago. His first venture was a hit—Language Management International in Colorado. The company took

software programs designed in the United States and engineered them to run on machines in Japan, Europe and Latin America. It was successful early on and Blondi and the other investors sold it to Berlitz.

"After that, I knew everything," Blondi said. That is, until his next venture.

Blondi became chief marketing officer for Cyclone Commerce, a Scottsdale-based software company that allowed businesses to securely send documents over the web. Previously companies were forced to fax or use overnight delivery services to transmit invoices and other documents to business partners. It was a great concept that never really achieved the growth the management team envisioned, he said.

"We were never really able to differentiate our product from others," Blondi said. The company struggled but the investors found a happy exit strategy. The company was acquired by Axway, now a subsidiary of the French-based Sopra Group.

Since then, Blondi has been involved in several companies—often brought in to run the company or to train the next CEO.

He is currently the CEO of Ethix Media, which has a product called Homeminders. Homeminders is a web-based software that lets a home owner track routine maintenance, such as changing the filters on the heating/cooling systems, and inventory possessions. The user is a homeowner, but the customer usually is a large company that sponsors the software and gives the software away as a branding tool.

Blondi said he likes opportunities where he can build something. "I am looking for a long-term engagement, not a month-long project," he said.

But he's not looking for a permanent position. Blondi is already putting his next venture, a Scandinavian-designed application designed to help small and mid-sized companies diagnose their online security vulnerabilities. He is an investor in this venture as well as the CEO.

Are You the Type?

Blondi didn't start out to become an entrepreneur. He graduated from Southern Illinois University with a degree in mathematics and physics. His first job out of college was working as a computer programmer for Sears.

"Yes, back then we actually wrote code as opposed to entering it," he quipped. "I wasn't very good at that, and I'm not joking.

"My boss at the time said, 'You actually talk better than you code.'"

So Blondi was given a position where he could talk—and taken away from programming computers. He functioned as a liaison with non-technical users. He listened, and conversed with them in plain English, and then told the programmers what the users needed. That position launched his career in the software business.

Today, young people show more interest in start-UPS and other smaller ventures compared with the 1970s, Blondi said. But large organizations, which are not considered as secure as they once were, have certain advantages.

"Those companies have been around for 100 years, and they really have training down," he said. "You could learn as much in two years there as you could in 10 years somewhere else."

Entrepreneurs hip has become more glamorous in the past 20-30 years. But, "you only hear about the success stories," Blondi said. "They only tell you the good stuff. There's a lot of pain and suffering in being an entrepreneur."

The job entails great dedication and a great deal of stress. Many ventures simply don't survive. In 2006, the Small Business Administration estimated that 671,800 firms started and 544,800 were terminated. Not all those failed. Some were sold to other businesses. But long-term success is elusive.

And there is nothing quite like having to call a friend or a relative who invested in a venture where you lost their money because of decisions you made, Blondi said.

Before starting down the road, prospective entrepreneurs should ask themselves tough questions.

"Am I cut out to be an entrepreneur? Is it something I really want to do?" he said. "It's OK if you don't want to be an entrepreneur."

"We talk about non-entrepreneurs like it's a bad thing," he said, but not everyone who is creative and successful in business is an entrepreneur. Investor Warren Buffet, who tops the Forbes list of the richest people in the world, is generally not considered to be an entrepreneur.

It's also important to remember that the company founder is not the only player in the start-up drama. In fact, the idea generators are usually in the minority in a start up. The other 80 percent need to be people who excel at the execution, Blondi said.

Often, company founders take an egocentric approach to running a start-up venture, but it's not the best approach. "I've found building consensus sometimes seems to slow the process," Blondi said. "But in the end, it makes things easier. You need that buy-in."

Bottom Line

- It's critical for entrepreneurs to get feedback in order to refine their ideas for a start-up business. Few can come up with ideas that don't need sharpening to succeed.
- A career as an entrepreneur is not for everyone. A high percentage of start-up ventures fail each year. It's an intense, demanding occupation. Anyone considering starting a company should decide if this fits their personality.
- Entrepreneurs rely on others to make the dreams for their successful companies come true. The extra time it takes to build consensus will often pay off.

Ask an Angel: Berkus on Building a Board of Directors

Mary Jane Grinstead

Dave Berkus, chairman emeritus and member of Tech Coast Angels, has invested in 68 small technology companies since 1993, earning an IRR of 97 percent. He served on the boards of 40 of these companies and was chair of 12 of those boards. Currently, Berkus is a board member of 10 private companies, chair of six of those, and an active member of four non-profit boards. He is co-author of *Better Than Money* and *Extending the Runway* (available at www.berkus. com with author royalties donated to charity). ACEF's Mary Jane Grinstead recently talked with Dave to get his advice on the best practices for boards of directors for early-stage companies.

ACEF: Let's start with the bottom line. How can the angels participating on boards of their portfolio companies assist those companies in meeting milestones and overcoming obstacles?

DB: The role of angels who are board members doesn't stop with the investment—in fact that's where their most important role begins. The responsibility for helping grow a company falls on the board members as well as on management. If investors insist on having board participation, as I think they should, then they should be trained to respond effectively as a part of the company team. Boards require time to nurture and grow. That time is well-spent when the crises hit; and crises will hit all early stage companies.

ACEF: You have a flair for helping entrepreneurs and seem to understand why they need an effective board of directors. Tell us about your approach.

DB: It all starts by recognizing the entrepreneur's perspective and experience, or more likely lack of perspective and experience, with a "real" board. Early stage boards look and act differently from later stage boards. So it is helpful if both angels and entrepreneurs remember this.

Before a company has outside investors, the role of the board, which is usually made up of friends and family, is more advisory than one of governance. When angel investors come in, our documents dictate that we have investors' rights which usually include providing for one or two members on the board at all times. We're almost always the first "real" board that the entrepreneur has had to deal with.

These early boards before funding were stacked with friends-and-family investors, and the entrepreneur hasn't yet bought into the process about needing people from outside, so I try to get into the entrepreneur's shoes and ask questions that will get them to buy in.

Some questions to ask the founder: Do you need a board? Is it advisors you seek or governance? Do you have outside investors? Do you need legal, operational, industry, or financial expertise to help you grow the company? How about a "sounding board" for management or a source of appeal for management issues?

At least one of these points will resonate with almost every entrepreneur. No one CEO can do it all well, and CEOs are often isolated when they need help the most.

ACEF: Any tips on recruiting for the board?

DB: Get references from investors and existing board members. If you have to pay a reasonable recruiting fee to find the right industry expert from the outside, consider doing that. Ensure that candidates are comfortable with company management and the rest of the board. Be sure that prospects have the time and willingness to attend meetings and be available between meetings for telephone access by the CEO.

ACEF: After you get the entrepreneur comfortable about the benefits of a board, do you talk about potential risks?

DB: Yes. Many entrepreneurs don't realize that the board can hire or fire the CEO or that even though the entrepreneur has and is keeper of the vision, the board can influence and control the strategy of deployment. There's always the risk that the entrepreneur and the board can get sideways and that the board could withhold approvals for funding for acquisitions or other initiatives.

I advise the entrepreneur not to stack the board with friends or investors but to find a balance between finance, operational, and industry expertise. You want a board that helps the entrepreneur and the company to get things done. On a five-person board, giving two seats to the investors, one seat to management, and two seats to carefully selected independent members usually works well.

ACEF: What about having an attorney at board meetings?

DB: If one board member is experienced in governance, I believe that you don't need to have an attorney on the board. I also prefer not to have attorneys as observers in board meetings, which is a bit more controversial. Attorneys certainly add value when they have the answer to a question, but who on the board is going to raise their hand if the attorney oversteps? And it's a poor board if the attorney is there to protect the CEO not the company, especially if it is not stated clearly in advance who the attorney represents.

ACEF: You have participated in dozens of boards. Is there typically a board member experienced in governance?

DB: (laughs) Yes, usually me. After running two public companies and two private ones, governance training has been part of my life going way back; so I become the governance officer by default. I also find myself on the audit committee of virtually every board where I serve.

Government is increasingly applying the rules that affect public corporations to smaller and smaller companies, and training in governance itself is something many angels lack.

Angels need to know that as a board member, their legal responsibility, or duty of loyalty, is to the corporation, not to the shareholders, the employees, or the vendors. There will be times when there are conflicts of interest because of this. For example, there is a legal transfer of loyalty at the moment of insolvency when the board's duty of loyalty legally changes to protection of the assets for the creditors, which means that the board must protect assets for the payroll and vendors, and for all the entities that come in front of the investors.

Then there is the duty of care, a legal duty to care for that corporation asset—to protect and grow it and defend it against all forms of attack. Even if it is not in the best interest of the investors we board members represent, as board members we can't vote for things that are against the best interests of the corporate entity itself.

ACEF: How do you suggest early stage boards organize?

DB: Small boards should emulate big company boards in many ways, which includes establishing audit and compensation committees. If needed for governance or if requested by management, a company may have additional committees for finance, human resources, or technology. It is important to have ongoing focus on board development, at least as a subcommittee of the board; to assess continually whether the board is composed of the best possible members and balance of skills; whether there are non-performing members who should be replaced, and if so how that is going to be done. Consider having annual board evaluations; setting fixed but renewable terms, and even when to "fire yourself."

Angels need to remember that when the company reaches the growth stage that calls for VC investment and the venture capitalists come in, the angels will lose a board seat. If we understand that there are stages of board development, then we won't get upset when that event happens and one of us gets asked to leave. Often the departing board member will be granted observation rights.

ACEF: How can angels participating on boards appropriately help the companies they serve?

DB: There are five easy-to-understand resource areas that define value added activities for a board: money, time, relationships, process, and context.

ACEF: Money—there's an obvious one. How can a board help an entrepreneur and a fledgling company not run out of it?

DB: By guiding the company not to spend precious dollars until they begin to see the first evidence of demand. That saves the company from pushing products based on evangelizing a product into the marketplace that is not receptive to the message, which is how most small companies die. When the company does have a strategic partner that is willing to put resources behind the company, product, or distribution, you have the fist evidence of demand. Put the money behind that one and search for another strategic partner, and then another. I would label this "demand pull" as opposed to "cost push."

Avoid the "tyranny of the new office." Think how many companies are stuck with a lease for an overpriced office at the critical stage of capital preservation. Focus on extending the cash. At the high end of the curve, rapid growth actually demands more cash, not less. Boards should hold the company to a disciplined, constant, cash forecast.

Like money, start-up companies and entrepreneurs never have enough time. Deliberate over-commitment leads to "time bankruptcy," which is just as serious as running out of cash. The board can guide the company to use its vision statement as a tool to filter time allocation.

Yet another "opportunity" for board members is to probe for and discover the greatest bottleneck in the company's product or service delivery process, then work to provide resources to eliminate that bottleneck and restore smooth operations and efficient use of capital.

I've seen more boards of our tiny size hire the expensive "C" level officer; contract with the P/R company; pay for a large booth at one or more trade shows, and then the results don't appear and the money quickly runs out. The message here is, don't bet the farm unless the crops are on fire. Probe for demand and back up that demand with the resources saved for the real opportunity.

ACEF: Relationships and process management are part of the mantra of angel investing. It seems that a board can be invaluable to the entrepreneur when it comes to networking.

DB: Unquestionably. An effective board constantly encourages the entrepreneur to leverage the golden rolodexes of the people on the board, recognizing that there is always someone who can and will help to get a product to market faster or reduce the cost of development.

Process management means getting from start of the company to successful product launch and growth safely and faster. If the inventor/entrepreneur hasn't built a company before, the board can help him or her figure out how to use fewer resources given the time to market and resulting burn of fixed costs.

And then there is the "every three million dollar crisis."

ACEF: What's that?

DB: Companies hit critical points at about every three million dollars of incremental revenue—or of gross profit if there are outside vendor product costs. These stages are where the entrepreneurs and their boards are likely to have disagreements and conflicts. To some extent, a board that has a good working relationship with the company founder and management team can rehearse these stages in advance; however, some conflict is unavoidable.

At $3 million with about 20 employees, it is often time to replace the weaker people in the company—and that could include the CEO's friends or even the CEO. Reporting or organizational management usually needs to be realigned. At $6 million in revenue with about 40 employees, the company will hit another bump, this time usually a cash crisis, and raising growth capital consumes at least half the CEO's time. If he or she was the bottleneck, all heck really breaks loose inside the company.

Assuming the company stays on track, another rough patch happens around $9 million. By now, the product is in second or third generation with new features. The high quality that the company thought was sacrosanct suffers from the rapid growth, and quality problems consume management. At the $12 million level, the problem often returns to operational, closing the ever-expanding circle of repeating crises.

ACEF: So if these bumps are likely, what can a board do to help a company manage through?

DB: From the beginning, provide the leadership to ensure that the entrepreneur follows a constant planning exercise that helps the company stay in sync or context with the market. This perspective doesn't come from investors or from the CEO, but from industry experts on the board who understand whether or not the company is flying with the prevailing winds of the marketplace or wasting money pushing product to an indifferent market.

The CEO is always going to have a gee-whiz idea that will take the market by storm. Independent board members with industry knowledge can supply an important balance, helping find that elusive receptive market for a new company or product. Think about Apple; only about a half-million iPods were sold in the first year because the product came out too early. If a product as big and successful as the iPod had market context issues, you can bet that most of the companies angels deal with are going to have these sorts of challenges, too.

The planning process should also include actively seeking great strategic partnerships, especially in the context of pre-thinking the company's exit strategy. I like to run a white board exercise with the company's board, asking them to name 10 companies that might be candidates to eventually buy the firm down the road.

Then we talk about how to create the most value for those candidates. Is our value to those companies in our patents, products, or distribution? If we discover that six of the 10 companies would want the same thing from our company if they knew that we could provide it better than anyone, then that discovered value becomes a core competency that the company will want to develop. In this way, boards can create credibility for future fundraising and liquidity events.

ACEF: How does a company pay an early stage board?

DB: Cash is nice, and typical in public companies, but very rare early on. Stock grants create taxable events and must be carefully managed. Options are the most typical form of board compensation because options align the board with management.

You typically see early stage funded companies offering one percent of the fully diluted value in common stock to each non-VC outside board member, vesting over two to four years. If there are both preferred and common classes of stock, there are pricing choices for the options. In any event, these board member non-qualified stock options (NSO) must be priced at the last transaction price or at a carefully derived share price after considerable research and discussion.

ACEF: How often should boards meet and what should an entrepreneur be expected to prepare?

DB: Monthly meetings are appropriate early on or if the company is in a directional crisis. Bi-monthly works well if the company is progressing and cash flow isn't a problem. The board package should include financials, projections, statements of progress, and a separate statement of concerns or problems authored by the CEO. At meetings, leave time and encourage the CEO to include other members of the management team to demonstrate depth of management and to give the board a better understanding of management issues.

ACEF: Any final observations.

DB: The education of angels who aspire to be good board members is important. We want to understand what is going on with the company, to effectively advise management, and to open our rolodexes for help, but we must keep our "noses in and our fingers out."

Once a board member steps across that line and interferes with management, it is almost impossible to cross back and repair the damage. Such improper moves by board members, although well-intentioned, create a stressful relationship with C-level management and make a much less effective board member.

We must constantly remember that we board members are not managing the company, only providing governance, resources, and direction to help management.

Why a CEO Needs to Have a Plan B: An Interview with Jack Stack

For nearly three decades, in good times and bad, Jack Stack has run his company as though disaster could strike at any moment. Now, with the economy cratering, he's glad he did.

BO BURLINGHAM

If you think times are tough now, consider that in the early '80s, the prime interest rate topped 21 percent, and unemployment was just shy of 11 percent. That was the economic environment confronting Jack Stack and 12 other managers of a small engine-remanufacturing plant in Springfield, Missouri, as they prepared to buy the factory from International Harvester in a desperate attempt to save their own jobs and those of the people they worked with. Their new company, Springfield ReManufacturing Corporation, survived that recession and went on to prosper for the next 26 years.

Today, Stack, the company's CEO, and his colleagues are weathering a recession of similar magnitude. But they find themselves in a far different situation. The enterprise, now called SRC Holdings, is a mini conglomerate of seven holding companies with 26 businesses whose 1,200 employees make automobile engines, irrigation pumps, home furnishings, and more. Its current health is no accident. Having launched the company to save jobs, Stack was determined never to be forced to lay people off. He spoke with editor-at-large Bo Burlingham (with whom he has co-authored two books) about how he has worked to keep that promise to his employees—and build a company that is bucking nearly every current economic trend.

Most American Manufacturers are in Terrible Shape Right Now. And Yet You Seem to Be Doing Well. What Do You Attribute that to?

Paranoia. We've always been terrified of being forced to lay people off, and so we've spent the past 26 years trying to make sure we would never have to do that.

Where Does that Paranoia Come from?

It goes back to our beginnings. When we started out in February 1983, we were at rock bottom. Everybody was at the bottom in 1983. It was ugly and painful, just like today. We'd bought our factory to save our jobs, but to do it we had to take on a huge amount of debt, $8.9 million, because we had very little money ourselves. Our debt-to-equity ratio was 89:1. Let me tell you, you're brain-dead in that situation. You're on life support. We had bank auditors literally camped outside our doors. If we'd had one little slip-up—if we'd been an hour late with a payment—they would have rushed in and closed us down, and 120 people would have been out on the street.

When you go through a period like that, you don't ever want to do it again. I am sure people who lived through the Great Depression developed some form of trapdoor thinking and contingency planning—whether it was having two or three jobs or investments or just not living outside their means. Anyway, that experience made us realize that a job is never secure. If you let yourself get lulled to sleep, you're going to get screwed—even if you have what you think is a fail-safe deal.

How Do You Keep from Getting Lulled to Sleep?

We constantly look for our vulnerabilities. We do forecasting to determine where they are, and then we ask ourselves a lot of what-ifs. What if we're getting wrong information? What if a market goes down? What if we have a collection problem with a major customer? What if interest rates go through the roof? What if there's a 9/11? The whole idea is to provide our people with job security and job opportunities. I think it's led us to go one step further than most companies do. A lot of businesses put up a plan to satisfy their bankers or because they think it's what you're supposed to do. But our culture is, "Let's find out where our weaknesses and vulnerabilities are and then build something to offset them."

How Does That Work in Practice?

We measure each piece of business by the amount of labor that goes into it. Then we see how concentrated our labor is. When we were starting out in the 1980s, more than 75 percent of our labor hours were in the truck market. We did some investigating and found out that the truck market has a recession every six years. So we had to ask ourselves what we'd do if we had a recession.

And the Answer?

We thought about what goes up in a down market, and we discovered that automobile parts go up, because people keep their cars longer and fix them. That's how we got into the automotive aftermarket business. That kind of thinking became part of our culture and our way of doing business.

So Is This All about Saving Jobs?

No, it's about creating jobs. That's our goal. And once you create them, you don't want to lose them. What we're doing here is helping people to get through life. I never want to have to take someone else's livelihood away because of mistakes I've made in not anticipating a problem—even if it's a problem I couldn't have seen coming. It's management's job to anticipate those problems and prepare for them. A layoff is a failure of management. But the people who usually pay for that failure are not the ones responsible for it.

It's Interesting to Me that Your Paranoia Actually Led You to Expand the Company in Some Very Ambitious Ways

Absolutely. The contingencies and trapdoors we developed eventually became new businesses. Our values drove our paranoia. Our paranoia drove our contingency planning. And our contingency planning drove our diversification. We knew the more we diversified, the safer we would be. So we spread out of our core competencies. We've spun off 55, 56 businesses as a result of this process.

A Lot of People Would Say You Took a Big Risk by Getting Outside Your Core Competencies. The Common Wisdom is That You're Supposed to Stick to Your Knitting

I think that's really bad advice in most cases. Sure, if we'd stayed in our core competency, we might have been very successful in the truck market. We could have reduced our expenses and increased our margins, but we would have been tremendously vulnerable. We would have had 100 percent of our eggs in one basket.

Certainly, Some People Have Been Successful by Sticking to Their Core Competencies

Oh, sure. It's not too bad a strategy if you plan to sell the business. You build up your earnings and your sales, and then you cash out. But to create something sustainable, you have to be totally paranoid. You have to be realistic that you're going to get hit with a lot of unknown events. If you diversify, you can handle those unknowns. But it takes a lot of courage to fix a weakness when it's not immediately painful.

Describe the Process that Leads to the Creation of the New Businesses

It's centered around our sales meetings, which we hold twice a year—one in June and one in October. We tell people, "Give us your honest-to-God forecast. We'd love to see 15 percent growth. If we get 6 percent or more, that's OK, but tell us what it would take to get to 15." Generally, we prefer to grow organically, increasing sales of products we already make and selling to customers and markets we already have. Organic growth is the most profitable kind. Your margins are always better when you grow with something you're already strong at.

But we want people to have new products and new markets lined up in case they can't reach their goals organically. Those are the contingencies and trapdoors. Let's say one company needs 100 people this year and projects it will need 106 people to handle its growth next year. At the sales meeting, its representatives tell us how they plan to do it in terms of product lines, customers, and the marketplace. But they also have to consider that they might be wrong. So we ask them to come to the meeting with an additional 15 percent of sales in what-ifs. What if they can't cover the 106 people? Because if they're wrong on the forecast, they're also wrong on somebody's life.

And 15 Percent Is the Magic Number?

We want at least 15 percent of our projected sales in research and development at all times. The whole idea of the trapdoor is that if something happens, we can rush that new product to market, or we can rush that product we already have to a new customer. We look at a variety of factors. For example, one of our companies makes agricultural machinery, and agriculture tends to be good in the spring and the fall, but there's a gap in the middle. We asked ourselves, "What sells in the summertime?" The answer: refrigeration units. So we put refrigeration units in there. It was a contingency. We began to develop a lot of contingencies like that, and some of the contingencies ultimately became businesses.

Is that Why You've Done So well Despite the Current Downturn?

Yes. Look at SRC Automotive. It remanufactures automotive and marine engines. Its biggest customers are Mercury Marine and General Motors. Our GM orders fell off a cliff in November. Up to then, we'd been doing 800 to 1,000 engines a month for them. In December, we sold 212 engines. Marine got hit hard, too. It was a tsunami. If we hadn't had these contingencies and trapdoors, we would have had no option but to lay off 35 percent of the work force and wait until the business came back. We figured that would be at least five or six months.

I Take it That's Not What You Did

Fortunately, we didn't have to. We were able to move some of the people into our other companies that needed the extra manpower and had jobs they could do. We also found a Missouri program that helped us out. Instead of laying people off, we put them on a four-day workweek, and they collect unemployment for the days they aren't working. On their days off, they wind up with about $10 less than what they'd been making, but that's a loss they can handle. Meanwhile, we bought time to execute our contingencies.

What Did You Do?

One of automotive's contingencies was to build natural-gas pumping units. They'd been looking at that opportunity for a year or more. When the cuts came, they went after the business. They also had their eye on remanufacturing engines for the postal service. So by February, automotive was back to a five-day workweek. March was a full month as well. In three months, they repositioned the company. And now, if their two main customers come back to normal levels, they'll be stronger than ever. In fact, they'll have to start hiring people.

That's Impressive

But understand, there's no way to develop new markets and new customers if you lay people off. How are they going to do natural-gas pumps or the post-office business if they've gotten rid of the people who do the work?

Is This the Process You Use in All the Companies?

More or less. Our program is the four Ps: people, profits, positive cash flow, and positioning. We're saying to ourselves, "Look, we got this far by creating jobs. We've done all this to build the type of culture we want—a culture that puts people at the center. What are we going to do to keep it? How much are we willing to invest in keeping it?" I'm willing to give up profits if the losses go to repositioning the company, so that when we come out of this thing, we're stronger than when we went in.

We had two months when we lost $200,000 while we were executing the contingencies and moving people around to keep them employed. But that's money we were going to lose anyway, and we were able to keep our cash flow positive by dropping our inventories. When you sell finished goods that were in inventory or when you don't buy as many parts to put in inventory, you have more cash. Of course, it doesn't hurt that we have so much cash in the bank—enough to carry us for three or four years.

Where Did That Come From?

That was the result of another contingency. A little more than 10 years ago, we started a joint venture with John Deere to remanufacture diesel engines for its agricultural and construction equipment divisions. We'd been looking at Deere for a while as a potential way to diversify SRC Heavy Duty. That particular contingency turned into a business fairly quickly. We became 50-50 partners with Deere in the joint venture, which we called ReGen Technologies, and we each had an option to buy the other out according to a formula we agreed upon in advance. Last year, we mutually decided that the time had come for us to exercise the option and sell our interest in ReGen to Deere. This was several months before the financial crisis. The deal closed at the beginning of November and put all that cash on our balance sheet. Suddenly, we looked like the smartest guys in the world.

You Have Been Thinking This Way for Decades. What Do You Say to People in Small Companies Who Are Scared That They Are Not Going to Be Able to Make It through This Recession?

Well, it's not so much what I would say as what I would ask. I'd ask, "How productive is your team? Are you leveraging the mental capacity of everybody in your organization?" Nine times out of 10, when I go into those small organizations you're asking me about, I find CEOs who have taken all the responsibility upon themselves. They're freaked out, because they believe they have to come up with all the answers. But that's what leads to failure, especially in this type of economic environment. People just don't understand that you do not have to take all the problems on yourself. Nobody is smart enough to take on a crisis like this one all alone. But people have been taught that it's the job of a CEO to have the answers.

What Should CEOs Be Thinking about If They Want to Emerge from the Crisis Stronger than When It Began?

If your sales are down and you're losing money, you're crazy not to be investing in repositioning. You have underutilized capacity. People are standing around. Don't lay them off. Have them come up with new products, new ideas, new services, new ways of doing things. Maybe you find something new to do with your underutilized capacity. Maybe you can change your products or go into different markets. That's how we got into making engines for pumping natural gas. Our automotive people were building engines for cars. Someone noticed that they could be refitted for other uses. Natural-gas pumping equipment looked promising, given the stricter emissions standards in California. They did the research, made some adjustments, built a prototype, worked out the quality procedures, and found customers. Each step required an investment. In a down period, while you may not have cash to invest, you do have excess people capacity. Most companies reduce it by having a layoff. That's what I call cutting to the bone. You wind up weaker as a result.

SRC Is an Employee-Owned Business. How Important Was Employee Ownership to Doing All This?

That's a great question, but it's probably a question that has to be answered by the employee owners, not me. Personally, I don't think we could ever have come this far if I owned 100 percent of the company. I know myself; I couldn't have handled all that wealth. I would have felt guilty. That's not the person I am and not the person I want to be. I just believed from the very beginning that the employees create the value.

You have often spoken about what you call the company's contingent liability to its employee owners. Eventually, they will want to cash in their stock, and the company will have to come up with the cash to pay them. Your awareness of that contingent liability has driven a lot of the innovation, hasn't it?

I think that is the best-kept secret of running a successful company. Knowing we have to cover the contingent liabilities pushed us to find answers. If your company is publicly owned,

you don't have that pressure, because there's a market for the stock. When you're privately owned, you definitely work in a different world.

Is That True Only of Employee-Owned Companies?

No, I think it applies to a lot of privately held companies, especially ones owned by families. It's different in companies founded by people who've already decided they're going to run it for five years and sell it. Granted, a lot of people tell themselves, "When push comes to shove, I can always sell the company." They don't think about how they're going to feel when they find out their employees don't want them to sell. You design a culture where people work 40 hours a week, make friends, raise kids, become members of a community. It's very hard to let go of it. But if you want to keep it, you have to be willing to ask yourself, "What are our vulnerabilities, and how can we address them?" I will say this: We did not walk away from that question. Our people had the courage to come up with answers. That was the beginning of creating the subsidiaries, which became our vehicles for innovation. They brought out the entrepreneurship in us. And we still have some trapdoors left that we haven't used.

What Do You Mean?

Well, 20 years ago, we bought a big piece of property here in Springfield for $250,000. Its value increased to about $4 million, but it's still on our books at the purchase price. We could sell it if we needed cash. We also helped start a bank that eventually was sold. The stock is on our books at less than $500,000, but it's worth $3.4 million.

Is There a Downside to Paranoia? Some People Might Say You Miss Opportunities If You Are Always Worrying That Something Could Come along and Whack You

I'd say you're a fool if you know you're going to get whacked and don't do something about it.

You Actually Enjoy Working in an Environment Like This One, Don't You? I Can Hear It in Your Voice

I think that it's really, really hard to win with a lead. I like coming from behind. And we're all coming from behind right now. An economy like this one creates opportunities. You bring in something new, but you don't let go of what you had before. When the economy comes back, you get a twofer. In the long run, it creates more jobs and more security.

Why Do You Prefer Coming from Behind? Is It the Challenge?

I think there's a sense of satisfaction when, regardless of how bleak the situation is, you find people succeeding. It gives you inspiration to see them going the extra mile. It gives you hope. In order to be courageous, you need to see things happening that generate hope. There's a lot of bad things going on, and we're totally influenced by the media, which tell us all about them. It's great to see people fighting back.

Top Ten Reasons Why Startups Fail (Venture Capital)

Entrepreneurship is for those with thick skin, and sheer tenacity to be able to hear lots of "no's" but not be deterred.

MOHANJIT JOLLY

I think most people are aware of the fact that very few startups actually succeed. That's precisely what makes entrepreneurs a rare breed. While knowing the risks, entrepreneurs follow their passion, try to change the world and hope for wealth creation for themselves and their shareholders.

It's the potential for that proverbial home-run (or a Sixer in cricket talk, I suppose) that drives entrepreneurs, especially technology entrepreneurs (and VCs) to get into the game in the first place. But, for a combination of reasons both within and outside one's control, startups fail. The list below is one compiled by my colleague, Tim Draper. I have tried to add my own little twist to give it some Indian spice and colour. So, here goes . . .

1. Startups Run out of Cash

One can argue whether that's the cause or effect of failure. Often, startups are too optimistic about when their product is going to be accepted by the market (the hockey stick that entrepreneurs and investors alike often talk about). I used to have a professor in Business School who was a turnaround specialist hired by large corporates in the US to help float a sinking ship, and actually have them become viable businesses.

He used to say, "You can run out of wives and girlfriends, but make sure you never run out of cash". I am guessing the latter will automatically lead to the former in most cases. But all kidding aside, there are often times when the entrepreneur is either too naive or highly arrogant when dealing with the situation of "cash crunch".

On the former, he/she is busy fighting other fires that he/she simply underestimates how long the cash will last (sales cycles are longer than expected, for example, or customers are more price sensitive than expected). I have also seen the latter, where an entrepreneur will not heed advice from Board or advisors (in terms of cutting the burn) simply because he/she thinks that his/her company is too valuable for the investors and other stakeholders to let die, and they will bridge the company. More often than not, the entrepreneur is wrong. In tough times, investors become a lot more disciplined about letting go of the non-performers, and not putting good money after bad.

2. Founders Don't Have Complete Faith in Each Other

They fight instead of delegate, trust and verify with each other. This is a tricky one. I often tell entrepreneurs that great companies are founded not by an individual but teams (2 or more founders). Gates and Allen, Brin and Page, Yang and Filo, Jobs and Wozniak and the list goes on and on . . . It's important to have one founder who is outward facing (customer/business centric) while another who in inward facing (operations centric).

But there has to be a clear delineation in roles and responsibilities, so that one doesn't step on the others' toes. The other aspect is to be brutally honest with each other, and actually have a transition plan, as a company scales. More often than not, founders are great at the early stages of a company, but a new seasoned management team is necessary to scale the business to tens of millions of dollars and beyond in revenue.

Sometimes, I have found myself in situations where two buddies who founded the company are no longer capable of running the company (i.e. the company has grown to a size beyond what the founders can handle). The truly remarkable founders/CEOs are ones who realise when they are no longer right people to be at the helm of the company.

They often step aside, or take on a role of a chairman/evangelist and let a more seasoned CEO steer the company forward. But for a variety of reasons, ranging from "giving up control", to "title creep (still needing to be CxO)", to sheer ego, founders end up in a tiff with each other or with the Board. Let me give you a specific example. There is a company where two co-founders (Founders A and B, close friends for many years) started a company with operations and market in India, while they were still in the US. The plan was for them to move to India. But for a variety of personal reasons, Founder A simply could not make the move to India. Founder B, as a result, ended up doing most of the work.

Even though founder A was no longer contributing, founder B didn't want to let him go due to the long personal friendship. Founder B, as a Board member, has a fiduciary responsibility to do the right thing, and let his buddy go (since he was no longer actively contributing to the company). The unvested equity held by founder A was no longer working towards creating value for the company. Founders often have a hard time choosing between a fiduciarily responsible decision and an emotional personal relationship. By having a detailed conversation around roles and transitions at the onset, founders (who are also good friends) can avoid awkward situations downstream.

3. CEOs Hire Weak Team Members

This is partially related to the previous point. Strong CEOs sometimes try to carry everyone with them rather than hiring people who stand up on their own. Again, there may be team members who are dear friends, but may actually not be the best person for the position. CEOs need to do what's optimum for the company and the shareholders, not their friends or their ego.

Most successful CEOs will utter the following words "always surround yourself with people smarter than you". Again, if entrepreneurs are honest with themselves and actually adhere to that mantra, they will build a strong company, and an equally strong culture of hiring better and hiring smarter. Many CEOs or executives, due to either ignorance or arrogance, end up settling for weaker team members.

The reason for hiring strong team members is simply that they will question the status quo, and the traditional way of thinking. They will be a resource for the CEO and the Board to help determine the company's overall strategy. For startups with constrained resources and continuous threat from incumbents, there needs to be a team with a combination of smart out-of-the-box thinking/questioning, scrappiness and uncompromising tenacity. Often founders, who are junior from an experience standpoint, do not want to let go of a lofty title. My recommendation is that one would often be much better off working at a director or manager level for a seasoned VP or CxO from the outside, than try to learn on the job as a CxO or SVP themselves.

4. They Want to Do Too Much

Usually, successful start-ups figure out a narrow niche that they can dominate and then expand from there. This is where the bowling pin analogy is helpful. Often entrepreneurs face a dilemma of "appearing big enough" to a VC especially during a fundraising discussion, but at the same time being able to focus on a particular segment of a market. There is also a balance between being flexible/nimble as a startup, but at the same time not looking completely lost or defocused.

Often, startups have to experiment and try a variety of approaches to products, channels, business models, but they also have to make sure that there is discipline and analysis behind the decision making. Bottom line: stay focused, become dominant is a very targeted segment or vertical, and with that success as foundation, expand into adjacent areas. Entrepreneurs should paint a long term big picture, in terms of a game changing vision, but be laser focused in their execution, especially when starting up. Admittedly, this is easier said than done (as with most of my articles).

5. They Go after Too Small a Market

Selling ice to Eskimos is a trivial but poignant example. You may have the best customised ice sculptures, but it doesn't mean a whole lot if the market is either too small or non-existent. This is often the case when entrepreneurs develop a technology looking for a problem, rather than developing a product having researched a market and determining that the opportunity exists, it's large and customers are willing to pay for the right product or service.

Another way of looking at this is to see how much "better, faster, cheaper" one can make a solution compared to something that already exists. Trying to improve existing solutions by 10 or 20% doesn't usually have an impact. Order of magnitude impact in terms of price/performance is a lot more interesting. Having said that, companies often are created not to address an existing market, but one that is anticipated to emerge.

In India, for example, several companies were created and funded prematurely relying on broadband penetration that was supposed to happen in India. Examples around mobile video or location based services are other areas where current market is tiny, but they will emerge. A very tough question to answer is one of timing—Should a startup wait for a market to be ripe, or build a solution while guesstimating market maturation? I am more a proponent of the former, since there is quantifiable opportunity that often does not require behaviour change, and complete customer education. There is a reference in terms of incumbent products/technologies against which the startup can measure its own offering, in terms of being significantly better, faster and/or cheaper.

6. They Don't Charge Enough from Their Customers to Survive

They often think their VCs are their customers and that a nice VC pitch is all they need to make to get more money. There is no better cash source than happy, marque price-insensitive customers. Just like many other challenges faced by a startup, determining a business model and more specifically pricing is one of them. Although it's ok to provide a discount for the early alpha/beta customers, it's usually not the right move to compete based simply on pricing.

Also, it's crucial to have a very good idea of costs of creating and delivering one's product or service, so that pricing and margins are enough to sustain a growing company. The aforementioned is an obvious statement, but one would be amazed at how often entrepreneurs don't actually have a good handle on their margins. In India, which happens to be a more price sensitive economy than most, it's extremely difficult to start with a low price and raise it over time. The reverse will likely be true. Bottom line: base the pricing on a quantifiable ROI to the customer, and have an incredibly capital efficient production and distribution base. Margins tend to shrink, not expand, as offerings get commoditised over time.

7. They Hire Too Many People up Front

Too many mouths to feed too early can sink a company. Keep a low burn until you have your business model in place. In some businesses it is crucial to have a team in place to be able to deliver the product or service. There is usually training involved, so people do need to be hired slightly ahead of revenue. But often, especially in good times, startups hire too many people prior to having clarity of the business model or revenue visibility.

Having a high burn without either having a product/service to sell, or a process to deliver that particular product or service, is the number one reason, in my mind, why startups fail. Startup investments happen in tranches or series of funding that are usually tied to a company hitting specific milestones. But if the burn is high, those early product milestones are not hit in time, and companies have an incredibly difficult time raising additional capital.

On the technology front, early hires are usually engineering centric to develop and refine the product. Once the product is getting close to market release (as alpha/beta), that's when sales, business development and customer facing hires come into play. The aforementioned is a slight generalisation and seems fairly obvious, but one would be amazed at how frequently this particular mistake is made, often by seasoned entrepreneurs. I have had experience with several companies where, due to the economic/market environment, a RIF (reduction in force) had to take place.

What's more amazing is that in most cases, after the RIF, the company's performance did not suffer in terms of revenue, and bottom line improved drastically. Lesson learned: companies can be much more capital and team efficient than they realize. Often it's only after a startup goes through the over-hiring and then laying-off cycle that entrepreneurs realise that they truly can do more with less.

8. Sheer Luck (or Lack Thereof)

Startups can and do get broadsided by competitors, new technologies, big companies changing direction, regulatory environment, etc. This is one that squarely belongs in the category that's completely "out of one's control". Startups' success depends on a blend of luck and skill.

One can argue about the percentage splits between the two. In India, this point may be more true than most places, given the regulatory environment that exists in many sectors. And given the mood of large organisations like the RBI, SEBI, or the various ministries and their dynamic mandates, startups can either tremendously benefit or completely get clobbered by the decisions made. In India, there are grey areas around topics like Service tax, which can cause significant burden or relief depending whether a company is liable or not.

Given my aerospace background, I had a chance to see direct impact on technology companies catering to the defense sector getting tremendous benefit when the Republicans were in the White House vs the Democrats. Finally, often cash rich incumbents can simply play a loss-leading pricing game to crush a startup.

9. They Don't Work Hard Enough or Fast Enough or Smart Enough

All those little decisions add up to an outcome. Awareness of the market dynamics subtleties are ignored or not analysed/understood as well as they should be. It's important, for example, in India to realise that this is primarily a cash based economy, and on top of that a pre-paid economy. So, trying to enter the Indian market with a credit-card-based purely online subscription model, may not work, especially if the product or service is to be delivered to a broad consumer base.

DFJ has companies in our portfolios who have faced the very same challenges, so the nimble startups have to keep their finger on the market pulse and continuously adjust (without throwing darts in the dark) based on market feedback. Although not often the case,

there are times when startups get a bit complacent. This could be due to over confidence in the technology, or on the other extreme, due to fatigue, especially if the company has been going on but been relatively flat for a number of quarters or years.

Sometimes technology entrepreneurs get a bit detached from their eventual customers, not realising that the needs of the market are changing, or the customer behaviour is morphing and as a result the product also needs to change. Lack of that adaptation, or not doing so fast enough, can also lead to a dire end. Let me give another hypothetical example. If a company relies on acquiring online merchants to be able to provide a service like search engine optimisation, or an advertising network to an online publisher, then it's crucial to have a process in place to be able to add those merchants seamlessly and quickly if the business is to scale. Yet, if that company has an Oracle like culture, and the QA process for every merchant addition takes 8–10 weeks, the company is doomed.

10. They Don't Take Enough Risks

Some start-up entrepreneurs think that they should operate as though they are big companies. This is wrong. They will never beat Microsoft or Google at their own game. They must get creative and do things differently, even at the risk of embarrassment. The incredibly successful entrepreneurs are those who thought monumental, not incremental.

11. Bonus Point (Buy 10, Get 1 Free, Recession Special)

Entrepreneurs get greedy. This may be ironic coming from a VC. The sole focus of the entrepreneur should be to create a large profitable long term entity. The big pain point for the entrepreneurs, and understandably so, is around dilution that they suffer when raising capital. That concern often leads to sub-optimal decision making.

For example, especially in times of financial uncertainty like today when valuations tend to be lower, founders/promoters tend to take less money to minimise dilution. My advice to entrepreneurs is "when offered capital, take it". It's almost always better to take more capital than less because it usually takes longer and more capital to hit key milestones.

Bottom line: Entrepreneurship is for those with thick skin, and sheer tenacity to be able to hear lots of "no's" but not be deterred. Having said that, passion alone cannot guarantee success and due in part to reasons given above, startups fail. What's equally important to realise is that it's "ok to fail".

I am obviously not implying that one should strive for failure. Silicon Valley is filled with entrepreneurs who failed their first and even second time before they finally had a success under their belts.

The learning involved in going through a rough startup experience can be tremendous. In India, I feel a sense of risk aversion among entrepreneurs where a stigma still lingers (whether real or perceived) around failure. I think only when that viewpoint changes, will we start seeing truly monumental ideas coming out of India, rather than the incremental "low risk, low reward" variety.

UNIT 5

Special Issues for the Entrepreneur

Unit Selections

Key Points to Consider

- What is a social entrepreneur?

- How does a social entrepreneur differ from a "regular" entrepreneur?

- How does microfinance work? Where in the world would it be most successful?

- What is the difference between a non-profit and a for-profit organization?

- How can entrepreneurs minimize the impact of their businesses on the environment?

- What are the benefits of "going global" for entrepreneurs?

- What products/services have the best potential for global sales?

- What are some of the problems and barriers to entrepreneurs "going global"?

- What exit strategies are available to entrepreneurs?

- How do the exit strategies differ among the various investors?

Student Website

www.mhcls.com

Internet References

Ashoka
   http://www.ashoka.org/

Bill & Melinda Gates Foundation
   http://www.gatesfoundation.org/Pages/home.aspx

Center for Advancing Social Entrepreneurship (CASE)
   http://www.caseatduke.org/

Center for Social Innovation
   http://www.gsb.stanford.edu/csi/

Grameen Foundation
   http://www.grameen-info.org/

Milken Institute
   http://www.milkeninstitute.org

Global Entrepreneurship Week
   http://www.unleashingideas.org/

VolunteerMatch.org
   http://www.volunteermatch.org/

This unit looks at three special issues for today's entrepreneur. The first issue examines social entrepreneurship in nonprofits and for-profit organizations. The second issue is learning how to be "born global" and understand the challenges facing global entrepreneurs. The third issue discusses the last stage in the entrepreneurial life cycle, the exit strategy whether it is increasing positive cash flows for the owners or selling out to a larger company and paying back the investors.

A social or nonprofit entrepreneur uses established, proven entrepreneurial management practices primarily in the public and nonprofit sectors to solve a range of social problems in the areas of health, safety, environmental protection, and community involvement. Social entrepreneurs create and manage not-for-profit projects, events, organizations, and programs that are measured by means other than bottom-line profits. The nonprofit sector they lead comprises 7 percent of U.S. gross domestic product—a number that grows even larger when health care and public education are included.

Increasingly, consumers, investors, business partners, employees and other stakeholders are choosing to deal with progressive companies that not only produce and deliver the goods and services but have acceptable, even exceptional, corporate values. Local communities now expect from companies a place of productive and healthful employment in the community. The communities also expect participation of company officials in community affairs, provision of regular employment, fair play, reasonable purchases made in the local community, interest in and support of local government, support of cultural and charitable projects.

Globalization represents one of the most influential forces in determining the future course of business. The term was first coined in the 1980s. We define globalization as the democratizing of access to local market knowledge, customer information, services, products, and capital across national, cultural, and linguistic boundaries. According to McKinsey and Company, 80 percent of the world's GDP will be sold across international borders by 2027, compared to about 20 percent in 2001. Multinational business activity will grow from approximately $5 trillion to $70 trillion by 2027. To understand how this is happening consider your desktop computer. It might have been assembled in Mexico with Chinese components; it uses chips designed in the United States, manufactured in Malaysia, and preinstalled with software applications that were jointly developed in India and Ireland.

Global expansion favors smaller, entrepreneurial companies. It gives them access to capital, technology, talent, and markets that previously only big firms could reach. Small firms with fewer than 500 employees make up 97.3 percent of U.S. exporting activities. A global entrepreneur seeks out and conducts new and innovative business activities across national borders. These activities may consist of exporting, licensing, opening a new sales office, or acquiring another venture.

The final articles in this unit support our belief that having a harvest goal in mind and creating an exit strategy to achieve

© The McGraw-Hill Companies, Inc/Jill Braaten, photographer

it are what separate successful entrepreneurs from the rest. Clearly, the main objective of professional entrepreneurs is to create economic value. It is unfortunate that little attention in the entrepreneurial world has been given to exiting a business venture, or what has come to be called harvesting the business.

But just because a venture team can build a successful business doesn't mean they can become rich from it. Investors who provide equity financing to high-risk ventures need to know how and when they are likely to realize a return on their investments before they commit any funds. They invest not for eternity but on average for three to seven years, after which they expect to make a profit that reflects the scale of the risk they have taken on in making their investment. An exit should be seen as a critical milestone that focuses on the transferring of ownership. It is at this stage in the entrepreneurial life cycle that the capital gains (or losses) occur, or, in other words, that there is a harvest (or exit) from the investment.

The harvest of a business is the venture team's and investors' combined strategy for achieving the final cash rewards on their capital investment. This unit also explores the last activity in the entrepreneurial life cycle. In his book *The Seven Habits of Highly Effective People,* Steven Covey says that one of the keys to being effective in life is "beginning with the end in mind." To paraphrase Covey, entrepreneurs need to visualize the end of their venture and then develop a plan to make it happen even though it may take 5, 10, 15 years, or more to build a venture of significant net worth.

The harvest of a business venture represents the ending of a long struggle to build financial values and represents an emotional end to a rewarding experience. But a harvest decision does not always mean that the entrepreneur will leave the company. If the entrepreneur is successful, significant value will have been created. The issue then becomes harvesting and distributing that value. The structuring of a harvest strategy depends on options available to the entrepreneur. Many of these options depend on an assessment of the value of the business, which is a most difficult task. When it comes to developing a harvest strategy for the entrepreneur and the investors, the entrepreneur will need to attempt to value the company's assets for which a great amount of incomplete and conflicting information may exist. Based upon the valuation, there can be a number of alternatives available to the entrepreneur to end the venture—some are straightforward, others involve more complex financial strategy. This unit presents the reader with a brief look at these options.

For almost all entrepreneurs, ending a venture is a huge undertaking. A venture worth harvesting is a venture that becomes a dominant part of their lives. Thus, the decision to harvest a venture cannot effectively be made apart from the entrepreneur's personal goals. Creating such a strategy can never begin too early in the venture because, as with planning in other situations, the process itself is more important than the plan. Entrepreneurs should look at the harvesting of a venture as a point in the future where preparation and opportunity meet, not necessarily when an opportunity is at an end.

Taking Social Entrepreneurship Seriously

J. GREGORY DEES

A cursory look at world affairs should convince any thinking and caring person, regardless of political ideology, that we have considerable room for improvement. Despite the tremendous strides in the quality of life that humankind has made in the past two centuries, many persistent problems remain and new ones have emerged. Rapid economic growth and various experiments with activist governments have not been sufficient to lift a huge portion of the world population out of poverty. Curable and preventable diseases still cause tremendous suffering and claim many lives, particularly among the poor. Access to education and the quality of education vary widely across the globe, even within some developed countries. Slavery and human trafficking are more serious and widespread than most of us care to admit. Violence and conflict abound on personal, tribal, national, regional, and global levels. The earth is warming, polar icecaps are melting, and bio-diversity is declining at an unusually high rate, raising serious questions about the impact on future generations, regardless of the cause. The list could go on and on. We may not all agree on our visions for an ideal world, but we can generally agree that the gap between reality and our notions of the ideal is still enormous.

One potentially promising strategy for improvement is to encourage and support social entrepreneurs, individuals, and organizations that bring to social problems the same kind of determination, creativity, and resourcefulness that we find among business entrepreneurs. One prime example is the 2006 Nobel Peace Prize winner Muhammad Yunus, who founded the highly successful Grameen Bank in Bangladesh to provide credit to the poor to help them move out of poverty. Two of the 2006 MacArthur Fellowship winners were also leading social entrepreneurs. Victoria Hale founded the Institute for OneWorld Health, a nonprofit pharmaceutical company that develops safe, effective, affordable medicines for developing countries, and Jim Fruchterman is a Silicon Valley engineer who created Benetech to craft technological solutions to social needs, ranging from literacy to human rights and landmine detection.

The concept of "social entrepreneurship" emerged in the 1980s from the work of Bill Drayton at Ashoka, funding social innovators around the world, and Ed Skloot at New Ventures, helping nonprofits explore new sources of income. It has come into its own in the last decade, capturing the imaginations of many thoughtful observers. For instance, David Gergen, Harvard professor and former advisor to four U.S. presidents, has described social entrepreneurs as the "new engines of reform." Numerous universities, including Harvard, Stanford, Columbia, New York University, Oxford, and Duke have launched centers or major initiatives in this arena. The World Economic Forum has openly embraced social entrepreneurship, and the Forum's founders, Klaus and Hilde Schwab, have created their own Foundation for Social Entrepreneurship. Jeffrey Skoll, eBay's first president, has devoted his foundation to "investing in, connecting, and celebrating social entrepreneurs." Actor and director Robert Redford hosted a Public Broadcasting series in 2005 on the "New Heroes," supported by the Skoll Foundation, to profile successful social entrepreneurs. Major media outlets from the *New York Times* to the *Economist* have run feature articles on this trend. The Manhattan Institute, with which Husock is affiliated, gives an annual Social Entrepreneurship Award. The embrace of this concept cuts across political and national boundaries, with activities and interest cropping up around the world.

Is this attention and excitement warranted? Does social entrepreneurship have the potential to create sustainable and scalable impact in arenas where government efforts have been ineffective? After studying this activity for over a decade, I am convinced that social entrepreneurs, operating outside of the constraints of government, significantly enhance our ability to find and implement effective solutions to social problems. Of course, the real test of any thesis of this sort lies in action and results. My goal in these pages is to convince readers that we should take social entrepreneurship seriously and make the necessary investment of resources, time, and energy to give this idea a serious and sustained test.

Government as Problem Solver

To put the current interest in social entrepreneurship in perspective, it is useful to think about human history as a series of experiments in social organization—from family, clan, and tribal structures to the elaborate governmental, corporate, and social structures of today. These experiments can be seen as a response to the question: How should we organize ourselves, publicly and privately, to move closer to the ideals of a good society? This article is not the place to trace the evolution of different forms of social organization, but it is helpful to look back briefly at a particular turning point in late eighteenth-century Europe that had ripple effects around the world.

The major social problem of the day was poverty. Some leading political thinkers, such as Thomas Paine and the Marquis de Condorcet, recognized the ineffectiveness of charity and, in the spirit of the Enlightenment, proposed more scientific and secular state-based alternatives. Charity was largely grounded in the practice of alms giving, typically organized by the church. The term comes from the Latin *caritas,* referring to a sentiment, compassion for others, which was not always a reliable or effective platform for action. It allowed givers to demonstrate their virtue, but charity at best provided temporary relief for the poor. This relief did not always reach all those that could benefit from it, and many feared it exacerbated the very problem at which it was directed, creating dependency and undermining the industriousness of the poor. According to historian Gareth Stedman Jones, in his book *An End to Poverty,* Paine, Condorcet, and their fellow travelers offered a secular and rational alternative. A republican state could take a scientific approach to administer aid to the poor in a more rigorous, fair, and effective way. Though their particular schemes were not immediately implemented, these thinkers planted the seeds for social democracy and the welfare state.

The Enlightenment positioned government as the main actor in resolving social problems that were not addressed by economic development. Building on the seventeenth-century scientific revolution, and with Newtonian mechanics as the paradigm, it made sense for the state to take on the central role in engineering a solution to poverty. Of course, this shift away from religious, sentimental approaches to poverty was taken to new heights in the late nineteenth and twentieth centuries by Karl Marx and his followers. Over the course of the past two centuries, the world has witnessed a variety of experiments in government-based efforts to tackle poverty, as well as other social and environmental problems. Over this period, a mixed religious and secular civil society continued to evolve and play a complementary role, but the hope for social problem solving has largely been on government.

While this focus on government as social problem solver led to some notable successes, such as increased access to education and health care for many, the experience also revealed the limits of government as the vehicle for social problem solving. It has become clear that large-scale, top-down government programs have serious drawbacks. No clear principles of "social mechanics" have emerged to guide central planning. Even physical science has moved beyond the billiard-ball world of Newtonian mechanics. Communism, socialism, and the welfare state have been subjected to the same kind of criticism that was leveled against the charity of old. They, too, run the risk of creating dependency, perhaps even more so because of the sense of entitlement they can create.

Government service delivery, including in the relatively successful arenas of education and health care, has been criticized as bureaucratic, ineffective, wasteful, too political, and antithetical to innovation. Because of the risks of fraud, waste, and abuse of power, bureaucracy became the dominant organizing method for government agencies. This is not an organizing mode that is conducive to creative problem solving. In hindsight, these shortcomings are not surprising given the incentives and decision mechanism common to governmental organizations. Government alone is clearly not the answer. After two centuries of aggressive experimentation with different forms of government, we have learned, at the very least, that government is a tool that is effective for some kinds of social interventions but not as effective for others. We do not need to enter the ideological debates about the appropriate role and size of government to recognize the potential value of bringing private initiative, ingenuity, and resources to the table.

Through various government efforts to solve social problems, we have learned that with all our scientific knowledge and rational planning, we still do not know in advance what will work effectively. Thus, progress in the social sphere depends on a process of innovation and experimentation akin to entrepreneurship in the business world. When the Austrian economist Joseph Schumpeter formulated his theory of economic development, he saw entrepreneurs playing a central role. They drove development by "carrying out new combinations." They could modify existing products or services, develop new ones, improve production and marketing processes, find new sources or supply, take existing products into new markets, or create new forms of organization. In so doing, as he later put it, they "reform or revolutionize the pattern of production." And they shift resources into areas of higher yield and productivity, to paraphrase J. B. Say, the eighteenth-century French economist who popularized the term "entrepreneur." To be sure, large firms engage in incremental innovations, but as Carl Schramm and Robert Litan of the Kauffman Foundation recently put it, "Radical breakthroughs tend to be disproportionately developed and brought to market by a single individual or new firm." Social entrepreneurs are needed to play the same innovating role with regard to social needs and problems.

Social and business entrepreneurs uncover or create new opportunities through a process of exploration, innovation, experimentation, and resource mobilization. This is an active, messy, highly decentralized learning process. Decentralization is critical because finding what works depends on having the right knowledge, being able to envision new combinations, and having the freedom to test ideas through action. The necessary knowledge cannot easily be centralized; much of it is local and dispersed among the population. As a result, some people will see opportunities and conceive of promising new combinations that others could not envision. Because of the creative nature of this process, centralizing social problem solving makes about as much sense as centralizing art production. Finally, since independent entrepreneurs must mobilize resources to continue to pursue their visions, they have to persuade financiers who are putting their money behind the idea and talented employees who are devoting their time and skills that this venture is worthwhile. This selection process provides a discipline, albeit imperfect, that helps narrow the funnel to those ideas that have better chances of working. When it works well, this decentralized process allows bad ideas to fall by the wayside, encourages lessons to be learned, and provides an incentive for continuous improvement of the more promising ones.

This entrepreneurial process is similar to the path of natural selection, involving a continuous cycle of differentiation, selection, and expansion. Just as high levels of biodiversity (differentiation) characterize a vibrant ecosystem, high levels of entrepreneurship characterize a vibrant economy and high levels of social entrepreneurship should come to characterize a healthy society. No "solution" is likely to bring us to an ideal state and keep us there forever. Society will change over time just as ecosystems change. New challenges will arise as we make progress on the old ones. Thus, the need for this independent innovation process has no foreseeable end.

Why can't government agencies do this? When compared to government agencies, independent social entrepreneurs have several distinct advantages. They have greater freedom of action and can usually move more quickly than public officials. They can explore a wider range of alternatives, largely because they are not as constrained by bureaucratic rules, legislative mandates, political considerations, and a fixed budget. Social entrepreneurs can tailor their efforts to different communities or markets in ways that would be difficult for government programs. Moreover, independent social entrepreneurs have access to private resources, while private contributions to government are relatively rare. Thus, social entrepreneurs are able to attract voluntary gifts of money, time, and in-kind donations, leveraging public money devoted to the same problem with philanthropy, social investment, or earned income from their business ventures.

The reliance on independent social entrepreneurs also provides society with greater opportunities to learn with less risk. Government programs usually represent relatively large bets on fairly standardized interventions with commitments to a certain course of action that can be very hard to modify once announced. As economists Douglas North and Robert Thomas observed, "government solutions entail the additional cost of being stuck with the decision in the future—that is, withdrawal costs are higher than those related to voluntary organizations." With social entrepreneurs we have more and smaller bets on varied efforts to tackle the same social problem. When we have high levels of uncertainly about the best approach, diversification and experimentation increase the opportunities for learning and success. Diversification of activity has the added benefit of reducing the costs of failure during this learning process. If some of the small bets fail, the impact will be far less than the failure of a large-scale government program. To the extent that these experiments are privately funded, this learning process does not come at great public expense.

Furthermore, some social innovations are unlikely to be very effective if they are carried out by governmental organizations. The private nature of social ventures can be a distinct advantage.

Consider Planned Parenthood, Alcoholics Anonymous, the Sierra Club, Habitat for Humanity, or community foundations. Could these work as well as branches of government? It seems unlikely. Boy and Girl Scouts would certainly take on a very different connotation if the government ran these programs. A rape crisis center might be effective in large part because it is run and staffed by volunteers who have been victims of rape themselves. Would victims of rape trust the center as much if it were government run? Additionally, in some cases, it is important to work across governmental levels and jurisdictional boundaries. The Nobel Prize winning organization, *Medecins Sans Frontieres* (Doctors Without Borders) captures this notion in its very name. It is much harder for government agencies to work effectively across boundaries. Since many social and environmental issues cut across these boundaries, it makes sense for the organizations tackling them to be organized accordingly. Thus, many innovative approaches to social problems are not only best started outside government, they are best kept outside government.

Social entrepreneurs have an important role to play, whether it is to complement or supplant government efforts. They are better positioned to innovate and experiment than government agencies. They have flexibility in how they serve their missions that should allow them to be more efficient and effective. They increase our chances of learning, and they bring private resources to the table. Unfortunately, until recently, they were not taken as seriously as they should be as an important driver of social progress. People tended to focus on government and markets as the main social forces, treating the "third sector" as marginal, rather than as a potential major engine for progress. Yet, independent social entrepreneurs have the potential to play the same role in addressing social needs that business entrepreneurs play in what economic Nobel Laureate Edmund Phelps calls "dynamic capitalism." Social entrepreneurship engages the problem-solving skills and local knowledge of many individuals and organizations in search of innovative solutions. As a result, it has some powerful advantages over centralized policy analysis and planning.

Charity and Problem-Solving

The recent rise of interest in social entrepreneurship is definitely not a case of the pendulum swinging away from government, back to charity, as much as some political commentators, such as Marvin Olasky, might like to see. Today's social entrepreneurs do not see themselves as engaged in "charity" in the traditional, alms-giving sense. They recognize its limits and weaknesses, as did the Enlightenment critics. Muhammad Yunus makes the point forcefully: "When we want to help the poor, we usually offer them charity. Most often we use charity to avoid recognizing the problem and finding a solution for it. Charity becomes a way to shrug off our responsibility. Charity is no solution to poverty. Charity only perpetuates poverty by taking the initiative away from the poor. Charity allows us to go ahead with our own lives without worrying about those of the poor. It appeases our consciences."

Other social entrepreneurs may not object as strongly to charity. However, even those who acknowledge a need for temporary relief tend to view their own work as fundamentally different. They aim to create sustainable improvements and are willing to draw on self-interest, as well as compassion to do it.

Social entrepreneurship represents another step in the continuing reinvention of the "third sector" over the past one hundred and fifty years. The Enlightenment brought not only a shift in political philosophy it also changed private charitable institutions. Many of them embraced the new rationality leading to the rise of what historian Gertrude Himmelfarb calls "scientific charity." This shift generated a relative boom of new organizations in the later nineteenth and early twentieth centuries. The movement included new religious charities with more "scientific" approaches, the creation of secular charitable institutions, professionally run philanthropic foundations, and the establishment of new helping professions, such as social work. The Salvation Army, YMCA, Boys and Girls Clubs, and many prominent third-sector organizations and major foundations trace their roots to this era.

Leading social entrepreneurs today are most aptly described as pragmatists. They are focused on achieving sustainable results and will use whatever tools are most likely to work. They embrace innovation, value effective management, and are open to a wide range of operational and business models. They are willing to adapt ideas and tools from business when these will help. They are even willing to use for-profit forms of organization or hybrid structures that include for-profit and nonprofit elements. When it is possible, social entrepreneurs will happily craft market-based solutions that rely only on self-interest, allowing scarce philanthropic or government resources to flow to areas that genuinely need subsidy. If they can find an overlooked market opportunity that also improves social conditions, they will gladly pursue it. Yunus's Grameen Bank is legally a for-profit institution owned by its borrowers and is now financially self-sustaining.

Recognizing that for-profit or hybrid organizations may have an important role in creating better social conditions, some new philanthropists are disregarding old sector boundaries. When Silicon Valley venture capitalists Brook Byers and John Doerr started the New Schools Venture Fund, they decided to use it to fund both nonprofit and for-profit ventures that have the potential to create major improvements in K-12 education. Recently, the giant Internet search company Google decided that instead of creating the typical nonprofit company foundation, it would create its philanthropic arm as a for-profit capable of investing in nonprofit or for-profit ventures with a social purpose, such as more fuel-efficient vehicles. The lines between for-profit and nonprofit are breaking down as social entrepreneurs and entrepreneurial philanthropists look for new ways to tackle a range of social issues from alternative energy to improvements in health care.

Today's social entrepreneurs are building on the tradition of Ben Franklin. When Franklin saw opportunities to improve life for his fellow citizens in Philadelphia, he pursued them in whatever form seemed most sensible. He created for-profit printing and publishing businesses to keep citizens informed, a voluntary firefighting association to protect the homes of members, a subscription-based lending library, and a philanthropically supported academy that became the University of Pennsylvania, just to mention a few examples. For each entrepreneurial venture Franklin adopted an economic, operating, and legal structure that was suitable given the circumstances. Social entrepreneurs operating today embrace this legacy of pragmatic private initiatives to improve social conditions. They do not see themselves as "charities" or even as "nonprofits," though they often use that legal form of organization. They are entrepreneurs who move comfortably across sector boundaries in search of the best ways to achieve sustainable impact.

A Supportive Infrastructure

The current boom in social entrepreneurship exists despite a relatively poor understanding of this work. Those who take it up often lack the resources and infrastructure they need to succeed at a significant scale. They are swimming against the current of cultural assumptions and biases. As a society, we have not openly embraced social entrepreneurship, do not appreciate the crucial differences between social entrepreneurship and charity, and have not yet constructed the kinds of cultural and institutional mechanisms social entrepreneurs need to be effective. Though today's social entrepreneurs represent a break from sentimental, alms-giving charity, their work is still inhibited by the old norms and assumptions of alms-giving charity that permeate the sector. Even social entrepreneurs who feel they can adopt a for-profit legal form do not find the kind of support they need to blend social and financial objectives. If we want to capitalize on this current wave of interest and test the potential of social entrepreneurship, we need to create an environment conducive to success. We need to support social entrepreneurs with a more efficient and robust infrastructure, appropriate public policy, and a change in the culture of the social sector.

The relatively efficient and effective markets that we know today evolved over centuries as appropriate institutions, public policies, and cultural values were developed. On the infrastructure side, capitalism grew with the increase in wholesale markets and fairs, bourses, banking instruments, insurance for trade voyages, and the like. Today we have very sophisticated financial markets, business schools engaged in both education and research, and many supportive associations for business organizations. The investment in developing this infrastructure has been tremendous. We need similar institutions to develop and make available to social entrepreneurs appropriate funding, talent, knowledge, and social capital. We also need to modify our current institutions to align them more with the requirements of social entrepreneurship, making significant changes in philanthropy, other financial services, research, and educational programs. Fortunately, a number of thoughtful players in this sector are working hard to develop new institutions.

On the policy side, capitalism relied upon clear property rights, systems for enforcing contracts, and a variety of supportive investments by governments. For social entrepreneurship to flourish, we need public policies that recognize and deliberately harness its potential. These policies should free social entrepreneurs to innovate and experiment, manage the risk of this experimentation, encourage private investors to support this activity, and allow those involved to reap appropriate rewards for their success. Even though Grameen Bank is a private initiative, it is owned in small part by the government of Bangladesh, and it required special legislation so that it could take savings deposits and operate as a formal financial institution. Without these deposits it would not have been able to grow nearly as rapidly. As social entrepreneurs experiment with new business models, we may need new legal forms of organization, such as the "community interest company" category recently created in the United Kingdom. As philanthropists and other financial backers experiment with the best ways to use their resources to support social entrepreneurs, we may need changes in the legal structures and rules for doing that kind of investing as well.

Capitalism required a culture that allowed for trust and a comfort with transactions beyond family and tribal boundaries, as well as a culture in which profit making is morally acceptable. Similarly, in the social sector, we need a culture that honors and taps into the altruistic impulses that have fueled charity in the past, but directs those impulses toward impact and performance. We need a culture that accepts failure as essential for learning and that honors effectiveness and efficiency as much as the culture of charity honors sacrifice. We also need a culture that does not make it shameful to earn a decent living serving social purposes. Building the right supports will not be easy, but it is essential if this approach is to achieve its potential.

Challenges to Moving Forward

By making social entrepreneurs a recognized, strategic element in the process by which we improve social conditions, we have the potential to make headway in arenas that have remained vexing. The worldwide potential for mobilizing socially entrepreneurial behavior, if we were to make a deliberate effort to promote it, is enormous. However, this idea is relatively new, is still experimental, and it may not work as well as proponents (including myself) expect it to, just as activist governments did not work as well as many expected it to. Several issues could be raised, but three stand out as especially important: social impact assessment, the selection-investment processes, and scalability.

Entrepreneurship works well in business because markets tend to reinforce value creation both for customers and for investors. Businesses that do not create sufficient value for these two groups usually wither and fail. The test is whether customers will pay enough to cover the costs of production and to generate an attractive return for investors. An attractive return is one that is comparable to or better than those generated by alternative investments of similar risk. Businesses with strong track records and indications of future potential can grow relatively rapidly because of the size of the financial markets and the ability of these markets to respond quickly. These measures are definitely not foolproof. Even seasoned business investors make serious mistakes. However, customer and financial markets work reasonably well to identify, select, and scale firms that are creating the most customer and investor value. The same cannot be said of social entrepreneurship.

Social impact is difficult to measure in a reliable, timely, and cost-effective fashion—especially for the most ambitious social ventures. How and when do we know that someone has been moved out of poverty in a sustainable way or that a strategy will slow global warming? Signs, symptoms, and leading indicators often must be used to provide clues to whether an intervention is having its intended impact. Many innovations that sound logical and promising fail in practice or produce unintended harms that offset the gains. Even with micro-finance, the innovation for which Yunus won the Nobel Peace Prize, attempts to demonstrate its impact in a rigorous and systematic way have produced mixed and sometimes confusing results. The stories of impact on individuals and their families are plenty and powerful, but methods for systematic evaluation have been a subject of debate. Even when the intended impact can be assessed reliably, it may be difficult to attribute causation without very well controlled studies that are costly and complicated. Children who participate in a voluntary after-school tutoring program may have better graduation rates than their classmates, but this could be driven by other factors, such as educated and motivated parents. Even when causation can be established, comparisons across organizations can be very difficult unless they have a very similar mission, strategy, operating environment, and target population. Even among domestic educational interventions, how do we compare Teach for America, the Gates Foundation's U.S. Libraries initiative, and Edison Schools? This does not mean the situation is hopeless. Innovators are working on this challenge and making some headway, but we need to develop better ways to identify the most promising innovations, sort out the failures, and learn from these experiments. In the meantime, we must operate with greater uncertainty, making our best judgments in light of imperfect data.

Even if we can find methods to measure impact more accurately, we need natural selection processes that direct resources and support to the most promising innovations and away from the failed experiments. Current mechanisms in the social sector are highly imperfect, for at least two reasons. First, performance evaluation is not highly valued in the culture of charity. Charity is about compassion, sacrifice, and temporary relief. It is easy to see if you get food to a hungry person. Your motivations are between you and your God or conscience. Why invest in performance assessment? Better for the money to go for programs. This culture is crumbling, especially among major foundations and new philanthropists, but it still holds more sway than we recognize. The second reason selection is weak is that "investors" in the social sector, particularly philanthropists, are motivated by more than social impact. They allocate their capital for emotive and expressive reasons as well. Some want to thank the hospice that cared for their loved one, not reward the best hospice in the country. Others choose to support Green Peace instead of the Nature Conservancy, not because of a dispassionate assessment of which organization is doing a better job, but because they identify with the ideology and confrontational tactics of Green Peace. Still others want to support a needy organization, rather than one that seems to be doing well, even if the latter could create more impact dollar for dollar. As things stand, effective and efficient organizations may not be rewarded with additional resources, while ineffective and inefficient ones may thrive because they have a moving story to tell. Resource flows still depend more on sentiment, popular causes, personal charisma, and marketing skills than on social value creation. We need to move toward selection and investment processes that better align personal satisfaction of resource providers with the potential for impact.

Social entrepreneurs often find it very hard to scale. When they do scale, the process is usually very slow, particularly when viewed relative to the size and growth of the problems being addressed. Even Habitat for Humanity, one of the greatest growth stories of the social sector, cannot keep up with the need for housing in its target population. This is partly because the infrastructure, policy, and culture needed to support the growth has been lacking. It is also partly because private resources devoted to the social sector have been relatively small compared to the problems being addressed and poorly allocated. The oft-touted intergenerational transfer of wealth that we are experiencing in the United States may help, but this infusion of capital could represent a one-time boom, rather than a sustainable solution. To reduce the need for outside funding, many social entrepreneurs are experimenting with earned income strategies. Developing new business models may help, but even profitable businesses often must tap into outside markets for growth capital. Social ventures tend to have smaller pools to tap into. While many people are at work on innovations in the private funding markets for social entrepreneurs, it is still not clear whether the amount of private capital available will be sufficient and appropriately directed to scale the most promising innovations, raising the question of government involvement.

Government-supported programs can scale rather rapidly, when the political will and funding are present. This is because government has the power to coerce compliance and mobilize resources through taxation. But how do we avoid the problems associated with government programs? We need to learn from prior efforts to combine social entrepreneurship with government support to see how this might be done most effectively. What can we learn from charter school legislation, which opened the door to more education entrepreneurs by providing access to public funding? What can we learn from the rapid spread of hospices throughout the United States after Medicare agreed to reimburse for hospice care? Even some of the paradigms of independent social entrepreneurship, such as Teach for America and Habitat for Humanity, rely on some government funding. In his essay on "The Age of Social Transformation," Peter Drucker envisioned a society in which "Many social sector organizations will become partners with government" through voucher programs. He noted that these organizations would also be competitors with government, concluding, "The relationship between the two has yet to be worked out—and there is practically no precedent for it." Working this out may be essential to assure the scalability of effective social innovations.

Social entrepreneurship is a promising development that may lead into a new era in which we more effectively harness private initiative, ingenuity, and resources to improve social and environmental conditions. We need to provide the right support and we need to address fundamental questions.

Further Readings

Bornstein, David. 2004. *How to Change the World: Social Entrepreneurship and the Power of New Ideas.* New York: Oxford University Press.

Dees, J. Gregory, and Beth Battle Anderson. "Sector Bending: Blurring the Lines between Nonprofit and For-Profit," *Society* 40, 4, May/June 2003. Reprinted in Peter Frumkin and Jonathan B. Imber (eds.), *In Search of the Nonprofit Sector.* New Brunswick, NJ: Transaction Publishers, 2004.

Mosher-Williams, Rachel, ed. 2006. *Research on Social Entrepreneurship: Understanding and Contributing to an Emerging Field,* ARNOVA Occasional Paper Series, vol. 1, no. 3.

Nichols, Alex. 2006. *Social Entrepreneurship: New Paradigms of Sustainable Social Change.* New York: Oxford University Press.

Yunus, Muhammad. 1999. *Banker to the Poor: Micro-Lending and the Battle Against World Poverty.* New York: PublicAffairs.

J. GREGORY DEES is adjunct professor and faculty director of the Center for the Advancement of Social Entrepreneurship at Duke University's Fuqua School of Business. He is coauthor of *Enterprising Nonprofits and Strategic Tools for Social Entrepreneurs.*

The Microfinance Revolution: An Overview

The Nobel Prize committee awarded the 2006 Nobel Peace Prize to Muhammad Yunus and the Grameen Bank "for their efforts to create economic and social development from below." The microfinance revolution has come a long way since Yunus first provided financing to the poor in Bangladesh. The committee has recognized microfinance as "an important liberating force" and an "ever more important instrument in the struggle against poverty." Although several authors have provided comprehensive surveys of microfinance, our aim is somewhat more modest: This article is intended as a non-technical overview on the growth and development of microcredit and microfinance. (JEL I3, J41, N80)

RAJDEEP SENGUPTA AND CRAIG P. AUBUCHON

In 2006, the Grameen Bank and its founder Muhammad Yunus were awarded the Nobel Peace Prize for their efforts to reduce poverty in Bangladesh. By providing small loans to the extremely poor, the Grameen Bank offers these recipients the chance to become entrepreneurs and earn sufficiently high income to break themselves free from the cycle of poverty. Yunus's pioneering efforts have brought renewed attention to the field of microfinance as a tool to eliminate poverty; and, since 1976 when he first lent $27 to 42 stool makers, the Grameen Bank has grown to include more than 5.5 million members with greater than $5.2 billion in dispersed loans. As microfinance institutions continue to grow and expand, in both the developing and developed world, social activists and financial investors alike have begun to take notice. In this article we seek to explain the rise in microfinance since its inception in the early 1980s and the various mechanisms that make microfinance an effective tool in reducing poverty.[1] We also address the current problems facing microfinance and areas for future growth.

In its broadest sense, microcredit includes the act of providing loans of small amounts, often $100 or less, to the poor and other borrowers that have been ignored by commercial banks; under this definition, microcredit encompasses all lenders, including the formal participants (such as specialized credit cooperatives set up by the government for the provision of rural credit) and those of a more informal variety (such as the village moneylender or even loan sharks). Yunus (2007) argues that it is important to distinguish microcredit in all its previous forms from the specific form of credit adopted at the Grameen Bank, which he calls "Grameencredit." Yunus argues that the "most distinctive feature of *Grameencredit* is that it is not based on any collateral, or legally enforceable contracts. It is based on 'trust,' not on legal procedures and system." For the purposes of this article and unless mentioned otherwise, our use of the term microcredit will, for the most part, follow Yunus's characterization of Grameencredit.

Although the terms microcredit and micro-finance are often used interchangeably, it is important to recognize the distinction between the two. As mentioned before, microcredit refers to the act of providing the loan. Microfinance, on the other hand, is the act of providing these same borrowers with financial services, such as savings institutions and insurance policies. In short, microfinance encompasses the field of microcredit. Currently, it is estimated that anywhere from 1,000 to 2,500 microfinance institutions (MFIs) serve some 67.6 million clients in over 100 different countries.[2]

Many MFIs have a dual mandate to provide financial as well as social services, such as health care and educational services for the underprivileged. In this sense, they are not always perceived as profit-maximizing financial institutions. At the same time, the remarkable accomplishment of microfinance lies in the fact that some of the successful MFIs report high rates of repayment, sometimes above 95 percent. This rate demonstrates that lending to underprivileged borrowers—those without credit histories or the assets to post collateral—can be a financially sustainable venture.

Not surprisingly, philanthropy is not a requirement of microfinance—not all MFIs are non-profit organizations. While MFIs such as Banco Sol of Bolivia operate with the intent to return a profit, other MFIs like the Grameen Bank charge below-market rates to promote social equity.[3] As will be discussed below, this distinction is important: As the microfinance industry continues to grow and MFIs serve a wider client base, the commercial viability of an MFI is often viewed as crucial for its access to more mainstream sources of finance. (We will return to this and related queries in the "The Evidence of Micro-finance" section of this paper.) The next section offers a brief history of the Grameen Bank and a discussion of its premier innovation of group lending contracts; the following sections describe the current state of microfinance and provide a review of some of the common perceptions on microfinance. The final section outlines the future of microfinance, particularly in the context of global capital markets.

A Brief History of the Grameen Bank

The story of the Grameen Bank is a suitable point to begin a discussion of microcredit and microfinance. After obtaining a PhD in economics in 1969 and then teaching in the United States for a few years, Muhammad Yunus returned to Bangladesh in 1972. Following its independence from Pakistan in 1971 and two years of flooding, Bangladesh found itself in the grips of a terrible famine. By 1974, over 80 percent of the population was living in abject poverty (Yunus, 2003). Yunus, then a professor of economics at Chittagong University in southeast Bangladesh, became disillusioned with economics: "Nothing in the economic theories I taught reflected the life around me. How could I go on telling my students make believe stories in the name of economics?" (See Yunus, 2003, p. viii.) He ventured into the nearby village of Jobra to learn from the poor what causes their poverty. Yunus soon realized that it was their lack of access to credit that held them in poverty. Hence, the origins of "microfinance" emerged from this experience when Yunus lent $27 of his own money to 42 women involved in the manufacturing of bamboo stools.[4]

Through a series of trials and errors, Yunus settled on a working model and by 1983, under a special charter from the Bangladesh government, founded the Grameen Bank as a formal and independent financial institution. Grameen is derived from the Bengali word *gram,* which means village; *grameen* literally means "of the village," an appropriate name for a lending institution that requires the cooperation of the villagers. The Grameen Bank targets the poor, with the goal of lending primarily to women. Since its inception, the Grameen Bank has experienced high growth rates and now has more than 5.5 million members (see Figure 1), more than 95 percent of whom are women.[5]

Lending to poor villagers involves a significant credit risk because the poor are believed to be uncreditworthy: That is, they lack the skills or the expertise needed to put the borrowed funds to their best possible use. Consequently, mainstream banks have for the most part denied the poor access to credit. The Grameen Bank has challenged decades of thinking and received wisdom on lending to the poor. It has successfully demonstrated this in two ways: First, it has shown that poor households can benefit from greater access to credit and that the provision of credit can be an effective tool for poverty alleviation. Second, it has proven that institutions do not necessarily suffer heavy losses from lending to the poor. An obvious question, though, is how the Grameen Bank succeeded where so many others have failed. The answer, according to most economists, lies in its unique

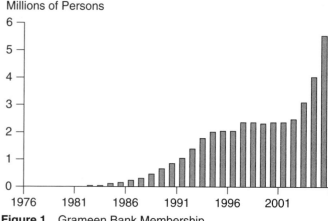

Figure 1   Grameen Bank Membership.

group lending contracts, which enabled the Grameen Bank to ensure repayment without requiring collateral from the poor.

The Group Lending Innovation

This Grameen Bank lending model can be described as follows: Borrowers organize themselves into a group of five and present themselves to the Bank. After agreeing to the Bank rules, the first two members of the group receive a loan. If the first two successfully repay their loans, then four to six weeks later the next two are offered loans; after another four to six weeks, the last person is finally offered a loan. As long as all members in the group repay their loans, the promise of future credit is extended. If any member of the group defaults on a loan, then all members are denied access to future credit. Furthermore, eight groups of Grameen borrowers are organized into centers and repayment is collected during public meetings. While this ensures transparency, any borrower who defaults is visible to the entire village, which imposes a sense of shame. In rural Bangladesh, this societal pressure is a strong dis-incentive to default on the loan. Initial loans are small, generally less than $100, and require weekly repayments that amount to a rate of 10 percent per annum.[6] Weekly repayments give the borrowers and lenders the added benefit of discovering problems early.

Group lending—or the joint liability contract—is the most celebrated lending innovation by the Grameen Bank. Economies of scale motivated its first use, and Yunus later found that the benefits of group lending were manifold. Under a joint liability contract, the members within the group (who are typically neighbors in the village) can help mitigate the problems that an outside lender would face. Outside lenders such as banks and government-sponsored agencies face what economists call agency costs. For example, they cannot ensure that the borrowed money be put to its most productive use (moral hazard), cannot verify success or failure of the proposed business (costly state verification/auditing), and cannot enforce repayment. It is not difficult to see how peers within the group can help reduce these costs, particularly in a situation where the promise of future credit depends on the timely repayment of all members in the group. Joint liability lending thus transfers these agency costs from the bank onto the community of borrowers, who can provide the same services more efficiently.

But perhaps the more difficult agency problem faced by lenders is that of adverse selection—ascertaining the potential credit risk of the borrower. Market failure occurs because safe borrowers (who are more likely to repay) have to subsidize risky borrowers (who are more likely to default). Because the bank cannot tell a safe borrower from a risky one, it has to charge the same rate to all borrowers. The rate depends on the mix of safe and risky borrowers in the population. When the proportion of risky borrowers is sufficiently large, the subsidy required (for the lender to break even on all borrowers) is so high that the lender has to charge all borrowers a significantly high rate. If the rates are sufficiently high, safe borrowers are unlikely to apply for a loan, thereby adversely affecting the composition of the borrower pool. In extreme cases, this could lead to market failure—a situation in which lenders do not offer loans because only the risky types remain in the market!

Economic theory helps show how joint liability contracts mitigate adverse selection (Ghatak and Guinnane, 1999). Under group lending, borrowers choose their own groups. A direct way in which this might help is when a prospective customer directly informs the bank about the reliability of potential joiners. Perhaps a more surprising result is that the lender can mitigate the adverse selection problem even when customers do not directly inform the bank but form themselves into like groups (peer selection). That is, given a joint liability clause, safe customers will more likely group together with other safe customers, leaving the risky types to form groups by themselves. This "assortative matching" mitigates the adverse selection problem because now the risky borrowers are the ones who must bail out other risky borrowers, while the safe borrowers have to shoulder a lesser subsidy. Consequently, all borrowers can be charged a lower rate, reducing the likelihood of a market failure.

Current State of Microfinance

Since the inception of the Grameen Bank, microfinance has spread to cover five continents and numerous countries. The Grameen Bank has been duplicated in Bolivia, Chile, China, Ethiopia, Honduras, India, Malaysia, Mali, the Philippines, Sri Lanka, Tanzania, Thailand, the United States, and Vietnam; the microfinance information exchange market (MIX) lists financial information for 973 MFIs in 105 different countries. Some MFIs have also begun to seek out public and international financing, further increasing their amount of working capital and expanding the scope of their operations. As MFIs have become more efficient and increased their client base, they have begun to expand their services through different product offerings such as micro-savings, flexible loan repayment, and insurance. We discuss these three different product offerings below.

At the time of their inception, many MFIs included a compulsory savings component that limited a borrower's access to deposited funds. This promoted long-term savings, but ignored the fact that many poor save for the short term to smooth consumption during seasonal lows of production. Figure 2 provides a look at the distribution of voluntary MFI savings by

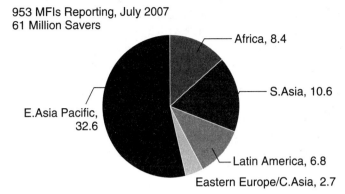

953 MFIs Reporting, July 2007
61 Million Savers

Figure 2 Savings by region.

Source: Microfinance Information Exchange Network; www.mixmarket.org.

region. As MFIs have become better versed in the microfinance market, they have applied their innovations in lending to the collection of deposits. One of the leading examples is SafeSave, located in Dhaka, Bangladesh, which uses the idea that frequent small deposits will guard against the temptation of spending excess income. To keep the transaction costs of daily deposits low, SafeSave hires poor workers from within the collection areas (typically urban slums) to meet with clients on a daily basis. By coming to the client, SafeSave makes it convenient for households to save; by hiring individuals from the given area, training costs and wages are also kept low. With this efficient model for both the bank and individuals, SafeSave has accumulated over 7,000 clients in six years.[7] Not surprisingly, microfinance deposits (like microfinance loans) break from traditional commercial banking experiences. The example of Bank Rakyat Indonesia (BRI) suggests that the poor often value higher liquidity over higher interest rates on deposit products. In 1986, after a year of field experiments, they offered two deposit products: The TABANAS product offered a 12 percent interest rate but restricted withdrawals to twice monthly, whereas the SIMPEDES product offered an interest rate of zero but allowed unlimited withdrawals. The SIMPEDES program saw the largest gain in popularity and to this day still offers a lower interest rate but maintains more accounts than the TABANAS program.[8]

The original Grameen Bank was one of the first MFIs that incorporated a compulsory savings requirement into their lending structure. Every client was required to make a deposit worth 5 percent of their given loan, which was placed into a group fund with strict withdrawal rules (generally no withdrawals before three years). In 2001, the Grameen Bank reviewed both its lending and savings policy and reinvented itself as Grameen II. At the heart of this change were more savings options and more flexible loans, which act as a form of insurance. New to Grameen II is a pension fund, which allows clients with loans greater than 8,000 taka ($138) to contribute at least 50 taka ($0.86) per month. The client receives 12 percent per year in compound interest, earning a 187 percent return after the mandatory 10-year wait. This scheme allows Grameen II to earn more money in the present and expand services, while delaying payment in the near future.

Table 1 Characteristics of Select Microfinance Institutions

	Grameen Bank, Bangladesh	Banco Sol, Bolivia	Compartamos, Mexico	Enterprise Development Group, Washington, D.C.
Established	1983	1992	1990	1993
Membership	6,948,685	103,786	616,528	250
Average loan balance (US$)	$69	$1,571	$440	$22,285**
Percent female	96.70%	46.40%	98.40%	30.00%
Group lending contracts?	Yes	Yes	Yes	No
Collateral required?	No	No	No	No
Portfolio at risk >30 days ratio	1.92%	2.91%	1.13%	N/A
Return on equity	1.95%*	22.81%	57.35%	N/A
Operational self-sufficiency	102.24%*	120.09%	181.22%	53%**

Note: *12/31/2005; **2004.

Source: Data for this table come from the Microfinance Information Exchange (MIX) Network, which is a web-based platform: www.mixmarket.org. Information was provided for the Enterprise Development Group because it is the only U.S.-based MFI that reports data on the MIX network. Some of the information for EDG was taken from their 2003/2004 annual report, available at www.entdevgroup.org. Comparable information is not available for the Southern Good Faith Fund, as the scope of their mission has changed and expanded to more training-based programs. A more comprehensive summary chart exists in Morduch (1999).

Grameen II serves as a good example of a second innovation in microfinance: flexible loan repayment. Group lending still exists and is an integral part of the process, but Grameen II introduced a flexi-loan that allows borrowers multiple options to repay their loan on an individual basis. Yunus (2002) stated that "group solidarity is used for forward-looking joint actions for building things for the future, rather than for the unpleasant task of putting unfriendly pressure on a friend." The flexi-loan is based on the assumption that the poor will always pay back a loan and thus allows the poor to reschedule their loan during difficult periods without defaulting. If the borrower repays as promised, then the flexi-loan operates exactly like the basic loan, using dynamic incentives[9] to increase the size of the loan after each period. If the borrower cannot make her payments, she is allowed to renegotiate her loan contract rather than default. She can either extend the life of the loan or pay only the principle for an extended period of time. As a penalty, the dynamic incentives of her loan are reset; she cannot access larger (additional) amounts of credit until the original loan is repaid. Because her default now poses no threat to the group promise of future credit, each member is accountable only up to their individual liabilities.

The third offering is the addition of insurance to microfinance loans. The most basic insurance is debt relief for the death of a borrower, offered by many MFIs, including Grameen. Other MFIs have begun experimenting with health insurance and natural disaster insurance. As with lending, agency problems present a dilemma for micro-insurance. To this end, some groups such as FINCA Uganda require life insurance of all borrowers, including "risky" and "healthy" alike and thus avoid the adverse selection problem. Other ideas include providing rain insurance to guard against catastrophes. This relies on the assumption that crop yields (and much of the developing economy) are tied to seasonal rain cycles. This innovation eliminates the problem of moral hazard associated with a crop loan. By tying performance to rain cycles, a farmer has no incentive to take crop insurance and then fail to adequately produce a crop during a season of adequate rainfall.

A more recent phenomenon in microfinance is the emergence of foreign investment in MFIs. As more and more MFIs establish positive returns, microfinance is being seen by many professional investors as a profitable investment opportunity. One of the most important developments for the MFIs was the June 2007 release of Standard & Poor's (S&P) report on the rating methodology for MFIs. By applying a common methodology, S&P will be able to send a stronger signal to potential investors about the quality of MFI investments. The process of debt offerings and securitization in the microfinance sector will be covered in greater detail below.

Microfinance Around the World

As Yunus and the Grameen Bank began to prove that microfinance is a viable method to alleviate poverty, their methodology and program began to spread around the world. It is difficult to know exactly how many MFIs there currently are, but Microfinance Information Exchange (MIX) estimates range from 1,000 to 2,500 serving some 67.6 million clients. Of these 67 million, more than half of them come from the bottom 50 percent of people living below the poverty line. That is, some 41.6 million of the poorest people in the world have been reached by MFIs. MFIs have expanded their operations into five different continents and penetrated both rural and urban markets. They have achieved success with a variety of credit products and collection mechanisms. Table 1 provides a comparison of several groups from around the world.

Banco Solidario (Bolivia)

Banco Solidario originally existed as the Fundacion para Promocion y el Desarrollo de la Microempresa (PRODEM), a non-governmental organization (NGO) in the mid-to-late 1980s and provided small capital loans to groups of three or more people dedicated to entrepreneurial activities. By 1992, PRODEM serviced 17,000 clients and disbursed funds totaling $4 million dollars. Constrained by the legal and financial regulations governing an NGO, the board of directors decided to expand their services and PRODEM became the commercial bank, Banco Solidario, later that year. Currently, Banco Sol has 48 branches in seven cities with over 110,000 clients and a loan portfolio of more than $172 million. As of March 31, 2007, Banco Sol reported a past-due loans level of only 1.78 percent. An important distinction between Grameen and Banco Sol is the latter's emphasis on returning a profit with poverty alleviation stated only as a secondary goal.

Banco Sol offers credit, savings, and a variety of insurance products. Their initial loan offering was based on Grameen-style joint-liability lending, offering a maximum of $3,000 per client to groups of three or four individuals with at least one year of experience in their proposed occupation. Using dynamic incentives, the size of the loan is gradually increased based on good repayment history. Annual interest rates average between 12 and 24 percent and can be anywhere from 1 to 60 months in length (120 months for a housing loan).[10] With these higher interest rates, Banco Sol does not rely on subsidies and, at the end of 2006, posted returns on equity of 22.8 percent.

Compartamos (Mexico)

Compartamos is the largest MFI in Mexico, servicing some 630,000 clients with an active loan portfolio of $285 million. Located in Mexico City, Compartamos is active in 26 Mexican states throughout the country and services primarily rural borrowers. Compartamos was founded in 1990 and began by offering joint-liability loans to female borrowers for income-generating activities. Compartamos has only recently expanded their services to allow men to borrow through their solidarity group and their individual credit program; still, around 98 percent of their borrowers are female. In 1998, Compartamos formed a strategic alliance with Accion International and transformed into a regulated financial institution, called a Sociedad Financiera de Objeto Limitado (SFOL). In 2002, Compartamos took a unique step for a MFI and became one of the first MFIs to issue public debt, listing themselves on the Mexican Stock Exchange. As an SFOL, Compartamos was limited to only offering credit for working capital. In order to offer more services, such as savings and insurance programs, Compartamos became a commercial bank in 2006.

Compartamos was one of the first MFIs to raise additional capital funds through the sale of domestic bond issuances. In 2002, Compartamos was the first MFI in Mexico and one of the first in Latin America to offer a bond sale. Because this was Standard and Poor's first attempt at rating a microfinance bond, they adapted their current methodology and rated the bond using their Mexican scale and assumed local buyers. S&P was impressed with the diversified portfolio of debt and offered Compartamos an MXA + (Mexican AA) rating. Reddy and Rhyne (2006) report that their most recent bond was rated an MXAA through the use of credit enhancements, allowing them

to place the bond with institutional investors. Their fifth issue to date was three times oversubscribed with 70 percent of the bond purchased by institutional investors. By accessing the commercial market, Compartamos has been able to lower the cost of obtaining funds and, in turn, offer better services to their borrowers, such as absorbing the costs of providing life insurance for all clients. Their efforts to improve operational efficiency have also created a self-sufficient MFI that has existed without subsidies for over a decade.

Good Faith Fund (United States)

The Good Faith Fund was modeled after the Grameen Bank and was one of the first MFIs to be established in America. In 1986, while governor of Arkansas, Bill Clinton invited Muhammad Yunus to visit and discuss microfinance. The initial program was started as the Grameen Fund, but the name was later changed to better reflect the fund's commitment to providing loans to micro-entrepreneurs. Loans weren't securitized with collateral; rather, they were guaranteed on "good faith" (Yunus, 2003, p.180).

As the Good Faith Fund grew, practitioners and academics alike began to question the effectiveness of a pure Grameen-style program in the United States. Much like the original Grameen Bank, the Good Faith Fund has relied on innovation and change to apply microlending to the rural economy of Arkansas. Taub (1998) argues that the Good Faith Fund is a successful poverty alleviation program, but that it is a poor economic development program. In Taub's words, "the Good Faith Fund has never been able to deliver a meaningful volume of customers, provide substantial loan services to the really poor, or achieve anything close to institutional self-sufficiency." He argues that important social differences arise because rural Arkansas is inherently different from rural Bangladesh and that these social differences cause the group lending model to fail.

Group lending failed for several reasons, but foremost was the inability of potential borrowers to form a group. In Bangladesh, where poverty rates and population density are much higher than the those in the United States, potential borrowers can more readily find other entrepreneurs. However, a close network of social ties among the poor does not exist in rural Arkansas. In response to this problem, Good Faith Fund personnel established a mandatory six-week training program for individual new members and then created groups from the training programs. These newly formed groups of relative strangers lacked the social cohesion to enforce contract payments, unlike group members in rural Bangladesh, who often live in the same village and have family/community histories together. Consequently, group lending was slowly phased out of the Good Faith Fund. Today, the Good Faith Fund focuses mainly on career training through their Business Development Center and Asset Builders program. They have also found a niche in loaning larger amounts of money to small- and medium-sized enterprises that are underserved by the commercial banking center. These loans provide the same service, but at $100,000 or more, they can hardly be considered "micro" credit.

The Evidence on Microfinance

In this section, we review some of the important questions on microfinance. Our assessment is based on numerous studies, technical surveys, and newspaper reports on microfinance. The attempt here is to be illustrative rather than provide a comprehensive review of microfinance.

Is Microfinance a Desirable Alternative to Informal, Exploitative Sources of Finance?

The spread of microfinance and the success of MFIs in various countries around the world prompts a question: Who served the poor before the microcredit revolution? It is well known that conventional banks, which act as creditors to most entrepreneurial activity in the modern world, have largely avoided lending to the poor. Instead, credit to the poor has been provided mostly by local moneylenders, often at usurious rates. Consequently, moneylenders are typically perceived as being exploitative, taking advantage of poor villagers who have no other recourse to loans. Therefore, it is not surprising that microfinance has been welcomed by most as an alternative to the abusive practices of village moneylenders. However, this common perception requires a more careful study: Why don't mainstream banks lend to the poor? In the banks' absence, do local moneylenders have monopoly power? More importantly, are these high interest rates charged by moneylenders welfare reducing?

We begin by listing the difficulties that arise in lending to the poor. First, early studies believed that poor people often lack the resources needed to invest their borrowings to the most productive use. In short, the poor borrow mostly to finance consumption needs (Bhaduri, 1977; Aleem, 1990). Second, even if loans could be earmarked for investment purposes, commercial banks would find it difficult to lend: Lack of credit histories and documented records on small entrepreneurs or farmers make it difficult for the bank to assess the creditworthiness of the borrower. Finally, there is the inability of the poor to post collateral on the loans. This reduces the bank's recourse to a saleable asset once the borrower defaults on the loan. Therefore, it is not difficult to see why commercial banks have avoided lending to the poor.

On the other hand, it is believed that local moneylenders could mitigate the problems faced by outside banks in lending to the poor. Local moneylenders are arguably better informed of borrower quality and have more effective means of monitoring and enforcing contracts than outside banks. In short, because of their social ties, information, and location advantage, these moneylenders are in a unique position to lend to the poor. Some observers argue that usurious interest rates in these markets can be explained by this "monopoly" that the local moneylenders enjoy. Several researchers have studied the market structure of rural credit markets in developing countries. Some argue that rural credit markets are more competitive than previously imagined because there is free entry for local moneylenders if not outside banks. While there is no broad consensus yet, most observers believe that despite free entry in these markets, moneylenders often enjoy some form of local monopoly power (in the manner of monopolistic competition), at least in the short run.

However, there are other reasons why money-lenders charge high interest rates. First, money-lenders have to compensate for the high transaction costs of issuing and servicing a small loan. Second, some observers believe that these funds have high "opportunity costs"—that is, moneylenders can earn high returns by investing in their own farms. Finally, and this is despite their local informational advantage, moneylenders face some of the same problems as commercial banks in identifying risky borrowers and securing collateral, particularly in poor rural areas. A simple numerical example helps illustrate this result[11]: Consider two lenders with the same cost of funds. Suppose now that the first lender operates in a prime market where borrowers faithfully repay all of their loans at 10 percent, giving him an expected 10 percent return. However, the second lender operates in a poor rural market where borrowers arguably have a higher rate of default, say 50 percent.[12] Consequently, her expected net return is thus $[(1 + \text{interest rate}) * (1 - \text{probability of default}) - 1]$. Therefore, for the second money-lender to earn the same 10 percent return, she must charge an interest rate equal to 120 percent: $(1 + 120\%) * (1 - 50\%) - 1 = 10\%$. This is not to say that some moneylenders don't engage in price setting, but it does give a simple example in which a moneylender can be competitive but still charge extremely high interest rates.

Do moneylenders reduce welfare because they charge high interest rates? To the extent that borrowers willingly accept these loan contracts, the answer is no.[13] These loan contracts do generate a positive surplus ex ante. That is, only those borrowers who expect to generate a rate of return from their investment that is higher than that charged by the moneylender will enter into these contracts. Clearly, this situation can be improved upon by offering lower rates: This would allow more borrowers—i.e., those who expect to generate a lower rate of return on their investment—to enter into loan contracts. However, this does not mean that a high interest rate per se reduces welfare. On the contrary, getting rid of moneylenders or preventing them from offering loans at these high rates can be welfare reducing; in their absence, entrepreneurs with the highest returns on their projects have no recourse to loans.

In contrast, MFIs can often offer lower interest rates than local moneylenders because of their higher efficiency in screening and monitoring borrowers, which results from both their economy of scale (serving more borrowers) and their use of joint liability lending mechanisms. This lowers the MFI's cost of lending relative to that of the local moneylender. To the extent that MFIs can provide loans at a lower rate than moneylenders, enabling more and more borrowers to enter the credit market, is an argument for both the efficiency (because of the reduced cost of funds) and welfare enhancement (because of an increase in the borrower pool) of microfinance.

How High are the Repayment Rates for MFIs?

This is widely regarded as the greatest achievement of microfinance. Many MFIs report high rates of repayment, often greater than 90 percent. These claims have driven considerable academic interest in why and how microfinance works.

Furthermore, these repayment rates are widely cited in popular media (*Business Week,* July 9 and 16, 2007; *Wall Street Journal,* September 23, 2007) and have been one of the reasons for the recent interest generated by microfinance in financial markets worldwide. Although the theories of joint liability contracts, progressive lending,[14] frequent repayments, and flexible collateral adequately explain these high rates of repayment, Morduch (1999) raises the important issue of validation. Because many of these repayment rates are self reported, it is important to understand the methodology used to calculate these repayment rates.

Morduch studies the repayment rates for the Grameen Bank for the 10-year period of 1985 to 1996. During this period, Grameen's average loan portfolio grew from $10 million to $271 million and membership expanded more than 12-fold to include 2.06 million members in 1996. For this decade, Grameen reports an average overdue rate of only 1.6 percent.[15] Morduch's contention is that the Grameen Bank does not follow conventional accounting practices and calculates the overdue rates as the value of loans overdue (for more than one year) divided by the *current portfolio,* instead of dividing by the *size of the portfolio when the overdue loans were issued.* Because the size of the loan portfolio expanded 27-fold during this 10-year period, the loan portfolio is significantly larger at the end of any one year than at the beginning. Morduch finds the adjusted average default rate to be 7.8 percent for the same 10-year period. He makes the point that "the rate is still impressive relative to the performance of government development banks, but it is high enough to start creating financial difficulties" (Morduch, 1999, p. 1590).

As for these financial difficulties, Morduch then focuses on reported profits, taking special care to examine the provision of loan losses. He finds that the bank is slow to write off bad loans, dropping only a modest 3.5 percent of its portfolio every year, again overstating the amount of profit. He calculates that instead of posting a total of $1.5 million in profits, the bank would have instead lost a total of $18 million. The implications to Morduch's findings are as follows: In the early 1990s, to operate without subsidies, the Grameen Bank would have had to raise interest rates on its general product from 20 percent to 50 percent, and this would have raised the average interest rate on all products to 32 percent. Morduch is careful to point out that it is unknown whether or not borrowers would defect, because for most borrowers the alternative is either no loan or an even higher interest rate on loans from a moneylender.

Although there is an apparent disagreement between Morduch's adjusted rates of repayment and the Grameen Bank's self reported rates, this alone does not mean that Grameen is a financial failure. In one case, the modest write-offs of bad loans offer proof of Yunus's organizational commitment to the poor and the belief that, given time, they will repay a loan. The since-implemented Grameen II Bank builds on this concept and allows borrowers to restructure a loan into smaller payments or to take a scheduled amount of time off, rather than default. Yunus describes the difference: "[The] overarching objective of the conventional banks is to maximize profit. The Grameen Bank's objective is to bring financial services to the poor, particularly women and the poorest and to help them fight poverty,

stay profitable and financially sound. It is a composite objective, coming out of social and economic visions." Given that the Grameen Bank's focus is largely on social objectives and not profit maximization, some have argued that it is not obligated to adopt standard accounting procedures. What is important is that Grameen is among the few transparent microfinance organizations and researchers have been able to review and evaluate their financial statements.

An important consideration here is that MFIs are known to charge considerably higher rates compared with similar loans from conventional banks. In their celebrated work, Stiglitz and Weiss (1981) showed that the high interest rate that a lender charges may itself adversely affect repayment rates by either discouraging creditworthy borrowers (adverse selection) or tempting the borrowers to opt for riskier projects (moral hazard). Consequently, the coexistence of high repayment rates (around 95 percent) and higher interest rates (a 30 to 60 percent interest rate is common) in microfinance has "puzzled" economists.

One explanation offered by some economists is that MFIs face an inelastic demand for loans. However, in a recent empirical study on the SafeSave program in Dhaka slums, Dehejia, Montgomery, and Morduch (2005) show that the elasticity of demand for microcredit may be significantly negative even though certain groups of borrowers (particularly the wealthier ones) do not reduce their demand when faced with higher interest rates. However, Emran, Morshed, and Stiglitz (2006) offer a more promising explanation for this puzzle. Departing from the traditional focus on credit markets in studies of microfinance, the authors examine the implications of missing or imperfect labor markets for poor women in developing countries (the typical customers of MFIs in Bangladesh). Emran, Morshed, and Stiglitz (2006, p. 4) demonstrate "the critical role played by the structure of the labor market in making the small-scale household-based investment projects 'credit worthy' in the face of very high interest rates, especially for the poor households with little or no collaterizable assets."

Is There More to Microfinance than Group Lending or Joint Liability Contracts?

The success of microfinance in generating high repayment rates led many economists to investigate the reasons behind this success. The mid-to-late 1990s witnessed a large increase in the number of journal articles on group lending contracts, as economists sought to explain how microfinance "succeeded" where traditional forms of lending had failed. Joint liability contracts were seen as the break from traditional lending mechanisms and economic theory was used to readily explain how these contracts helped to improve repayment rates. The growth of the literature on group lending contracts in the mid-1990s offers the impression that all MFIs operate as such, but the reality is that MFIs use a variety of lending techniques, such as dynamic and progressive loans, frequent repayment schedules, and non-traditional collateral to ensure high repayment rates among poor, underserved borrowers. These mechanisms were either introduced independently or in conjunction with joint liability programs such as Grameen's and in many cases operate along-side group contracts. Practitioners and theorists alike have now realized that these mechanisms can operate with individual contracts and in certain cases (e.g., in areas of low population density) offer better repayment results than group lending schemes.

The mechanism of progressive lending guards against the borrower's strategic default at the end of a loan cycle, because by definition she has little or no collateral to be seized in the event of default. Instead, MFIs have offered small initial loans, with the promise of future credit for timely repayment. The offer of future credit serves as a powerful incentive for a micro-entrepreneur trying to grow her business. In this scenario, a borrower will default only if her current income is greater than her future expected profits. With a small initial loan for a beginning entrepreneurial venture, this is unlikely. To further increase the likelihood of repayment, MFIs use dynamic lending, in which the size of the loan is gradually increased with each successive loan repayment. Now, the expected future profits are almost certainly greater than current earned income because the size of the loan continues to grow.

Another mechanism used by MFIs is that of frequent repayments, which often begin even the week after the loan is disbursed. By requiring small repayments before the business venture has reached maturity, MFIs are essentially requiring that borrowers have a second source of income and, hence, borrow against their current consumption. This allows MFIs to screen against high-risk borrowers from the beginning because borrowers will be able to repay the loan even if their venture fails. Indeed, weekly repayments give the borrowers and lenders the added benefit of discovering problems early. Armendáriz de Aghion and Morduch (2005) also suggest that frequent repayments provide better customer service, contrary to the belief that more repayments raise the transaction costs for the borrower by requiring more travel to and from payment centers. Instead, frequent repayments help borrowers with savings constraints such as seasonality of income, family members dropping by to borrow funds, or discretionary spending by one or more of the family members. When coupled with dynamic incentives, frequent loan repayments begin to resemble savings deposits that will be paid with interest (the graduated size of the next loan). This allows families to break free of certain savings constraints (such as those noted above) because the loan is paid each week, before the money can be spent on anything else.

The final mechanism is the requirement of nontraditional collateral, which was introduced by banks such as Bank Rakyat Indonesia (BRI). This feature breaks from the commercial practice that collateral submitted must have a resale value equal to the loan. In a group lending contract, joint liability often serves as collateral, but BRI operates on the "notional value" of an item and allows collateral to be any item that is important to the household, regardless of market value. This may include the family's sole domestic animal, such as a cow, or it may be land that is not secured by title. Neither item could be sold for much of a profit without significant transaction costs to the bank, but both items would be even more difficult and costly for the family to do without.

Armendáriz de Aghion and Morduch (2000) offer evidence of the success of individual loans that use progressive/dynamic incentives, frequent repayments, and nontraditional collateral to guarantee a loan. Using data from Eastern Europe and Russia, they demonstrate that individual loans can generate repayment rates greater than 90 percent (and above 95 percent in Russia). In industrialized settings, borrowers are more likely to face more competition, making it more costly to form a borrowing group. In this scenario, loan products will go to different entrepreneurs, with different expected payoffs—hence, necessitating different loan amounts. A group contract can be inefficient because it imposes a ceiling on the loan size equal to that given to the smallest member of any potential group. They conclude by suggesting that in areas that are relatively industrialized, individual loan models may perform better than traditional group lending models.

Is Microfinance an Important Tool for Poverty Alleviation?

Microfinance started as a method to fight poverty, and although microfinance still fulfills this goal, several institutions have sought to make a distinction between the "marginally poor" and the "very poor." The broadest definition distinguishing these two groups comes from the Consultative Group to Assist the Poorest (CGAP), which defines the poor as individuals living below the poverty line and the poorest as the bottom half of the poor. The World Bank estimates that in 2001, some 1.1 billion people had consumption levels below $1 and another 2.7 billion lived on less than $2 per day.[16] As microfinance continues to grow, questions have started to focus on who is the optimal client. Should microfinance target the marginally poor or the extremely poor?

Morduch (1999) tries to answer this question by considering two representative microfinance clients, one from each poverty group described above. The first client belongs to a subsidized microfinance program and her income is only 50 percent of the poverty line. The second client belongs to a financially sustainable program that accordingly charges higher interest rates. To ensure repayment of the loan at the higher rate, the second borrower is chosen to be marginally poor, that is, with an income of 90 percent of the poverty line. Using the widely used "squared poverty gap" (Foster, Greer, and Thorbecke, 1984) measure of poverty, Morduch suggests that a dollar increase in income for the very poor borrower has a five times greater impact than the same dollar for the marginally poor borrower.

This simple example would suggest that, in terms of poverty alleviation, MFIs should focus on the poorest borrowers first, but this is not always the case. As MFIs seek to become financially independent, they find themselves serving only the marginally poor. This is an important distinction between Grameen and Banco Sol of Bolivia: The latter's emphasis is on returning a profit, and alleviating poverty is seen only as a secondary goal. Not surprisingly, Banco Sol charges higher interest rates,[17] does not rely on subsidies, and at the end of 2006 posted returns on equity of 22.8 percent.[18]

This apparent dichotomy between financial independence and poverty alleviation also gets to the heart of a different problem. At what point does a successful MFI begin to look like a regular bank? If the MFI successfully serves poor clients, then those clients should be able to use their loans to lift themselves out of poverty. Because of the nature of progressive and dynamic loans, successful borrowers earn access to larger loans, helping them break free of poverty even faster.

The Grameen Bank has found a way to make this dichotomy work for them and now uses their economy of scale to create a financially independent bank without raising interest rates. In 1995, the Grameen Bank decided not to request any more funds from donors and instead began to fund the bank from collected deposits. With more than two decades of successful borrowers behind them, Grameen has had a chance to build up savings deposits slowly, to the point that it is now self-sustainable, based on the amount of funds provided by members. In a rough sense, it is now the more-successful poor that are subsidizing new clients. This is a significant step, especially considering that, from the decade of 1985 to 1996, Armendáriz de Aghion and Morduch (2005) calculate that Grameen accepted $175 million in subsidies, including both direct donations and "soft" donations such as soft loans, implicit subsidies through equity holdings, and delayed loan loss provision.

Is Microfinance Sustainable or Even Profitable?

With all of the positive publicity surrounding microfinance, it may be surprising to learn that not all MFIs are sustainable or able to return a profit. Despite their rapid growth and sound operations based on strong theoretical platforms (such as using group loans, dynamic incentives, and frequent repayments), less than half of all MFIs return a profit and most still require the help of donors and subsidies. A lack of financial sustainability doesn't necessarily indicate a failing MFI, but rather raises questions about the mission and direction of that particular MFI. Even with subsidies, many MFIs remain the most cost-effective method to alleviate poverty; and, as we argued previously, subsidies can help change the profile of the targeted client from the poor to the extremely poor.

For an MFI to be sustainable can mean one of two things: The organization can be operationally sustainable or it can be financially sustainable. An MFI that is operationally sustainable raises enough revenue to cover the cost of operating the business—paying loan supervisors, opening branch offices, etc. Subsidies might still be used to issue loans or cover defaulted loans. An institution that is financially sustainable does not require any subsidized inputs or outside funds to operate. Instead, it raises money through its lending operations. The *MicroBanking Bulletin* (2003) surveyed 124 MFIs with a stated commitment to becoming financially sustainable. In their survey, the *Bulletin* found that only 66 operations were sustainable, a rate just slightly above 50 percent. As Armendáriz de Aghion and Morduch (2005, p. 232) note, all 124 programs asked for help in managing their accounting standards and,

hence, "in terms of financial management, [these 124 programs] are thus skimmed from the cream of the crop." Similar sustainability data do not exist for the other 2,000+ MFIs; but, without similarly strong commitments to financial sustainability, the percentage of sustainable operations is likely to be much lower than 50 percent.

Subsidized credit is financed in a variety of forms, some of which have been discussed briefly with the Grameen Bank example. MFIs also secure funds from donors, many of whom want to alleviate poverty but have not seen strong returns in the nongovernmental organization (NGO) or government sector. For many, donations and subsidies are intended as a method to get MFIs started. But without any accountability or empirical research, it is difficult for donors to decide at what point an MFI should forgo its dependence on outside funds. Lacking in this debate is a clear understanding of how subsidies affect the supply and demand of loans. Without subsidies, interest rates may rise; and, as standard demand theory suggests, fewer loans will be requested. Moreover, rising interest rates without subsidies may exclude poorer projects, thus raising average returns. But, they may also increase the moral hazard problem; at higher interest rates, only risky borrowers apply for a loan, thus increasing the default rate and lowering returns. Finally, it is unclear what affect subsidized lenders have on the overall credit supply. Do they segment the credit market while serving the very poor or do they squeeze out other lenders, reducing overall efficiency for the market?

In some instances, government institutions collaborate with local MFIs; but, more often than not, government organizations and MFIs are at odds with one another, despite the fact that both share the stated goal of reducing poverty. A prime example of the failure of government subsidized initiatives in the market for microcredit is the Integrated Rural Development Program (IRDP), which allocated credit based on social targets in rural India, giving 30 percent of credit to socially excluded groups and 30 percent to women. Armendáriz de Aghion and Morduch (2005) report that between 1979 and 1989 IRDP offered over $6 billion in subsidized credit but generated loan repayment rates below 60 percent, with only 11 percent of borrowers taking out a second loan. During the same decade, the Grameen Bank also accepted subsidies in a variety of forms, but did not change their lending model to include social targets. During this time, the Grameen Bank saw its membership grow to half a million members, with repayment rates above 90 percent. The experience of the Grameen Bank and IRDP during the late 1970s and early 1980s is important because of the similarities between regions. Both Bangladesh and India are densely populated, rural, agrarian economies with high rates of poverty. Therefore, it is likely that the Grameen Bank's comparative success during this period is indicative of a more efficient lending model rather than variances in their lending environment.

In sum, even if many MFIs are not financially sustainable, the microfinance movement may still be the best per-dollar investment for alleviating poverty. Further research is needed to show whether financial sustainability is even a desired objective, and future work could help understand how different subsidy mechanisms can best balance financial sustainability with the desired social objectives.

Could Competition Among MFIs Lead to Better Results?

At first glance, standard economic theory suggests that competition should improve the performance of MFIs and lead to better service and lower interest rates. With such a large poor population and high rates of growth, there is also a large market to support more MFIs. Historically, though, competition has failed to increase services and often decreases the rate of repayment. When clients have access to alternative sources of credit, MFIs lose the leverage they gain from dynamic incentives and progressive loans (i.e., future loans are contingent on repayment).

During the late 1990s, Bolivia and Banco Sol experienced a microfinance crisis. As the success of Banco Sol increased and commercial banks began to see the profitability in an MFI model, competition increased. General economic theory suggests that competition is inherently good, but for the early MFIs, competition reduced efficiency by weakening the incentives: As credit options increased for borrowers, the incentives inherent in a dynamic or progressive loan became weaker. This proved difficult for Banco Sol, whose model relies on group lending and dynamic incentives. The competition mainly came from Acceso FFP, a Chilean finance company that paid its employees on an incentive system. Within three years, Acceso had 90,000 loans, and Banco Sol lost 11 percent of its clients. Regulated MFIs in Bolivia saw their loan overdue rates increase from 2.4 percent to 8.4 percent in just over two years. Because of the increased competition, Banco Sol saw its return on equity fall by 20 percentage points to only 9 percent in 1999 (Armendáriz de Aghion and Morduch, 2005, p. 127).

In their study of 2,875 households from 192 villages in Thailand, Ahlin and Townsend (2007, p. F43) reach a similar conclusion. They note that, with increased access to credit, borrowers do not respond to dynamic incentives. Moreover, strong social ties, such as the clustering of relatives in a village, can also lower repayment rates in the same manner of competition. In their words, "this result has not been seen in the previous empirical research, nor focused on in the theoretical models."

In the early years of competition in the micro-finance sector, MFIs struggled to maintain a credible threat of denying future credit on default. In recent times, however, new regulation has helped to promote competition in Bolivia as lenders started to share more information on borrowers. By law, Banco Sol and other regulated financial intermediaries are now required to report the name and national identification number of delinquent borrowers to the Superintendent of Banks and Financial Institutions. This information is available to all financial intermediaries through both formal and informal agreements. This agreement helped to strengthen the threat of dynamic incentives, and, as a result, competition among lenders has led to an increase in their client base.

Does Microfinance Have Any Social Impact in Terms of Female Empowerment and Education?

Any review of microfinance is incomplete without a discussion of its impact on women. The Microcredit Summit Campaign Report (2000) lists over a thousand programs in which 75 percent of the clients were women. Yunus (2003) recounts the initial difficulties overcoming the social mores in rural Bangladesh and lending to women in this predominantly Islamic nation. However, his efforts were rewarded and 95 percent of the Grameen Bank's current clients are women.

This focus on women follows largely from Yunus's conviction that lending to women has a stronger impact on the welfare of the household than lending to men. This has been confirmed by a large volume of research on microfinance. In countries where microfinance is predominant, country-level data reveal signs of a social transformation in terms of lower fertility rates and higher literacy rates for women. Pitt and Khandker (1998) show that loans to women have a positive impact on outcomes such as children's education, contraceptive use, and the value of women's non-land assets. Khandker (2005) finds that borrowing by a woman has a greater impact on per capita household expenditure on both food and non-food items than borrowing by a man. Among other things, this also improves nutrition, health care, and educational opportunities for children in these households. Smith (2002) validates this assertion using empirical data from Ecuador and Honduras to compare microfinance institutions that also offer health services with institutions that offer only credit. He notes that, "in both countries, health bank participation significantly raises subsequent health care over credit-only participation." In particular, he found that participation in MFIs that offer health services reduces the tendency to switch to bottle feeding as incomes rise. He notes that breast-feeding children under age two is a key health-enhancing behavior.

A pro-female bias in lending works well for the MFIs. Practitioners believe that women tend to be more risk averse in their choice of investment projects, more fearful of social sanctions, and less mobile (and therefore easier to monitor) than men—making it easier for MFIs to ensure a higher rate of repayment. Various studies from both Asia and Latin America have shown that the repayment rates are significantly higher for female borrowers compared with their male counterparts.

However, critics have argued that microfinance has done little to change the status of women within the household. A much-cited paper by Goetz and Gupta (1996) points to evidence that it is mostly the men of the household and not the women borrowers who actually exercise control over the borrowings. Moreover, micro-finance does little to transform the status of women in terms of occupational choice, mobility, and social status within the family. Therefore, microfinance hardly "empowers" women in any meaningful sense. Although this may truly be the case, there is no denying the fact that micro-finance has provided heretofore unrealized working opportunities for women with limited skills in traditional activities.

Can the Microfinance Experiment Be Successfully Replicated Anywhere in the World?

Although the microfinance revolution has recorded success in most developing countries of the world, it has achieved little success in some of the more developed nations. The most notable example here is the Good Faith Fund in Arkansas, where microfinance has failed to deliver the same rapid growth and poverty alleviation as it has in the developing world. This seems reasonable given the relatively smaller percentage of those living in poverty and the much larger safety net afforded the poor through welfare and unemployment programs. As Yunus (2003, p. 189) states, "In the developed world, my greatest nemesis is the tenacity of the social welfare system . . . [M]any calculate the amount of welfare money and insurance coverage they would lose by becoming self-employed and conclude the risk is not worth the effort." Yunus correctly addresses a motivating factor for the relatively weak success of microfinance in the United States, but studies have found other reasons why microfinance has failed to deliver: e.g., a lack of entrepreneur opportunities for the poor, lack of group structure, and the multitude of options facing the U.S. poor.

Why Did Microfinance Initiatives Fail in the United States? In their study of U.S. micro-finance, Edgcomb, Klein, and Clark (1996) find that micro-enterprise accounts for only 8 to 20 percent of all jobs—because of the availability of wage jobs and public assistance. When compared with the 60 to 80 percent of jobs supplied by micro-enterprise in the developing world, the pool of potential microfinance beneficiaries in the United States is substantially smaller. Schreiner and Woller (2003) make the point that the characteristics of the poor are different in the two regions. In the developing world, jobs are relatively scarce and hence the unemployed are more likely on average to include individuals that are highly skilled or better motivated to become entrepreneurs. In contrast, in the United States, where poverty is much less prevalent, most individuals with the aforementioned characteristics can find jobs. Furthermore, the amount of small business regulation in the United States poses problems; a micro-entrepreneur must know their proposed business but must also understand local and federal tax laws and regulations. To compete with much larger national markets, small business owners must further understand and excel at marketing their products in both local and larger markets. The lack of highly skilled or better-motivated workers among the poor in the United States, combined with the higher entry costs for successful micro-enterprise, makes successful microfinance initiatives more difficult. Schreiner (1999) finds that, in absolute terms, only one person in a hundred was able to move from unemployment to self-employment through micro-enterprise.

Taub (1998) offers a slightly different explanation: He found that the markets for the borrowers differed between regions. In Bangladesh, most small entrepreneurs engage in goods-producing activities that, when combined with their small local markets, offers an almost immediate stream of revenue. This feature allows the Grameen Bank and others to require weekly repayments, which is often cited as a primary reason for their high repayment rates. In the United States, most entrepreneurs engage in service-producing activities because it is difficult to compete against the economies of scale in goods production and distribution within the U.S. market. These service businesses provide a relatively unreliable source of income, particularly in the early stages. This risk, combined with the safety net afforded to the poor through welfare, discourages many potential entrepreneurs from starting a new venture. In support of this point, Taub found that the likely borrower comes from a family with at least one source of steady income, so that their new venture is unlikely to substantially hurt their family resources.

In the late 1980s, the Good Faith Fund demonstrated the difficulty of forming a cohesive group structure to enforce joint liability loans. Schreiner and Woller (2003) offer four basic failures of group formation in the United States. First, they suggest that the impersonal nature of U.S. market interactions reduces the need for social reputations and hence the group loses the ability to punish delinquent borrowers. Second, the U.S. poor are diverse and hence it is difficult to find other poor potential entrepreneurs to guarantee a group loan. In U.S. markets, there is also a limit to the potential number of small-business ideas. In developing countries, a group of borrowers may all enter the basket-making market with success because of the much larger local economy. The group guarantees the loan but also offers advice to help succeed in the market. In the United States, the demand for micro-businesses is much smaller and diverse groups of people must start diverse business ventures. There is little value to the group outside of a loan guarantee because group members don't share the same risk to their businesses. Third, defaults are often not enforced in group settings, as found by Hung (2003). Finally, groups often break down in the United States because the poor have access to other forms of credit. This credit may be more attractive because it doesn't require the transaction costs of dealing with a group.

For the United States, pure Grameen-style group lending schemes have failed to deliver substantial results, but that is not to say they have not benefited the poor. Rather, microfinance operations in the United States have often switched to individual lending operations that require borrowers to attend mandatory small business training programs or offer loans to attend specialized schooling for particular professions. A fundamental difference is that microfinance in the United States helps place the poor into existing wage-earning jobs rather than create new jobs. The additional training substantially raises costs to the point that many U.S. MFIs are not self-sustaining, instead relying on grants and subsidies. Edgcomb, Klein, and Clark (1996) found that the average cost to make and service a loan was $1.47 per dollar lent, with a range of costs from

$0.67 to $2.95. Without charging usurious interest rates, it can be difficult to earn such a similarly high return, particularly with the smaller microfinance market. Taub (1998) reports that from 1989 to 1992, the Good Faith Fund averaged only 18 new loan customers per year.[19] In the following years, the average number of new loan customers rose into the mid 20s, before a change in management and change in focus substantially reduced those numbers. With small loans, averaging just $1,600 per year for the first four years, it became impossible for the Good Faith Fund to even come close to matching the combined staff salaries of $450,000.

Due in part to these high-cost structures, Bhatt, Tang, and Painter (2002) found direct evidence that nearly a third of MFIs started in California in 1996 had ceased to exist by 1998. Instead of focusing on becoming self-sufficient, Schreiner (2002, p. 82) argues for more quantitative evaluation of MFIs. He claims that "the dirty secret in micro-enterprise is that few evaluations are really tests. . .[E]valuations were funded and conducted by people who already believed that micro-enterprise was worthwhile." Schreiner thus concludes that a main goal in helping alleviate poverty should be to evaluate the efficiency of MFIs and, if need be, reallocate resources to other training programs that specialize in poverty alleviation, not economic development.

The Future of Microfinance

The number of MFIs has been growing steadily, and the top 100 MFIs are increasing their client base at a rate of 26 percent per year.[20] To fund this spectacular growth, MFIs have turned to a variety of sources, many of which rely on funding from local sources to guard against foreign currency risk. MFIs are currently moving into the international market and confronting challenges such as developing standard rating methods; guarding against foreign currency risk and country risk; and meeting the large volume requirements for an international offering. But, according to Reddy (2007) of Accion International, "Many believe that savings mobilized from local depositors will ultimately be the largest source of capital for microfinance. Foreign capital provides 22 percent of funding for the 'Top 100' MFIs, but savings is the first source of capital, representing 41 percent of all assets in 2005."[21] Many MFIs have a mandatory or suggested savings rate; and, for larger loans, MFIs will often require borrowers to deposit 5 percent of the loan back into a savings account. Some, but not all, have restrictions on when and how that money can be accessed.

Although not the main source of funding, foreign capital still represents a significant portion of current funding for the top 100 MFIs. As Elizabeth Littlefield of CGAP found, U.S. investment in foreign microfinance in 2006 was $4 billion, which is more than double the 2004 total of $1.6 billion. This funding comes from two main sources: international financial institutions and microfinance investment vehicles. To access this foreign investment, MFIs are beginning to use new vehicles of debt-structured finance, including collateralized debt obligations (CDOs) and securitization.

To date, one of the most well-known international debt issues was structured by Blue Orchard Finance in 2004. This deal, worth $40 million, linked 90 investors with nine MFIs in Latin America, Eastern Europe, and Southeast Asia. The main innovation of the Blue Orchard deal was the introduction of a tiering system (of five tranches) that allowed for different risk appetites among investors. Microfinance is also beginning to raise money in the equity market, through organizations such as Accion Investments, which has invested $12.4 million in five institutions (Reddy and Rhyne, 2006).

In 2006, the first securitized microfinance receivables went on the market from the Bangladesh Rural Advancement Committee (BRAC). BRAC is an NGO that lends money to the extremely poor, focusing mainly on offering women credit to develop their own income-generating activities. The transaction was structured by RSA Capital, CitiGroup, the Netherlands Financing Company, and KfW Bank of Germany and has securitized $180 million in receivables over a period of six years.

According to CitiGroup, 65 percent of the loans are to the extremely poor, who borrow from $50 to $100. BRAC offers three loans, based primarily on the land holdings of the borrower. For those with less than one acre of land, borrowers can obtain from $50 to $500 at a flat 15 percent rate, payable over one year through 46 weekly installments. The marginally poor, those who own more than one acre of land and are involved in agricultural enterprise, can qualify for loans between $166 and $833 with a flat 15 percent interest rate. This product must be repaid in equal monthly installments, with a 12- or 18-month horizon. Finally, BRAC offers larger loans to entrepreneurs to start their own business. These loans are monthly products (12, 18, or 24 months) with a 15 percent interest rate.[22] BRAC employs a dynamic lending scheme, wherein timely repayments guarantee future access to credit. This mechanism is similar to a joint lending liability, except in this case borrowers are liable to their future selves.

International Financing Review Asia honored the BRAC deal with the title of best securitization in Asia Pacific for 2006 because "one of the most impressive aspects of the transaction is the way that it deals with the sheer complexity of a dynamic pool that will contain about 3.3 million short tenor loans for which the average outstanding principal is around US$95."[23] The security was given an AAA rating from the local Bangladesh markets, with CitiGroup and Netherlands Financing Company each purchasing one-third of the certificates. The remaining one-third was split among CitiGroup Bangladesh and two local Bangladeshi banks.

This deal differs from the collateralized debt obligations that Blue Orchard Loans for Development issued in April 2006, in which funding for 21 MFIs from 12 countries was packaged into a $99.1 million commercial investment. The main difference between a CDO and securitization is that a CDO relies on the ability of the MFI to repay the loan, unlike a securitized loan that relies on the underlying borrowers to repay. A CDO is another vehicle to bring mainstream investors to microfinance, but is still limited by the ability to rate the creditworthiness of differing MFIs. To help with this issue, S&P released a rating methodology for microfinance in June 2007. By applying a common methodology, S&P will be able to send a stronger signal to potential investors about the quality of MFI investments. It is unclear yet whether the 2007 subprime mortgage meltdown in the United States will have an effect on investors' risk appetites for more collateralized securities and whether microfinance securities will be viewed as "subprime" loans.

Walter and Krauss (2006) argue that the opposite should be true—namely, that microfinance can reduce portfolio volatility—and their empirical tests show that microfinance institutions have a low correlation to general market movements. They suggest that this phenomenon is brought on by the continuous and diverse funding through international donor agencies and because micro-entrepreneurs may be less integrated into the formal economy. When markets enter a downturn, micro-entrepreneurs may experience a countercyclical effect, as consumers shift their consumption downward to cheaper goods.

Outside of international credit markets, microfinance has continued to receive grassroots support and popular media coverage. Organizations such as Kiva.org serve as intermediaries and connect individual donors with micro-entrepreneurs. Kiva.org allows individuals to choose a business, originate their own micro-loan, and in return receive electronic journal updates and payments from their borrower. Most loans are small, between $50 and $100 and have repayment terms from six months to a year, but the lender does not receive any interest on their loan. Rather, journal updates and progress reports serve as interest, letting lenders know that their money has been put to good use. At the end of the year, providers can start the cycle anew or withdraw. To date, 128,547 individuals have lent over $12 million with a self-reported repayment rate greater than 99 percent. Popular media outlets such as the *Wall Street Journal* (September 23, 2007, August 21, 2007, October 21, 2006), *New York Times* (March 27, 2007, December 10, 2006), National Public Radio (September 7, 2007, June 19, 2007, April 6, 2007), and others have given Kiva.org frequent and broad exposure, making the microfinance movement as accessible to lenders as the Grameen Bank made microcredit accessible to borrowers.

Conclusion

With the recognition of the Nobel Peace Prize in 2006, Muhammad Yunus's vision of extending credit to the poor has reached a global level. Microfinance is not a panacea for poverty alleviation; but, with committed practitioners, a wealth of theoretical work, and a surging demand for both international and individual investment, micro-finance is a poverty-alleviation tool that has proven to be both effective and adaptable. Through innovations in group lending and dynamic incentives, MFIs have been able to successfully lend to those traditionally ignored by commercial banks, because of their lack of collateral and credit scores. The poor have responded in kind, by repaying their loans with significant repayment rates. As MFIs have grown and reached new clients, they have continued to innovate by offering individual loans, savings options, and life insurance and seeking new forms of capital in domestic and international

markets. Microfinance has spread to five continents and hundreds of countries, yet its success in U.S. markets has been ill-defined, as lenders struggle with higher transaction costs of offering loans and starting micro-enterprises. As more and more MFIs become self-sufficient and continue to expand their client base, it will be the duty of all parties concerned with poverty relief to look for other ways to innovate. For now, microfinance remains a viable solution to economic development and poverty alleviation, both in Bangladesh and around the world. With more transparency from institutions and better rating standards, the influx of investment capital from international markets will continue to drive microfinance toward Yunus's goal of a poverty-free world.

Notes

1. Other, more technical surveys of microfinance include Ghatak and Guinnane (1999), Morduch (1999), and Armendáriz de Aghion and Morduch (2005).

2. Microfinance Information Exchange (MIX) lists financial profiles and data for 973 MFIs. The high estimate of 2,500 comes from a survey conducted by the Microcredit Summit Campaign in 2002.

3. The social objectives of the Grameen Bank are summarized by the 16 decisions in their mission statement. The statement is available at http://grameen-info.org/bank/the16.html.

4. Yunus (2003) describes his conversation with Sufiya, a stool maker. She had no money to buy the bamboo for her stools. Instead, she was forced to buy the raw materials and sell her stools through the same middleman. After extracting interest on the loan that Sufiya used to buy the bamboo that morning, the moneylender left her with a profit of only 2 cents for the day. Sufiya was poor not for lack of work or skills, but because she lacked the necessary credit to break free from a moneylender. With the help of a graduate student, Yunus surveyed Jobra and found 41 other women just like Sufiya. Disillusioned by the poverty around him and questioning what could be done, Yunus lent $27 dollars to these 42 women and asked that he be repaid whenever they could afford it.

5. Grameen Bank, annual reports (various years). Data can be viewed at www.grameen-info.org/annualreport/commonElements/htmls/index.html.

6. See www.grameen-info.org/bank/GBGlance.htm. Other sources put the annual rates charged by MFIs at around 30 to 60 percent.

7. See www.savesafe.org.

8. The SIMPEDES program does also use a lottery system to give rewards, often worth 0.7 percent of deposits. More details are available at the BRI web page: www.bri.co.id/english/mikrobanking/aboutmikrobanking.aspx.

9. Dynamic incentives threaten to exclude defaulted borrowers from future loans.

10. Banco Sol, accessed July 27, 2007; www.bancosol.com.bo/en/intro.html.

11. This example in Armendáriz de Aghion and Morduch (2005) is drawn from the early work of Bottomley (1975).

12. Of course, Yunus believes that this wrong assumption is the root of all the problems that the poor have in obtaining credit.

13. Bhaduri (1973) points to some degree of coercion in rural credit markets, particularly in situations where landlords double as moneylenders.

14. Progressive lending is a type of dynamic incentive in which access to larger amounts of credit becomes available after each successfully repaid loan.

15. In comparison, nonperforming loans averaged between 1 and 1.5 percent for all U.S. commercial banks for the decade of 1995 to 2005. (Source: Federal Financial Institutions Examination Council.) Braverman and Gausch (1986) found that government credit programs in Africa, the Middle East, Latin America, South Asia, and Southeast Asia all had default rates between 40 and 95 percent.

16. World Bank, "Poverty Analysis"; data can be viewed at http://web.worldbank.org.

17. Annual interest rates average between 12 and 24 percent and can be anywhere from 1 to 60 months in length (120 months for a housing loan). The data are from Banco Sol, accessed 7/27/07; www.bancosol.com.bo/en/intro.html.

18. MIX Market financial data are from BancoSol, accessed 8/2/07; www.mixmarket.org/en/demand/demand.show.profile.asp?token=&ett=280.

19. At the time of Taub's study, population density in Bangladesh was 814 per square kilometer, while the population densities of Arkansas counties served by the Good Faith Fund were only 36, 9, 8, 9.1, and 10.33 per square kilometer (Jefferson, Lincoln, Desha, Chicot, and Ashley counties, respectively).

20. MIX Market analysis of top 100 MFIs; www.mixmarket.org.

21. Data taken from MIX Market analysis of the top 100 MFIs; www.mixmarket.org.

22. See BRAC's economic development and microfinance information at www.brac.net/microfinance.htm.

23. CitiGroup: "Innovative BRAC Microcredit Securitization honored in Bangladesh," accessed 1/16/07; www.citigroup.com/citigroup/press/2007/070116b.htm.

References

Ahlin, Christian and Townsend, Robert M. "Using Repayment Data to Test Across Models of Joint Liability Lending." *Economic Journal,* February 2007, *117*(517), pp. F11–51.

Aleem, Irfan. "Imperfect Information, Screening, and the Costs of Informal Lending: A Study of a Rural Credit Market in Pakistan." *World Bank Economic Review,* September 1990, *4*(3), pp. 329–49.

Armendáriz de Aghion, Beatriz and Morduch, Jonathon. "Microfinance: Beyond Group Lending." *Economics of Transition,* July 2000, *8*(2), pp. 401–20.

Armendáriz de Aghion, Beatriz and Morduch, Jonathon. *The Economics of Microfinance.* Cambridge, MA: MIT Press, 2005.

Bhaduri, Amit. "A Study in Agricultural Backwardness Under Semi-feudalism." *Economic Journal,* March 1973, *83*(329), pp. 120–37.

Bhaduri, Amit. "On the Formation of Usurious Interest Rates in Backward Agriculture." *Cambridge Journal of Economics,* December 1977, *1*(4), pp. 341–52.

Bhatt, Nitan, Tang, Shui Yan and Painter, Gary. "Microcredit Programs in the United States: The Challenges of Outreach and Sustainability," in J. Carr and Z.-Y. Tong, eds., *Replicating Microfinance in the United States.* Washington, DC: Woodrow Wilson Center Press, 2002.

Bottomley, Anthony. "Interest Rate Determination in Underdeveloped Rural Areas." *American Journal of Agricultural Economics,* May 1975, *57*(2), pp. 279–91.

Braverman, Avishay and Gausch, J. Luis. "Rural Credit Markets and Institutions in Developing Countries: Lessons for Policy Analysis from Practice and Modern Theory." *World Development,* October/ November 1986, *14*(10/11), pp. 1253–67.

Dehejia, Rajeev; Montgomery, Heather and Morduch, Jonathon. "Do Interest Rates Matter? Credit Demand in the Dhaka Slums." Unpublished manuscript, March 2005.

Edgcomb, Elaine; Klein, Joyce and Clark, Peggy. "The Practice of Microenterprise in the US: Strategies, Costs, and Effectiveness." Washington, DC: Aspen Institute, 1996.

Emran, M. Shahe; Morshed, A.K.M. Mahbub and Stiglitz, Joseph E. "Microfinance and Missing Markets." Unpublished manuscript, October 2006.

Foster, J.; Greer, J. and Thorbecke E. "A Class of Decomposable Poverty Measures." *Econometrica,* 1984, *52*, pp. 761–66.

Ghatak, Maitreesh. "Screening by the Company You Keep: Joint Liability Lending and the Peer Selection Effect." *Economic Journal,* July 2000, *110*(465), pp. 601–31.

Ghatak, Maitreesh and Guinnane, Timothy. "The Economics of Lending with Joint Liability: Theory and Practice." *Journal of Development Economics,* October 1999, *60*(1), pp. 195–228.

Goetz, Anne Marie and Gupta, Rina Sen. "Who Takes the Credit? Gender, Power, and Control Over Loan Use in Rural Credit Programs in Bangladesh." *World Development,* January 1996, *24*(1), pp. 45–63.

Hung, Chi-kan Richard. "Loan Performance of Group-Based Microcredit Programs in the United States." *Economic Development Quarterly,* November 2003, *17*(4), pp. 382–95.

Khandker, Shahidur R. "Microfinance and Poverty: Evidence Using Panel Data from Bangladesh." *World Bank Economic Review,* September 2005, *19*(2), pp. 263–86.

MicroBanking Bulletin. "Focus on Savings," July 2003, No. 9, pp. 72–76; www.mixmbb.org.

Microcredit Summit Campaign Report 2000, 2000; www.microcreditsummit.org/campaigns/report00html#overview.

Morduch, Jonathon. "The Microfinance Promise." *Journal of Economic Literature,* December 1999, *37*(4), pp. 1569–614.

Pitt, Mark M. and Khandker, Shahidur R. "The Impact of Group-Based Credit Programs on Poor Households in Bangladesh: Does the Gender of Participants Matter?" *Journal of Political Economy,* October 1998, *106*(5), pp. 958–96.

Reddy, Rekha M. "Microfinance Cracking the Capital Markets II." *InSight,* May 2007, *22*, pp. 1–17.

Reddy, Rekha M. and Rhyne, Elisabeth. "Who Will Buy Our Paper: Microfinance Cracking the Capital Markets?" *Insight,* April 2006, *18*, pp. 1–19.

Rhyne, Elisabeth. *Mainstreaming Microfinance: How Lending to the Poor Began, Grew, and Came of Age in Bolivia.* Bloomfield, CT: Kumarian Press, 2001.

Schreiner, Mark. "Lessons for Microenterprise Programs from a Fresh Look at the Unemployment Insurance Self-Employment Demonstration." *Evaluation Review,* October 1999, *23*(5), pp. 503–26.

Schreiner, Mark. "Evaluation and Microenterprise Programs in the United States." *Journal of Microfinance,* Fall 2002, *4*(2), pp. 67–91.

Schreiner, Mark and Woller, Gary. "Microenterprise Development Programs in the United States and in the Developing World." *World Development,* September 2003, *31*(9), pp. 1567–80.

Smith, Stephen C. "Village Banking and Maternal and Child Health: Evidence from Ecuador and Honduras." *World Development,* April 2002, *30*(4), pp. 707–23.

Stiglitz, Joseph and Weiss, Andrew. "Credit Rationing in Markets with Imperfect Information." *American Economic Review,* June 1981, *71*(3), pp. 393–410.

Taub, Richard P. "Making the Adaptation Across Cultures and Societies: A Report on an Attempt to Clone the Grameen Bank in Southern Arkansas." *Journal of Developmental Entrepreneurship,* Summer 1998, *3*(1), pp. 353–69.

Walter, Ingo and Krauss, Nicolas A. "Can Microfinance Reduce Portfolio Volatility?" Working paper, November 9, 2006; http://ssrn.com/abstract=943786.

Yunus, Muhammad. "Grameen Bank II: Designed to Open New Possibilities." Grameen Bank, October 2002; www.grameen-info.org/bank/bank2.html.

Yunus, Muhammad. *Banker to the Poor: Micro-Lending and the Battle Against World Poverty.* New York: Public Affairs, 2003.

Yunus, Muhammad. "What Is Microcredit?" Grameen Bank, September 2007; www.grameen-info.org/bank/WhatIsMicrocredit.htm.

RAJDEEP SENGUPTA is an economist and **CRAIG P. AUBUCHON** is a research associate at the Federal Reserve Bank of St. Louis. The authors thank Subhayu Bandyopadhyay, Patrick Pintus, and George Fortier for helpful comments and suggestions

The Hidden Economy of Nonprofits

We know surprisingly little about nonprofits. Does it matter? Do they?

RONALD A. WIRTZ

If you would, draw a picture of the face of nonprofits. Perhaps you envision a food shelf providing meals for the hungry. Or maybe the United Way or Boy Scouts. Possibly the Red Cross or Salvation Army. Many might picture a religious organization or countless other entities serving the less fortunate or children or both. Whatever your choice, it is more than likely a face drawn from the compassionate history of charities.

Now, try to describe the collective body of nonprofits. Is it big or small? Growing or shrinking? Which parts of the body are healthy, and which ones sick? And here are a few extra credit questions: How has that body changed over time? What helps its different parts grow, and what causes them to die? How does it interact with the other two members of the economic family: for-profits and the government? What does the nonprofit sector accomplish in the course of a year, and is it running faster, or more efficiently, than the year before?

What's that? You've got a cake burning in the oven? Call it the what's-his-name syndrome: We recognize the face, but we don't know much else about the economic traits and activities of the nonprofit sector.

Whoa, you might be saying—we're talking about nonprofits here. Next you'll be squeezing Mother Teresa into a supply-and-demand curve. What's the point?

One key reason to develop a clearer understanding of nonprofits is that they "are growing disproportionately" to the economy as a whole and are slowly assuming a larger share of the overall economy, said Kirsten Grønbjerg, Efroymson Chair in Philanthropy at the Center on Philanthropy at Indiana University. The sector has changed considerably, having seen explosive growth in terms of total organizations, organizational mix, employment, revenues and assets. You might say the nonprofit meek are inheriting the earth. Said Grønbjerg, "Clearly, it would seem to be useful to understand what's driving this."

But in spite of this growth, we know comparatively little about the nonprofit sector. What we do know—or think we know—with relative certainty merely scratches the surface, and yet still comes with a lot of measurement caveats. Very few historical and trend data are available on the many smaller "activity fields" that make up the nonprofit sector. The matter

Ten Years of Nonprofit Growth

	Number of Nonprofits		
	1996	2006	Change
Public charities	535,857	850,312	58.7%
Private foundations	58,944	100,029	69.7%
Noncharitable organizations	491,066	459,287	−6.5%
Total	1,085,867	1,409,628	29.8%

Source: National Center for Charitable Statistics at the Urban Institute.

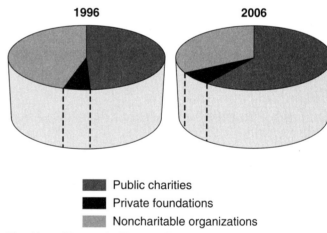

1996 **2006**

■ Public charities
■ Private foundations
■ Noncharitable organizations

Ten-Year Change in Types of Nonprofits

gets worse as we attempt to understand more sophisticated economic benchmarks, like output or productivity.

So you might say the nonprofit sector is something of a hidden economy. We know it's widespread and growing, but we don't have good measures for its economic activity or overall contributions, and those measures that we do have likely undervalue it. We obsess over for-profit sectors and their performance, but we're largely ignorant about nonprofits.

"Nonprofits are an afterthought in the economy, so all stats are relative to business," said David La Piana, corresponding via e-mail. He is president of La Piana Associates, a consulting firm to nonprofits based in Emeryville, Calif. "Nonetheless, nonprofits are a significant economic component and employer. We are missing something important by not [understanding] their output."

In some ways, the economics and activities of nonprofits are almost akin to how Secretary of Defense Donald Rumsfeld described the difficulties in Iraq: There are known-knowns, known-unknowns and unknown-unknowns. For example, the Internal Revenue Service has collected data on nonprofit organizational growth over time. OK, good start. But these data are fraught with methodological gaps that lead to both overcounting and undercounting the nonprofit universe (more on this in a bit). Without reliable data at the most fundamental level—organizations, employment—more difficult economic measures like output and productivity are beyond our grasp, and economists are hard-pressed to offer more than a shrug regarding the sector's performance and influence in the broader economy.

The Known-Knowns

First, a little housekeeping. People generally lump all nonprofits together as a group—as does a lot of research on this topic—when in reality the term "nonprofit" covers many types of organizations, with widely varying missions, sizes, revenue streams and other organizational and sectoral characteristics.

At their root, nonprofits are political creations, granted a federal exemption from paying various taxes on the theory that they offer some type of quasi-public service, and because people connected with the organization don't receive private gain from it. In all, several dozen nonprofit categories are notched into the federal tax code.

Here's what we know about the nonprofit sector: It's large, and it's growing rapidly. In terms of employment and/or gross receipts, in fact, it's believed to be larger than the finance and insurance industry, construction, wholesale trade or durable goods manufacturing. As a group, the number of U.S. nonprofits registered with the IRS has jumped by 30 percent since 1996, tallying more than 1.4 million, according to the National Center for Charitable Statistics, which uses IRS tax returns to compile a comprehensive database on nonprofits. By comparison, over a similar 10-year period (1993-2003), the number of private establishments (not including sole proprietorships) increased by about 14 percent, according to U.S. Census figures.

When it comes to trend-spotting in the sector, three types or groupings—public charities, private foundations and noncharitable organizations—encompass all nonprofits and also offer useful insights into sector trends. Public charities and private foundations both fall under the tax-code umbrella of 501(c)(3)s: They are exempt from federal and other taxes, and donations to such organizations are deductible from income taxes. Noncharitable organizations—essentially, everything besides 501(c)(3)s—are also tax exempt, but contributions to them are not deductible. Overall growth among nonprofits masks a markedly different pace among these three main groups. The number of public charities, for example, has risen by almost 60 percent in the past decade and now totals 850,000; foundations grew by 70 percent, topping 100,000 this year. In contrast, noncharitable organizations saw their numbers decline by almost

7 percent across the country—to 460,000—driven in part by the decrease in fraternal and other social associations. As a result, the nonprofit sector is becoming increasingly concentrated in 501(c)(3)s; their share of the sector has typically grown about 10 to 15 percentage points in many states over the past decade, often making up 55 to 70 percent of all nonprofits in a given state.

And though most nonprofits are small, as a group they are getting bigger and richer. In the past decade, gross annual receipts have doubled to $2.6 trillion, with total assets reaching $3.3 trillion—and these are conservative figures because of who is counted (more on this below). The explosion in revenue and assets tends to be concentrated in larger nonprofit organizations, particularly health care and education.

Charitable donations are also growing, and many smaller humanitarian organizations still depend heavily on such giving. But the sector is increasingly less dependent on donations for growth: The $260 billion in charitable donations received last year made up only about 10 percent of all nonprofit gross receipts. Fees for service now provide easily the largest chunk of nonprofit revenue, much of it in health care and education. In Wisconsin, for example, these two nonprofit subsectors make up about one-fifth of nonprofits but lay claim to about three-fourths of gross receipts.

Though national data on nonprofit employment aren't particularly solid, the rise in total nonprofit organizations, along with solid data from Minnesota (one of few states to track the sector), suggests that nonprofit employment is going gangbusters. From 1993 to 2004, nonprofit employment in Minnesota grew by 48 percent to more than 250,000 workers—an annual average growth rate of 4.4 percent. That's better than twice the private sector's employment growth rate for Minnesota and the nation—both of which came in at about 20 percent-over the same period.

And Now for the Footnotes

That might feel like strong statistical footing, but don't let go of the proverbial railing. Even these fairly straightforward measures of nonprofit economic activity are rife with caveats.

For example, the biggest pot of data on nonprofits comes from the IRS, which requires organizations to register with it in order to receive tax-exempt status; it also requires organizations with revenue over $25,000 to file an annual 990 tax return. Though it offers easily the best historical record of nonprofit growth, "there [are] problems with the IRS tracking of nonprofits," according to Kevin Rafter, a research associate at the Institute for Nonprofit Organization Management (INOM) at the University of San Francisco. "It has precision issues."

And how. IRS data do the seemingly impossible feat of simultaneously undercounting, overcounting and double counting. The data undercount because numerous types of organizations are exempt from filing 990s, most notably religious organizations, estimated to number 330,000. The data also overcount the total number of nonprofits because defunct organizations are not regularly purged from records. Rafter and others believe the dead weight could be 20 to 30 percent—possibly higher—of all organizations. IRS data also double count organizations at times, because some organizations register two entities, a 501(c)(3) so donations can be tax deductible and a 501(c)(4) to gain the unrestricted ability to lobby politically.

GuideStar is a leading online source of nonprofit information, much of it gleaned from 990s. Last year, GuideStar CEO Robert Ottenhoff wrote in the *Nonprofit Quarterly* that filing exemptions and errors in the returns that are filed create "a gaping hole in providing nonprofit data."

David Renz, director of the Midwest Center for Nonprofit Leadership at the University of Missouri-Kansas City, called the 990 data "terribly inaccurate," compounded by the fact that the IRS has "no motivation to get it right." As nontaxed entities, nonprofits do not represent a revenue stream to go after in terms of possible abuse. Any IRS efforts would be an exercise in data accuracy only. That might not matter if there were other data agencies to fall back on. But surprisingly, federal data offices like the Bureau of Labor Statistics and the Bureau of Economic Analysis offer virtually nothing on the sector—or at least nothing specific. Technically, nonprofit organizations and workers are counted in major government surveys, like the BLS's Occupational Employment Statistics survey. But the OES does not distinguish between nonprofit and for-profit workers. Given the small-minority status of nonprofits in terms of the total private market, data and trends on nonprofits simply get lost in the for-profit wash. With the assistance of some academic researchers, the BLS is developing better nonprofit measures for its Quarterly Census of Employment and Wages, but BLS officials say they won't be available for some time.

Don't You Love Me?

Why doesn't the government track the nonprofit sector? There are many reasons, some of them simple, others less so. Several sources noted that little attention is paid to the nonprofit sector data because most see nonprofits as economically insignificant. Rather than having a clear and purposeful role in the economy, "nonprofits are seen to fill a role left over from government and the for-profits," said Rafter, from INOM. Some likely view the sector as economically "trivial," according to Grønbjerg, from Indiana University. "There is probably a tendency to assume that whatever is important is in the for-profit sector."

That perception of nonprofits likely filters down to the priorities of data-gathering agencies. "It's a matter of administrative necessity and convenience. We're not willing to pay the costs" of getting good nonprofit data, Renz said. His organization produces a unique regional data set on the nonprofit industry in the greater Kansas City region. "I've tried to get government and foundation funding, and they don't care."

But even if time, interest and resources were all available, measuring the nonprofit sector in economic terms offers some unique challenges. In a nutshell, "some of the results are hard if not impossible to quantify or to verify," said Patrick Rooney, director of research at the Center on Philanthropy at Indiana University, via e-mail. Nonprofit motivations and outcomes are more nebulous and "sometimes completely intangible. It is a far cry from outputs and prices from the for-profit sector. But it is still important."

Employment offers a small window on the problem. Even if accurate data were gathered on workers drawing compensation from nonprofit organizations, such data would miss the contribution of volunteer labor to the nonprofit sector. Currently, only crude estimates of volunteer labor exist, and a very modest understanding of its value to organizations.

When it comes to even more sophisticated economic measures—like output and productivity—the matter quickly gets complicated. Technically speaking, total output by nonprofits is included in gross domestic product, according to Gabriel Medeiros, of the BEA's Current Industry Analysis Division, also corresponding by e-mail. Nonprofits are also included in value-added measures (equal to compensation and a measure of capital consumption) that are used for GDP figures. But these figures do not represent a genuine calculation of nonprofit output, but rather sort of a better-than-nothing measure.

"There are many reasons why nonprofit output is hard to pin down," said Medeiros. For starters, measuring the value of services, whether for-profit or nonprofit, is tougher than measuring the value of goods. "There are more imputations made when it comes to services. . . . Services are a lot harder to price," he said. In addition, many nonprofit services either have no price or the price charged has been subsidized by other revenue streams.

Because of this and other difficulties, nonprofit output is calculated by the BEA on an inputs (or expense) basis, according to Medeiros. A lot gets lost in the translation, mostly because many nonprofit inputs are nonmonetary. Renz gives an example of a regional mental health clinic in the Kansas City region. It operates on an all-volunteer basis, and even the facility was donated. The only expenses are for utilities like heat, water and electricity, which means "the (expense) measure of input doesn't have any bearing to output" of this mental health facility.

The lack of an accurate output yardstick has a ripple effect on other measures that economists and others typically find useful, like productivity—a measure "we know nothing about in the nonprofit sector," said Shawn Sprague, with the BLS Division of Major Sector Productivity, via e-mail. It's a pretty simple matter, really: Productivity is an efficiency measure for how well economic inputs are converted into outputs. Without real output measures, nonprofit productivity simply cannot be computed accurately. If you want to go through the calculations—outputs divided by inputs over time—the sector's productivity rate is negligible because annual inputs and outputs are the same.

Mere Academic Debate?

This might all seem very ethereal—interesting to discuss, but ultimately impractical—but the push to measure has already swept much of the nonprofit sector as nonprofit organizations, their boards and funders have taken a keen interest in outcomes, efficiency and performance measurement.

Over the past few years, very public controversies have arisen over the sector's performance and efficiency. In 2003, former U.S. Senator and presidential candidate Bill Bradley created a furor when he suggested that charities were wasting $100 billion a year, mostly on inefficient fundraising and administrative practices, as well as overlapping program services.

More recently, the Michael and Susan Dell Foundation, one of the nation's largest charitable foundations, has challenged nonprofits to become more efficient.

Even at the level of individual organizations, the nonprofit sector struggles with the notion of output measurement—and for many of the same basic reasons seen at the broader, sectoral level. In a recent paper on nonprofit organizational effectiveness, Robert Herman and David Renz, both of the Midwest Center for Nonprofit Leadership, wrote that nonprofits struggle to measure effectiveness at the organizational level because they lack "the simple criterion of bottom-line profit or loss. . . . The reality is the [nonprofit] effectiveness is more complicated."

So in the place of identifiable outcomes, financial and other input measures often serve as proxies for effectiveness and performance outcomes. For example, much attention is paid by nonprofit watchdog groups and others (notably United Way) to overhead costs and administrative efficiency (known in nonprofit circles as financial or funding ratios). Those with small funding ratios are touted as more efficient because more of an average dollar goes directly for services, rather than administrative costs.

Online firms like GuideStar and Charity Navigator have carved a niche in making such information available for hundreds of thousands of organizations, thanks to IRS 990 records.

But some are also beginning to question whether the goal of administrative efficiency might discourage nonprofits from making necessary investments in their infrastructure. Taken to the extreme, it turns into a race to the administrative bottom and assumes that all administrative costs are inefficient and wasteful, when in fact good administrative infrastructure is essential to good programs.

An obsession over economic and financial measurement might also be missing the point entirely about the role of nonprofits in society, ignoring important noneconomic contributions that nonprofits make to community and individual quality of life, according to Grønbjerg, from Indiana University. What's important "is not so much what (nonprofits) do, but what difference they make in the community" in terms of quality of life. "We are particularly far away from knowing anything about noneconomic contributions."

Still, La Piana, from California, believes it's fair to ask about nonprofit outcomes. "If nonprofits are in business to combat social problems . . . then asking what are they accomplishing is valid. On the other hand, it is a bit like asking if the growth of hospital emergency rooms is reducing the number of car wrecks." La Piana points out that nonprofits often deal "with the results of social problems, not the causes. Child abuse services often do more to help children and families than to prevent abuse, for example. But it is a discussion to have. I have no patience with nonprofits that say it is impossible to measure what they do. It is extremely difficult, but also essential to do so."

Don't Know What I Don't Know

So, given the many gray areas and all the measurement difficulties, is it worth the trouble to try to get a better handle on what nonprofits contribute to the nation's economy?

"Yes, it is important," said Charles Weinberg, who does research on nonprofits as a marketing professor at the University of British Columbia. "If we don't understand a major part of the economy, how are we going to know how the economy operates?"

Better economic data on nonprofits are important "for the same reason that for-profit businesses devour economic statistics—so they can identify trends and stay ahead of them," according to Woods Bowman, a DePaul University economist, and formerly with the Chicago Fed, corresponding via e-mail.

But to many, it's still a matter of out-of-sight, out-of-mind. "To the extent you don't know, you don't know why you should care" about the fact that comparatively few macro data on the industry are available, said Renz, in Kansas City. But he said there are very good—and urgent—reasons for getting a better economic understanding of the nonprofit sector.

"Why it is more important now—to a degree that it concerns me, and I'm not alone—is that nonprofits are an agent of government service delivery," Renz said. The federal government has been abdicating more of that system to nonprofits, and given the resources at stake, not to mention social stability considering the populations served, the system's reliability and efficiency are paramount.

"There are significant policy implications when you don't understand the health of the delivery system. . . . If you're going to take this imprecise information (on nonprofits) and make policy, you're really playing the blind-man-and-the-elephant game," said Renz.

So what's the holdup, you might ask? Most point back to the lack of systematic attention and data-gathering from traditional research agencies, particularly the federal government and academia. To Weinberg, the fundamental problem is a dearth of economists and academics who are interested in the nonprofit sector as a research focus. He's particularly puzzled by the fact that many areas of organizational and economic research on the for-profit sector are saturated. That means economists and academics can have a major impact on discovery within the nonprofit field. Yet there is little allure for newcomers.

Why? "It's a positioning problem," says Weinberg, the marketing expert. The sector doesn't receive much attention in the classroom or from scholars, and it is widely called the "third sector," which appears to denote its value—and thus prestige—vis-à-vis research in (or on) the private sector or government. "That's not a good marketing position to be in."

Some, like Bowman, from DePaul, argue that research on the nonprofit sector is really not so far behind. "We know less about it than the for-profit sector primarily because it is a newer field of inquiry," its genesis coming in the early 1970s after federal legislation required more reporting by organizations. He adds that the sector "is arguably more complex, so in a sense there is more to know."

And neither should one be left with the impression that no research whatever exists on the nonprofit sector. In fact, there's a growing body of research at the micro and organizational level on such topics as board governance, management, fundraising and charitable giving, performance measurement and other matters. With 27 chapters, the forthcoming second edition of

Walter Powell and Richard Steinberg's *The Nonprofit Sector: A Research Handbook* promises to make a notable contribution to the economic, political and historical understanding of nonprofits, and will fill in "some conspicuous gaps," according to the editors. But the book—several years in the making—is a case study in the slow-moving nature of nonprofit research.

Medeiros, from the BLS, believes more information will be available in the future. With a growing service economy, "there has been greater interest in the services measures, and both Census and the BLS I'm sure have been fighting for a bigger budget so that they can try to measure that sector of the economy appropriately." But any real progress, he said, "depends largely on the budget climate."

Rafter, from INOM, hopes that the researchers will continue to produce better data on the sector, but sees something of a chicken-and-egg scenario. There are very few data on nonprofits, he says, because there is very little demand for it, and there's low demand because people know so little. Rafter has done work in producing regional snapshots of the nonprofit sector in California, and he said, "people are not knocking down our door for it."

But as more data become available, and they're tailored to geography, subsector, mission and other specific targets, the sector will start demanding more information because of its intrinsic value in understanding trends. Rafter believes much of the demand will come from foundations and other philanthropists who are beginning to require new metrics for evaluating their grant-making.

Currently, he said, "the data are very imperfect. But I have hope that in 10 to 20 years they will be much better."

Eminence Green

The story of how Patagonia founder Yvon Chouinard took his passion for the outdoors and turned it into an amazing business.

Susan Casey

These words, a quotation from the legendary Sierra Club executive director David Brower, are the first thing you see when you walk into Patagonia headquarters in Ventura, Calif., and really, you can't miss them, given that they're etched into the front door.

The next thing you see, posted on a whiteboard above the reception desk, is today's surf report: "3–5 feet, check water quality." Not too promising. Which is why most of the 350 employees who work at this campus, a block's worth of sunny, yellow Mission-style buildings, are actually in residence. Write "double overheads, offshore wind" on that board, however, and watch the place clear out.

"There is no business to be done on a dead planet."

—(Fortune Magazine)

Freeform work environments have become common enough that barefoot employees, cavorting pets and organic chefs hardly merit a second glance. But Patagonia is no Web startup. It's a 35-year-old outdoor-clothing and equipment company. And yet, looking around at the bicycles, the surfboards, the solar panels, the Tibetan prayer flags, the shed full of convalescing owls and hawks, it's clear that you're not in traditional corporate-land, either. The place is all business, but it's business conducted upside down and inside out. Everything about it flies in the face of consultants' recommendations about How to Maximize Profits and Cut Costs. Simply put, it's radical. Which is exactly how Patagonia's founder, Yvon Chouinard, likes it.

"This company is an experiment," says the 68-year-old Chouinard, leaning back on a redwood chair in his office. Though he's given to provocative statements—"I don't think we're going to be here 100 years from now as a society, or maybe even as a species"—anyone expecting a pugnacious character would be surprised. He speaks softly, with a California drawl. Athletically built and small-statured, forged by a life spent in

nature's wildest corners, he looks more like a river guide than an executive.

And again, this is no accident. To Chouinard, the average suit ranks somewhere between alcoholic and criminal on the respect scale, and American business, when powered by the endless consumption and discarding of stuff, is unimaginative at best and evil at worst, responsible for clear-cutting forests, polluting oceans, and bulldozing wetlands to make way for the next condo development. Its modus operandi is unsustainable growth, which he compares to an "out-of-control tumor."

"I would never be happy playing by the normal rules of business," he writes in his book "Let My People Go Surfing," a combination memoir and green-business primer. "I wanted to distance myself as far as possible from those pasty-faced corpses in suits I saw in airline magazine ads . . . I wanted to be a fur trapper when I grew up."

Except he didn't end up skinning muskrats. Instead, he heads a company that made $270 million in revenues last year. No, that's not a huge number. Most of the company's competitors—Nike (Charts, Fortune 500), Adidas, and Timberland, to name a few—are much bigger. But from day one, Patagonia has punched above its weight—helped create a whole outdoor lifestyle, in fact. And decades before recycling became common practice, Patagonia was reusing materials. It was one of the first companies in America to provide onsite day care, both maternity and paternity leave and flextime. It used its lushly designed mail-order catalog to speak out about issues like genetically modified food and overfishing, proving that a company can benefit from having a voice and a moral compass, and that a clothing-company owner who quotes Thoreau ("Beware of any enterprises that require a new set of clothes") isn't necessarily a paradox.

Along the way, Patagonia's conscience has rubbed off on others, from smaller enterprises like Clif Bar to larger ones like Levi Strauss and the Gap (Charts, Fortune 500). Even Wal-Mart (Charts, Fortune 500): "The one thing that impresses me is the power of the people who work at Patagonia," says Matt Kistler, a senior vice president at Sam's Club, the warehouse-store division of Wal-Mart. "I was very impressed to see how involved in sustainability their employees are. They're tremendously knowledgeable and want to do the right thing."

So how did this antibusinessman's experimental little company become so influential? How did Chouinard hack his own contrarian path to success by putting the Earth first, questioning growth, ignoring fashion, making goods that don't break or wear out, telling customers to buy less, discontinuing his own profitable products, giving away chunks of earnings and saying things like, "If you're not pissing off 50 percent of the people, you're not trying hard enough"? And given Chouinard's intention to prove that "business can make a profit without losing its soul," how did he get so cozy with Wal-Mart?

To answer these questions you have to go back to 1957, to a garage in Burbank, Calif.

The 'Dirtbag' Way

Born in rural Maine to French-Canadian parents, Chouinard had an early education in rugged living and recalls watching his father once do his own dental work with pliers. When Yvon was 8, la famille Chouinard moved to Burbank. Speaking little English and saddled with a girl's name, Chouinard spent much of his time alone, exploring the nearby ocean, forests and lakes. School chafed (with the exception of shop class); social success was elusive. At 15 he followed several "fellow misfits" into the local falconry club, where he learned to rappel down from raptors' cliff-top nests. And at this point, everything changed. Climbing was it.

Life became a circuit of passions, with only occasional interruptions for school (two years in community college) and work (a stint at his brother's detective agency, where he spied on starlets for the main client, Howard Hughes). There was surfing in Baja, fly-fishing in the Tetons, and—especially—climbing in Yosemite. Chouinard gravitated to the famed Camp IV, where elite climbers congregated to scale the park's 2,000- to 3,000-foot granite walls. As much a '60s subculture as a base camp, Camp IV's residents shared a disdain for the establishment, a reverence for nature, and a genius for scaling sheer, vertical rock. Chouinard was in heaven.

But there was the problem of gear. Yosemite's difficult climbs called for a new generation of tools. Back in Burbank, Chouinard installed a coal forge in his parents' garage and became a self-taught blacksmith, hammering out pitons—three-inch strips of steel used for anchoring climbing ropes. Chouinard's pitons were stronger and more elegant than their predecessors, a triumph of minimalist engineering. He sold them out of the back of his car for $1.50 and tried to live on the proceeds.

It wasn't easy. There were lean years of Dumpster diving and, during one particularly fallow time, subsisting on cat food. There was a summer spent living in an abandoned incinerator. And in 1962, Chouinard was arrested with a climbing buddy in Winslow, Ariz., and spent 18 days in jail for "wandering around aimlessly with no apparent means of support." (Upon release, he was given 30 minutes to get out of town.) But what he describes as the "dirtbag" way—living as close to the wild as possible with as little as possible—never seemed like privation. Rather, this was freedom.

Chouinard managed to keep climbing even when he was drafted and sent to Korea for two years in the 1960s. Upon return he made a series of big-wall ascents that established him as one of the era's greats. He expanded his business, which he now called Chouinard Equipment, and moved it to Ventura—and he met his match: a rock-climbing art student named Malinda Pennoyer. They married in 1970.

Over the years, Chouinard Equipment grew and morphed and existed mainly to fund its owner's wilderness adventures. Malinda threw herself into the work, and in 1972 they branched into clothing, launching a new company called Patagonia. Among its early offerings were rugby shirts, corduroy knickers and boiled-wool mittens. Meanwhile the outdoor industry itself was taking off, with more people doing the kinds of activities that required these clothes.

Which is how Yvon Chouinard, who intended to spend approximately zero days of his life behind a desk, became a businessman. But he and Malinda were crystal clear: This would be business on their terms. It wouldn't release toxins into rivers or cause nervous breakdowns or chase endless growth. It wouldn't make disposable crap that people didn't really need. Anything it produced would be of the highest quality, manufactured in the most responsible way. When the surf was up or the powder wafted down, employees would be where they ought to be: outside. If an employee's child was sick, the parent would also be where he ought to be: at home. They would keep Patagonia privately held and say no to anything that compromised their values.

Scaling the likes of Yosemite's El Capitan, Chouinard had learned big lessons. The biggest was that reaching the summit had nothing to do with where you arrived and everything to do with how you got there. Likewise, he thought, with business: The point was not to focus on making money; focus on doing things right, and the profits would come. And they did.

Pradagonia

On a winter Saturday afternoon the Patagonia store on Manhattan's Upper West Side is jammed with shoppers eyeing Houdini full-zip shells, Plush Synchilla hoodies, Micro Puff Polarguard vests and Recycled Capilene underpants. Unlike, say, Abercrombie & Fitch (Charts), where anyone over 23 is greeted with a hostile stare, there is no one type of customer here. There are couples pushing double-wide strollers, teenagers and grandparents, and even a woman in high heels clicking across the sustainably harvested Douglas fir floor.

None of them is suiting up for Everett anytime soon, and many would be surprised to hear Chouinard's criteria about what makes the merchandise appealing: "You should be able to wash travel clothes in a sink or a cooking pot, then hang them out to dry in a hut and still look decent for the plane ride home."

It's ironic that although Chouinard detests trendiness, he instructs Patagonia designers to ignore the current fashions and tells his customers that "the more you know, the less you need," people often refer to this store, and the other 22 like it, as Patagucci and Pradagonia.

As always, there is plenty of fleece on the shelves. In 1977 the company created its breakthrough product, a jacket made of polyester pile that, unlike natural fibers, repelled moisture while retaining heat. It was stiff and ungainly but worked like a charm in environments where looking odd was preferable to getting hypothermia.

Refinements continued. Working with fabric manufacturer Malden Mills, Patagonia created a finer, softer version called Synchilla in colors like sea-foam green and garnet red. Sales exploded, and the company became known for the "fleece jacket." Later, when Patagonia discovered it could make Synchilla using discarded soda bottles, Chouinard saw a way to reconcile his expanding business with his angst over manufacturing's destructive effects: by conducting an "environmental assessment" of all materials. Could recycled materials be used in a product? Could the product itself be recycled? Which materials caused the most harm to the environment, and which the least?

"We didn't have any of the answers," Chouinard recalls. "There was no book you could pick up and say, Here's what we need to do. We didn't know that making clothes out of a synthetic was better than making them out of a natural material. And so what about rayon? It's made out of cellulose, which is made out of trees—that seems like a good product. But then you find out they use really toxic chemicals to convert it." It turned out that hemp was the most responsible fiber but only if grown in cold, wet climates. Wool, too, could be good or bad: "If you get it from sheep grazing in alpine meadows," Chouinard says, "that's damaging as hell."

Greener Materials

Conventionally grown cotton was especially heinous. Heavily dependent on noxious pesticides, insecticides and defoliants, it's an environmentalist's nightmare crop. "To know this and not switch to organic cotton would be unconscionable," Chouinard says. In 1994 he gave his managers 18 months to make the change. Given that organic cotton, rare at the time, cost between 50 percent to 100 percent more, and that a fifth of Patagonia's business came from cotton products, this was no small risk. There was pushback from the ranks; suppliers defected. Chouinard delivered his ultimatum: Do it, or we never use cotton again.

The gamble paid off. Patagonia's cotton sales rose 25 percent and, more important, established an organic-cotton industry so that other companies could cross over. Demand grew and prices decreased, leading to even more demand. In 2006, Wal-Mart became the world's largest purchaser of organic cotton.

You'd think this would make Chouinard happy. And it does, to a point. He's ecstatic over Wal-Mart's green initiatives. But when executives from Sam's Club came to Ventura last month to meet him, he told them they needed to go further. "Even organic cotton is bad," he says. "It's better to make clothes out of polyester if you can recycle them into more clothes, and keep doing it—like we do with aluminum cans—instead of growing more organic cotton and selling cheap clothes that people just throw away."

In the early 2000s, the Japanese fabric company Teijin, a partner of Patagonia's, invented a process by which used polyester can be almost endlessly recycled. Patagonia, which makes a line of polyester base layers known as Capilene, encouraged customers to send back their worn-out underwear. (It now also accepts products made from fleece, nylon and organic cotton.) Recycling polyester, Chouinard says, is a home run: "We use 76 percent less energy than if we'd made it out of virgin petroleum."

The questioning continued. Chlorine disappeared from Patagonia's wool products, replaced by a patented slow-wash technique. Instead of adding antimicrobial silver, a groundwater pollutant, to its underwear lines, it used a product made of crushed crab shells for odor control. It became the first California company to use renewable sources like wind and solar to power all its buildings, and one of the first to print catalogs on recycled paper.

After discovering that airfreight requires more energy than shipping by ground or sea—at least eight times more, according to Luke Tonachel at the Natural Resources Defense Council—the company advised customers to "ask yourself if you really need that pair of pants sent overnight."

But Patagonia does offer that option, which brings up an inconvenient truth: No matter how careful the choice of materials or methods, all companies leave a footprint. This is Chouinard's conundrum, and you get the sense it keeps him up at night. "Patagonia will never be completely socially responsible," he writes gloomily at the end of his book. "It will never make a totally sustainable, nondamaging product. But it is committed to trying."

Surf's Up

"This is our sweatshop," Chouinard says, and the roomful of workers sitting behind sewing machines bursts out laughing. The place is idyllic. Rolls of fabric are stacked like a psychedelic patch of giant flowers; sunlight and bird song stream through open windows that look onto a playground of the company's day-care facility. Walking around headquarters with Chouinard is like going on a sprawling house tour: Here is the Infant Room, the day-care annex for newborns; here, in a onetime slaughterhouse, is the first Patagonia store; here is the original blacksmith shop where Chouinard Equipment was born. "I still come out here and make fireplace tools," Chouinard says.

He greets employees by name, and they light up when they see him. But the laidback ambience is misleading. Competition to be here is stiff; Patagonia receives more than 900 applications for every job opening. The people who get hired are anything but slackers, and Chouinard is an unrepentant perfectionist. "He has an easygoing persona, and he's a California guy," says Casey Sheahan, Patagonia's 51-year-old CEO. (He got the job in March 2006.) "But he does demand excellence. People in this company would run through walls for him."

That would be a shame. The walls are gorgeous, filled with nature photographs and paintings, including many of Mount Fitzroy, the South American peak that inspired Patagonia's logo. The images evoke the solidity and timelessness that Chouinard has tried to instill in his brand, which makes it startling to hear what he has to say next: "We're in the middle of a revolution. Every ten years we have to blow this place up."

The reason for the upheaval? Climate change. "We're getting into the surf market, because it's never going to snow again, and the waves are going to get bigger and bigger," Chouinard says. "I see an opportunity." In response, he is opening Patagonia watersports shops along the coasts and in Hawaii. The first, in Cardiff-by-the-Sea, Calif., opened in June 2006.

Like his stand on organic cotton, Chouinard's vision of a stormier, more aquatic world caused some heels to dig in. No midsized, well-established company has ever broken into the surf industry, his skeptics remind him; it's all edgy startups or billion-dollar juggernauts like Billabong. "People just do not like change," he says. "You've got all these people hired to create a mountain-sports company, and now you're telling them to go 50 percent watersports." He sighs. "Now it's accepted. But there's still grumbling."

This "Ocean Initiative" has its roots in a Quonset hut across the parking lot, where his son Fletcher, 31, is crafting a line of surfboards made with nontoxic materials that Patagonia claims are stronger, lighter and more eco-friendly than its competitors'. Surf legend Gerry Lopez has signed on to the effort, as have Chris, Keith and Dan Malloy, professional surfer siblings who have serious industry clout.

Another watersports product Chouinard shows off with pride is a new wetsuit. Anyone who has spent time encased in neoprene knows that it can be stiff, uncomfortable, and smelly. Chouinard, who surfs about 200 days a year, was determined to improve on this. "He told me he wanted to make the perfect wetsuit material," says Tetsuya O'Hara, 44, Patagonia's manager of raw material sourcing and development. O'Hara, who previously developed sailcloth technologies for the America's Cup, began with a new, nonpetroleum neoprene made from crushed limestone and then added a lining of recycled polyester and, of all things, organic wool. The Patagonia suit is pricey ($470), but in-house testing showed it to be 90 percent warmer than other wetsuits, as well as stretchier, stronger and naturally odor resistant.

Compared with fleece, surf gear may seem like a sideline, but this is classic Chouinard—activism mixed with reluctant capitalism. If anything, he's more concerned with Patagonia's growing too fast. (Typical revenue growth is a modest 3 to 8 percent a year. And a fair chunk of the company's haul is given away—$26 million donated to grass-roots organizations since 1985.) That kind of attitude can get you fired in corporate America. But as the guy who owns 100 percent of the company—he gets calls regularly from would-be buyers—he can do what he wants.

"Everybody tells me it's an undervalued company," he says, "that we could grow this business like crazy and then go public, make a killing." He shakes his head. "But that would be the end of everything I've wanted to do. It would destroy everything that I believe in." Chouinard's good friend and fellow environmentalist Tom Brokaw has heard him put it far more succinctly: "He says, 'I don't want a Wall Street greaseball running my company.' That is a direct quote.'"

The Revolution Has Started

Could it be that the world is finally catching up to Yvon Chouinard? These days he's a standing-room-only ticket at Stanford and Harvard business schools. Yale, which awarded him an honorary doctorate in humane letters in 1995, recently offered him a fellowship to teach courses merging business with environmental studies. "I mean, can you imagine that?" he says, laughing. "I got a degree in auto mechanics at John Burroughs High School. But there's no surf in New Haven."

The appeal of his message has gone way beyond students—other companies are paying attention too. In 2001 he created One Percent for the Planet, an alliance of businesses that pledge to donate 1 percent of gross revenues to environmental causes. To date, 500 organizations have signed on.

Wal-Mart is not among them, but Chouinard's greatest cause for optimism nevertheless comes from Bentonville, Ark. "The revolution really has started," he says with a slow, curling and just slightly subversive smile. "I'm blown away by Wal-Mart. If Wal-Mart does one-tenth of what they say they're going to do, it will be incredible. And hopefully America will get a government that we need rather than one we deserve, that will put pressure on business to clean up its act. But the most powerful pressure will come from the consumer. Oh, my God, it's going to be really powerful."

As Chouinard sees it, there's only one downside to this good news: It's probably too late. "There's a race between running out of water, topsoil or petroleum. I don't know what's going to be first. Or maybe it will all happen at once."

Locusts, high water, whatever; you can bet that Chouinard will be out there, on a Patagonia surfboard. "I'm a very happy person," he says. "I never get depressed, even though I know that everything's going to hell."

From *Fortune*, April 2, 2007. Copyright © 2007 by Fortune Magazine. Reprinted by permission.

Managing Global Expansion: A Conceptual Framework

ANIL K. GUPTA AND VIJAY GOVINDARAJAN

There at least five reasons why the need to become global has ceased to be a discretionary option and become a strategic imperative for virtually any medium-sized to large corporation.

1. The growth imperative. Companies have no choice but to persist in a neverending quest for growth if they wish to garner rewards from the capital markets and attract and retain top talent. For many industries, developed country markets are quite mature. Thus, the growth imperative generally requires companies to look to emerging markets for fresh opportunities.

Consider a supposedly mature industry such as paper. Per capita paper consumption in such developed markets as North America and Western Europe is around 600 pounds. In contrast, per capita consumption of paper in China and India is around 30 pounds. If you are a dominant European paper manufacturer such as UPM-Kymmene, can you really afford not to build market presence in places like China or India? If per capita paper consumption in both countries increased by just one pound over the next five years, demand would increase by 2.2 billion pounds, an amount that can keep five state-of-the-art paper mills running at peak capacity.

2. The efficiency imperative. Whenever the value chain sustains one or more activities in which the minimum efficient scale (of research facilities, production centers, and so on) exceeds the sales volume feasible within one country, a company with global presence will have the potential to create a cost advantage relative to a domestic player within that industry. The case of Mercedes-Benz, now a unit of DaimlerChrysler, illustrates this principle. Historically, Mercedes-Benz has concentrated its research and manufacturing operations in Germany and has derived around 20 percent of its revenues from the North American market. Given the highly scale-sensitive nature of the auto industry, it is easy to see that Mercedes-Benz's ability to compete in Europe, or even Germany, hinges on its market position and revenues from the North American market.

3. The knowledge imperative. No two countries, even close neighbors such as Canada and the United States, are completely alike. So when a company expands its presence to more than one country, it must adapt at least some features of its products and/or processes to the local environment. This adaptation requires creating local know-how, some of which may be too idiosyncratic to be relevant outside the particular local market. However, in many cases, local product and/or process innovations are cutting-edge and have the potential to generate global advantage. GE India's innovations in making CT scanners simpler, transportable, and cheaper would appear to enjoy wide-ranging applicability, as would P&G Indonesia's innovations in reducing the cost structure for cough syrup.

> **Going international needs no grand design, but neither should a company wander aimlessly into the global jungle.**

4. Globalization of customers. The term "globalization of customers" refers to customers that are worldwide corporations (such as the soft-drink companies served by advertising agencies) as well as those who are internationally mobile (such as the executives served by American Express or the globe-trotters serviced by Sheraton Hotels). When the customers of a domestic company start to globalize, the company must keep pace with them. Three reasons dictate such an alignment. First, the customer may strongly prefer worldwide consistency and coordination in the sourcing of products and services. Second, it may prefer to deal with a small number of supply partners on a long-term basis. Third, allowing a customer to deal with different supplier(s) in other countries poses a serious risk that the customer may replace your firm with one of these suppliers even in the domestic market. Motivations such as these are driving GE Plastics to globalize. Historically, it supplied plastic pellets to largely U.S.-based telephone companies such as AT&T and GTE. As these firms globalized and set up manufacturing plants outside the U.S., GE Plastics had no choice but to follow them abroad.

5. Globalization of competitors. If your competitors start to globalize and you do not, they can use their global stronghold to attack you in at least two ways. First, they can develop a first-mover advantage in capturing market growth, pursuing global scale efficiencies, profiting from knowledge arbitrage, and providing a coordinated source of supply to global customers. Second, they can use multi-market presence to cross-subsidize and wage a more intense attack in your own home markets. It is dangerous to underestimate the rate at which competition can accelerate the pace of globalization. Look at Fuji's inroads into the U.S. market, historically dominated by Kodak. The trend is happening in other industries as well, such as in white goods, personal computers, and financial services.

In the emerging era, every industry must be considered a global industry. Today, globalization is no longer an option but a strategic imperative for all but the smallest firms. The following framework and set of conceptual ideas can guide firms in approaching the strategic challenge of casting their business lines overseas and building global presence:

- How should a multiproduct firm choose the product line to launch it into the global market?
- What factors make some markets more strategic than others?
- What should companies consider in determining the right mode of entry?
- How should the enterprise transplant the corporate DNA as it enters new markets?
- What approaches should the company use to win the local battle?
- How rapidly should a company expand globally?

Choice of Products

When any multiproduct firm chooses to go abroad, it must ask itself whether it should globalize the entire portfolio simultaneously or use a subset of product lines. Firms can make this choice randomly and opportunistically or in a well thought out and systematic manner.

Consider the case of Marriott Corporation, which was essentially a domestic company in the late 1980s. It had two principal lines of business: lodging and contract services. Besides other activities, the lodging sector included four distinct product lines: full-service hotels and resorts ("Marriott" brand), mid-price hotels ("Courtyard" brand), budget hotels ("Fairfield Inn" brand), and long-term stay hotels ("Residence Inn" brand). On the other hand, contract services included the following three product lines: Marriott Management Services, Host/Travel Plazas, and Marriott Senior Living Services (retirement communities). As the company embarked on globalization, it had to confront the question of which one or more of these product lines should serve as the starting point for its globalization efforts.

Global expansion forces companies to develop at least three types of capabilities: learning about foreign markets, learning how to manage people in foreign locations, and learning how to manage foreign subsidiaries. Until firms develop these capabilities, they cannot avoid remaining strangers in a strange

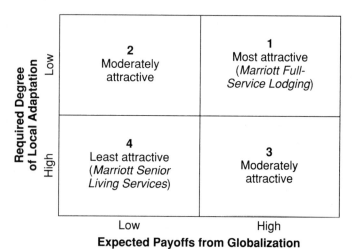

Figure 1 A framework for choice of products: attractiveness of product lines as launch vehicles for initial globalization.

land, with global expansion posing a high risk. Engaging in simultaneous globalization across the entire portfolio of products compounds these risks dramatically. So it is often wiser to choose one or a small number of product lines as the initial launch vehicles for globalization. The choice should adhere to the twin goals of maximizing the returns while minimizing the risks associated with early moves abroad. These initial moves represent experiments with high learning potential. It is important that these experiments succeed for the firm because success creates psychological confidence, political credibility, and cash flow to fuel further rapid globalization.

Figure 1 presents a conceptual framework to identify those products, business units, or lines of business that might be preferred candidates for early globalization. Underlying this framework are two essential dimensions by which to evaluate each line of business in the company's portfolio—one pertaining to potential returns (expected payoffs) and the other to potential risks (required degree of local adaptation).

The first dimension focuses on the magnitude of globalization's payoffs, which tend to be higher when the five imperatives (listed at the beginning of the article) are stronger. Looking at the case of Marriott, it is clear that such imperatives are much stronger for full-service lodging than they are for the retirement community business. The primary customers of full-service lodging are globe-trotting corporate executives. In such a business, worldwide presence can create significant value by using a centralized reservation system, developing and diffusing globally consistent service concepts, and leveraging a well-known brand name that assures customers of high quality and service. In contrast, none of these factors is of high salience in the retirement community business, thereby rendering the imperatives for globalization much less urgent.

The second dimension of our framework concerns the extent to which different lines of business require local adaptation to succeed in foreign markets. The greater the extent of such adaptation, the greater the degree to which new product and/or service features would need to be developed locally rather than cloned from proven and preexisting concepts and capabilities. Because any new development involves risk, the greater the degree of required local adaptation, the greater the risks of failure—particularly when such development entails the already significant "liability of foreignness." Marriott exemplifies these principles. Compared with full-service lodging, the retirement community business is a very local business and thus requires more local adaptation.

Combining both dimensions, as indicated in Figure 1, full-service lodging emerges as a particularly attractive candidate for early globalization. As the spearhead for globalization moves, it provides Marriott with a high return/low risk laboratory for developing the knowledge and skills needed for foreign market entry and managing foreign subsidiaries. Having thus overcome the "liability of foreignness," Marriott would be better positioned to exploit the globalization potential of its other lines of business.

To reiterate, hardly any line of business today is devoid of the potential for exploitation on a global scale. However, any multiproduct firm that is starting to globalize must remember that a logically sequenced rather than random approach is likely to serve as a higher-return, lower-risk path toward full-scale globalization.

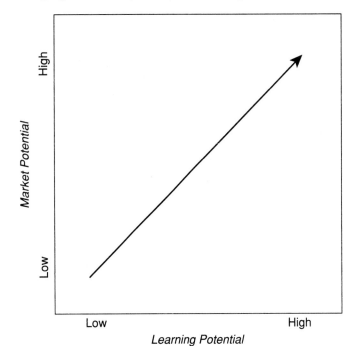

Figure 2   Drivers of a market's strategic importance.

Choice of Strategic Markets

Not all markets are of equal strategic importance. This is a central tenet of the conceptual framework presented in Figure 2. The following two dimensions determine the strategic importance of a market: (1) *market potential,* and (2) *learning potential.*

The concept of market potential encompasses both current market size and growth expectations for a particular line of business. For instance, one of the critical markets for AOL is Japan because 45 percent of the PCs sold in Asia are there. It is important to remember that, notwithstanding the importance of the size of a country's economy, market potential does not always go hand in hand with the country's GDP. A blindness to this reality has led some authors to conclude that companies are not global unless they are present in the triad of Europe, Japan, and North America. Such simplistic conclusions can often be dramatically fallacious. If you are managing ABB's power plant business, the bulk of your market for new power plants lies outside the triad.

There are two drivers of the learning potential of any market. The first is the presence of sophisticated and demanding customers for the particular product or service. Such customers (1) force a company to meet very tough standards for product and service quality, cost, cycle time, and a host of other attributes, (2) accelerate its learning regarding tomorrow's customer needs, and (3) force it to innovate constantly and continuously. France and Italy are leading-edge customer markets for the high fashion clothing industry—a fact of considerable importance to a company such as Du Pont, the manufacturer of Lycra and other textile fibers.

The second driver of a market's learning potential is the pace at which relevant technologies are evolving there. This technology evolution can emerge from one or more of several sources: leading-edge customers, innovative competitors, universities and other local research centers, and firms in related industries.

As indicated in Figure 2, the strategic importance of a market is a joint function of both market potential and learning potential. No firm is truly global unless it is present in all strategic markets. Nevertheless, despite their obvious importance, the timing of a firm's decision to enter strategic markets must also depend on its "ability to exploit" these markets. Going after a strategic market without such an ability is generally a fast track to disaster.

The ability to exploit a market is a function of two factors: (1) the height of entry barriers, and (2) the intensity of competition in the market. Entry barriers are likely to be lowest when there are no regulatory constraints on trade and investment (as in the case of regional economic blocks) and when new markets are geographically, culturally, and linguistically proximate to the domestic market. Even when there are low entry barriers, the intensity of competition can hinder a company's potential for exploiting a market. For example, the large U.S. market in the retailing industry has historically proven to be a graveyard for foreign entrants such as Marks & Spencer, precisely because of the intensity of local competition.

Figure 3 presents a conceptual framework that combines the two key dimensions—"strategic importance of market" and "ability to exploit"—to offer guidelines on how a firm can engage in directed opportunism in its choice of markets. The firm's stance toward markets that have high strategic importance and high ability to exploit ought to be to enter rapidly. By comparison, the firm can afford to be much more opportunistic and ad hoc with respect to markets that have low strategic importance but are easier to exploit. In the case of markets that have

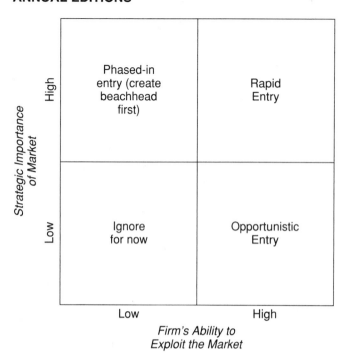

Figure 3 A Framework for choice of markets.

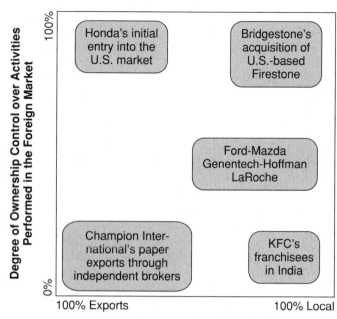

Exports versus Local Production

Figure 4 Alternative modes of entry.

high strategic importance but are also very difficult to exploit, we recommend an incremental phased approach in which the development of needed capabilities precedes market entry. One attractive way for a company to develop such capabilities is to first enter a *beachhead market:* one that closely resembles the targeted strategic market but provides a safer opportunity to learn how to enter and succeed there. Some commonly used examples of beachhead markets are Switzerland and/or Austria for Germany, Canada for the U.S., and Hong Kong or Taiwan for China. Finally, the firm should stay away from those markets that are neither strategic nor easy to exploit.

Mode of Entry

Once a company has selected the country or countries to enter and designated the product line(s) that will serve as the launch vehicles, it must determine the appropriate mode of entry. The entry mode issue rests on two fundamental questions. The first concerns the extent to which the firm will export or produce locally. Here, the firm has several choices. It can rely on 100 percent export of finished goods, export of components but localized assembly, 100 percent local production, and so on.

The second question deals with the extent of ownership control over activities that will be performed locally in the target market. Here also, the firm faces several choices: 0 percent ownership modes (licensing, franchising, and so on), partial ownership modes (joint ventures or affiliates), and 100 percent ownership modes (fully-owned greenfield operations or acquisitions). Figure 4 uses these two dimensions to depict the array of choices regarding mode of entry that are open to any firm, and includes examples illustrating the variety of available options.

Choosing the right mode of entry is critical because the choice, once made, is often difficult and costly to alter. Inappropriate decisions can impose unwanted, unnecessary, and undesirable constraints on future development options.

Turning to the first question, greater reliance on local production would be appropriate under the following four conditions:

- *Size of local market is larger than minimum efficient scale of production.* The larger the size of the local market, the more completely local production will translate into scale economies for the firm while holding down tariff and transportation costs. One illustration of this argument is Bridgestone's entry into the U.S. market by acquiring the local production base of Firestone instead of exporting tires from Japan.

- *Shipping and tariff costs associated with exporting to the target market are so high* that they neutralize any cost advantages associated with producing in any country other than that market. This is why cement companies such as Cemex and Lafarge Coppee engage heavily in local production in every country they enter.

- *Need for local customization of product design is high.* Product customization requires two capabilities: a deep understanding of local market needs, and an ability to incorporate this understanding in the company's design and production decisions. Localizing production in the target market significantly enhances the firm's ability to respond to local market needs accurately and efficiently.

- *Local content requirements are strong.* This is one of the major reasons why foreign auto companies rely heavily on local production in markets such as the EU, China, and India.

Turning to the second question, given the differing costs and benefits of local market activities, neither alliances nor complete ownership are universally desirable in all situations. Unlike the complete ownership mode, alliance-based entry modes have the advantages of permitting the firm to share the costs and risks associated with market entry, allowing rapid access to local know-how, and giving managers the flexibility to respond more entrepreneurially and much more quickly to dynamic global competition than the conquer-the-world-by-yourself approach. However, a major downside of alliances is their potential for various types of conflict stemming from differences in corporate goals and cultures.

Taking into account the pros and cons, then, alliance-based entry modes are often more appropriate under the following conditions:

- *Physical, linguistic, and cultural distance between the home and host countries is high.* The more dissimilar and unfamiliar the target market, the greater the need for the firm to rely on a local partner to provide know-how and networks. Conceivably, the firm could obtain the requisite local knowledge and competencies through acquisition. However, in highly dissimilar and unfamiliar markets, its ability to manage an acquired subsidiary is often very limited. Ford's decision to enter the Indian market through the joint venture (JV) mode rested partly on the company's need to rely on an experienced and respected local partner, Mahindra & Mahindra.

- *The subsidiary would have low operational integration with the rest of the multinational operations.* By definition, tighter integration between a subsidiary and the rest of the global network increases the degree of mutual interdependence between the subsidiary and the network. In this context of high interdependence, it becomes crucial for the subsidiary and the network to pursue shared goals, and for the firm to be able to reshape the subsidiary according to the changing needs of the rest of the network. Shared ownership of the subsidiary puts major constraints on the firm's ability to achieve such congruence in goals and have the requisite freedom to reshape subsidiary operations as needed.

- *The risk of asymmetric learning by the partner is (or can be kept) low.* In a typical JV, two partners pool different but complementary know-how into an alliance. Ongoing interaction between their core operations and the alliance gives each an opportunity to learn from the other and appropriate the other's complementary know-how. In effect, this dynamic implies that the alliance often is not just a cooperative relationship but also a learning race. If Firm A has the ability to learn at a faster rate than Firm B, the outcome is likely to be asymmetric learning in favor of Firm A. Thus, over time, Firm A may seek to dissolve the alliance in favor of going it alone in competition with a still-disadvantaged Firm B.

- *The company is short of capital.* Lack of capital underlay Xerox's decision in the 1950s to enter the

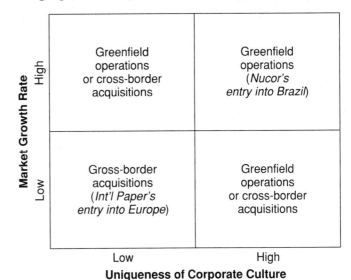

Figure 5   Greenfield vs. cross-border acquisition.

European market through an alliance with the Rank Organization of the U.K.

- *Government regulations require local equity participation.* Historically, many countries with formidable market potentials, such as China and Brazil, have successfully imposed the JV option on foreign entrants, even when all other considerations might have favored the choice of a complete ownership mode.

A company that decides to enter the foreign market through local production rather than through exports faces a secondary decision. It must decide whether to set up greenfield operations or use an existing production base through a cross-border acquisition. A greenfield operation gives the company tremendous freedom to impose its own unique management policies, culture, and mode of operations on the new subsidiary. In contrast, a cross-border acquisition poses the much tougher challenge of cultural transformation and post-merger integration. However, setting up greenfield operations also has two potential liabilities: lower speed of entry, and more intense local competition caused by the addition of new production capacity as well as one more competitor. Taking into account both the pros and the cons, Figure 5 provides a conceptual framework to determine when greenfield operations and/or cross-border acquisitions are likely to be the more appropriate entry modes.

This conceptual framework has two dimensions. The first pertains to the uniqueness of the globalizing company's culture. Nucor is a good example of a newly globalizing firm with a very strong and unique culture. It is significantly different from other steel producers in its human resource policies, egalitarian work environment, performance-based incentives, team-work, decentralization, and business processes. The more committed a company is to preserving its unique culture, the more necessary it becomes to set up greenfield operations when entering foreign markets. This is because building and nurturing a unique culture from scratch (as would be feasible in the case of greenfield operations) is almost always much easier than transforming an entrenched culture (as would be necessary in the case of a cross-border acquisition).

Aside from corporate culture considerations, the impact of entry mode on the resulting intensity of local competition must also carry considerable weight in a firm's decisions. If the local market is in the emerging or high growth phase (such as the auto industry in China and India), new capacity additions would have little downside effect on the intensity of competition. In contrast, when the local market is mature (such as the tire industry in the U.S.), new capacity additions will only intensify an already high degree of local competition. Within the forest products industry, Indonesia-based Asia Pulp & Paper has used the greenfield mode for expanding into other high-growth Asian markets. In the same industry, the U.S.-based International Paper has pursued a different path and relied on the acquisition mode for its expansion into the mature European market.

Transplanting the Corporate DNA

Having decided on a mode of entry for a particular product line into a particular target market, the challenge of building global presence moves on to implementing actual entry. Among the first issues the globalizing company must address is how to transplant the core elements of its business model, its core practices, and its core beliefs—in short, its DNA—to the new subsidiary. The following example illustrates the challenge of transplanting the corporate DNA.

After acquiring 2,000 employees from Yamaichi Securities, Merrill Lynch & Co. counted on an American-style investment advisor approach to build a high-trust image in the securities brokerage industry in Japan. Historically, says Sugawara (1999), the industry has been

> tainted by unsavory practices.... One well-known abuse ... is "churning"—in which sales people persuade naive investors to buy and sell a lot of securities so the sales people can boost their commissions. Merrill Lynch promised that there would be no churning. Instead, its sales people were instructed to try to get an overall picture of customers' finances, ascertain their needs and then suggest investments. Something got lost in the translation, however. Japanese customers have complained that Merrill Lynch sales people are too nosy, asking questions about their investments instead of just telling them what stocks to buy.

As this example illustrates, obstacles to transplanting the corporate DNA can emerge from any of several sources: local employees, local customers, local regulations, and so forth. Given such obstacles, every company needs to develop clarity regarding what exactly its "core" (as distinct from "peripheral") beliefs and practices are. Such clarity is essential for knowing where the company should stay committed to its own beliefs and practices and where it should be willing to adapt. Having achieved this clarity, the company needs to build mechanisms to transfer core beliefs and practices to the new subsidiary. Finally, and most important, it needs to embed these beliefs and practices in the new subsidiary.

Clarifying and Defining the Core Beliefs and Practices

Core beliefs and practices can be defined at any of varying levels of abstraction. Take Wal-Mart's practice of promoting "Made in America" goods in its U.S. stores. Assuming that promoting the origin-of-manufacture is a core practice for Wal-Mart, the company can define the practice in more or less abstract terms. A more abstract definition would be, "Wherever we operate, we believe in promoting locally manufactured products." On the other hand, a less abstract definition would be, "We promote products that are made in America." As this example points out, defining core beliefs and practices in more abstract terms permits a higher degree of local adaptation. At the same time, if the core beliefs and practices become too abstract, they could lose much of their meaning and value.

Notwithstanding its criticality, the definition of what constitutes a company's core beliefs and practices is and must always be the result of learning and experimentation over time. This is because the answers will almost certainly vary across industries, across firms within an industry, and, for the same firm, across time. As observed astutely by a senior executive of a major global retailer, "Cut your chains and you become free. Cut your roots and you die. Note, however, that differentiating between the two requires good judgment, something that you acquire only through experience and over time."

Transplanting Core Beliefs and Practices to the New Subsidiary

Transplanting core beliefs and practices to a new subsidiary, whether a greenfield operation or an acquisition, is always a transformational event—the challenge of transformation being greater in the case of an acquisition. The likelihood is very high that the transplanted beliefs and practices are likely to be at best partially understood and, in the case of an acquisition, will often be seen as alien and questionable. As such, transferring core beliefs and practices to a new subsidiary almost always requires transferring a select group of committed believers ("the DNA carriers") to the new operation. The size of this group would depend largely on the scale of the desired transformation effort. If the goal is to engage in a wholesale replacement of an entire set of preexisting beliefs and practices (as in the case of ABB's acquisitions in Eastern Europe), then it may be necessary to send in a virtual army of DNA carriers. On the other hand, if the goal is to create a new business model (as in the case of Mercedes-Benz's Alabama plant), then the transplants would need to be much fewer in number and would need to be very carefully selected.

Obloj and Thomas (1998) describe rather vividly how the invasion process worked in the case of ABB Poland:

> The transformation began with an influx and invasion of external and internal ABB consultants that signaled clearly the introductory stage of organizational change. Their behavior was guided by their perception of the stereotypical behavior of an inefficient state-owned firm typically managed by a cadre of administrators who do not understand how to manage a firm in a market economy. They did not initially perform any sophisticated diagnosis or analysis of local conditions or develop a strategic vision for the transformation process. Rather, they forcefully implemented market enterprise discipline in the acquired former state-owned firms by a series of high-speed actions. They implemented massive training efforts aimed at exposing employees and managers of acquired firms to the principles of the market economy, modem management principles, and the ABB management system. This was adopted in all acquired firms following Percy Barnevik's dictum that the key to competitiveness is education and reeducation.

Embedding the Core Beliefs and Practices

While the process of transplanting the corporate DNA starts with transferring a select group of DNA carriers to the new subsidiary, it can be regarded as successful only when the new beliefs and practices have become internalized in the mindsets and routines of employees at the new subsidiary. Achieving such internalization requires (1) visibly explicit and credible commitment by the parent company to its core beliefs and practices, (2) deepening the process of education and reeducation within the new organization right down to middle managers and the local work force, and (3) concrete demonstration that the new beliefs and practices yield individual as well as corporate success.

The approach taken by the Ritz-Carlton chain at its new hotel in Shanghai, China illustrates how a company can go about successfully embedding its core beliefs and practices in a new subsidiary. Ritz-Carlton acquired the rights to manage this hotel, with a staff of about 1,000 people, under its own name as of January 1, 1998. The company believed that, consistent with its image and its corporate DNA, the entire operation required significant upgrading. As one would expect, the company brought in a sizable contingent of about 40 expatriates from other Ritz-Carlton units in Asia and around the world to transform and manage the new property. What is especially noteworthy, however, is the approach the managers took to embed the company's own standards of quality and service in the hearts, minds, and behavior of their local associates. Among its first actions in the very first week of operations under its own control, the company decided to start the renovation process from the employee's entrance and changing and wash rooms rather than from other starting points, such as the main lobby. As one executive explained, the logic was that, through this approach, every employee would see two radical changes in the very first week: one, that the new

standards of quality and service would be dramatically higher, and two, that they, the employees, were among the most valued stakeholders in the company. This approach served as a very successful start to embedding the company's basic beliefs in every associate's mind: "We Are Ladies and Gentlemen Serving Ladies and Gentlemen."

Winning the Local Battle

Winning the local battle requires the global enterprise to anticipate, shape, and respond to the needs and/or actions of three sets of host-country players: customers, competitors, and government.

Winning Host Country Customers

One of the ingredients in establishing local presence is to understand the uniqueness of the local market and decide which aspects of the firm's business model require little change, which require local adaptation, and which need to be reinvented. The global firm faces little need to adapt its business design if it targets a customer segment in a foreign market similar to the one it serves in its home market. However, if the firm wants to expand the customer base it serves in a foreign market, then adapting the business model to the unique demands of the local customers becomes mandatory.

Consider the case of FedEx when it entered China. As an element of its entry strategy, FedEx had to choose who its target customers should be: local Chinese companies or multinational corporations. The company chose to target multinational companies—a customer segment identical to the one it has historically served. Given the choice, FedEx was able to pretty much export the U.S. business model into China, including the use of its own aircraft, building a huge network of trucks and distribution centers, and adopting U.S.-style aggressive marketing and advertising. On the other hand, had FedEx selected local Chinese firms as its targeted customer segment, winning host country customers would have required a significantly greater degree of local adaptation of the business model.

Domino's Pizza is a good example of a company that has benefited from adapting its business model when it entered India. Unlike KFC, Domino's was successful in its initial entry into India, primarily because it tailored its approach to the Indian culture and lifestyle. Even though pepperoni pizza is one of the most popular items for Domino's in other markets, the company dropped it from the menu to show respect for the value Hindus place on the cow. Domino's also tailored other toppings, such as chicken, ginger, and lamb, to suit Indian taste buds.

Winning against Host Country Competitors

Whenever a company enters a new country, it can expect retaliation from local competitors as well as from other multinationals already operating there. Successfully establishing local presence requires anticipating and responding to these competitive threats. Established local competitors enjoy several advantages: knowledge of the local market; working relationships with local customers; understanding of local distribution channels; and so on. In contrast, the new firm suffers from the "liability of newness." When a global firm enters a market, local competitors will feel threatened and will have a strong reason to retaliate and defend their positions. Such response constitutes entry barriers. In such a context, four possible options are available to the new invader:

1. Enter by acquiring a dominant local competitor.
2. Enter by acquiring a weak local competitor who can be quickly transformed and scaled up.
3. Enter a poorly defended niche.
4. Engage in a frontal attack on the dominant and entrenched incumbents.

Acquire a Dominant Local Competitor

Acquiring a dominant local firm will prove to be successful if the following three conditions are met: (1) there is significant potential for synergies between the acquisition target and the global firm; (2) the global firm has the capability to create and capture such synergies; and (3) the global firm does not give away the synergies from a huge acquisition premium up-front.

A case of successful entry through acquisition of a dominant local competitor is Accor, the French hospitality company, which entered the U.S. market by acquiring Motel 6—the best managed market leader in the budget lodging category. On the other hand, Sony paid a huge premium to acquire Columbia Pictures; to date, however, it has had great difficulty in justifying this premium—despite the significant potential synergies between Sony's hardware competencies and the "content" expertise of Columbia Pictures.

Acquire a Weak Player

Acquiring a weak player in the foreign market is an attractive option under the following conditions:

1. The global firm possesses the capabilities that are required to transform the weak player into a dominant player; and
2. The global firm has the ability to transplant the corporate DNA in the acquired firm very quickly.

The sheer act of acquiring a weak player signals to other local competitors that they will soon be under attack. It is therefore to be expected that local competitors will retaliate. If the global firm is unable to transform the weak player within a very short time, the player could become even weaker under attack from local competitors.

Consider Whirlpool's entry into Europe in 1989 by acquiring the problem-ridden appliance division of Philips. Unfortunately, Whirlpool could not quickly embed the capabilities to turn around Philips's struggling appliance business. In the meantime, two European rivals—Sweden's Electrolux and Germany's Bosch-Siemens—got a wake-up call from Whirlpool's European entry. Quite naturally, the two invested very heavily in modernization, process improvements, new product introductions, and restructuring—all with a view to improving their competitiveness. The net result was a disappointment for Whirlpool in terms of its ambition to consolidate the white goods industry in Europe. By 1998, Whirlpool had 12 percent market share in Europe (half of its expected position) and was also underachieving in profitability. To quote Jeff Fettig, Whirlpool's head of European operations: "We underestimated the competition."

Enter a Poorly Defended Niche

If acquisition candidates are either unavailable or too expensive, the global firm has no choice but to enter on its own. Under such circumstances, it should find a poorly defended niche for market entry under the following conditions:

1. Such a niche exists.
2. The global firm can use that niche as a platform for subsequent expansion into the mainstream segments of the local market. That is, the mobility barriers to move from the niche market to the mainstream segments are relatively low.

In the early 1970s, the Japanese car makers entered the U.S. market at the low end, a segment that was being ignored by the U.S. car companies and was thus a "loose brick" in their fortress. The Japanese companies used their dominance of the lower end segment to migrate to the middle and upper ends very effectively.

Frontal Attack

The global company can choose a head-on attack on the dominant and entrenched incumbents provided it has a massive competitive advantage that can be leveraged outside its domestic market. If this were not true, taking on an 800-pound gorilla with all the liability of "newness" could prove suicidal. Lexus succeeded in its frontal attack on Mercedes and BMW in the U.S. market mainly because of a dominating competitive advantage in such areas as product quality and cost structure. For instance, Lexus enjoyed a 30 percent cost advantage. For Mercedes, given the high labor costs in Germany where it manufactured its automobiles, such a cost advantage could not be neutralized quickly.

Managing Relationships with the Host-Country Government

Local government can often be a key external stakeholder, particularly in emerging markets. Two points are worth noting in this context.

1. The global firm can ill afford to ignore non-market stakeholders such as the local government. For instance, the Chinese government recently banned direct selling. This action has an important bearing on such firms as Mary Kay Cosmetics and Avon, which depend on a highly personalized direct marketing approach.

2. Managing the non-market stakeholders should be seen as a dynamic process. Instead of simplistically reacting to existing government regulations, the firm should also anticipate likely future changes in the regulatory framework and even explore the possibility of helping shape the emerging framework. Instead of appeasement or confrontation, persistence and constructive dialogue with the local government are often critical elements of winning the local battle.

Enron's entry into India is a telling example of an active approach to transforming the entering firm's relationship with host governments. In 1995, mostly due to ideological and political reasons, the Maharashtra government put a sudden halt to Enron's partly built, $2.5 billion power plant. Yet by 1999, not only had Enron won back the original contract for the 826-megawatt unit, it even succeeded in getting a go-ahead to triple the capacity to 2,450 megawatts, representing India's largest foreign investment and Enron's biggest non-U.S. project. Instead of giving up, Enron persisted and helped shape evolving public policy. In the process, the company learned a lesson, but so did the Indian government.

Speed of Global Expansion

Having commenced the journey of globalization, a company must still address one major issue in building global presence: How fast should it expand globally? Microsoft's worldwide launch of Windows 95 *on the same day* epitomizes using globalization for aggressive growth. By moving quickly, a company can solidify its market position very rapidly.

However, rapid global expansion can also spread managerial, organizational, and financial resources too thin. The consequence can be to jeopardize the company's ability to defend and profit from the global presence thus created. Witness PepsiCo's helter-skelter rapid expansion in Latin America during the first part of the 1990s. In most cases, Pepsi's ambitious agenda resulted in market positions that have proven to be both indefensible and unprofitable.

Taking into account the pros and cons, an accelerated speed of global expansion is more appropriate under the following conditions:

- *It is easy for competitors to replicate your recipe for success.* This possibility is obvious for fast food and retailing companies such as KFC and Starbuck's, where it is easy for competitors to take a proven concept from one market and replicate it in another unoccupied market with a relatively small investment. However, this phenomenon is observable in other, very different types of industries as well, such as personal computers and software. The rapid globalization of companies like Compaq, Dell, and Microsoft reflects their determination to prevent replication and/or pirating of their product concepts in markets all around the world.

- *Scale economies are extremely important.* Very high economies of scale give the early and rapid globalizer massive first mover advantages and handicap the slower ones for long periods of time. This is precisely why rapid globalizers in the tire industry, such as Goodyear, Michelin, and Bridgestone, now hold considerable advantage over slower ones, such as Pirelli and Continental.

- *Management's capacity to manage (or learn how to manage) global operations is high.* Consider experienced global players like Coca-Cola, Citicorp, Unilever, and ABB. Should such a company successfully introduce a new product line in one country, it would be relatively easy and logical to globalize it rapidly to all potential markets around the world. Aside from the ability to manage global operations, the speed of globalization also depends on the company's ability to leverage its experience from one market to another. The faster the speed with which a firm can recycle its learning about market entry and market defense from one country to another, the lower the risk of spreading managerial and organizational capacity too thinly.

Becoming global is never exclusively the result of a grand design. At the same time, it would be naive to view it as little more than a sequence of incremental, ad-hoc, opportunistic, and random moves. The wisest approach would be one of *directed opportunism*—an approach that maintains opportunism and flexibility within a broad direction set by a systematic framework. Our goal here has been to provide such a framework.

References

D.A. Blackmon and D. Brady, "Just How Hard Should a U.S. Company Woo a Big Foreign Market?" *Wall Street Journal,* April 6, 1998, p. A1.

S. Ghoshal, "Global Strategy: An Organizing Framework," *Strategic Management Journal,* September–October 1987, pp. 425–440.

V. Govindarajan, "Note on the Global Paper Industry," case study, Dartmouth College, 1999.

G. Hamel and C.K. Prahalad, "Do You Really Have a Global Strategy?" *Harvard Business Review,* July–August 1985, pp. 139–148.

K. Iverson and T. Varian, *Plain Talk: Lessons from a Business Maverick* (New York: Wiley, 1997).

J.P. Jeannet and H.D. Hennessy, *Global Marketing Strategies* (Boston: Houghton Mifflin, 1998).

Jonathan Karp and Kathryn Kranhold, "Enron's Plant in India Was Dead: This Month, It Will Go on Stream," *Wall Street Journal,* February 5, 1999, p. A1.

T. Khanna, R. Gulati, and N. Nohria, "Alliances as Learning Races," *Proceedings of the Academy of Management Annual Meetings,* 1994, pp. 42–46.

K. Obloj and H. Thomas, "Transforming Former State-owned Companies into Market Competitors in Poland: The ABB Experience," *European Management Journal,* August 1998, pp. 390–399.

G. Steinmetz and C.J. Chipello, "Local Presence Is Key to European Deals," *Wall Street Journal,* June 30, 1998, p. A15.

G. Steinmetz and C. Quintanilla, "Whirlpool Expected Easy Going in Europe, and It Got a Big Shock," *Wall Street Journal,* April 10, 1998, p. A1.

S. Sugawara, "Japanese Shaken by Business U.S.-Style," *Washington Post,* February 9, 1999, p. E1.

R. Tomkins, "Battered PepsiCo Licks Its Wounds," *Financial Times,* May 30, 1997, p. 26.

"Xerox and Fuji Xerox," Case No. 9-391-156, Harvard Business School.

ANIL K. GUPTA is a professor of strategy and international business at the University of Maryland, College Park, Maryland. **VIJAY GOVINDARAJAN** is the Earl C. Daum 1924 Professor of International Business at Dartmouth College, Hanover, New Hampshire.

From *Business Horizons,* Vol. 43, Issue 2, March/April 2000, pp. 45–54. Copyright © 2000 by Kelley School of Business. Reprinted by permission of Elsevier Inc. via Rightslink.

The Global Entrepreneur

A new breed of entrepreneur is thinking across borders—from day one.

Daniel J. Isenberg

For a century and more, companies have ventured abroad only after establishing themselves at home. Moreover, when they have looked overseas, they haven't ventured too far afield, initially. Consumer health-care company Johnson & Johnson set up its first foreign subsidiary in Montreal in 1919–33 years after its founding in 1886. Sony, established in 1946, took 11 years to export its first product to the United States, the TR-63 transistor radio. The Gap, founded in 1969—the year Neil Arm-strong walked on the moon—opened its first overseas store in London in 1987, a year after the *Challenger* space shuttle disaster.

Companies are being born global today, by contrast. Entrepreneurs don't automatically buy raw materials from nearby suppliers or set up factories close to their headquarters. They hunt for the planet's best manufacturing locations because political and economic barriers have fallen and vast quantities of information are at their fingertips. They also scout for talent across the globe, tap investors wherever they may be located, and learn to manage operations from a distance—the moment they go into business.

Take Bento Koike, who set up Tecsis to manufacture wind turbine blades in 1995. The company imports raw materials from North America and Europe, and its customers are located on those two continents. Yet Koike created his globe-girding start-up near São Paulo in his native Brazil because a sophisticated aerospace industry had emerged there, which enabled him to develop innovative blade designs and manufacturing know-how. Tecsis has become one of the world's market leaders, having installed 12,000 blades in 10 countries in the past decade and racked up revenues of $350 million in 2007.

Standing conventional theory on its head, start-ups now do business in many countries before dominating their home markets. In late 2001, Ron Zwanziger, David Scott, and Jerry McAleer teamed up to launch their third medical diagnostics business, even though Zwanziger lives in the United States and Scott and McAleer live in England. They started Inverness Medical Innovations by retaining the pieces of their company that Johnson & Johnson didn't acquire and immediately gained a presence in Belgium, Germany, Ireland, Israel, the United Kingdom, and the United States. The troika didn't skip a beat. In seven years, they wanted to grow the new venture into an enterprise valued at $7 billion and believed that being born global was the way to do it. They're getting there: Inverness Medical's assets were valued at $5 billion as of August 2008.

Today's entrepreneurs cross borders for two reasons. One is defensive: To be competitive, many ventures, like Tecsis and Inverness Medical, have to globalize some aspects of their business—manufacturing, service delivery, capital sourcing, or talent acquisition, for instance—the moment they start up. That may sound obvious today, but until a few years ago, it was standard practice for U.S. venture capitalists, in particular, to require that the companies they invested in focus on domestic markets.

The other reason is to take the offense. Many new ventures are discovering that a new business opportunity spans more than one country or that they can use distance to create new products or services. Take RacingThePlanet, which Mary Gadams founded in 2002 to stage marathons, each 250 kilometers long and lasting seven days, in the world's most hostile environments. Her team works out of a small Hong Kong office, but the company operates in the Gobi Desert in Mongolia, the Atacama Desert in Chile, the Sahara Desert in Egypt, and Antarctica. Distance has generated the opportunity: If the deserts were accessible, participants and audiences would find the races less attractive, and the brand would be diluted. RacingThePlanet isn't just about running; it's also about creating a global lifestyle brand, which Gadams uses to sell backpacks, emergency supplies, clothing, and other merchandise, as well as to generate content for the multimedia division, which sells video for websites and GPS mapping systems. The company may be just six years old, but brand awareness is high, and Racing The-Planet is already profitable.

In this article, I'll describe the challenges start-ups face when they are born global and the skills entrepreneurs need to tackle them.

Key Challenges

Global entrepreneurs, my research shows, face three distinct challenges.

Distance. New ventures usually lack the infrastructure to cope with dispersed operations and faraway markets. Moreover,

How Diaspora Networks Help Start-Ups Go Global

Many entrepreneurs have taken advantage of ethnic networks to formulate and execute a global strategy. The culture, values, and social norms members hold in common forge understanding and trust, making it easier to establish and enforce contracts.

Through diaspora networks, global entrepreneurs can quickly gain access to information, funding, talent, technology—and, of course, contacts. In the late 1990s, for instance, Boston-based Desh Deshpande, who had set up several high-tech ventures in the United States, was keen to start something in his native India. In April 2000, he met an optical communications expert, Kumar Sivarajan, who had worked at IBM's Watson Research Center before returning to India to take up a teaching position at the Indian Institute of Science in Bangalore. Deshpande introduced Sivarajan to two other Indians, Sanjay Nayak and Arnob Roy, who had both worked in the Indian subsidiaries of American high-tech companies. The trust among the four enabled the creation of the start-up Tejas Networks in two months' time. Deshpande and Sycamore Networks, the major investors, wired the initial capital of $5 million, attaching few of the usual conditions to the investment. Tejas Networks has become a leading telecommunications equipment manufacturer, generating revenues of around $100 million over the past year.

The research that my HBS colleague William Kerr and I have done suggests that entrepreneurs who most successfully exploit diaspora networks take these four steps:

Map networks. The members of a diaspora often cluster in residential areas, public organizations, or industries. For instance, in Tokyo, Americans tend to work for professional service firms such as Morgan Stanley and McKinsey, live in Azabu, shop in Omotesandō, and hang out at the American Club.

Identify organizations that can help. Many countries have offices overseas that facilitate trade and investment, and they open their doors to people visiting from home. These organizations can provide the names of influential individuals, companies, and informal organizations, clubs, or groups.

Tap informal groups. Informal organizations of ethnic entrepreneurs and executives are usually located in communities where immigrant professionals are concentrated. In the United States, for instance, they thrive in high-tech industry neighborhoods such as Silicon Valley or universities like MIT.

Identify the influentials. It can be tough to identify people who have standing with local businesses and also within the diaspora network. A board member or coach that both respect is an invaluable resource for a would-be entrepreneur.

physical distances create time differences, which can be remarkably tough to navigate. Even dealing with various countries' workweeks takes a toll on a start-up's limited staff: In North America, Europe, China, and India, corporate offices generally operate Monday through Friday. In Israel, they're open Sunday through Thursday. In Saudi Arabia and the UAE, the workweek runs Saturday through Wednesday, but in other predominantly Muslim countries like Lebanon, Morocco, and Turkey, people work from Monday through Friday or Saturday.

A greater challenge for global entrepreneurs is bridging what the British economist Wilfred Beckerman called in 1956 "psychic distance." This arises from such factors as culture, language, education systems, political systems, religion, and economic development levels. It can heighten—or reduce—psychological barriers between regions and often prompt entrepreneurs to make counterintuitive choices. Take the case of Encantos de Puerto Rico, set up in 1998 to manufacture and market premium Puerto Rican coffee. When founder-CEO Angel Santiago sought new markets in 2002, he didn't enter the nearby U.S. market but chose Spain instead. That's because, he felt, Puerto Ricans and Spaniards have similar tastes in coffee and because of the ease of doing business in Spanish, which reduced the psychic distance between the two countries. When two years later, Encantos de Puerto Rico did enter the United States, it focused initially on Miami, which has a large Hispanic population.

Context. Nations' political, regulatory, judicial, tax, environmental, and labor systems vary. The choices entrepreneurs make about, say, where to locate their companies' headquarters will affect shareholder returns and also their ability to raise capital. When the husband-and-wife team of Andrew Prihodko, a Ukrainian studying at MIT, and Sharon Peyer, a Swiss-American citizen studying at Harvard, set up an online photo management company, they thought hard about where to domicile Pixamo. Should they incorporate it in Ukraine, which has a simple and low tax structure but a problematic legal history? Or Switzerland, where taxes are higher but the legal system is well established? Or Delaware, where taxes are higher still but most U.S. start-ups are domiciled? Prihodko and Peyer eventually chose to base the company in the relatively tax-friendly Swiss canton of Zug, a decision that helped shareholders when they sold Pixamo to NameMedia in 2007.

Some global entrepreneurs must deal with several countries simultaneously, which is complex. In 1994, Gary Mueller launched Internet Securities to provide investors with data on emerging markets. Three years later, the start-up had offices in 18 countries and had to cope with the jurisdictions of Brazil, China, and Russia on any given day. By learning to do so, Internet Securities became a market leader, and in 1999, Euromoney acquired 80% of the company's equity for the tidy sum of $43 million.

Resources. Customers expect startups to possess the skills and deliver the levels of quality that larger companies do. That's a tall order for resource-stretched new ventures. Still, they have no option but to do whatever it takes to retain customers. In 1987, Jim Sharpe acquired a small business, XTech, now a

How Social Entrepreneurs Think Global

Atsumasa tochisako is an unlikely entrepreneur. When he was in his mid-fifties, he left a senior position at the Bank of Tokyo-Mitsubishi to set up Microfinance International, a global for-profit social enterprise (FOPSE, for short), based in Washington, D.C. Having also been stationed in Latin America for many years, Tochisako had observed the large cash remittances coming from immigrants in the United States, as well as the exorbitant charges they paid commercial banks and the poor service they received. Sensing a business opportunity and the chance to do some good, he decided to provide immigrant workers with inexpensive remittance, check-cashing, insurance, and microlending services.

MFI was international from its birth in June 2003, with operations in the United States and El Salvador. Since then, it has expanded into a dozen Latin American countries and further extended its reach by allowing multinational financial institutions, such as the UAE Exchange, to use its proprietary Internet-based settlement platform.

Like Tochisako, many entrepreneurs today combine social values, profit motive, and a global focus. Social entrepreneurs are global from birth for three reasons. First, disease, malnutrition, poverty, illiteracy, and other social problems exist on a large scale in many developing countries. Second, the resources—funds, institutions, and governance systems—to tackle those issues are mainly in the developed world. Third, FOPSEs that tackle specific conditions can often be adapted to other countries. For instance, in 2002, Shane Immelman founded The Lapdesk Company to provide portable desks to South African schoolchildren, a third of whom are taught in schoolrooms that don't have adequate surfaces on which to write. The company asks large corporations in South Africa to donate desks—with some advertising on them—for entire school districts. By doing so, these companies are able to meet the South African government's requirement that they invest part of their profits in black empowerment programs. Since then, Immelman has adapted the business model to Kenya, Nigeria, and the Democratic Republic of Congo and has launched programs in India and Latin America.

manufacturer of faceplates for telecommunications equipment. Initially, the company made its products in the United States and sold them overseas through sales representatives and distributors. However, by 2006, Cisco, Lucent, Intel, IBM, and other XTech customers had shifted most of their manufacturing to China. They became reluctant to do business with suppliers that didn't make products or have customer service operations in China. So Sharpe had no choice but to set up a subsidiary in China at that stage.

Competencies Global Entrepreneurs Need

All entrepreneurs must be able to identify opportunities, gather resources, and strike deals. They all must also possess soft skills like vision, leadership, and passion. To win globally, though, they must hone four additional competencies.

Articulating a global purpose. Developing a crystal clear rationale for being global is critical. In 1999, for example, Robert Wessman took control of a small pharmaceuticals maker in his native Iceland. Within weeks, he concluded that the generics player had to globalize its core functions—manufacturing, R&D, and marketing—to gain economies of scale, develop a large product portfolio, and be first to market with drugs as they came off patent. Since then, Actavis has entered 40 countries, often by taking over local companies. Wessman faced numerous hurdles, but he stuck to the strategy. Actavis now makes 650 products and has 350 more in the pipeline. In 2007, it generated revenues of $2 billion and had become one of the world's top five generics manufacturers.

Alliance building. Start-ups can quickly attain global reach by striking partnerships with large companies headquartered in other countries. However, most entrepreneurs have to enter into such deals from positions of weakness. An established company has managers who can conduct due diligence, the money to fly teams over for meetings, and the power to extract favorable terms from would-be partners. It has a reasonable period within which to negotiate a deal, and it has options in case talks with one company fail. A start-up has few of those resources or bargaining chips.

Start-ups also have problems communicating with global partners because their alliances have to span geographic and psychic distances. Take the case of Trolltech, an open-source software company founded in 1994 in Oslo by Eirik Chambe-Eng and Haavard Nord. In 2001, the start-up landed a contract to supply a Japanese manufacturer with a Linux-based software platform for personal digital assistants (PDAs). The dream order quickly turned into a nightmare. There were differences between what the Japanese company thought it would get and what the Norwegian supplier felt it should provide, and the start-up struggled to deliver the modifications its partner began to demand. Suspecting that Trolltech wouldn't deliver the software on time, the Japanese company offered to send over a team of software engineers. However, when it suggested that both companies work through the Christmas break to meet a deadline—a common practice in Japan—Trolltech refused, citing the importance of the Christmas vacation in Norway. The relationship almost collapsed, but Chambe-Eng and Nord managed to negotiate a new deadline that they could meet without having to work during the holiday season.

Supply-chain creation. Entrepreneurs must often choose suppliers on the other side of the world and monitor them without having managers nearby. Besides, the best manufacturing locations change as labor and fuel costs rise and as quality problems show up, as they did in China.

Start-ups find it daunting to manage complex supply networks, but they gain competitive advantage by doing so. Sometimes the global supply chain lies at the heart of the business opportunity. Take the case of Winery Exchange, cofounded by Peter Byck in 1999. The California-based venture manages a 22-country network of wineries and breweries. Winery Exchange works closely with retail chains, such as Kroger, Tesco, and Costco, to develop premium private label products, and it gets its suppliers to produce and package the wines as inexpensively as possible. The venture has succeeded because it links relatively small market-needy suppliers with mammoth product-hungry retailers and provides both with its product development expertise. In 2006, Winery Exchange sold 2 million cases of 330 different brands of wine, beer, and spirits to retailers on four continents.

In addition to raw materials and components, start-ups are increasingly buying intellectual property from across the world. Hands-On Mobile, started by David Kranzler, is a Silicon Valley-based developer of the mobile versions of Guitar Hero III, Iron Man, and other games. When the company started in 2001, the markets for mobile multimedia content were developing faster in Asia and Europe than in the United States, and gamers were creating attractive products in China, South Korea, and Japan. Kranzler realized that his company had to acquire intellectual property and design capacity overseas in order to offer customers a comprehensive catalog of games and the latest delivery technologies. Hands-On Mobile therefore picked up MobileGame Korea, as well as two Chinese content development companies, which has helped it become a market leader.

Even start-ups can thrive by using distance to gain competitive advantage.

Multinational organization. In 2006, I conducted a simulation exercise called the Virtual Entrepreneurial Team Exercise (VETE) for 450 MBA students in 10 business schools in Argentina, Austria, Brazil, England, Hong Kong, Liechtenstein, the Netherlands, Japan, and the United States. The teams, each composed of students from different schools and different countries, developed hypothetical pitches for Asia Renal Care, a Hong Kong-based medical services start-up, that had raised its first round of capital in 1999. They experienced a slice of global entrepreneurial life in real time, using technologies like Skype, wikis, virtual chat rooms, and, of course, e-mail to communicate with one another. The students learned how to build trust, compensate for the lack of visual cues, respect cultural differences, and deal with different institutional frameworks and incentives—the competencies entrepreneurs need for coordination, control, and communication in global enterprises. The would-be entrepreneurs' emotions ranged from elation to frustration, and their output varied from good to excellent.

Start-ups cope with the challenges of managing a global organization in different ways. Internet Securities used a knowledge database to share information among its offices around the world, increasing managers' ability to recognize and solve problems. Racing-The-Planet used intensive training to ensure that volunteers perform at a consistently high level during the events it holds. Trolltech worked round the clock to meet deadlines, passing off development tasks from teams in Norway to those in Australia as the day ends in one place and begins in the other. Inverness Medical hired key executives wherever it could and organized the company around them rather than move people all over the world.

Still, there are no easy answers to the challenges of managing a start-up in the topsy-turvy world of global entrepreneurship. Take the case of Mei Zhang, who founded WildChina, a high-end adventure-tourism company in China, in 2000. Three years later, Zhang hired an American expatriate, Jim Stent, who had a deep interest in Chinese history and culture, as her COO. Zhang moved to Los Angeles in 2004, anointing Stent as CEO in Beijing and appointing herself chairperson. Thus, a Chinese expatriate living in the United States had to supervise an American expatriate living in Beijing. And when the two amicably parted ways in 2006, Zhang started managing the Chinese company from Los Angeles. These are contingencies no textbook provides for.

Entrepreneurs shouldn't fear the fact that the world isn't flat. Being global may not be a pursuit for the fainthearted, but even start-ups can thrive by using distance to gain competitive advantage.

DANIEL J. ISENBERG (disenberg@hbs.edu) is a senior lecturer at Harvard Business School in Boston.

Harvesting Firm Value: Process and Results

J. WILLIAM PETTY

For most within the academic community, entrepreneurship has come to be viewed as a process involving the relentless pursuit of a potential investment opportunity without regard to resources currently owned (Stevenson and Gumpert, 1985; Stevenson and Sahlman, 1987). The objective of this pursuit depends in part on the nature of the opportunity itself. For micro-firms, the goal is mostly to provide a "preferred" lifestyle. For mega-firms, or entrepreneurial firms, on the other hand, the objective is to create economic value. Although micro- and mega-firms have some similarities, there are real differences between them, an important one being the opportunity for the mega-firm to harvest a terminal value from the investment that is not present for the micro-firm. Thus mega-firms are of primary interest to us within the context of harvesting a venture.

Most of the academic literature in entrepreneurship has concentrated on the earlier stages of the entrepreneurship process, namely, identifying and exploiting an opportunity. Little attention has been given to exiting or what has come to be called *harvesting the business,* which is the focus of this chapter.

Harvesting an entrepreneurial firm is the approach taken by the owners and investors to realize terminal after-tax cash flows on their investment. It defines how they will extract some or all of the economic value (cash flows) from the investment. Also, from the entrepreneur's perspective, the issue of harvesting is about more than money, involving personal and nonfinancial aspects of the harvest as well. Even an entrepreneur who realizes an acceptable value for a firm may come away disappointed with the overall outcome of the harvest.

How Important Is Harvesting?

There is little in the way of hard evidence as to the exact significance of the harvest; that is, it cannot be said precisely how much of the value realized from a venture is attributable to a successfully implemented harvest strategy. However, from intuition alone, one would expect that few events in the life of the entrepreneur, and for the firm itself, are more significant than the harvest.

In one sense, the harvest is not as important as successfully identifying an opportunity or even growing the firm. These two phases of the entrepreneurial process are without question the primary value-creating activities. However, *the availability and effectiveness of the exit ultimately determine the value to be realized from the venture.* While value must first be created, it must then be realized for any real

benefit. Thus, the terminal liquidity, or lack thereof, provided by the harvest will ultimately determine the value received from the venture. The inability to harvest at a *fair* value would be much like buying a stock, watching its value increase over time, but not being allowed to capture the value by selling the stock. However, the stock analogy fails to capture the complexity of the harvest relative to selling a publicly traded stock.

The significance of the problem may also be viewed from a macro perspective by considering the large number of family-owned firms that will be faced with the prospects of the harvest. It has been estimated that 18 percent of the financial assets held by U.S. households, or $2.4 trillion, is invested in privately held firms, mostly family-owned businesses—$300 billion more than these same households have invested in publicly traded companies (Paré, 1990). Many of these privately owned firms were founded by entrepreneurs in the 1950s and 1960s who are or soon will be contemplating and executing a harvest or exit strategy. The same situation also exists in Europe. As many as 17,000 European companies received equity venture capital during the past decade (Batchelor, 1992). Most of those investments have yet to be harvested.

The harvest is also of prime importance to outside investors. These investors typically have a priori expectations about their investment that include either taking the firm public or being acquired by other investors (Freear et al., 1990). Investors, be they professional venture capitalists or private informal investors, have an obvious vested interest in the exit mechanism used to liquidate their investment. While not having the same personal significance for the firm's investors as it does for the entrepreneur, the effectiveness of the harvest affects the amount and timing of the after-tax cash flows to be received, which in turn determines the eventual return earned on the investment. From experience, they realize that time can exact a fierce penalty on the rate of return. A successful entrepreneurial venture returns at least 40 percent compounded annually to investors over a holding period of four to five years. To achieve such a return requires a terminal cash-flow multiple of 5.4 times the original investment. However, the same yield over 10 years requires 28.9 times the original investment. Thus, an investment in a high-risk venture that is unrealized after 10 years is thought to be long past its "sell-by" date in all but a few rare instances. Consequently, venture capitalists are reluctant to make an investment without having some idea as to how an exit will be arranged.

In short, the opportunity to exit successfully from a venture is thought to be a significant factor in the entrepreneurial process, both for the entrepreneur and for any investors providing risk capital.

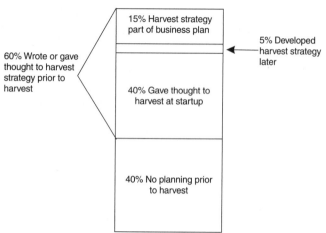

Figure 1 Developing the harvest strategy.

In examining the literature on harvesting the venture, there are four areas of interest:

1. Developing a strategy.
2. The value-creating process.
3. The process of the harvest.
4. The European experience in harvesting.

When Does the Harvest Begin?

The typical prescription for developing a harvest strategy is simple: *Now, not later.* Timmons (1994) suggests that entrepreneurs build a great company but do not forget the harvest; he also advises that entrepreneurs should keep harvest options open and think of harvesting as a vehicle for reducing risk and for creating future entrepreneurial choices and options. Thus, crafting a harvest strategy is viewed as something to be done early on and as an ongoing process along with growing the business, even well before the impending need or desire to harvest.

Given the conventional wisdom of the need for a harvest strategy even before the event, a natural question would be, Do entrepreneurs ever follow this advice? To answer this question, one must rely on limited empirical evidence. Holmburg (1991) surveyed CEOs at computer software firms that went public between 1980 and 1990. He found that 15 percent had a written harvest strategy as part of the original business plan; 5 percent developed a formal exit strategy subsequent to preparing the business plan; 40 percent had given some thought to the harvest; and the final 40 percent did not give any consideration to the harvest beforehand (Figure 1). Similar results were found in another study where 40 percent of the CEOs surveyed did not consider the harvest at the outset of the venture (Hyatt, 1990). Thus, it can be concluded—based on our limited information—that roughly 60 percent give some advance thought to the harvest, either informally or formally. However, only 20 percent appear serious in their efforts.

You Cannot Harvest What You Have Not Created

Valuing a firm when the stock is not traded in the market-place is difficult in the best of circumstances. But even worse is forecasting the value of a startup some five or 10 years into the future. Financial contracting requires some estimate of the venture's terminal value and an assumed horizon date for the harvest (Sahlman and Summer, 1988). The problem is one of assigning value to an asset for which the greatest amount of incomplete and conflicting information exists. To be even more precise, founders and early-stage investors are in reality purchasing an option on the future cash flows to be exercised if the firm does well; the option characteristics are especially apparent when staged commitments are allowed.

The possible approaches for determining a company's value are legion. However, most investors in entrepreneurial firms rely on some multiple of earnings, be it net income, operating income, or earnings before interest, taxes, depreciation, and amortization (EBITDA). For instance, a multiple of EBITDA plus the firm's cash is often used to estimate firm value. Outstanding debt is subtracted to determine the value of the equity. This approach, while simple, begs an important question: What *should* determine harvest value? Two basic perspectives can be used in answering the question: either the accountant's "map of the territory" or the economist's. An accountant would say that earnings drive firm value—the larger the earnings, the greater the firm value. The economist's map of firm value, on the other hand, is based on the present value of future cash flows.

To the extent that a willing buyer is prepared to pay some multiple of earnings for a firm, value—at least from all appearances—is based on earnings. But there is little in the way of an economic rationale or any empirical evidence to suggest that a firm's value is closely linked to earnings (Brennan, 1995). Instead, many believe that value ought to be determined by finding the present value of future cash flows discounted at the opportunity cost of funds for the given level of risk (Copeland et al., 1994). Nevertheless, the conventional wisdom that earnings matter continues to carry the day for most investors.

The issue of valuation as it relates to the harvest strategy is important; one cannot structure the deal without some notion of what the harvest value will be. However, the issue can be expressed more fundamentally by asking, Will economic value be created with the capital that is being invested in the venture? Given that a start-up company is not traded publicly, one cannot depend on the capital markets for that information. Even so, firm value can correctly be represented as the capital invested in the business plus any value created by earning economic rates of return that exceed the cost of capital; or stated negatively, firm value is equal to the capital invested, less the value destroyed by earning rates of return less than the firm's opportunity cost of funds.

As a firm moves in time toward the harvest, there are two questions that are of primary importance. First, are the current owners and managers effectively creating firm value? The answer to this question can be answered easily from historical financial data by estimating the economic value added (EVA) over time. The economic value added from a firm's operations in year t (EVA_t) could be estimated as follows (Stewart, 1991):

$$EVA_t = (\text{return on capital}_t - \text{cost of capital}_t) \times \text{invested capital}_t$$

where return on capital is measured as *economic* income divided by the amount of capital (cash) invested in the company over its life, and cost of capital is the investors' opportunity cost of funds—a concept almost totally alien to most entrepreneurs. This single measurement of economic value added, which is seldom considered by large companies (much less smaller companies), can tell us a great deal about the value-creating ability of a company, an issue of import if there is to be any value to harvest.

The second and related question is, Could new owners do more with the company than the founders? If so, then the firm would have greater value in the hands of new owners. That is, growing a venture to the point of diminishing returns and then selling it to others better able to carry it to the next level is a proven way to create value. How this incremental value will be shared between the old and the new owners largely depends on the relative strengths of each party in the negotiations, i.e., who wants the deal the most.

With the foregoing as a backdrop, the next step is to examine the actual harvesting process.

The Harvesting Process

For the most part, designing a harvest strategy is limited to one of several options. The more common ways to harvest include the following:

- Restructuring the company's goals and strategies in order to increase the cash flows extracted from the business by the owners and investors.
- Being acquired by or merged into another, usually larger, company.
- Private sale for cash, debt, and/or equity to: (1) another company or group of investors; (2) management, frequently through a leveraged management buyout;
  (3) employees, usually in the form of an employee stock option plan; or (4) family members.
- Public stock offering.

How do entrepreneurs view these options? Again drawing on Holmburg's (1991) study of the computer software CEOs who took their firms public, each respondent was asked to reflect back to the start-up stage of the company and to rank the probability at that time that the firm would use one of four alternative harvest strategies at some point in the future. The options included an initial public offering, being acquired by a larger company, merging with another firm, and a leveraged buyout by employees. Somewhat of a surprise, 65 percent of the CEOs considered an initial public offering as their most likely choice; 30 percent assigned the highest probability to being acquired by a larger company, and the remaining 5 percent thought a leveraged buyout by employees would occur. These results are supported by another recent survey of 100 CEOs where more than half planned on going public from the initial start-up phase (Hyatt, 1990). The discussion that follows briefly explains several of the above options.

Increasing the Firm's Free Cash Flows

A firm's free cash flows represent the amount of cash that can be distributed to its investors—debt and equity—after all operating needs have been met. Specifically,

$$\text{Free cash flows} = \substack{\text{operating} \\ \text{profits after} \\ \text{tax}} + \text{depreciation} - \substack{\text{investments} \\ \text{required to} \\ \text{grow the firm}}$$

In a firm's early years, everything goes into growing the company. All available cash is devoted to growth, which means that the last term in the above equation is large. For most growth firms, the free cash flows are significantly negative in the early years. As a firm and its industry mature, the opportunity to grow declines, which can result in sizable amounts of free cash flows.

Many of the fights in the 1980s between management and corporate raiders occurred in mature industries, such as oil and steel, over the use of the firm's cash flows. Management was using them to invest in unrelated businesses, usually with dismal results, while the raiders thought the newly acquired firms should not have been acquired because the result was a loss of focus. So the raiders attempted to take over these widely diversified businesses in an attempt to return them to their core businesses—and to return the cash flows to the investors. A substantial part of the academic literature in this area focused on this debate (e.g., Donaldson, 1994; Bhide, 1989).

Within the context of harvesting, the concern is not so much about the battle over the use of the free cash flows as it is in converting them into a way of harvesting an entrepreneurial firm. Specifically, at some point, an entrepreneur and any investors in the venture may decide to slow or even discontinue the company's sales growth rate. Rather than reinvesting all the cash flows back into the company, the owners begin cashing out of their investment. Only the amount of cash is retained that is necessary to maintain current markets—there is no effort to grow the present markets or expand into new markets. The free cash flows can then be harvested without affecting current operations. For many ventures, this event may occur as a natural consequence of maturing markets where competition has removed any growth opportunities that earn returns greater than the firm's cost of capital. The mistake at this point is for the entrepreneur not to harvest. Thus, restricting a company's growth is a viable strategy for harvesting the venture, but it requires some time to accomplish.

Increasing the firm's free cash flows has two potential advantages. First, the owners can retain the ownership of the company if they are not ready to sell. Second, the strategy is not dependent on finding an interested buyer and going through the often time-consuming and energy-draining experience of negotiating the sale, nor does the owner face the exciting, but at times frustrating, process of a public stock offering.

There are, however, some disadvantages as well. In harvesting the business, the desire is to maximize the after-tax cash flows going to the company's owners and investors. If the firm simply distributes the cash flows as dividends, the income will be taxed both as corporate income and again as personal dividend income to the stock-holders. There are ways, within limits, to avoid this problem, but it may not provide the entrepreneur as much discretionary cash flow as an outright sale. Another disadvantage of this strategy is the chance that the firm may not be able to sustain its competitive advantage while simultaneously harvesting the venture. If so, the end result may be an unintended liquidation. Finally, for the entrepreneur who is simply tired of the day-to-day operations, harvesting the venture by siphoning off the free cash flows over time may be asking for too much in the way of patience. Unless there are other individuals within the company who are qualified to provide the needed managerial leadership, then the strategy may be too emotionally draining.

Merging or Being Acquired

In terms of mergers and acquisitions, the literature has mostly been concerned with the rationale and success of acquiring or merging with another company, especially in an unrelated business (Weston et al., 1990). The predominant question has been, What can management accomplish through corporate diversification that the owners cannot achieve through their own diversification and with a lot more ease?

The 1980s came to be known as the decade of the deals and as a time of hostile takeovers, which to many instinctively felt wasteful and harmful. But not all was bad about the 1980s. The decade's merger and acquisition (M&A) activity allowed the shareholders of a significant number of privately held companies to realize the value "locked-up" in their companies via a market-based transaction. In other words, the M&A activity of the 1980s allowed many entrepreneurs the opportunity to harvest their investment that might not have otherwise been possible.

The financial issues related to selling a firm are basically the same with any exit strategy, namely, how to value the company for the purpose of the sale and how to structure the payment. However, financial matters, while not insignificant by any means, are not the only issues of importance when it comes to selling the firm and may not even be the primary concern.

To gain some understanding into this process, Petty et al. (1994) collected a sample of acquisition transactions of privately held companies reported in *Mergerstat Review* between 1984 and 1990. The sample was limited to acquisitions valued between $5 million and $100 million. Also, 278 venture-backed companies that were acquired between the years of 1987 and 1990 were identified through the *Venture Economics* database, which included the names of venture capitalists who had participated in the financing. With this combined listing, background information about the buyer and seller and about the acquisition itself was collected from the Dow Jones News Retrieval Service.

The issues addressed in the study fell into one of three areas: 1) the decision to sell, 2) the selling process, and 3) the post sale. Using these issues as guidelines, phone interviews were conducted of a limited sample of the entrepreneurs—efforts to interview venture capitalists were essentially unsuccessful. Some of the conclusions reached from the interviews were as follows:

1. Some of the entrepreneurs were significantly disappointed with the acquisition process and the final outcome. They came to realize that the firm served as the base for much of what they did, both in and out of the business arena. This sentiment existed more with owners of the low-tech firms, especially service firms, than with the high-tech companies.

2. The most prevalent reason for selling the company related to estate planning and the opportunity to diversify their investments. A second reason for the sale related to the need for financing growth, which the firm or the owner did not have the capacity to provide.

3. The harvest did provide the long-sought-after liquidity, but some entrepreneurs found managing money more difficult, and less enjoyable, than they had expected and less rewarding than operating their own company.

4. The disillusionment of selling the firm was particularly evident when the entrepreneur continued in the management of the company but under the supervision of the acquiring owners. The differences in corporate culture became a significant problem for both companies involved in the transaction, but more so for the selling entrepreneur.

5. A number of the selling owners were disappointed in the advising they received from the "experts." After the fact, they wish they had talked to other entrepreneurs who had been through the experience of a company sale.

6. Most entrepreneurs relied on their staff and advisors to determine a fair price for their company. Thus, they would talk in terms of cash flows and earnings, most often the capitalization or multiple of the earnings or cash flows, and seldom the present value of future cash flows. However, most of the entrepreneurs felt they had a sense of what they would accept for the firm, and that instinct had a greater influence than did the supporting computations. Most often, the price was not a serious issue.

7. There is considerable downside risk if the acquisition is not consummated. During the negotiations, management's focus and attention shifts from company operations to consummating the sale. Members of the existing management team may be promised promotions after the acquisition, which are not fulfilled after the negotiations fail. Hence, there is a real risk of losing part of the management team and certainly taking several months to regain the firm's focus.

In addition to selling the firm or being acquired by independent purchasers or acquirers, the harvest strategy can be accomplished by selling to the firm's own management or its employees, as described in the following two sections.

Management Buyout

As already observed, the 1980s will long be remembered—not so favorably by some managers and employees—for the unfriendly takeovers and corporate restructurings, involving corporate raiders and takeover artists, such as Carl Icahn and T. Boone Pickens. These paragons—or parasites some might say—popularized financial engineering, in which an attempt to buy a company is made for the purpose of restructuring it and selling it off in pieces to the highest bidder. To finance the deal, heavy amounts of debt are incurred, with as much as 90 percent of the financing coming from high-yield debt, thus the name *leveraged buyout*. If the leveraged buyout is performed not by outsiders but by the firm's own management, we have a *management buyout* (MBO).

The MBO has been used by some to thwart outside raiders and by others to refocus current management's vision. The evidence is clear that MBOs can contribute significantly to a firm's operating performance by increasing management's focus and intensity and that the benefits accruing from MBOs are not short-term in duration. (See Kaplan, 1989 and 1991, for an analysis of the operating effects of large-firm MBOs, and Wright et al., 1992b, for smaller-firm MBOs.)

Given the empirical evidence of increased efficiencies produced from an MBO and the proven longevity of these benefits, an MBO should be considered a potentially viable means for transferring firm ownership—both for large and small businesses. In like manner, an MBO can serve as a possible means for harvesting a venture. While the managers within many entrepreneurial businesses frequently have a strong interest and incentive to buy the business, they often lack the financial capacity to do so. An MBO can resolve this intractability. It simply means that they must be prepared to live in a glass house and with the unforgiving nature of debt financing.

If an MBO is used to consummate the sale, not only is the new owner exposed to financial risk, so is the selling owner. Also, to the extent that the entrepreneur accepts debt in consideration for the company, there is a potential complication to be resolved. The deal must then be structured to minimize potential agency problems. Specifically, if the new owners have placed little if any of their own money in the deal, they may be inclined to take risks that are not in the best interest of the selling entrepreneur; they simply have nothing to lose if the company fails. Also, if the terms of the deal include an earnout where the final amount of the payment depends in part on the subsequent profit performance of the company, the buying owners have an incentive to do things that lower the firm's profits during the earnout period. Thus, the entrepreneur needs to take great care in structuring the deal; otherwise, there will most likely be disappointment with the outcome.

In addition to their recent popularity in the United States, management buyouts have come to be used in Europe as well. In Europe, the venture capital industry has had a significant role in MBOs, especially for smaller firms. Wright et al. (1992a) evaluated a sample of 182 venture-backed MBOs and found the same improvement in operating efficiencies and longevity as did researchers in the United States. Also, European managers who undertake MBOs typically anticipate their exit to be in the form of a public offering, but almost invariably the firm is sold to a third party. This last finding will become clearer at a later point in the chapter.

Employee Stock Ownership Plan

Employee stock ownership plans (ESOPs) were designed to increase productivity by linking employee compensation to company performance and by giving employees a role in management through their voting rights as share-holders. The research to date suggests that ESOPs have indeed been effective toward these ends. For instance, using both Tobin's (Tobin, 1969) and accounting performance variables, Park and Song (1995) found that average performance significantly increases after establishing or expanding an ESOP (see also Beatty, 1995). There are also tax advantages with ESOPs that are not available with other retirement plans.

In response to the above benefits, owners of small and midsize firms have been the primary users of ESOPs when they are ready to sell (Englander, 1993). The opportunity for employees to invest in employer stock and the significant tax savings not available with other retirement plans—for employers and employees alike—makes the ESOP potentially attractive as a way to harvest the venture (Beatty, 1995).

A *leveraged* ESOP particularly fits the needs of an entrepreneur wanting to harvest a venture. This type of ESOP borrows money to buy the company's stock. By having access to borrowed money, the leveraged ESOP can make large purchases of the stock at one time, conceivably purchasing the entire company. Figure 2 presents a flow chart of the sequence of events when a leveraged ESOP is used to provide an employee retirement plan and, in conjunction, to allow the present owners to sell their stock. The firm first establishes an ESOP and guarantees any debt borrowed by the ESOP for the purpose of buying the company's stock. Next, the ESOP borrows money from a lender, and the cash is used to buy the owner's stock. The shares are held by a trust, and the company makes annual tax-deductible contributions to the trust so it can pay off the loan. As the loan is paid off, shares are released and allocated to the employees.

While an ESOP benefits the owner by providing a market for selling stock, it also carries with it some tax advantages that make the approach attractive to owner and employee alike. Some of the benefits are as follows:

1. If the ESOP owns at least 30 percent of the firm after purchasing the shares, the seller can avoid current tax on the gain by using the proceeds to buy other securities.

2. If the ESOP owns more than 50 percent of the company, those who lend money to the ESOP are taxed on only 50 percent of the income received from such loans. Thus, the lender can afford to offer a lower interest rate, usually about 1½ percentage points below a company's normal borrowing cost.

3. The dividends that a business pays on the stock held by the ESOP are allowed as a tax-deductible expense; that is, the dividends are treated like interest expense when it comes to taxes.

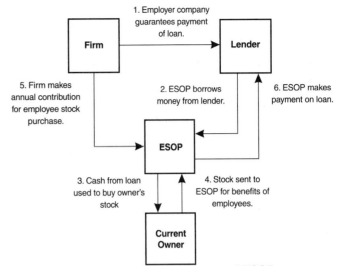

Figure 2 The Harvest: using the leveraged ESOP.

Source: Adapted from D. R. Garner, R. R. Owen, and R. P. Conway. *The Ernst & Young Guide to Raising Capital.* New York: John Wiley & Sons, 1991, p. 282.

Despite the advantages ESOPs offer, they are not appropriate for all companies. If the entrepreneur does not want the employees to have control of the company, then an ESOP is not an option. Also, the ESOP must cover all employees, and the owners are required to disclose certain information about the company, such as its performance, and its key executives' salaries, which for some entrepreneurs is not palatable. Finally, using an ESOP can place the employees in double jeopardy, where both their jobs and their retirement funds depend on the success of a single business. Even so, an ESOP has considerable potential when crafting a harvest strategy.

The next section looks at the option for harvesting the venture that most would love to attain, but few do.

Initial Public Offerings

An initial public offering (IPO) is not in and of itself a primary means for harvesting a venture. While founders and the shareholders clearly benefit from an IPO, its principal purpose in most situations is to facilitate the raising of future capital. Simply put, publicly traded stock provides for greater liquidity, which allows the company to raise capital on more favorable terms than if it were privately held. These perceptions are borne out in Holmburg's (1991) study, where he asked the CEOs of firms that had gone public to indicate the level of importance of some 17 different possible motivations for the public offering. The items receiving the highest percentage of "very important" responses are as follows:

Raise capital for growth	85%
Raise capital to increase working capital	65%
Facilitate acquiring another firm	40%
Establish a market value for the firm	35%
Enhance the firm's ability to raise capital	35%

For all practical purposes, the CEOs clearly considered financing future growth as the primary impetus for going public. Without a strong IPO market, young high-growth firms would have limited access to the public capital markets, but equally bad, they would have less access to private investors who rely on the IPO market to harvest their investment. However, at the same time, the IPO market is beneficial to the founding entrepreneur in the form of increased liquidity and the enhancement of future options, both of which reduce the investor's risk exposure. So it may not be a pure harvest in the same way of other approaches where cash is received, but the investor captures some of the same advantages accruing to the firm.

Understanding the IPO Process

The IPO process can be one of the most exhilarating, but also frustrating and exhausting, experiences an entrepreneur will encounter (Sutton and Beneddetto, 1990). Managements of large companies, much less small ones, do not like being exposed to the vicissitudes of the capital markets and to the world of investment bankers.

In a survey of the *Inc.* magazine's top 100 firms, the CEOs who had participated in public offerings indicated they spent 33 hours per week on the offering for 4 months (Brokaw, 1993). The cost of the IPO process seemed excessive and exorbitant to many. They found themselves not being understood and having little influence in the decisions being made. Disillusionment with the investment bankers, and much of the entire process itself frequently occurred. At some point, the owners wondered where they had lost control of the process, a feeling generally held by most entrepreneurs involved in a public offering.

The chronology of a public offering is relatively straightforward, namely:

- The management decides to go public.
- An investment banker is selected to serve as the underwriter, who in turn brings together a group of investment houses to help sell the shares.
- A prospectus is prepared.
- The managers, along with the investment banker, go on the road to tell the firm's story to the brokers who will be selling the stock.
- On the day before the offering is released to the public, the decision is made about the actual offering price.
- All the work, which by now has been months, comes to fruition in a single event—offering the stock to the public and waiting for the consequence.

During this process, the firm's owners and managers are answering such questions as:

- What do we need to do in advance of going public?
- What are the legal requirements?
- Who should be responsible for the different activities and how should we structure our team to make it all happen?
- How do we choose an investment banker?
- How do we determine an appropriate price for the offering?
- How is life different after we are a public company?

While the foregoing issues are important, they do not represent the complete story. The missing element is the shift in power that occurs during the process. When the chain of events begins, the company's management is in control. They can dictate whether or not to go public and who the investment banker will be. However, after the prospectus has been prepared and the road show is underway, the firm's management, including the entrepreneur, is no longer the primary decision-maker. Now the investment banker has control of the decisions. Finally, the marketplace, in complement with the investment banker, begins to take over, and ultimately it is the market that dictates the final outcome.

In addition to the issue of who controls the events and decisions in the IPO process, one other matter is important—understanding the

investment banker's motivations in the IPO process. Stated differently, who is the investor banker's primary customer here? Clearly, the issue firm is rewarding the underwriter for the services being performed through the fees paid and a participation in the deal. But the economics for helping with an IPO may not be as rewarding for the investment banker as other activities, such as involvement with corporate acquisitions. The investment bank is also selling the securities to its customers on the other side of the trade. Thus, it becomes unclear as to what is driving the pricing decision by the investment banker (Sahlman, 1988). This potential agency problem may be one of the reasons for the upfront underpricing of IPOs (Welch, 1996).

While the process of going public may prove frustrating and exasperating, the eventual outcome frequently is not. In a survey of firms listed on the French *Second Marché* (secondary market), most CEOs were very satisfied with their decision (Desroches and Belletante, 1992). The firm owners thought the external image of the firm was improved in the eyes of the suppliers, customers, and others after the offering, along with an increased effectiveness in the level of communications, strategy, and other internal management-related aspects. They disliked, however, the fluctuations in the firm's share price, which they did not believe reflected firm performance. Similar results were observed by Desroches and Jog (1989) in a study of 194 firms that went public in Canada. They concluded that CEOs do not convey a significant loss of control and actually welcome the more structured decision-making which resulted from going public. Although they did not like the valuation of their shares by the marketplace, their conclusion was that going public does imply significant and positive changes to the status of the firm, management structure, and the entrepreneur.

While the Canadians were overwhelmingly pleased with the outcome of going public, they like the French, disliked the feeling of powerlessness about the firm's stock price and the belief that the market price does not reflect the true value of the firm. This view is one that is held by managers across the board, without respect to firm size. The perception is that the capital markets are myopic; that management is under pressure for short-term performance and can no longer look to the share-holder's long-term best interests (Jones et al., 1992).

While there are certainly anomalies, as explained in the next section, there is absolutely no empirical evidence that the capital markets are short-sighted, while management can see more clearly into the long-term future. If anything, it is management that is myopic, not the markets (Miller, 1994).

Understanding the IPO Market

If contemplating a public offering, management needs to have an understanding of the basic nature and peculiarities of the new-issues market. In this area, there is no lack of empirical work about the outcomes of new offerings. Specifically, three anomalies have been found:

1. There is a large amount of empirical literature validating IPO underpricing, dating back 20 years—all finding that the distribution of initial returns to be highly skewed, with significant positive means (Ibbotson, 1975). The average first-day return of a new issue falls somewhere between 10 percent and 15 percent. These results are even more pronounced for smaller, younger companies going public than for their older, more established counterparts. For instance, the average initial return on IPOs with an offering price of less than $3.00 was found to be an amazing 42.8 percent, whereas the average initial return on IPOs with an offering price of $3.00 or more was only 8.6 percent (Chalk and Peavy, 1987). Moreover, underpricing persists in every country with a stock

market, although the amount of under-pricing is different from country to country (Loughran et al., 1994).

2. There are cycles in both the volume of new issues and the magnitude of first-day returns. The periods of high average initial returns are known as "hot issue" markets. (Hot issue markets were first identified by Ibbotson and Jaffe, 1975.) The cycles in underpricing allow one to predict next month's average initial return based upon the current month's average with a high degree of accuracy, i.e., the first-order autocorrelation of monthly average initial is 0.66. Likewise, high-volume months are almost always followed by high-volume months, where the autocorrelation is 0.89 (Ibbotson et al., 1994).

3. New issues tend to underperform for up to five years after the offering (Loughran, 1993). For IPOs during the period 1975 to 1984, the total return from the end of the first day of trading to three years later was 34.5 percent, compared with the return on the NYSE of 61.9 percent (Ritter, 1991). Again these findings were even more pronounced for younger firms than for established firms. There is also reason to believe that the earnings per share of companies going public typically grows rapidly in the years before going public, but then actually declines in the first several years after the IPO (Jain and Kini, forthcoming).

Ibbotson et al. (1994) described the IPO market pricing as a puzzle to those who otherwise believe in efficient capital markets and argued that the anomalies are interrelated by periodic overoptimism by investors which causes many firms to rush to market, resulting in disappointing returns to long-term investors when the issuers fail to live up to overly optimistic expectations. They also found that firms that issue during low-volume periods typically experience neither high initial price runups nor subsequent long-run underperformance and that the patterns are much more pronounced for smaller, younger companies going public than for their older, more established counterparts. Their finding is consistent with evidence by Hanley and Ritter (1993) suggesting inefficiencies in markets for smaller-cap stocks.

In short, the IPO market has somewhat a personality of its own and one that acts a bit different from the rest of the capital markets—a fact that needs to be understood by an entrepreneur wanting to take a firm public.

A Venture Capital Perspective of IPOs

Many venture capitalists believe that an IPO produces a higher price than an outright sale. That belief is encouraged by the fact that the average valuation of IPOs between 1988 and 1992 was $106.9 million versus $37.4 million for private sales. But the companies floating IPOs are mostly stars or potential stars, whereas those that are sold include not only stars but also many mediocrities with no hope of going public.

The gains realized through IPOs were almost five times greater than the next most profitable method of harvesting the venture, according to a study of how 26 venture capital funds exited 442 investments from 1970 to 1982 (Soja and Reyes, 1990). That study found that 30 percent of the exits were through IPOs, 23 percent private sales, 6 percent company buyouts, 9 percent secondary sales, 6 percent liquidations and 26 percent write-offs.

A study of 77 high-tech companies backed by venture capital that had IPOs between 1979 and 1988 found that the times returns (amount returned ÷ amount invested) on the venture capital investment

at the initial offering price was 22.5 times for the first round; 10 times for the second round; and 3.7 times for the third round (Bygrave and Stein, 1989). Four years after the IPO the times return was 62.7 times for the first round, 38.1 times for the second, and 13.5 times for the third.

The average compound annual rate of return for the first round of venture capital at the time of the IPO was 220 percent; four years after the IPO (about seven years after the first round of venture capital), it had declined to 57 percent. So although the times return increased from 22.5 times to 62.7 times, the rate of return declined because of the longer holding period—another indication of underpricing of new issues.

According to industry wisdom, venture capitalists financing seed and start-up high-technology companies are looking for compound annual returns of 50 percent or more; for second-stage financings they tend to look for 30 to 40 percent; while third-round investors may expect returns of 25 to 30 percent (Morris, 1985).

A rule of thumb is a return in five years of seven times the first venture capital (a compound rate of return of 48 percent). The evidence in the above studies gives some credence to these expected returns. However, in the latter 1980s, the returns of funds started in the 1980s fell far short of expectations, mainly owing to the public's loss of interest in speculative IPOs during the latter 1980s. As a result, many venture-backed companies were unable to go public. Thus, venture funds were unable to reap their expected harvests. The return of a "hot" IPO market in the 1990s has provided hopes of a return to the earlier years. However, based on limited evidence, the returns probably have only returned to the 15 to 20 percent range.

The European Experience with Harvesting

To understand the environment for harvesting in Europe, one can draw on the comprehensive work edited by Bygrave et al. (1994). In this study, realizing investment value is the result of collective efforts of a group of researchers who carefully examined the harvesting process across Europe.

The organized venture capital industry in Europe is little more than 12 years old, in contrast to 50 years for the U.S. industry. There were a few players in Europe before 1980, most notably the U.K. firm now named 3i, and at least one unsuccessful American-style venture capital firm that was set up in the 1960s. But it was during the entrepreneurial era of the 1980s that European venture capital grew explosively. From 1984 through 1992, the venture capital funds under management in Europe grew from ECU 3.6 billion to ECU 38.5 billion (EVCA, 1991–93). More recently, the total capital under management in Europe approximates that of the United States.

Unlike the United States, however, where entries and harvests have been roughly in balance, the amount of money being invested in portfolio companies by European venture capital funds far exceeds the amount being divested. For instance, over five years (1988 to 1992), ECU 21.2 billion was invested in portfolio companies but only ECU 9.4 billion was divested. Of course, some of that imbalance is because the total pool of venture capital continues to grow. But that is only a partial explanation because the amount of new funds raised has been declining since it peaked in 1989. If the 1990 to 1992 trend continues, a log jam of unrealized investments is building up.

By the end of 1992, most people within the European venture capital industry agreed that much of the investment-divestment imbalance was due to the relative scarcity of viable harvest options. For instance, of 158 MBOs completed in the period 1983 to 1985 in the

United Kingdom, more than 70 percent had not been harvested successfully by June 1992 (Wright et al., 1992a). That lack of successful exits is particularly acute with smaller MBOs.

At the start of the 1990s, frustration on the part of venture capitalists in the United Kingdom and the Netherlands over the lack of exit options gave rise to a number of new initiatives designed to facilitate harvesting. Among them were proposals for a pan-European private secondary market for venture capital investments and for a local participation market for Dutch venture capital investment. (Onians, 1993; Elbertse, 1993).

During the 1980s, a number of European countries set up second- and third-tier stock markets in order to facilitate IPOs by small companies that could not meet the requirements of the main markets. These markets include the Unlisted Securities Market (USM) in the United Kingdom, the *Second Marché* in France, and the Parallel Market in the Netherlands. A surge in venture capital in the United Kingdom, France, and the Netherlands coincided with a boom in these countries' secondary markets. However, despite these efforts to create equity markets for private firms, the results have been unsuccessful. For instance, the USM is to be closed at the end of 1996 to be replaced by the Alternative Investment Market (AIM). In addition, a pan-European exchange is being formed called the EASDAQ in an effort to create the equivalent of the NASDAQ in the United States. So at the present, Europe continues to lack a well-established market for IPOs.

Given the limited accessibility to the IPO market as an exit strategy, venture capitalists in Europe have primarily resorted to company sales as their exit mechanism of choice—41 percent of all exits in Europe come through the company being sold, compared with 10 percent exits through IPOs. Here too, however, the number of corporate sales has decreased in recent years. In the United Kingdom, the number of sales of MBOs averaged 39 per year from 1981 through 1988, but fell to 15 in 1989, 8 in 1990, and 3 in 1991. Fortunately, trade sales in other European nations have not been as severely affected. Even so, the European venture industry, along with the entrepreneurs in whose companies they have invested, is experiencing severe problems in realizing the value created through its investments.

Current State of Affairs and the Need for Research

Based on the prior research, several things can be said about harvesting with reasonable certitude:

- To harvest value, it must first be created. Whether a firm is high-tech or low-tech, small or large, economic value is created only by earning rates of return that exceed the investors' opportunity cost of the funds—including the owners'. Value is destroyed by earning rates of return that are less than the opportunity cost of the funds—again including the equity owners. Creating value and capturing the value are not the same thing. Without the opportunity to harvest, a firm's owners and investors will be denied a significant amount of the value that has been created over the firm's life.
- Harvesting is more than merely selling and leaving a business. It is about capturing value (cash flows), reducing risk, and creating future options.
- There are four fundamental approaches to harvesting a venture: 1) Restructuring the company's goals and strategies in order to increase the cash flows extracted from the business by the owners and investors; 2) selling to outsiders, management, employees, and/or family members; 3) being

acquired or merged into another business; or 4) issuing stock to the public.
- Investors providing high-risk capital—particularly venture capitalists—generally insist on an exit strategy as part of the terms of the deal. As a result, the accessibility to venture capital is driven by the availability of harvest options.
- Return distributions resulting from venture-backed harvests and IPOs are known.
- The window of opportunity for harvesting quickly opens and closes. That is, there are waves of IPOs and merger and acquisition opportunities.

Besides what is known about harvesting an entrepreneurial firm, there are also some impressions based on intuition and anecdotal evidence, including:

- Few events in the life of the entrepreneur, and for the firm itself, are more significant than the harvest.
- Some entrepreneurs are averse to thinking about the harvest, while others begin the venture to harvest it.
- The decision to harvest is frequently the result of an unexpected crisis rather than a well-conceived strategy.

Finally, some things are still not known about the harvest. The following questions are begging further research:

- How much difference does an effective harvest strategy make in releasing the value within the firm for the benefit of the owners and investors?
- What is the entrepreneur's perspective about the harvest? How do these expectations compare to the final outcome?
- How important is timing in the harvest? How does the entrepreneur know when to harvest?
- What can be done to increase the effectiveness of the harvest?
- How do the entrepreneur's personal preferences and situation affect the harvest?
- What can be done by the entrepreneur to enhance the probability of a successful harvest?
- A better understanding of the actual process of the harvest is needed. Some things are known about the outcomes but little about the process, e.g., 1) What are the catalysts that bring the entrepreneur and investors to the decision to harvest? 2) How do they make a choice as to the approach to be taken in harvesting? 3) What does the entrepreneur need to know before going through an IPO?

These questions and many others go unanswered. There is so much that could be done. The primary limitations are the researcher's own creativity and the limited availability of quality data. Gaining access to the needed information is no small matter in this area. Nevertheless, given some creativity and diligence, numerous research questions could be addressed, and the importance of the topic calls us to take up the challenge.

References

Batchelor, C. 1992. Enterprise looks for a way out. *Financial Times,* December 22.

Beatty, A. 1995. The cash flow and informational effects of employee stock ownership plans. *Journal of Financial Economics* 38(2):211–230.

Bhide, A. 1989. The causes and consequences of hostile take-overs. *Journal of Applied Corporate Finance* 2(2):n36–59.

Brennan, M.J. 1995. A perspective on accounting and stock prices. *Journal of Applied Corporate Finance* 8(1):43–52.

Brokaw, L. 1993. The first day of the rest of your life. *Inc.* 15(5):144.

Bygrave, W.D., and M. Stein. 1989. A time to buy and a time to sell: A study of venture capital investments in 77 companies that went public. In N.C. Churchill et al. (eds.): *Frontiers of Entrepreneurship Research.* Wellesley, MA: Babson College, 288–303.

Bygrave, W. D., M. Hay, and J. B. Peeters, (eds.). 1994. *Realizing Investment Value.* London: Pitman Publishing.

Chalk, A., and J. Peavy. 1987. Initial public offerings: Daily returns, offering types and the price effect. *Financial Analyst Journal* 27(4): 65–69.

Copeland, T., T. T. Koller, and J. Murrin. 1994. *Valuation: Measuring and Managing the Value of Companies.* New York: John Wiley and Sons.

Desroches, J. J-Y., and B. Belletante. 1992. The positive impact of going public on entrepreneurs and their firms: Evidence from listing on the "Second Marché" in France. In N. C. Churchill et al. (eds.): *Frontiers of Entrepreneurship Research.* Wellesley, MA: Babson College, 466–480.

Donaldson, G. 1994. *Corporate Restructuring: Managing the Change Process from Within.* Cambridge, MA: Harvard Business School Press.

Elbertse, E. 1993. Developing exit mechanism in your market. Presentation at European Venture Capital Association business seminar on exiting in Europe, Venice, February 11–12.

Englander, D. W. 1993. Cashing out through ESOPs. *Small Business Reports* 18(10):43–45.

European Venture Capital Association (EVCA). 1991–93. *Venture Capital in Europe: EVCA Yearbooks.* Zaveman, Belgium.

Freear, J., J. A. Sohl, and W. E. Wetzel. 1990. Raising venture capital: Entrepreneurs' views of the process. *Frontiers of Entrepreneurship Research,* 223–265.

Holmburg, S. 1991. Value creation and capture: Entrepreneurship harvest and IPO strategies. In N. C. Churchill et al. (eds.): *Frontiers of Entrepreneurship Research.* Wellesley, MA: Babson College, 191–204.

Hyatt, H. 1990. The dark side (of going public). *Inc.* 12(6):46–56.

Ibbotson, R.G. 1975. Price performance of common stock new issues. *Journal of Financial Economics* 2(3):235–272.

Ibbotson, R.G., and J.F. Jaffe. 1975. Hot issue markets. *Journal of Finance* 30(4):1027–1042.

Ibbotson, R.G., J.L. Sindelar, and J.R. Ritter. 1994. The market's problems with the pricing of initial public offerings. *Journal of Applied Corporate Finance* 7(1):66–74.

Ibbotson, R.G., J.L. Sindelar, and J.R. Ritter. 1993. Initial public offerings. *Journal of Applied Corporate Finance* 1(2):37–45.

Jain, B. and O. Kini (Forthcoming). The post-issue operating performance of IPOs. *Journal of Finance.*

Jones, S., M. B. Cohen, and V. V. Coppola. 1992. Going public. In Sahlman, W. A., and Stevenson, H. H. (eds.): *The Entrepreneurial Venture.* Cambridge, MA: Harvard Business School Publications.

Kaplan, S. 1989. The effects of management buy-outs on operating performance and value. *Journal of Financial Economics* 24:217–254.

Kaplan, S. 1991. The staying power of leverage buyouts. *Journal of Financial Economics* 29:287–313.

Loughran, T. 1993. NYSE vs. Nasdaq returns: Market microstructure or the poor performance of IPOs? *Journal of Financial Economics* 33:241–260.

Loughran, T., J. Ritter, and K. Rydqvist. 1994. Initial public offerings: International insights. *Pacific-Basin Finance Journal* 2(3):165–199.

Miller, M. 1994. Is American corporate governance fatally flawed? *Journal of Applied Corporate Finance* 6(4):32–39.

Morris, J.K. 1985. The pricing of a venture capital investment. In S. E. Pratt and J. K. Morris (eds.): *Pratt's Guide to Venture Capital Sources,* 9th edition. Wellesley Hills, MA: Venture Economics.

Onians, R. 1993. A European secondary market. Presented at EVCA business seminar on Exiting in Europe, Venice, February 11–12.

Paré, T. P. 1990. Passing on the family business. *Fortune* 127(9):50.

Park, S., and M.H. Song. 1995. Employee stock ownership plans, firm performance, and monitoring by outside blockholders. *Financial Management* 24(4):52–65.

Petty, J.W., B.E. Bygrave, and J.M. Shulman. 1994. Harvesting the entrepreneurial venture: A time for creating value. *Journal of Applied Corporate Finance* 7(9):48–58.

Ritter, J. 1991. The long-run performance of initial public offerings. *Journal of Finance* 46(3):3–27.

Sahlman, W. A. 1988. Aspects of financial contracting in venture capital. *Journal of Applied Corporate Finance* 1(4):23–36.

Sahlman, W. A. 1989. Teaching notes accompanying CML Group, Inc. *Going Public.* Cambridge, MA: Harvard Business School Publishing Division.

Soja, T.A., and J.E. Reyes. 1990. *Investment Benchmarks: Venture Capital.* Needham, MA: Venture Economics.

Stevenson, H.E., and D.E. Gumpert. 1985. The heart of entrepreneurship. *Harvard Business Review* 63(2):85–94.

Stevenson, H.E., and W.A. Sahlman. 1987. Entrepreneurship: A process, not a person. Working paper 87-06, pp. 1–49.

Stewart, G.B., III. 1991. *The Quest for Value.* New York: Harper-Collins, pp. 136–140.

Sutton, D.P., and M.W. Beneddetto. 1990. *Initial Public Offerings.* Chicago: Probus Publishing Company.

Timmons, J. 1994. *New Venture Creation.* Chicago: Irwin, p. 654.

Toben, J. 1969. A general equilibrium approach to monetary theory. *Journal of Money, Credit, and Banking* 1:15–29.

Welch, I. 1996. Equity offerings following the IPO: Theory and evidence. *Journal of Corporate Finance* 2:227–259.

Weston, J.F., K. Chung, and S. Hoag. 1990. Theories of mergers and tender offers. In *Mergers, Restructuring and Corporate Control.* Englewood-Cliffs, NJ: Prentice Hall, 190–222.

Wright, M., K. Robbie, Y. Romanet, S. Thompson, R. Joachimsson, J. Bruining, and A. Herst. 1992a. Realizations, longevity and the life-cycle of management buy-outs and buy-ins: A four-country study. Presented at the European Federal for Economic Research (EFER) Forum, London Business School, December 12–14.

Wright, M., S. Thompson, and K. Robbie. 1992b. Venture capital and management-led buyouts: European evidence. *Journal of Business Venturing* 7(1):47–71.

Wright, M., S. Thompson, K. Robbie, and P. Wong. 1992c. Management buy-outs in the short and long term. In N. C. Churchill et al. (eds.): *Frontiers of Entrepreneurship Research.* Wellesley, MA: Babson College, 302–316.

From *Entrepreneurship 2000,* Upstart Publishing Company, 1997, pp.71-94. ©1997 by J. William Petty. Reprinted by permission of the author.

Choosing Your Exit Strategy

Wᴉʟʟɪᴀᴍ H. Pᴀʏɴᴇ

Your exit strategy impacts many directions that you might choose in growing your business. Not considering your exit strategy early may indeed limit your options in the future. It is not a matter of whether you will sell, or otherwise dispose of, your interest in this business. Your only decisions are when and how.

It Pays to Plan Ahead

It's always a good idea to plan your exit strategy early. It's also important that your founding operating partners and investors agree with it. If you wish to sell the business in five years, but your operating partner wants to own and manage it with you for 15 years, you have a problem. If you suggest to key employees that you have no plans to exit the company and then sell within two years, they are likely to be dissatisfied and could disrupt the sale. If you decide you would like to give your shares to your heirs, angel investors may object and choose an exit strategy that does not complement your future plans.

If you wish to share equity with employees or with heirs, it helps to start early, when the company valuation (and share price) is low. U.S. tax laws severely limit gifts to heirs; hence, it will take many years to pass the business on to your children. Assuming the company experiences consistent growth, sharing equity with employees can be rewarding at any stage in the business cycle. However, transferring total ownership to the employees, including the sale of your shares, is more easily accomplished and costs less when you start early.

If you choose to fund the early growth of your company using venture capital (VC), you are usually setting out on a course leading to an initial public offering (IPO), or to the sale of the company. Before seeking VC funding, it is mandatory that the entrepreneur contemplate the management and control issues that accompany VC funding and eventual public ownership.

Finally, if you plan to seek a business partner and/or outside financing from angel investors, banks or venture capitalists, someone will surely ask about your long-term plans regarding the business, and specifically, how long you plan to be with it. You need to have a thoughtful response.

Is Selling the Best Way Out?

Liquidation of ownership in your business is a very personal decision, and it is yours to make as the entrepreneur. Some founders say that creating a business and selling it within a few years is a travesty to the employees who helped build it. Others have said they couldn't possibly go public, because a "big brother" would constantly be looking over their shoulders. From my perspective, there is no incorrect exit strategy. You, your partners, your investors and your employees are building a business. Your exit strategy is simply a very important part of your business plan.

Selling your business to another individual or independent business is one of four usual choices for liquidating your equity. It's a huge decision and generally one that is difficult to make. One day you own the company, and the next day you do not. To optimize the terms of the sale, the new owner may insist you continue to operate the business for an agreed-upon period of time. From another perspective, then, you move from controlling owner to employee in one quick step.

Proceeds from the sale of a private company usually consist of cash, shares of a public company, shares of a private company or a combination of the above. This is generally a move toward greater liquidity in your personal estate. You are selling illiquid shares of your private company for cash and/or shares of a company that will eventually become liquid.

This allows the successful entrepreneur, who often has nearly 100 percent of his or her assets tied up in the business, the option of diversifying his or her portfolio of investments. Some entrepreneurs sell to other private companies and achieve asset diversification by becoming part of the larger, merged business. While immediate liquidity may not be their primary driver, founders who take this course usually move closer to a liquidation opportunity.

The disadvantages of selling your business are also obvious. You have given up your "baby." You are no longer in control. You may have passed up the opportunity to grow the business (and the value of your shares) in the future.

When Should You Sell?

It may be time to begin working on selling your business when you are losing sleep (or your hair) because you realize one or more of the following:

- Your business is a very valuable asset.
- Ownership represents nearly 100 percent of your net worth.
- Some power outside your control (competitor, government, act of God, etc.) could take that away from you.

Personally, I like investing in small, well-run companies positioned to be "discovered" by an attractive buyer. As an investor, I prefer niche or boutique businesses in which:

- The investment required to achieve break-even in cash flow is less than $500,000.
- The annual revenue potential within the first five to ten years is $5 million to $20 million.
- The likelihood that a large public company might be interested in purchasing the company is significant. In other words, these companies plan to sell to an attractive public company as the business approaches a preset valuation.

Is Going Public Better than Being Acquired?

Offering shares of your company to the public markets is viewed by some as an exit strategy. In my opinion, it is not. Initial public offerings, or IPOs, involve issuing new shares for cash at a time when the business is challenged with an opportunity to grow, which would be facilitated with an infusion of cash. However, going public generally limits your exit options and, by default, defines your exit strategy. Once the shares trade in public markets, significant employee ownership (that is, more than 50 percent) or control by your heirs is unlikely.

Selling ownership to public markets generally provides the cash for growth, while offering the principals of the company the promise of some future liquidity of their shares. Liquidation by the entrepreneur can be accomplished, but it is likely to require many years, unless, of course, the entire company is subsequently sold. Control by the founders is generally possible, but the company acquires a new set of investors with a short-term perspective on defining success. Dealing with the demands of the market makers and the Securities and Exchange Commission (SEC) will become a reality. And, in volatile markets, it may not be desirable.

Selling to Your Employees

Employee ownership can be very rewarding and can take several forms. Most of us are familiar with Employee Stock Ownership Plans, or ESOPs, which are managed like a pension plan with all company contributions used to buy company stock. But, an ESOP is only one arrow in the equity-compensation quiver.

Motivated employees can be given appropriate incentives through other forms of equity, such as stock options, stock-purchase plans and performance-based stock bonuses. These plans generally allow the founder to maintain control of the company as his or her shares are diluted by those shares made available to the employees. Equity compensation as part of a corporate culture fosters a great working environment conducive to a high-growth business.

Under certain conditions, it is possible for the founder to sell shares back to the company, or to the ESOP. However, the legal ramifications of this strategy are many and should be explored well in advance.

Passing Control to Your Heirs

Transferring ownership to the founder's heirs is more common than most entrepreneurs might imagine, although tax laws in the United States limit this option. It requires patience and endurance. Gifts by a single U.S. citizen to each heir, without paying gift tax, are limited to $10,000 a year, and the tax implications of passing a business to your heirs through your estate are daunting. It's best to take action early in the life of the business, when the share price is low and the entrepreneur has many years to give some of it away.

For high-tech entrepreneurs, this option may not be feasible, because high-tech products may have limited life spans. However, there are plenty of entrepreneurs building significant businesses outside of the high-technology arena. The long-term prospects for a well-run commodities business, for example, justify planning to pass ownership along to the following generation.

If you haven't done so already, I suggest you develop your exit strategy now. Get a good understanding of your options. Then, talk to your spouse, parents, friends and business advisors. Use all these insights to develop a strategy that meets your needs. Once you have developed your plan, think about structuring your company to meet those needs.

Test-Your-Knowledge Form

We encourage you to photocopy and use this page as a tool to assess how the articles in *Annual Editions* expand on the information in your textbook. By reflecting on the articles you will gain enhanced text information. You can also access this useful form on a product's book support website at *http://www.mhcls.com*.

NAME: DATE:

_____

TITLE AND NUMBER OF ARTICLE:

_____

BRIEFLY STATE THE MAIN IDEA OF THIS ARTICLE:

_____

LIST THREE IMPORTANT FACTS THAT THE AUTHOR USES TO SUPPORT THE MAIN IDEA:

_____

WHAT INFORMATION OR IDEAS DISCUSSED IN THIS ARTICLE ARE ALSO DISCUSSED IN YOUR TEXTBOOK OR OTHER READINGS THAT YOU HAVE DONE? LIST THE TEXTBOOK CHAPTERS AND PAGE NUMBERS:

_____

LIST ANY EXAMPLES OF BIAS OR FAULTY REASONING THAT YOU FOUND IN THE ARTICLE:

_____

LIST ANY NEW TERMS/CONCEPTS THAT WERE DISCUSSED IN THE ARTICLE, AND WRITE A SHORT DEFINITION:

We Want Your Advice

ANNUAL EDITIONS revisions depend on two major opinion sources: one is our Advisory Board, listed in the front of this volume, which works with us in scanning the thousands of articles published in the public press each year; the other is you—the person actually using the book. Please help us and the users of the next edition by completing the prepaid article rating form on this page and returning it to us. Thank you for your help!

ANNUAL EDITIONS: Entrepreneurship, 6/e

ARTICLE RATING FORM

Here is an opportunity for you to have direct input into the next revision of this volume.
We would like you to rate each of the articles listed below, using the following scale:

1. **Excellent: should definitely be retained**
2. **Above average: should probably be retained**
3. **Below average: should probably be deleted**
4. **Poor: should definitely be deleted**

Your ratings will play a vital part in the next revision.
Please mail this prepaid form to us as soon as possible.
Thanks for your help!

RATING	ARTICLE
	1. Wanted: Entrepreneurs (Just Don't Ask for a Job Description)
	2. An Idea Whose Time Has Come
	3. Creative Disruption
	4. The World Discovers the Laffer Curve
	5. Building Entrepreneurial Economies
	6. The Role of Small and Large Businesses in Economic Development
	7. Success Rules!
	8. The Greatest Entrepreneurs of All Time
	9. The Secrets of Serial Success
	10. Startups in a Downturn
	11. So, You Want to Be an Entrepreneur?
	12. The B!g Idea
	13. How to Build a Bulletproof Startup
	14. Market Research on the Cheap
	15. 20 Reasons Why You Need a Business Plan
	16. How to Write a Great Business Plan
	17. Outline for a Business Plan: A Proven Approach for Entrepreneurs Only
	18. The 10 Biggest Business Plan Mistakes
	19. Writing a Compelling Executive Summary
	20. The People's Bank
	21. Angel Investment Criteria
	22. Venture Capital 101: What Is Venture Capital?
	23. Pursuing Venture Capital
	24. Evaluating a Venture Capital Firm to Meet Your Company's Needs

RATING	ARTICLE
	25. Perfecting Your Pitch
	26. Writing and Negotiating Term Sheets with a View toward Success
	27. How Entrepreneurs Craft Strategies That Work
	28. Seven Keys to Shaping the Entrepreneurial Organization
	29. Characteristics of a Successful Entrepreneurial Management Team
	30. Managing Growth
	31. Three Strategies for Managing Fast Growth
	32. The Zappos Way of Managing
	33. Give Me the Bad News: Successful Entrepreneurs Need Negative Feedback
	34. Ask an Angel: Berkus on Building a Board of Directors
	35. Why a CEO Needs to Have a Plan B: An Interview with Jack Stack
	36. Top Ten Reasons Why Startups Fail (Venture Capital)
	37. Taking Social Entrepreneurship Seriously
	38. The Microfinance Revolution: An Overview
	39. The Hidden Economy of Nonprofits
	40. Eminence Green
	41. Managing Global Expansion: A Conceptual Framework
	42. The Global Entrepreneur
	43. Harvesting Firm Value: Process and Results
	44. Choosing Your Exit Strategy

BUSINESS REPLY MAIL
FIRST CLASS MAIL PERMIT NO. 551 DUBUQUE IA

POSTAGE WILL BE PAID BY ADDRESSEE

McGraw-Hill Contemporary Learning Series
501 BELL STREET
DUBUQUE, IA 52001

ABOUT YOU

Name
_____

Date
_____

Are you a teacher? ❏ A student? ❏
Your school's name
_____

Department
_____

Address _____ City _____ State _____ Zip _____

School telephone #
_____

YOUR COMMENTS ARE IMPORTANT TO US!

Please fill in the following information:
For which course did you use this book?
_____

Did you use a text with this ANNUAL EDITION? ❏ yes ❏ no
What was the title of the text?
_____

What are your general reactions to the Annual Editions concept?
_____

Have you read any pertinent articles recently that you think should be included in the next edition? Explain.
_____

Are there any articles that you feel should be replaced in the next edition? Why?
_____

Are there any World Wide Websites that you feel should be included in the next edition? Please annotate.
_____

May we contact you for editorial input? ❏ yes ❏ no
May we quote your comments? ❏ yes ❏ no